MW01600564

Richard Brinsley Sheridan

TRANSITS:
LITERATURE, THOUGHT & CULTURE

Series Editor
Greg Clingham
Bucknell University

Transits is the next horizon. The series of books, essays, and monographs aims to extend recent achievements in eighteenth-century studies and to publish work on any aspects of the literature, thought, and culture of the years 1650–1850. Without ideological or methodological restrictions, *Transits* seeks to provide transformative readings of the literary, cultural, and historical interconnections between Britain, Europe, the Far East, Oceania, and the Americas in the long eighteenth century, and as they extend down to present time. In addition to literature and history, such "global" perspectives might entail considerations of time, space, nature, economics, politics, environment, and material culture, and might necessitate the development of new modes of critical imagination, which we welcome. But the series does not thereby repudiate the local and the national for original new work on particular writers and readers in particular places in time continues to be the bedrock of the discipline.

Titles in the Series

For a complete list of titles in this series,
please visit http://www.bucknell.edu/universitypress

TRANSITS

Richard Brinsley Sheridan

THE IMPRESARIO IN POLITICAL AND CULTURAL CONTEXT

EDITED BY JACK E. DEROCHI AND DANIEL J. ENNIS

LEWISBURG
BUCKNELL UNIVERSITY PRESS

Published by Bucknell University Press
Co-published with The Rowman & Littlefield Publishing Group, Inc.
4501 Forbes Boulevard, Suite 200, Lanham, Maryland 20706
www.rowman.com

10 Thornbury Road, Plymouth PL6 7PP, United Kingdom

British Library Cataloguing in Publication Information Available

Library of Congress Cataloging-in-Publication Data
Richard Brinsley Sheridan : the impresario in political and cultural context / edited
by Jack E. DeRochi and Daniel J. Ennis.
     p. cm.— (Transits: literature, thought & culture, 1650–1850)
  Includes bibliographical references and index.
  ISBN 978-1-61148-480-9 (cloth : alk. paper)—ISBN 978-1-61148-481-6
(electronic) 1. Sheridan, Richard Brinsley, 1751–1816—Criticism and
interpretation. 2. Politics and literature—England—History—18th century. 3.
London (England)—Social life and customs—18th century. I. DeRochi, Jack E.
II. Ennis, Daniel James, 1970–

  PR3684.R53 2013
  822'.6—dc23   2012037579

Printed in the United States of America

For two Jennifers.

CONTENTS

CONTENTS

ACKNOWLEDGMENTS

T HE EDITORS WISH TO THANK Coastal Carolina University and Winthrop University for their support of research and travel for this project, as well as the conference organizers of the 2009 American Society for Eighteenth-Century Studies Annual Meeting and of the 2010 Southeastern American Society for Eighteenth-Century Studies Conference, as both conference programs included sessions on Richard Brinsley Sheridan and thus allowed some arguments in this volume an early airing. Thanks, too, to the staff at the London Metropolitan Archives, the archivists at the Victoria and Albert Museum, and the librarians at Kimbel Library at Coastal Carolina University and Dacus Library at Winthrop University. The collection was enriched by the generosity of the staffs of the British Museum, the Mander and Mitchenson Collection, University of Brisol Theatre Collection, The Art Archive and the Harvard Theatre Collection. We received valuable editorial assistance from Kate Parker and Rose Pleasant, and welcome feedback from our colleagues in eighteenth-century studies, particularly Misty G. Anderson, Paula R. Backscheider, and Brian Corman.

.

INTRODUCTION

Jack E. DeRochi and Daniel J. Ennis

I S A NEW COLLECTION OF ESSAYS on Richard Brinsley Sheridan worthwhile? Sheridan himself might respond with The Puff Direct, noting that the essays herein are "strongly drawn—highly colored—funds of genuine insight—mines of invention—neat arguments—Attic salt." He might call out certain contributors to this volume and praise their scholarly performances, assuring readers that while every single one of the essays are "astonishingly great," certain scholars "never appeared to more advantage" and that "it is not in the power of language to do justice" to so much insight. Having mentioned the contributors, he would wind up with unqualified universal praise for the volume itself: "[i]n short, we are at a loss which to admire most, the unrivalled genius of the contributors, the great attention and liberality of the editors, the wonderful abilities of the book-jacket designer, or the incredible exertions of all the performers." The Puff Direct—as deployed in Sheridan's 1779 afterpiece *The Critic*—was the kind of multivalent riff in which Sheridan specialized. Charmingly afflicted with the very vices he tweaked in his plays, Sheridan had composed his share of puffs, and was fully aware of their cynical creativity and commercial utility. A generation has passed since we've taken a good long look at Sheridan, and in those years the study of the London stage in the late eighteenth and early nineteenth centuries has been transformed by new methodologies, nuanced re-readings, and acts of recovery that have radically revised the theatre and, larger, the cultural history of the era. This collection puts its puffing and puff-worthy subject in the midst of this diverting conversation.

A man himself closely attuned to fashion and taste, Sheridan would perhaps smile knowingly were he to learn of the vicissitudes of his standing since his death in 1816. He would probably be momentarily annoyed to learn that his relatively limited number and range of dramatic works—not his decades of political activity—became the basis of his enduring fame. But he might weep for joy to know he still matters at all, as he wept in 1813 when he heard of Lord Byron's great compliment:

> Whatever Sheridan has done or chooses to do has been, *par excellence*, the best of its kind. He has written the best comedy (*School for Scandal*), the best drama (*The Duenna*) . . . the best farce (*The Critic*) . . . the best address (Monologue on Garrick); and, to crown all, delivered the very best oration (the famous Begum speech) ever conceived or heard in this country.[1]

Byron's opinion of Sheridan has been more quoted for effect than deployed as a defensible critical position, but it has provided a template for most estimations of Sheridan's importance since the playwright's death: he produced little, but what he chose to produce was first-rate. Sheridan's truncated case for literary immortality consists of about three hundred pages of dramatic writing all produced in the second half of the 1770s, and a speech, delivered in 1787, that would turn out to be the early occurring high point of a quixotic political career. This record has frustrated attempts to fix his legacy, especially since much of his influence of Georgian culture was a function not of his pen, but his personality. Even Sheridan's champions have been ambivalent, with each generation of admirers infusing the body of commentary with backhanded compliments and praise so equivocal it seems hardly worth the effort. Brander Matthews, writing in 1904, declared that "Sheridan *was* a wit; and he was but little else."[2] W.A. Darlington, in 1933, covers as many bases as possible in summing up the playwright's standing—he is an "object of envy, admiration, scorn—but above all, affection."[3] Allardyce Nicoll, in 1967, declares the dramatist-politician both "perplexed" and "perplexing."[4] Brean S. Hammond, two decades later, notes that Sheridan "touched greatness and let it slip through his alcoholically palsied fingers."[5]

This critical tradition has caused Sheridan's reputation to oscillate, not prosper, with the passage of time. In 1778 the *London Magazine* made an early prediction that he would become "the first comic author of the age," but his place in the top rank of "authors" from the eighteenth century has never been secure.[6] Fixing Sheridan's place in the canon has, for two centuries, consisted of rolling his legacy up Parnassus and watching it roll back down for lack of gravitas. One such stone-roller, writing in a 1927 volume of *The North American Review*, registers both fascination and resignation: "What other figure in all English literature can match him for sheer volatility?"[7] Whereas Sheridan's plays have held the attention of producers, directors, and actors decade after decade, his literary legacy has only been one of serial come-backs from scholarly neglect, a pattern that has led to a critical tradition dominated not by two centuries of increasingly sophisticated and insightful commentary, but instead by a series of "rediscoveries." Moreover, Sheridan's pyrotechnic biography has consistently held great appeal since the playwright's death; most recently, biographies by Fintan O'Toole and Linda Kelly—published in the same year (1997)—reaffirm our moth-like attraction to the Sheridan flame. At the same time, each subsequent academic generation has been compelled to re-introduce Sheridan's plays to the canon and the classroom, and thus his works tend to float in a shallow pond of periodic critical appreciation. This volume attempts to erase that gap between stage and page and to break this pattern of advance and retreat: too often, the critical tradition has placed the literary Sheridan, the managerial Sheridan, and the political Sheridan on parallel tracks. But those tracks really ought to weave amongst each other, and those crossing points reveal the performative Sheridan, the personality who produced a spectacular life of scenes.

We begin, fittingly, with an essay on the "lives" of Sheridan, taking into account both his variegated career and the competing accounts of the man that spring up almost immediately after his death and still emerge with surprising regularity. Life as inspiration for works is conspicuous early in Sheridan's career, and we devote a chapter to the tones and colors of Sheridan's early poetry and their resonances in his more famous plays. The next section of this collection indeed focuses on Sheridan's theatre, and provides fresh readings of Sheridan's most famous dramatic pieces (*The Rivals* [1775], *The Duenna* [1775], *The School For Scandal* [1777], *The Critic* [1779], and *Pizarro* [1799]), while also recovering pieces that have not yet been given full consideration in the light of our current understanding of Sheridan's world and world-view. Sheridan's rarely read poems are mined for the early gold that would, refined, gild the later plays. Sheridan's influence on other writers (particularly women writers) is reconsidered, and in this reconsideration we find his influence on the British theatre consists not just in his own dramatic works, but in the shaping (and occasional disfiguring) of the plays of the many writers who submitted to Sheridan's authority as owner-manager of Drury Lane. The last section of this collection treats not Sheridan as politician, but as politician-performer. His public image was viewed through a lens of character, and his greatest political moment was seen by his contemporaries as drenched in theatricality.

Readers of this collection will find a Sheridan firmly in the world in which he thrived and failed and thrived and failed again: theatrical and political London—the spheres profligately overlapped—of the late-eighteenth and early nineteenth centuries. In this project we seize with enthusiasm the critical tools that have transformed literary and cultural study in the last two decades, and adopt methodologies that have energized the examination of eighteenth-century drama in particular. Cultural studies approaches to the London stage, dramaturgical analyses of production conditions, ideologically aware considerations of the role of performance in the public sphere—these approaches allow us to lift Sheridan's comedies out of the played-out realm of generic discussion. Sheridan is such a singular figure that the scholarly tendency has been to name his parts—to parse his wit; to track his plays against a comedic progression that runs from Plautus to Shaw; to relate the illustrative anecdote; to retell the *bon mot* delivered in the presence of greats like Samuel Johnson, William Pitt and the Duchess of Devonshire—in other words, to succumb to what Mita Choudhury calls "the dazzle." It is time, however, for Sheridan to be fully situated in that rich intersection of language, gender, power, politics, and performance that was Georgian Great Britain.

James Morwood and David Crane, the editors of *Sheridan Studies* (published in 1995), heretofore the only book-length collection of criticism devoted to the playwright, identify their volume as "the first systematic attempt to establish Sheridan as a major figure in the history of English Comedy and as the outstanding playwright between Congreve and Wilde."[8] As such, the editors took on the task of inserting Sheridan into a critical conversation that, in the 1970s and 1980s, had left the playwright a marginal figure, rarely discussed in the journal literature, hardly worth a monograph. As John Loftis put it in 1977, reservations about Sheridan's status as a truly important dramatist had "largely been conveyed by silence."[9] Studies of Sheridan in the years immediately preceding *Sheridan Studies* proved a handy place for discussions of "laughing comedy,"[10] and were sustained by a few new editions of *The School for Scandal*, but overall did not make for a very diverting scholarly neighborhood.[11] Thus Morwood and Crane's collection had to contain introductory chapters such as Mark S. Auburn's "Theater in the Age of Garrick and Sheridan" and Jack D. Durant's "Sheridan and Language," essays pitched to remind readers why Sheridan had on occasion been thought to be a first-rank talent. Sheridan's political career is sectioned off, for the most part, covered in essays by Christopher Clayton and Marc Baer.[12] Basic reminders of who Sheridan was and what world he inhabited were necessary for a project of Sheridan rehabilitation, and *Sheridan Studies* laid the groundwork for a gradual increase in the number and quality of articles and book chapters in the following decade.[13]

"Establishing" Sheridan as a major figure was thus attempted and achieved in a critical context in which canonicity was contested territory, and another collection devoted to the maintenance of Sheridan's status as a major figure would be, to use Sir Peter Teazle's phrase, mere "sporting with reputation." Nonetheless, we can declare Morwood and Crane's mission accomplished. Between 1995 and the appearance of this volume, Sheridan has finally enjoyed sustained critical attention, and now appears to be firmly established in the dramatic hierarchy, not just wedged in a Great Tradition between Congreve and Wilde, but also captured in mid-conversation with Hannah Cowley and Elizabeth Inchbald. In the years since *Sheridan Studies* appeared, in the words of Jonathan Mulrooney, "scholars of British theatre in the long eighteenth century have produced some of the most imaginative and exciting work in contemporary cultural studies."[14] Mulrooney calls Sheridan "one of the two major playwrights of the eighteenth century" (the other, Goldsmith), but while Sheridan is indeed now safely acknowledged as a "major playwright," getting at Sheridan's larger role in eighteenth-century British culture requires a more expansive view of the man's career—"playwright" just scratches the surface.

This collection capitalizes not just on the foundational work in Sheridan studies, but upon that revelatory work on the Georgian theatre published in the last two decades. Some of the contributors in this collection have published on Sheridan in other venues, but one of the main cases for this volume of essays is that the insights of the last two decades of scholarship on Sheridan suggest he has a new and interesting role to play in the history of British culture. A generation of scholars, steeped in interdisciplinarity and with a range of nuanced views about high and low art, drama and spectacle, theatre and literature, have transformed the study of the Georgian stage from a backwater to a *Pizarro*-style cataract, with editions and essays, monographs and databases bursting forth. The emergence of a scholarship of women playwrights from the era, for example, allows us to focus attention on Sheridan's role as arbiter of taste, and for too long he's been cast (if he appears at all) as the heavy in some gendered war, rejecting good women playwrights as the dutiful son of the patriarchy. More interesting is his struggle to find plays that made money while clinging to the shreds of a retrograde gendered worldview. Exciting new work on the theatre as an institution for political discourse has made Sheridan an even more compelling figure, since as an artist he worked in Whiggish colors, and as a politician he flirted with radical opposition, but as a businessman—in the loosest sense of the word—he understood that cooperating with hegemony can pay the bills. The now-commonplace assumption that contemporary celebrity culture has its roots in the eighteenth century encourages Sheridan's plays be re-read in the context of star-making and publicity; it was

Sheridan, after all, who created a character "so covetous of popularity, that he had rather be abused than not mentioned at all."[15] Sheridan's company at Drury Lane was not just a means to put plays on the stage, but is itself a work of some kind of celebrity art, with Sheridan less composer than overwhelmed conductor, as a symphony of Siddonses and Kembles, Abingdons and Yateses swirled around him. It no longer matters that readers accept Sheridan the playwright as "significant" (although we should add, as an aside to the Pit, that he certainly is!)—it is a far more enlightening project to integrate Sheridan's career into a new cultural history that is no longer segregated into "literature" and "performance."

Given his ubiquitous personality—his reputation, his transgressions and his successes—it is difficult to separate Sheridan the dramatist from any of his other personae, since, for Sheridan, all depended upon the stage. Sheridan's lineage suggests that he was indeed destined to write for public performance and, perhaps, to behave spectacularly. His mother, Frances Sheridan (1724–1766) wrote two fairly successful comedies, *The Discovery* and *The Dupe*, both produced at Drury Lane in 1763. Although David Garrick declined to produce her *Trip to Bath* (later renamed *The Journey to Bath*), this play passed its genetic material on through her son's career, as Frances's Mrs. Tryfort served as a model for Richard's Mrs. Malaprop. Richard's father, Thomas Sheridan (1719–1788) was a renowned actor, managed the Smock Alley Theatre in Dublin, and was a somewhat successful dramatist in his own right. Sheridan-*père* gained renown as a teacher of elocution, a subject for which he wrote *British Education: Or, the Source of Disorders of Great Britain* (1756) and *A Course of Lectures on Elocution* (1762). Richard Brinsley Sheridan was born in Dublin into this theatrical family in 1751.

After his mother's death in 1766, Sheridan moved with his father to Bath, where Thomas sought to open an "Academy for the regular instruction of Young Gentlemen in the Art of reading and reciting and Grammatical Knowledge of the English tongue," and it was there that Richard met his future wife, Elizabeth ("Eliza") Linley. A remarkable beauty and admired singer, Eliza was a prize sought by various men in Bath, including the dastardly Captain Thomas Mathews—the married villain of most Sheridan biographies. Although most accounts disagree about the precise details of the events that followed, it seems clear that Richard and his sister Elizabeth helped Eliza develop a scheme to escape the aggressive propositions of Mathews and her endless number of singing engagements. In March, 1772, Eliza did not join her family at a concert in Oxford; Sheridan arrived at her lodging in Bath with a post-chaise and an elaborately stage-managed plan to chaperone Eliza all the way to a convent in France, where the singer would sequester herself until her troubles passed. At some point during their harrowing and romantic journey, Richard and Eliza decided they should marry instead, the only honorable explanation for their journey and Eliza's potential return to England.

It was in the Bath hothouse of romance and intrigue that Sheridan began writing, and his early poetry—which includes longer works such as *The Ridotto of Bath* (1771) and *Clio's Protest; or, the Picture Varnished* (1772) as well as a variety of shorter pieces—is given its first significant critical attention by Robert Jones in his essay "Sheridan's Early Style." Sheridan's poetry was ultimately topical and inspired by the comings and goings of the Bath glitterati, but it reveals a sharp eye for the foibles of others, especially his romantic rivals. Sheridan's collaboration with his friend Nathaniel Halhed, a translation and adaptation of *The Love Epistles of Aristænetus* (1771), is a clever collision of classical cultural capital and sly eroticism. Jones's examination of Sheridan's verse reveals a young author developing a style, using poetry to "push at boundaries and penetrate hypocrisies" and explore social and sexual mores—especially those that spring from masculine friendships—that would later be revisited in the plays of the 1770s. In the "critical vacuum" that is Sheridan's pre-*Rivals* career, Jones finds young Sheridan posturing, caught between a desire to be noticed and a conception of gentlemanly behavior—a position Sheridan would occupy for much of his later career.

Sheridan's Bath period looms large not just in matters of style, but also in the ways Sheridan's life has been "read" in the nineteenth and twentieth centuries. Jack DeRochi, in his essay "The Many Lives of Richard Brinsley Sheridan," examines the elopement episode to illustrate the challenges facing the biographer of Sheridan. Narrowing his focus to four biographies—Thomas Moore's *Memoirs of the Life of the Right Honourable Richard Brinsley Sheridan* (1825), Margaret Oliphant's *Sheridan* (1883), Walter Sichel's *Sheridan* (1909), and Fintan O'Toole's *A Traitor's Kiss: The Life of Richard Brinsley Sheridan, 1751–1816* (1997)—DeRochi traces four main hermeneutical threads that often intertwine and underpin Sheridan biographies. Moore's biography, for example, constructs an image of the playwright that is most flattering: Sheridan is, above all else, a man of great wit and sentiment who cannot resist coming to the aid of the helpless damsel. For Oliphant, the quintessentially Victorian biographer, Sheridan's role in Eliza's escape from the clutches of Thomas Mathews is hardly admirable. In fact, this early event is no different from other "mad" moments to the scolding Oliphant; to her, Sheridan's life became nothing more than "a sort of vulgar drama," as the man of great promise descended to a man of great failure. Sichel's biography represents a shift to a common scholarly approach to Sheridan's life in the twentieth century.

Reading Sheridan's life through the lens of his plays and dramatic pursuits, Sichel establishes the elopement as an early example of Sheridan's propensity for spectacle. Departing a great deal from the twentieth-century interpretive constructions that Sichel's work appears to influence, O'Toole's biography makes Sheridan a distinctly Irish figure, one who continually seeks to reveal and combat the oppression of the marginalized: rescuing Eliza Linley was simply an early manifestation of a life in the service of the vulnerable. In all four biographies, DeRochi argues, the elopement episode "foregrounds the remainder of [each biographer's] treatment of Sheridan" as a playwright and a Member of Parliament.

Sheridan's courtship of Eliza initiated first of his many famous—today we might say "celebrity"—relationships with women. As Marianna D'Ezio argues in her essay "Sheridan and Women," Sheridan could not avoid intrigue in either his personal or professional relations with the opposite sex. D'Ezio suggests that the common contention that Sheridan sought to prevent the success of female playwrights requires more careful scholarly deliberation, since the context of Sheridan's relationships with women is complex and paradoxical. His marriage to Eliza was directly influenced by his problematic relationships with his father and brother. His pursuit of women of the Devonshire set is brought about, at least in part, by his attempt to rise in social class: as D'Ezio writes, "Sheridan had no right of birth to be admitted to mix with the society of Devonshire House, but his friendship with Georgiana became his passport to high society." And, taking this a step further, such upward mobility required men and women both to reject standard dictates of "purity" and "decorum," but such "decorum" operated in full force when Sheridan required Eliza to quit the stage.

In "Sheridan and Women," the Drury Lane Manager's interactions with female playwrights are read in the light of the many prologues and epilogues Sheridan contributed to productions of plays by women, and D'Ezio reminds us of the many women writers, from Frances Burney to Elizabeth Griffith, who praised Sheridan for his patronage and assistance. As for Hannah Cowley's accusation of Sheridan's plagiarism, D'Ezio contends that the "borrowing" of various texts was an aspect of the theatrical culture of the time: using another's text was a matter of business, and Sheridan's own words found their way to others' texts as well. Finally, D'Ezio argues we may trace, through the course of his many plays, the challenges with women he faced in his own life. Comparing Lydia from *The Rivals* to Lady Teazle in *A School for Scandal* and Nell in *The Camp*, D'Ezio believes Sheridan's "middle-class morality had thus been transported . . . and demolished in a nonsense 'doctrine' that corrodes femininity at all levels of society," that is, the "frivolous" Lydia has become the upward-scheming Lady Teazle. Yet throughout his career, Sheridan surrounded himself with accomplished women and, far from continually subverting feminine power, Sheridan consistently exposes aristocratic and patriarchal coding that inherently corrupts the moral imagination of women.

This coding is evident in the fallout from the elopement. Both patriarchs were displeased with their children's decision to escape to France: Thomas Sheridan was determined not to have a son marry beneath his rank, and Thomas Linley was determined to have his daughter return to her profitable singing career. The young couple returned separately to Bath after Thomas Linley followed them to France and convinced Eliza he would not over-burden her with so many concerts. Richard, on the other hand, returned only to discover that Mathews had smeared his reputation in the *Bath Chronicle*, an act that Sheridan believed required retribution. He and Mathews had two separate duels, both carefully staged for public consumption despite the putative privacy of their locations. The first injured neither man and appeared to have righted Sheridan's reputation with the fashionable community; the second left Richard grievously wounded. These duels, fought in the public prints as well as in the field, gave Sheridan his first taste of not just celebrity, but spectacle, and the elopement episode contributed to the poetry Jones finds "vaunting," the masculine public persona D'Ezio brands "passionate," and a play, *The Rivals*, that made Sheridan famous.

The talk of elopement and abortive duels in *The Rivals* was drawn from Sheridan's life and whimsically represented on the stage, but as David Haley points out in his essay "The Literary Origins of Sir Lucius O'Trigger," a key character in *The Rivals* comes not from life but from the stage history. Haley sheds new light on the complicated genealogy of O'Trigger, a "Stage Irishman" who, in Sheridan's hands, becomes a very complex character. The type first appeared on the Restoration stage in the person of Teague, a simple but fiercely loyal servant to the oppressed Cavaliers in Robert Howard's *The Committee* (1665). Haley tracks post-Teague Irish characters through a century of British drama—from Thomas Sheridan's *The Brave Irishman* (1755) to Richard Cumberland's *The West Indian* (1771)—and shows how in *The Rivals* the stage Irishman is complicated by his simultaneous deployment as another character type, the gentleman fortune-hunter. In so doing, Sheridan looked back past the works of Cumberland and Howard, all the way back to William Davenant's *News from Plymouth* (1635). Besides allowing Sheridan to gain aesthetic distance from his biographical experience, Davenant's play gave him a model—ultimately Jonsonian—for using the stage Irishman to present more sophisticated social situations and to both critique and celebrate a somewhat nostalgic conception of "honor."

The first performance of *The Rivals* was not greeted with enthusiasm but, after substantial revision and trimming, Sheridan's play announced his presence as an accomplished playwright. Revised and re-staged, *The Rivals* went through fifteen consecutive performances in its first season at Covent Garden and gave Sheridan immediate literary credibility. In May, Sheridan brought forward *St. Patrick's Day; or, The Scheming Lieutenant*, a short farce that he wrote in forty-eight hours that remained a popular afterpiece through the following theatrical seasons. It was *The Duenna*, however, that secured Sheridan's reputation. Working with both Eliza's father and brother—both named Thomas Linley and both skilled musicians—Sheridan wrote the most popular comic opera of the eighteenth century: *The Duenna* was performed over seventy times from its opening on November 21, 1775, until the end of the theatrical season the following June, shattering records that had been established by *The Beggar's Opera* earlier in the century.

Mita Choudhury, in her essay "Reflections upon Maintaining a Competitive Edge: *The Duenna* and her Peers at Drury Lane," points out that despite its success, *The Duenna* has attracted relatively little critical commentary, and the commentary that does exist tends to focus on the problematic character of Don Isaac. Isaac, punished at the end of the opera, per dramatic convention, is in Choudhury's words, a "diminutive outsider of Falstaff proportion" whose elimination is necessary for the comedy's resolution. But the success of *The Duenna* had far-reaching implications for the London stage, and Choudhury considers how Sheridan's dramaturgy affected the repertories of both Covent Garden, the house where *The Duenna* made its initial impact, and Drury Lane, the theatre Sheridan was later able to acquire because both *The Rivals* and *The Duenna* had yielded immense profit.

After the impressive success of these early dramas, Sheridan's life took on a dizzying pace. Accepting Samuel Johnson's invitation to join The Literary Club, finding time to transmute Vanbrugh's bawdy *The Relapse* into the effectively mild *A Trip to Scarborough*, and learning on the fly to manage his newly acquired theatre, Sheridan might have rested on his 1777 laurels. Instead, *A School for Scandal* opened in May, enthralling a bejeweled audience of the London *ton* that included Frances Anne Crewe and the Duchess of Devonshire. Garrick wrote the prologue, and one anecdote will suffice to illustrate the extent to which *School's* reception contributes to the Sheridan aura. Frederick Reynolds tells of walking past the Drury Lane on the night of the play's opening and hearing such a roar that he felt certain the theatre was collapsing, only to discover the next morning that "the noise did not arise from the *falling* of the house but from the *falling* of the screen in the fourth act; so violent and tumultuous were the applause and laughter."[16]

With that, Sheridan reached what Thomas Moore refers to as "the summit of his dramatic fame."

The School for Scandal bulks so large in Sheridan's career that, after the playwright's death in 1816, its powers remained undiminished: it was one of the most-produced plays of the nineteenth-century London stage. John Vance's "The Rule of *Scandal*: Sheridan in the Age of Wilde and Shaw" gives an account of the revivals of Sheridan's magnum opus from 1890 to 1919, a period during which Sheridan held his place just behind Shakespeare as a repertory stalwart; *The School for Scandal* was a play that seemed always in production on some world stage. Vance goes on to explore a phenomenon that suggests that admiration for Sheridan's craft went hand-in-hand with fascination with Sheridan the man. The Victorians wrote and produced many plays set in the eighteenth century, and Victorian audiences, like twenty-first century filmgoers, were treated to dramatic representations of Sheridan himself: this dramatist had finally become a "real" dramatic character.[17]

Perhaps more revealing of *Scandal*'s effect is its omnipresent influence on the titles of comedies and prose pieces throughout the end of the eighteenth century. Emily Friedman's "Schools Beyond *Scandal*, 1776–1800" examines how Sheridan's great play took advantage of a "popular extant naming tradition" to become the dominant rhetorical move for conspicuously sentimental critique of the public domain. Although the end of the eighteenth century saw many "schools"—schools for "children, Christians, happiness" as Friedman points out—it never observed one as deftly critical as Sheridan's brand of societal education, and certainly not one as immensely popular. The cultural effect of Sheridan's masterpiece is striking, as plays, novels, and prose pieces in the 1780s, 1790s and beyond embrace the new "school" model, signaling to readers and audiences the public application of the work that follows. In this way, according to Friedman, Sheridan's *Scandal* dramatically alters the rhetorical conception of "'school' into texts that become spaces of discipline, rigor, and hopes of social transformation."

The Critic (1779) was the last of Sheridan's remarkable successes as a playwright proper. As a lengthy afterpiece, *The Critic* became a consistent draw for London theatre audiences even as it poked fun at those who fill the theatre night after night. As Daniel J. Ennis explains in his essay "*Naumachia* and the Structure of *The Critic*," the grand dénouement of *The Critic* does not consist of sparkling dialogue but of wordless spectacle, as Puff announces his play will end with a noisy recreation of the English defeat of the Spanish Armada—a dramatic-mechanical recreation of a naval battle known as a *naumachia*. What follows is a remarkable stage direction that urges the modern reader to picture an elaborate battle scene: the simulated fleets engage, patriotic tunes are performed, and the considerable theatrical machinery available at the time produces a patriotic moment for the play's audience.

Sheridan's long career as theatre manager and owner was more tumultuous and controversial than his brief career as a playwright. The Sheridan era at Drury Lane was marked by increasingly tangled finances, and the snarl of mortgages necessary for a man of Sheridan's moderate prosperity to acquire and operate the capital-devouring Drury Lane marked the beginning of a lifetime accrual of debt. Sheridan compounded his troubles with legendary disorganization. Almost from the beginning of Sheridan's management, Drury Lane actors and playwrights complained about not being paid. Mail went unread and bills unopened, and one observer notes that Sheridan coped by avoidance:

> Sheridan's habit was to keep his visitors distributed variously, according to their rank and intimacy with him. Some . . . penetrated the library; others tired the chairs in the parlors; and the tradesmen lost their time in the hall, the butler's room, and other scenical diversions of the premises. A door opening above stairs, moved all their hopes below . . .[18]

Sheridan's liberality often outstripped his earnings, and the Drury Lane was destined to continually appear on the precipice of complete bankruptcy, the period Mark Auburn calls "distracted management."[19]

Sheridan's careening career at the helm of a theatre that no longer had new Sheridan-penned hits to generate income is illuminated by Stephen Gores, whose essay "The Lees and Sheridan: An Unexamined Connection" explores how the Lee family—a clan involved in British theatre for most of the long eighteenth century—is a neglected factor in assessments of Sheridan as theatre manager. The Lees and Sheridans had many connections: John Lee acted with Thomas Sheridan in Dublin in 1751 and originated the role of Sir Lucius O'Trigger in Richard's *The Rivals* more than two decades later. John's daughter Sophia wrote an "Epithalium" to celebrate the marriage of Richard Sheridan and Eliza Linley in 1773. As Richard Sheridan drifted away from writing plays, the Lee connection shows how Sheridan the manager operated through a network of marriage and familial alliances. Gores points out that, in 1781, Sophia consulted Thomas Sheridan regarding the libretto for her musical adaptation of Frances Sheridan's story, *Nourjahad*, and in 1787, another daughter of John Lee, Harriet, saw her comedy *New Peerage* staged at Drury Lane, the first of three Lee pieces to beat the odds and gain Sheridan's favor (Sophia's *Almeyda* appeared in 1797 and her *Assignation* in 1807). Gores shows that, while the Lees have gone virtually unnoticed by theatre historians and

Sheridan's biographers, this multi-generational Lee-Sheridan connection gives us new insight into the tightly knit world of the British theatre and the ways Sheridan made production decisions.

After his election to parliament in 1780, Sheridan wrote little, but he did have one last hit in him: August von Kotzebue's *De Spanier of Peru*, translated, adapted, and re-titled *Pizarro* (1799). Daniel O'Quinn points out that upon its appearance and for decades after, *Pizarro* generated a disproportionate number of lengthy reviews, critical notices, and visual representations. O'Quinn's essay, "Spectacular Dialectics: *Pizarro* and the Perilous Bridge between Tragic Emotion and Visual Excess," examines how Sheridan's production choices reflected a strategic view of his era's politics and, rather than being problematically inconsistent, constitute a "utopian dialectic" wherein apparent contradictions are actually stage-friendly stylistic choices and politically nuanced oppositional art. This dialectic culminates in the most spectacular element of *Pizarro*, the "bridge" scene that included elaborate effects on a massive scale. Embedded within this spectacle, O'Quinn argues, is a "Whig fantasy" that allowed the spectators to imagine a more just political order. *Pizarro* has always been the odd duck of Sheridan studies. It appears twenty years after Sheridan's last major play, *The Critic*, and its triple derivation from a misunderstood flash-in-the-pan German source has made it difficult to integrate into Sheridan's oeuvre. It rarely appears in single-volume selections of Sheridan's plays, despite its enormous commercial success and contemporary critical interest. O'Quinn's essay, by invoking Sheridan's stance on the pressing political questions of the 1790s, and by mining the "thick record" of response to *Pizarro*, converts the outlier for the playwright into a watershed for the theatrical politician.

As in the theatre, in Parliament Sheridan enjoyed a few bursts of astonishing success, but long years of crisis and frustration. Sponsored by the Duchess of Devonshire, Sheridan was first elected to Parliament as a representative of Stafford, and immediately joined the Whig opposition of Charles Fox and Edmund Burke. Sheridan would stay in the Opposition for most of his thirty-two years in office, distinguishing himself as the speaker most capable of matching Pitt's rhetorical skills on issues like absentee ownership and free trade in Ireland. It was the impeachment trial of Warren Hastings, however, that made Sheridan's career: his two speeches—one in the House of Commons, the other in the House of Lords—made Sheridan the most celebrated orator of the age. His first important address on Hastings, the "Begums Speech" that Byron so admired, was delivered on February 7, 1787, and lasted over five hours; it was immediately lauded in newspapers and on the streets of London as the most important speech of the preceding century. Pitt himself admitted that the speech "surpassed all the eloquence of ancient and modern times, and possessed everything that genius or art could furnish, to agitate and controul the human mind."[20] Hastings, once thought to be immune from prosecution, was arrested on May 21, 1787. The subsequent trial in the House of Lords began on February 13, and Sheridan delivered a speech that began on June 3 and finished, remarkably, on June 13, when he collapsed into Burke's awaiting arms with the memorable "My Lords, I have done!" Although the trial lasted seven years and eventually resulted in Hastings' acquittal, Sheridan's political fame was assured.

Glynis Ridley, in her essay "Sheridan's Courtroom Dramas: The Impeachment of Warren Hastings and the Trial of the Bounty Mutineers," argues that Sheridan's two celebrated speeches were written and delivered in full and conscious awareness of the entertainments, not only from rival theatres but also from other criminal trials that competed for the attention of Londoners. In particular, Ridley draws attention to another celebrated legal case that reveals the spectacular nature of Sheridan's political performances: the trial of the Bounty Mutineers. It was Hastings' misfortune to become a synecdoche for all that was feared about over-ambitious and unstable servants of empire. It was Sheridan's misfortune that the brilliance of his oratory in the first two years of the trial could not compensate for supporting leaden performances for a further five years. As Ridley has before noted of the Hastings impeachment, "a seven-year continuous run for a play is a sign of success—in a trial, it is a disaster." Ridley shows the relationship between stage and courtroom, and between one courtroom and others in the 1780s and 1790s, revealing the influence that the events surrounding the Bounty and Begums had on Sheridan's future writing and oratory.

Following the Hastings' speech, Sheridan's most important role may have been as the Prince of Wales's primary confidante during the Regency crisis, a development that chagrined Charles Fox. Sheridan and Fox never completely split, however, and the two remained allies throughout the French Revolution, a period that brought about the final rift between Sheridan and Burke. Sheridan spoke passionately about the French right to liberty, arguing that their project was analogous to the English revolution in 1688—an argument that Burke disdained, believing that the revolt in France was destroying the essential paternalistic aspect of the nobility necessary for stable government. In 1794, Sheridan joined Fox in his condemnation of Pitt's suspension of *habeas corpus* when many Whigs like Burke defected to the Prime Minister's position. To that end, Sheridan went so far as to defend Horne Tooke, Thomas Hardy, and other members of the London Corresponding Society during their trial for treason later that year, and further spoke for the restoration of *habeas corpus* in Parliament in January of 1795. Although believing that certain circumstances required war, Sheridan was willing to take the unpopular position of arguing for England to make peace with France after Napoleon rose to power. Similarly, always one to defend the oppressed and disenfranchised, Sheridan repeatedly spoke in favor of Catholic emancipation in Ireland and called for the end of slavery in England.

Starting with his election to Parliament in 1780, and with increasing frequency in the late eighteenth and early nineteenth centuries, Sheridan's political activities generated not just written criticism and commentary, but a great deal of graphic satire. As David Francis Taylor points out in the final essay in this collection, "Caricaturing Sheridan," Sheridan appeared in close to five hundred political cartoons. These satires reveal multifaceted public perceptions of Sheridan and constitute a "counter-biography," illustrating and commenting upon Sheridan's political fortunes as well as tracking his increasing radicalism. Through a series of readings of key caricatures, Taylor maps the ways in which artists like Isaac Cruikshank, William Dent, and James Gillray represent the friction between theatrical and political cultures in the Georgian period. Visual representations of Sheridan serve to problematize notions of the theatricality of politics—and indeed the politics of theatricality—that are now a critical commonplace in surveys of the late eighteenth century. These depictions, rich with the iconography of the theatre, reflect and even generate disjunctions between the "stages" of Westminster and Drury Lane.

In accounts of Sheridan's career—especially ones that organize Sheridan's life into a pre-1780 playwright period and the post-1780 political period (that is to say, all of them)—the final resting place of Sheridan's body away from his political heroes and colleagues is freighted with meaning and not a little sentiment. Most of Sheridan's political ambitions had not been realized, of course, but it was of those moments of political passion—fighting good fights on behalf of the Begums, defending *habeus corpus*—of which Sheridan was most proud. John Timbs, writing in 1862, declared that if Sheridan "could have spoken out when they were burying him, he would have protested loudly against the place where they laid him, as Poets' Corner was his aversion: he would have liked to be placed near Fox &c."[21] This view is essentially identical to that expressed in Sheridan's recent *Dictionary of National Biography* entry, penned by A. Norman Jeffares: "Sheridan would have preferred to be interred near Fox, and recognized as a statesman, but was buried on

13 July in Poets' Corner in Westminster Abbey."[22] Most of Sheridan's biographers read his grave as a final irony.[23]

But the Poet's Corner gambit only works if one both bifurcates Sheridan's career and ignores many of the occupants of Poet's Corner. Entombed near Sheridan are not just his literary peers—there's John Gay, here's Nicholas Rowe—but a brace of truer colleagues, men whose political activity and literary aspiration crossed and merged—there's Geoffrey Chaucer, here's Thomas Macaulay. Sheridan the impresario performed his politics, wrote speeches for characters (including the character of "Richard Sheridan, M.P."), and one can find among his moldering neighbors poets-politicians galore, from Abraham Cowley to Matthew Prior. Indeed, if we mean by poet "versifier," Sheridan does not belong in Poet's Corner at all (neither does Garrick, really) but as a poet-maker—an artist whose words moved people, an arranger of smaller units into larger, greater things—Sheridan rests right where he belongs: among actors and musicians and scribblers, with nobles, princes, and ministers but a few steps away.

Notes

1. Thomas Moore, *Memoirs of the Life of the Right Honourable Richard Brinsley Sheridan*. 5th ed., 2 vols. (London: Longman, Rees, Orme, Brown, and Green, 1826), 2:440.

2. Brander Matthews, ed., *Sheridan's Comedies: The Rivals and The School for Scandal* (New York: Thomas Y. Crowell, 1904), xii.

3. William Aubrey Cecil Darlington, *Sheridan* (London: Duckworth, 1933), 139.

4. Allardyce Nicoll, Review [untitled], *The Review of English Studies, New Series* 18, no. 71 (August1967), 344.

5. Brean S. Hammond, Review [untitled], *The Review of English Studies, New Series* 38, no. 149 (February1987), 83.

6. T. M., "Memoirs of Richard Brinsley Sheridan, Esq." *The London Magazine, or, Gentleman's Monthly Intelligencer*, vol. 47 (November, 1778), 484.

7. J. Brooks Atkinson, "Sheridan—Whom the Gods Loved," *The North American Review* 223, no. 883 (December1926–February 1927), 645.

8. Headnote to *Sheridan Studies*, James Morwood and David Crane, eds. (Cambridge: Cambridge University Press, 1995), n.p.

9. John Loftis, *Sheridan and the Drama of Georgian England* (Cambridge: Harvard University Press, 1977), 1.

10. As evinced in Marlies K. Danziger's slim volume entitled, simply, *Oliver Goldsmith and Richard Brinsley Sheridan* (New York: Frederick Ungar Publishing, 1978).

11. Cecil Price's edited 1971 Oxford edition of *The School for Scandal* is the best of a bunch that included versions issued or reprinted by Barron's Educational Publishing (1977), West Publishing (1975), Longman (1977), Meridian (1986) and Penguin (1988).

12. The most comprehensive is Christopher Clayton's "The Political Career of Richard Brinsley Sheridan," in *Sheridan Studies*, eds. Morwood and Crane, 131–50.

13. The shift away from the genre-oriented studies of Loftis, Morwood and Auburn is best seen in more recent work by Frank Donoghue, "Avoiding the 'Cooler Tribunal of the Study': Richard Brinsley Sheridan's Writer's Block and Late Eighteenth-Century Print Culture," *ELH* 68 no. 4 (Winter 2001): 831–56.; Julie Stone Peters, "Theatricality, Legalism, and the Scenography of Suffering: The Trial of Warren Hastings and Richard Brinsley Sheridan's *Pizarro*," *Law and Literature* 18 no. 1 (2006), 15–45; and James Thompson, "Sheridan, *School for Scandal* and Aggression," *Comparative Drama* 42 no. 1 (2008): 89–98.

14. Jonathan Mulrooney, "Reading Theatre, 1730–1830" in *The Cambridge Companion to British Theatre, 1730–1830*, eds. Jane Moody and Daniel O'Quinn (New York: Cambridge University Press, 2007), 249.

15. Sheridan, *The Critic,* in *The Dramatic Works of Richard Brinsley Sheridan*, ed. Cecil Price, 2 vols. (Oxford: Clarendon Press, 1973), 2:502.

16. Frederick Reynolds, *The Life and Times of Frederick Reynolds*, 2 vols. (Philadelphia: H. C. Cary and I. Lea, 1826), 1:74.

17. True contemporary Sheridians viewed the 2008 film *The Duchess* not for Keira Knightley's star turn as Georgiana, but for Aidan McArdle's subtle playing of a sympathetic and observant Sheridan himself. He appears—tragically—in too few scenes, but reminds us that we have not seen the playwright in a widely released film since 1994's *The Madness of King George*, when Barry Stanton represented him as the rather lumpy and conspiratorial henchman of Charles James Fox.

18. James Boaden, *Memoirs of the life of John Philip Kemble, esq, including a history of the stage, from the time of Garrick to the present period* (Philadelphia: Robert H. Small, 1825), 116.

19. Mark S. Auburn, "Richard Brinsley Sheridan," *Restoration and Eighteenth-Century Dramatists: Third Series*, ed. Paula R. Backscheider, vol. 89. *The Dictionary of Literary Biography* (Detroit: Gale Research, 1989), 319.

20. Quoted in Linda Kelly, *Richard Brinsley Sheridan: A Life* (London: Pimlico, 1998), 141.

21. John Timbs, *Lives of Wits and Humourists: R. Brinsley Sheridan, Richard Porson, Rev. Sydney Smith, Theodore Hook. James, and Horace Smith* (London: Richard Bentley, 1862), 98.

22. *Oxford Dictionary of National Biography*, s.v. "Sheridan, Richard Brinsley (1751–1816)" (by A. Norman Jeffares), http://oxforddnb.com (accessed June 2, 2011).

23. In her biography, Kelly remarks that Sheridan "would have protested loudly" but "Posterity has justified his place in Poet's Corner" (*Sheridan: A Life,* 308–9).

1

THE MANY LIVES OF
RICHARD BRINSLEY SHERIDAN

Jack E. DeRochi

Without means, without connexion, without character (which might be false at first and made him mad afterwards from desperation), he beat them all, in all he ever attempted. But alas! Poor human nature!

—Lord Byron, Letter to Thomas Moore, 1818[1]

CONSIDERED ALONGSIDE his more famous encomium of Sheridan's talents—"Whatever Sheridan has done or chooses to do has been, *par excellence*, the best of its kind"—Byron's impassioned letter to Thomas Moore captures the alluring enigma of Sheridan's figure for present-day Sheridan scholars. While it is not surprising that Sheridan's life has garnered so much biographical attention, the diversity of Sheridan's accomplishments presents difficult questions for present-day Sheridan studies: is Sheridan a great playwright who happened to make speeches? An influential Member of Parliament who happened to write plays? Or, if we consider that the drama of his (in)famous personal life may exceed the drama of his plays, is Sheridan simply a drunk profligate who possessed a large measure of wit?

E. H. Mikhail, in his collection of firsthand accounts of Sheridan, pointedly remarks, "Sheridan's character is so full of contradictions that it is difficult to assess. His biographers have been painstaking but hardly penetrative."[2] Indeed, far from being comprehensive in their approach, biographers appear simply to select various sides of Sheridan's multiple "contradictions." The disparate portrayals in two 1997 biographies, Linda Kelly's *Richard Brinsley Sheridan: A Life* and Fintan O'Toole's *A Traitor's Kiss: The Life of Richard Brinsley Sheridan*, are illustrative examples. Kelly argues that, despite Sheridan's wishes to be known as an important

Member of Parliament, "Posterity has justified his [final resting] place in Poet's corner." In stark contrast, O'Toole concludes his biography with a demonstrably political bent, suggesting when "the show" of Sheridan's funeral was over, it was the Member of Parliament's political radicalism that remained most influential, bringing the figure of William Godwin to his grave a dozen times to reflect on Sheridan's calls for revolution in England.[3] Taken together, these works reflect the contradictory perspectives that continually reappear throughout Sheridan's biographical history.[4] Over the last two centuries, Sheridan's figure has in fact undergone countless revisions. From his death until the beginning of the twentieth century, seven different biographers tackled the Sheridan conundrum, and no fewer than eighteen full-length biographies have been written between 1900 and today, a number that does not include the dozens of brief biographical sketches and accounts that introduce various editions of his plays or speeches.[5] The sheer volume and diversity of these biographical treatments illustrate the enticing yet enigmatic figure that Sheridan presents.

When we examine these different biographies and their answers to the questions above, we discover of course that Sheridan's life becomes a signifier for the biographer's ideological intent as much as the playwright's complexity. As Paula Backscheider remarks in *Some Reflections on Biography*, "The most invisible person in a biography is the most powerful—the author. At every moment his or her voice can be heard—but it isn't." When biographers encounter specific events in their subject's life, they inherently make value judgments—"we decide what kind of person we are writing about and assign motive over and over"—and thus reveal their own interpretive prism.[6] Taking Backscheider's argument a step further, and recognizing the unitary function of the narrative form, a historical figure becomes confined by the biographer's unifying conception of his or her character. Given this inherent aspect of biography, Sheridan's life—with its flashes of multifarious accomplishments and failings—becomes a study of oppositional hermeneutics. A survey of Sheridan's biographical history reveals four competing themes that underpin most of the divergent accounts: Sheridan as a sentimental wit, best represented by Thomas Moore's *Memoirs of the Life of the Right Honourable Richard Brinsley Sheridan* (1825); Sheridan as an arriviste, in Margaret Oliphant's *Sheridan* (1883); Sheridan as a spectacular marvel, in Walter Sichel's *Sheridan: From New and Original Material; including a Manuscript Diary by Georgina, Duchess of Devonshire* (1909); and Sheridan as an Irish romantic, in Fintan O'Toole's *A Traitor's Kiss: The Life of Richard Brinsley Sheridan, 1751–1816* (1998).[7] From these divergent themes come four distinct portraits of the same man.

One particular episode exposes the thematic centering of these four Sheridan biographies, a scene that reveals their ideological entrapment of Sheridan's character: his dramatic and scandalous elopement with Elizabeth Linley.[8] Was their marriage an act of love or conquest? Was the elopement part of an elaborate scheme or the act of youthful passion? Was Sheridan a Machiavellian villain or a sentimental hero? Moore's, Oliphant's, Sichel's, and O'Toole's answers to these questions—which naturally occur early in their treatments—shape their distinctive constructions of Sheridan's biography. Moreover, the rhetorical framing of the elopement becomes paradigmatic for each biography, foregrounding the remainder of the Sheridan portrait as a playwright, Member of Parliament, and manager of Drury Lane.

Before we delve into these divergent rhetorics, we should remind ourselves of certain facts of the events: facts that appear most certain from the many letters exchanged between the significant parties. Elizabeth Linley, the famously beautiful and accomplished young singer, was surrounded by countless suitors in Bath during the years of 1770–1772, when the family of Sheridans arrive. The "dramatic" Sheridans—Richard, his older brother Charles, sister Elizabeth, and father Thomas—soon became intimate friends with the "musical" Linleys, Elizabeth Sheridan and Elizabeth (Eliza) Linley becoming close confidantes. At the time, an older gentleman, Walter Long, was betrothed to the sixteen-year-old Eliza. However, for one reason or another, their engagement did not yield a marriage, and Long released Eliza from her commitment, giving her a £3,000 settlement to repair her reputation.

As for other suitors, Captain Thomas Mathews (the villain by most accounts, secretly married but pursuing Eliza) and Charles Sheridan were the greatest rivals to Richard's growing affections. After a short period of time, Charles ceased his own pursuit and moved eight miles away from Bath in order to rid himself of his youthful and inappropriate passion. After Charles's departure, Eliza attempted to discourage Captain Mathews' ambition, but he refused to relent and professed that he would commit suicide if Eliza did not acquiesce to his desires. At this point, Eliza became quite fearful because of Mathews' social status in Bath. Her closest friends and confidantes, Elizabeth and Richard Sheridan, helped her devise a plan: she would escape secretly to France, take refuge in a convent until she was twenty-one, and indemnify her father by granting him a large portion of her £3,000 settlement from Long.

On March 18, 1722, Eliza feigned illness and did not accompany the Linleys to perform at Oxford. At the same time, Richard left a letter for Thomas

Linley and arranged for a post chaise, complete with a waiting woman whom he paid to travel with and protect Eliza; the three traveled to London and arranged passage to France. Sometime in England, or perhaps after their entry into France, Richard and Eliza recognized their emotional attachment to one another and realized that marriage would have been the only proper motive for their escape from Bath. They married in a village outside of Calais and, once Eliza was settled within the convent in Lille, Richard returned to England to pacify both families and obtain the financial wherewithal to support his new wife. They "remarried" months later in England after many other escapades (including Richard's two duels with Mathews), as their Catholic marriage in France would not have been recognized by either family.

Sheridan's elopement with Eliza Linley becomes a biographical flashpoint for his biographers, formatively shaping the remainder of their narrative figuring. Studying the treatment of this episode by four significant biographies from four distinct time periods, we can better comprehend the competing hermeneutics in interpreting Sheridan's place in English literary and cultural history.

Sheridan, the Sentimental Wit

Although not the first biography,[9] Thomas Moore's *Memoirs of the Right Honourable Richard Brinsley Sheridan* (1825) has gone through numerous editions and printings.[10] The popularity of his biography assuredly stems from Moore's own poetic fame as well as his firsthand knowledge of Sheridan's family toward the end of the playwright's life—an authority that Moore routinely asserts throughout the work. In the "Preface," for example, he expresses his gratitude to Charles Sheridan, Richard's son, who provided "the chief part of the materials upon which the following Memoirs of his father are founded."[11] Because of his intimate knowledge of Sheridan, Moore confidently presents an image of a man who, despite his limited foundation, attained distinction in drama and Parliament based on his wit, preparedness, and sensitivity. The famous problematical moments—his elopement with Eliza, for example—are the natural and understandable consequences of the fullness of Sheridan's sentimental personality.[12]

This combination of wit and sentimentality is precisely, according to Moore, what made Sheridan the unavoidable champion of Eliza's affections:

> But in love, as in everything else, the power of a mind like Sheridan's must have made itself felt through all obstacles and difficulties. He was not long in winning the entire affections of the young "Syren"—though

the number and wealth of his rivals, the ambitious views of her father, and the temptations to which she herself was hourly exposed, kept his jealousies and fears perpetually on the watch. (1:45)

Moore further establishes Sheridan's sentimental aspect by consistently making references to his youth, shyness, and sense of propriety. Richard apparently hides his amorous feelings from everyone, including his older brother Charles and best friend Nathaniel Halhed, both men having already publicly declared their attractions. Moore suggests that Sheridan himself—"at this time little more than twenty, and his companion just entering her eighteenth year" (66)—in these early years at Bath becomes the model for the shy and young lover Falkland in *The Rivals* (1775).

Although his wit and youthful earnestness seem destined to attract Eliza's affections, Sheridan is not a domineering figure, and it is Eliza, not Richard, who first envisions her flight to France. When Mathews' persecution reaches its climax, Eliza, already in love with Sheridan, conceives of a plan to escape: "In consequence of this persecution . . . she adopted, in early 1772, the romantic resolution of flying secretly to France and taking refuge in a convent." For his part, Sheridan simply performs the role of advisor, though he was "not slow in offering to be the partner of it" (65).

With Sheridan marked as a sentimental hero and Eliza as a determined heroine, Moore introduces the elopement crisis by first establishing the villain of the history, Captain Mathews, a figure that is immediately identifiable by early nineteenth-century novel readers:

> Captain Mathews, a married man and intimate with Miss Linley's family, presuming upon the innocent familiarity which her youth and his own station permitted between them, had for some time not only rendered her remarkable by his indiscreet intentions in public, but had persecuted her in private with those unlawful addresses and proposals, which a timid female will sometimes rather endure, than encounter that share of the shame, which may be reflected upon herself by their disclosure. (64)

Mathews becomes the villain, allowing Sheridan to become the chivalric defender, for Eliza "terrified by [Mathews'] perseverance," "at length confided her distresses" to her protector. Sheridan, who had by this time admitted his own affections for Eliza to his sister, "lost no time in expostulating with Mathews upon the cruelty, libertinism, and fruitlessness of his pursuit" (64).

Sheridan's actions are equally justified by Moore's portrayal of Eliza's father at this time. Although Mathews is the conspicuous antagonist, Thomas Linley's oppressive demands are consistently apparent. When Eliza grows fearful of Mathews, she is—in Moore's depiction—equally "dreading the consequences of her father's temper, if this violation of his confidence and hospitality were exposed to him." Her determination to flee stems understandably from her "increasing dislike for her profession, which made her shrink more and more from the gaze of many, in proportion as she became devoted to the love of one" (65). And, after settling in the convent in France, Eliza consents to return with her father only after "a promise being given that, as soon as [a few singing] engagements were accomplished, she should be allowed to resume her plan of retirement." Eliza's decision occurs, naturally, only after Richard serves as mediator, giving a "few words of private explanation . . . which had the effect of reconciling [Thomas Linley] to his truant daughter" (70). Again, as with his depiction of Mathews, Moore's portrayal of Thomas Linley creates an important implication for Sheridan: while his youthful enthusiasm to assist in Eliza's escape may not warrant praise, it should not elicit condemnation.

Moore's description of the events that transpire during their journey to Calais, however, reveals the biographer's unease with Sheridan's behavior when Moore quickly transitions Sheridan from the role of chivalric protector to romantic lover to dutiful husband in barely three sentences. Moore frames this transition with rhetorical hedges: "On their leaving Dunkirk, as was natural to expect," Sheridan ceased being simply "the chivalrous and disinterested protector" to become a "mere selfish lover." Moore mitigates any potentially negative impression of Sheridan by reminding us, only two sentences later, that "[i]t did not, we may suppose, require much eloquence, to convince her to become Richard's wife." After this brief lapse into momentary criticism, Moore quickly returns to the firmer rhetorical ground of the sentimental mode, shaping Sheridan's character as the heroic protector by drawing our attention to a letter Richard writes his brother. Richard assures Charles, "All is well, I hope, and I hope, too, that though you may have been ignorant, for some time, of our proceedings you never could have been uneasy lest any thing should tempt me to depart, even in a thought, from the honour and consistency which engaged me at first" (67–68).

Introduced in the elopement episode, these notes of wit and sentimentality resonate throughout Moore's biography. Most telling are the echoes of this rhetoric when Moore describes Sheridan's political career. An early speech of Sheridan's presents, appropriately, "a strain of feeling so youthful and romantic, that they are more fit to be addressed to one of those parliaments of Love, which are held during the times of Chivalry" (355). It is Sheridan's famous pair of speeches during the impeachment trial of Warren Hastings, not surprisingly, that together reveal Moore's dominant hermeneutic, deliberately establishing Sheridan's figure as the honorable protector of the oppressed. Like Eliza's abuse at the hands of Captain Mathews, the oppression of India by the English (and Hastings specifically) was sufficient to "lay hold of the imagination as well as the feelings, and to furnish eloquence with those strong lights and shadows, of which her most animated pictures are composed." Resonating with romantic overtones, India becomes, in Moore's description, the feminized innocent while England's oppressive commercialism becomes the masculine oppressor: the virgin India—"the sanctity of Zenanus"—is raped by British commercialism—"violated by search-warrants"—as the phallic English government "transplant[s]" itself into the iconic "holy and peaceful shade of the Bramins" (440–41). Given the heightened (sexual) tension of the political moment, Sheridan becomes once again the chivalric hero of the feminine, one uniquely capable of fanning the embers of sentimentality.

Although Moore's biography dwells a good deal on the fame which the speeches brought Sheridan, the vast majority of his narrative focuses on the Sheridan's wit, imagination, and preparation that delivered "that celebrated Speech [to the House of Commons], whose effect upon its hearers has no parallel in the annals of ancient or modern eloquence" (450). Moore's agenda is conspicuously manifest in his presentation of Sheridan's second speech, for which he provides numerous excerpts interspersed with his own evaluative commentary. Recognizing an inherent oversight in Hastings' defense, Sheridan "thus shrewdly and playfully exposes all the persons concerned" and accurately "describes the feelings of the people of the East with respect to the unapproachable sanctity of their Zenanas" (493–95). Likewise, "[a]nticipating the plea of state-necessity," Sheridan "breaks into the following rhetorical passage" (499) that provides readers with another "specimen of that lofty style" (501). Moore uses the end of the speech unequivocally to illustrate Sheridan's wit and mastery of the moment:

> We now come to the Peroration, in which, skillfully and without appearance of design, it is contrived that the same sort of appeal to the purity of British justice, with which the oration opened, should, like the repetition of a solemn strain of music, recur at its close. . . .The pompous and Jesuitical style in which this singular doctrine is expressed, in a letter addressed by [Hastings] . . . is thus ingeniously tuned to account by the orator, in winding up his masterly statement to a close. (516–17)

[25]

Moore concludes, after explaining the important distinction between hearing and reading a speech, that "[g]ood sense and wit were the great weapons of his oratory—shrewdness in detecting the weak points of an adversary, and infinite powers of raillery in exposing it" (520).

Building upon his earlier construction of Sheridan's character, Moore effectually shapes an image of a sentimental hero of wit. Although ultimately unsuccessful in this particular enterprise—Hastings was found not guilty after a seven-year-long trial—Sheridan's political sensibilities were as chivalric and noteworthy as were his romantic intentions to rescue Eliza Linley. When seen in the appropriate context, suggests Moore, Sheridan's performance signifies "truth and good sense taking refuge from the equivocations of lawyers . . . [and] a great guiding light" (541). This interpretive lens softens the impact of Sheridan's conspicuous flaws as a husband and theatre manager. At the end of his portrayal, Moore's final moral assessment of Sheridan is marked by unmistakably sentimental tones: "There are few persons . . . to whose kind and affectionate conduct . . . so many strong and honourable testimonies remain" (2:482).

Sheridan, the Arriviste

Margaret Oliphant's eminently Victorian biography, *Richard Brinsley Sheridan* (one of several biographies in the "English Men of Letters" series) constructs in 1883 a different hermeneutic from Moore's for examining Sheridan's character.[13] Compartmentalized as one of many misadventures in a chapter titled simply "Youth," Sheridan's elopement introduces the reader of Oliphant's biography to the playwright's desire and willingness to portray certain roles to accomplish certain ends. Whereas Moore nostalgically views Sheridan as a sympathetic figure of the past, Oliphant perceives Sheridan to be the classic example of the misguided promise of the preceding age. She bluntly explains how Sheridan's "view of life was not a profound one. It was the vulgar sort of drama, a problem without any depths—to be solved by plenty of money and wine and pleasure . . . [To] Sheridan there was nothing to find out in [life] any more than there is anything to find out in the characters of his plays" (107–8).[14]

Oliphant's diminution of Sheridan's character begins early in the biography when she links him with Goldsmith and other "Anglo-Irish" whom we should rightly recognize as "brilliant" and "witty," but also "improvident" and "reckless" (1). She spends a good deal of time discussing Samuel Johnson's overt dismissal of Richard's father, Thomas Sheridan, not to establish a paradigm for viewing Sheridan as separate from his father; instead, Sheridan will always be linked to his father's social status and his apparent grandiose views of his own importance.[15] After thus briefly chronicling Sheridan's beginnings and early education, Oliphant arrives at the elopement episode, where her focus centers particularly on the figure of Eliza: "[i]t is the presence of this lady which gives interest and romance to the early chapter of Sheridan's life, and the record cannot go further without bringing her in" (17).[16] Oliphant presents the elopement episode as distinctly Eliza's crisis—thereby casting Sheridan to a subordinate role—devoting several pages simply to the figure of Eliza Linley, her family, and her universally acknowledged beauty: "[t]here flourished in Bath in those days a family called by Dr. Burney a nest of nightingales." The Linleys' position at Bath was synonymous with "Handel's at Windsor," their house was "always open, hospitable, and bright." As for Eliza, "Her voice was as lovely as her face, and she was the *prima donna* of her father's concert. . . . in Bath the young men were all at her feet, and not only the young men, as was natural, but the elder and less innocent members of society." Too much attention has been paid, suggests Oliphant, to Eliza's relationship with Captain Mathews, for emphasizing the Captain's low character erroneously establishes Sheridan as somehow different from Eliza's numerous devoted gallants: "[t]he affair [with Mathews] has occupied too much space, we think in the story of Sheridan's life. . . . The Maid of Bath, as she was called, had many admirers" (17–20). Eliza is, therefore, not simply a victim requiring Sheridan's heroic actions, but rather a victim of all male attention. Sheridan appears at best as only a partial improvement. Thus, his escape with Eliza is the first significant event in Sheridan's life, and he is not portrayed as the principal player.

Aside from portraying him as one of several would-be suitors, Oliphant likewise lowers Sheridan's heroic status by reminding the reader of his essential familial and class realities. Whereas Moore sees in Sheridan a character that transcends his milieu, Oliphant asserts that his poverty and low rank may have been Sheridan's ultimate motivation:[17] "he was very young, very poor, without any prospects that could justify him in entering the lists on his own account" (21). Later in her narrative, Oliphant questions Sheridan's financial ability to assist Miss Linley's escape to France:

> It is a curious commentary, however, upon the prodigality of the penniless class to which Sheridan belonged that he could manage to start off suddenly upon this journey out of Thomas Sheridan's household, where money was never abundant, a boy of twenty, with nothing of his own—hurrying up to London with post-horses, and hiring magnificently "the wife of one of his servants" to attend upon his love. (25)

This lengthy speculation ends with Oliphant's unmistakable association of poverty to the immorality of the preceding age: "there is nothing more remarkable than the ease with which these impecunious gallants procure post-chaises, servants, and luxuries in those dashing days" (26).

Within this context, Oliphant narrates Richard and Eliza's elopement. Perceiving in the young couple's decision the obvious trappings of romance, Oliphant consistently undercuts any positive estimation of Sheridan's character and dismisses their decision as sentimental nonsense. To begin, Eliza's character is perfectly recognizable, according to Oliphant. Citing a letter from Eliza to a confidante, in which she laments having engaged in correspondence with Captain Matthews, Oliphant declares, "The letter, indeed, is Lydia Languish from beginning to end—the Lydia Languish of real life without genius to trim her utterance into just as much as is needful and characteristic . . . something between Clarissa Harlowe and Julia Mannering" (20). As the innocent yet "long-winded" heroine, Eliza's situation presented an opportunity for Richard to "immediately [assume] the position of the young lady's guardian"; in this role, he became intimate friends with the Captain, which enabled him to discover the older suitor's "villainous designs," while simultaneously maintaining Eliza's confidence. While this characterization would suggest that Oliphant held some regard for Sheridan, it is at this moment in the narrative that she reminds the reader of his poverty—"he was very young, very poor, without any prospects." After this brief speculation, the reader is encouraged to question the romantic nature of his motivations; suddenly, his choices seem disingenuous at best, duplicitous at worst. For Oliphant, it was Sheridan's economic status that enabled him to secure the sentimental Eliza's affections, for he uses his poverty as a rhetorical device and is able to convince "Miss Linley that his love for her was subdued in friendship" (21) because he would not have dared to hope otherwise. Sheridan's poem for Eliza in fact explains how his counsel regarding her current circumstances originate solely out of filial love, "for well did she know that my heart meant no wrong." As a result, Sheridan's figure thus appeals to the sentimental Eliza, who "no doubt would have derived a certain comfort from the romantic circumstances altogether—the villain on one hand, threatening to lay his death at her door; the modest, self-suppressed adorer, on the other, devoting himself to her service" (23).

Unlike Eliza, however, Oliphant is unwilling to view Sheridan as the romantic protector; instead, she paints a figure whose intentions are simultaneously chivalric and manipulative: "[t]he two young creatures laid their foolish heads together in this crisis of fate—the girl thoroughly frightened, the youth full of chivalrous determination to protect her, and doubtless not without a hotheaded young lover's hope to turn it to his advantage." Thus, in Oliphant's biography, it is Sheridan who proposes that she should go to France and seek shelter in a convent; he will return to England to ensure that Eliza's actions are judged properly. It is important to note, however, that Sheridan is not cast as the unapologetic rake, for Oliphant concedes that the "Rash young lover" may simply be following youthful exuberance: "[i]t would seem [he] was very honest and really meant to carry out this mad project." Despite these concessions, the continual allusions to Sheridan's background gives a dark tinge to what might simply be a portrait of youthful, innocent sentimentalism. As a result, the reader perceives, within the gaps of Oliphant's narrative, a manipulative aspect of Sheridan's character: "[b]ut when they were fairly launched upon their adventurous career either common sense or discreet acquaintances soon made it apparent to the young man that a youth and a maiden, however virtuous, cannot rove about the world in this way without comment, and that there was but one thing to be done in the circumstances." Before once again speculating about Sheridan's ability to attain the money for such an adventure—"the prodigality of the penniless class"—Oliphant concludes this part of the elopement episode by returning to Eliza's problematic situation. As before, Oliphant again refrains from outright criticism of Sheridan's behavior, but there remains a conspicuous implication of the events so described: "[p]erhaps Miss Linley had begun to feel something more than the mere 'preference for the youngest,' which she had so calmly announced, or perhaps it was only the desperate nature of the circumstances that made her yield" (23–25).

Although she refrains from outright derision at this point, the rhetoric with which Oliphant introduces and narrates the elopement foreshadows her subsequent treatment of Sheridan's works and career in Parliament, when her criticisms are not so veiled. Before Oliphant approaches his famous speeches during the Hastings' impeachment, she efficiently addresses the young couple's desire to become members of the social elite despite their conspicuous inability to afford such an expensive lifestyle: "[w]hen he established himself in London with his beautiful young wife, they had neither means nor prospects to justify the life they immediately began to lead, making their house, which had no feasible means of support, into a little social centre, and collecting about it a crowd of acquaintances, much better off than they." For Oliphant, as with the elopement episode, Sheridan is an uncompromising arriviste, whose decisions are consistently motivated by both his desire to rise in society and his awareness of the limits of his familial past. Because Richard and Eliza had "been brought up in an atmosphere of publicity," they were naturally inclined to believe "that to make 'good friends' is to make your fortune." As a result, his invitation to join Johnson's Literary Club was not sufficient in its own right to bring Sheridan pleasure—instead, it was his relationships with Fox and Burke, which originated in the Literary Club, that were the most intoxicating: "[s]ocial success so great and rapid is always rare, and the contrast between the former life of the poor player's penniless son . . . without a sixpence in his pocket, and that of the distinguished young dramatist . . . making a close alliance with two of the first statesman of the day, invited everywhere . . . must have been overwhelming" (112–15).

This is the appropriate lens for considering Sheridan's sudden desire for public office, according to Oliphant, for otherwise "it is a little difficult to make out how it was that, just as he had achieved brilliant success in one career, he should have so abruptly turned to another" (120).[18] Sheridan's sudden ambitions for political office were not based in public service any more than his playwriting had been based on his desire to become a man of letters—"[t]here is no appearance that Sheridan cared very much for literary fame." Therefore, argues Oliphant, there is one conspicuous motivation that underpins all of Sheridan's decisions:

> Social success was what he aimed at—he wanted to be among the first, not in intellect, but in fact; to win his way into the highest elevation, and to stand there on an equality with whosoever should approach. . . . He would not creep into favour or wait for invitations into great houses, but boldly . . . himself invited the great world and became the host and entertainer of persons infinitely more important than himself. . . . And no doubt his determination to acquire for himself . . . a position in which he should be on the same level as the greatest—not admitted on sufferance, but an indispensable part of society—had something to do with the earnestness with which he threw himself into public life. (120–22)

Sheridan possessed some level of political sincerity—he was dutifully loyal to Fox and the Whig party—but, Oliphant maintains, he simply did not possess the same enthusiasm or passion as Burke. Instead, he was a "light-hearted adventurer in politics," seeking the honor and prestige of political and social significance.

The Hastings trial, therefore, presented to Sheridan the most conspicuous opportunity for him to ensure his reputation, not the moment to promote his underlying political ideology. Despite praising Sheridan for his elocutionary accomplishment, remarking how Sheridan was the perfect spokesman for such a rightful cause for humanity, Oliphant nonetheless reminds the reader that Sheridan's passionate sympathy for the Begums was not inherent, but grew steadily as he recognized the potential for a spectacular performance of oratory: "it was an extraordinary piece of good-fortune for Sheridan . . . that he should happily have lighted upon a subject for his greatest effort, which should not only afford scope for all his gifts . . . but at the same time should secure for himself as the magnanimous advocate a large share of sympathy of the audience." Similar to the elopement episode and his earlier contrivances to enter the highest society, Sheridan's greatest moments in Parliament were nonetheless motivated—at least in part—by self-promotion:

> His subject, his oratorical power, the real enthusiasm which inspired him, even if that enthusiasm took fire at its own flame, was more on account of Brinsley Sheridan than of the Begums, all helped in the magical effect. . . . He was the champion of humanity, the defender of the weak and helpless. No doubt, in the flow of interest in his own subject to which he'd worked himself up, he felt all this more fervently even than his audience, which again added infinitely to his power. (141)

To Oliphant, the Hastings' speeches represent the apex of Sheridan's life, for his fame would immediately begin its descent into "the dark side of life" (143). However, the consistent portrayal of this moment in terms of class—"this was what the player's son, the dramatist and stage-manager . . . had come to" (140)—and self-interest reinforces the over-arching hermeneutic of her biography. Beginning with her construction of his elopement with Eliza, Oliphant cautions the reader about perceiving him through a sentimental lens like the one Moore provides. Although Richard Brinsley Sheridan had momentary flashes of genius as a playwright and politician, his life presents a standard narrative of individuals born in unpromising circumstances who reach for greatness that is beyond their grasp.

Sheridan, the Spectacular

In 1909, Walter Sichel published a "scholarly" biographical treatment of Sheridan—an attempt to provide a comprehensive biography of the famous figure based on extensive research into primary source materials. As he writes in his Introduction, "A Comprehensive Life of Sheridan has long been needed. He has too often been drawn in profile, yet he touched the world at every point" (1:vii).[19] Published thirty years after Oliphant's influential treatment, Sichel's work intends to fill in the many gaps of our historical understanding of Sheridan. After discovering the diary kept by the Duchess of Devonshire, for example, Sichel "establishes what I long suspected from other evidence, that the Prince of Wales's well-known 'Letter to Mr. Pitt' was composed not by Burke . . . but by Sheridan." Because of his manner of research, discovering and analyzing such artifacts, Sichel asserts a more substantive and academic authority for his two-volume biography and thanks the Sheridan family, who gave him access to peruse documents other biographers overlooked.

Despite purporting a scholarly objectivity, Sichel's work nonetheless betrays an underlying ideology from the very opening by arguing the importance of rescuing Sheridan from the "individualism" of nineteenth-century biographies that sought "to play a solo upon a great man." For Sichel, Sheridan's is a figure too complex for such confinement: "[t]he career of Sheridan rejects this barbarous simplicity of treatment—as Hamlet repudiated the artless fingering of Guildestern. The multiplicity of this man and his connections requires an orchestra, in the conduct of which it will tax all our powers to harmonise the discords" (1:1). Adding to this sensational language, Sichel's frequent comparisons of Sheridan's life to various dramas likewise contributes to the grand effect of Sheridan's figure.[20] The rhetorical distinction is striking: while biographers frequently examine Sheridan's plays for their autobiographical elements, Sichel's work labors to establish the Sheridan biography through external texts. By creating such a prism, Sheridan's life becomes an embodiment of intertextuality, and the moments that compose his character appear all the more spectacular, given their literary and dramatic resonance. This is most apparent in Sichel's narration of the elopement episode, when Sheridan is cast in the role of "Count Almaviva," and Sichel's writing seems, quite frankly, as operatic as the scene he narrates.

While Sichel occasionally offers a semblance of moral evaluation in his chapter on the elopement, he devotes most of the chapter to tamping down such inclinations by continually drawing our attention to characters and plotting we should already recognize. The lengthy chapter begins with a reminder:

> Everyone remembers Count Almaviva in Beaumarchais's first part of his Figaro trilogy—the deliverer in domino of beauty in distress. Moonlight and serenade flit around him, Rosina beckons from her balcony, Bartolo's dark shadow looms in the background, while Figaro's ironic smile and unabashed resource blend with each phantom of a scene which is the triumph of operatic sentiment. (1:318–19)

By framing his narrative in this way, Sichel controls the reading of the event itself, establishing the scene as part of a larger romantic comedy—the "first act is elopement; the second, duel; the third, retreat; the fourth marriage"—before declaring that "[s]ome stock must be taken of the *dramatis personae* before the curtain rises" (1:318–19). Framing his discourse in this manner, Sichel portrays Sheridan as a character type—the romantic hero specifically—which inherently discourages the reader from condemning his behavior too harshly. After devoting several pages to the important "characters" in his text, Sichel commences with the elopement itself. [21]

In his descriptions of Mathews, Sichel likewise omits nothing in establishing the sensational aspect of his villainy. Mathews affords Eliza no respite, "brandishing a pistol before her" and "insisting on a renewal of their friendship." Eliza considered suicide, wrote a will and "[s]at down with a bottle of laudanum," when "Sheridan suddenly entered, saw the phial, dissuaded her from pursuing so fell a purpose and besought her to wait . . . he promised to stop Mathews pursuit." Unlike Moore and Oliphant, Sichel perceives the scheme to escape to France as one hatched by Eliza, Elizabeth Sheridan, and Richard together. Eliza and Richard are essentially equal characters in a drama, where Richard performs the necessary role of chivalric hero. As evidence, Sichel connects Sheridan's motivation to many of the lyrics written for *The Duenna* in 1772 and 1773, specifically "Carlos's Song," for which "chivalry animates the strain" (1:337–40). Again diminishing any moral questioning, Sichel suggests that Eliza was as enraptured by the spectacle of their elopement as well: "the suffering, as well as the romance, appealed to her, for as Sheridan was afterwards to write in his *Duenna* (1775), 'In the heart's attachments, a woman never likes a man with ardour, till she has suffered for his sake'" (1:346).

Sichel's propensity to rely on theatrical rhetoric enables him to heighten the spectacle of Sheridan's famous Begum Speech as well. In Parliament, Sheridan appears as a sincere actor in "a drama, and in part a tragedy"; the indictment is inherently "melodramatic" with "the unraveling of threads furnished a plot fraught with the . . . complexity of sensation." Sheridan, himself now a character in Sichel's drama, is attracted to both the sentimental and sensational aspects of the Hastings' plot. While the particulars of the indictment appeal to Sheridan's moral sensibilities—"Women and princesses had been misused, bribes and money had been taken and extorted. Sheridan was chivalrous, and he despised lucre"—the potential spectacle offers an undeniable political benefit, for "[h]ere was the unrivalled opportunity for all the powers at Hastings' command: eloquence, raillery, dramatic presentation" (2:122–23).

Avoiding an exploration of Sheridan's motivation, Sichel's emphasis is—yet again—on the theatrical effect of Sheridan's performance. As for Sheridan's speech in the House of Commons, Sichel notes that we have "some faint idea of the unexampled sensation caused by the speech." Examining the evidence of Sheridan's second speech to the House of Lords, he reiterates this point: "[t]here are parts of the Westminster Hall performance so infinitely superior as to prove that the speech in the senate which caused an even greater sensation will never be adequately known. The effect cannot be exaggerated."[22] Sichel next itemizes the famous attestations of Burke, Fox, Pitt, and Burgess to finally assert "all other topics were effaced. Nobody could talk of anything but Sheridan's speech." Finally, Sichel's narration evolves into a sensational novel itself: "[a] stillness succeeded in which pin could be heard to drop. For nearly six hours he riveted his audience by an utterance exceedingly rapid though singularly distinct, and at the close his voice sank to a whisper. The House, for the first time within record, broke into applause, and Sheridan's friends rushed up to him and hung about his neck" (2:127–28).

Although highly affected, Sichel's tome illustrates another method of unifying Sheridan's multi-dimensional figuring as a poet, dramatist, theatre manager, and politician. For Sichel, such a figure requires a theatrical framing, where the reader is less inclined to offer a moral summation of Sheridan's life and more encouraged to marvel at the spectacular nature of Sheridan's contributions. Sichel closes his biography in the similar vein he began, arguing that Sheridan's figure resists the confinement of normal biography, and readers will only comprehend his significance through an admiration of spectacle. Like other persons from other ages, Sheridan's life is "a drama" and his "being" will "continue to live in a romance of its own, long after [it] vanished from the stage." Because of its essential "picturesqueness," Sichel continues, Sheridan's "providence is not history but wonderland" (2:389).

Sheridan, the Irish Radical

We see a new dramatic shift in Sheridan's biographical history in Fintan O'Toole's *A Traitor's Kiss: The Life of Richard Brinsley Sheridan*. Contrasting Moore, Oliphant, and Sichel (and all others previously noted), O'Toole returns to Ireland to solve the biographical conundrum, arguing that the lack of a recent "Irish biography" has allowed Sheridan to become simply a "colorful flaw" in our understanding of eighteenth-century culture. It is only through the playwright's Irishness, suggests O'Toole, that we can resolve several of Sheridan's contradictory impulses: "he lived in two different places—a real England and a passionately imagined Ireland—at the same time" (v).[23]

Although O'Toole categorizes Moore's *Life of Sheridan* to be an early Irish biography, implying that *A Traitor's Kiss* returns us to a previously correct understanding of the playwright, the blatant ideological intent of this most recent biography is distinctive from Moore's. From the very first chapter of his work, which chronicles the "bloody characters" of Sheridan's Irish ancestry, O'Toole presents a Sheridan strikingly different from Moore's sentimental wit. Through the course of his life, Sheridan becomes an Irish politico, one continually battling the oppressive constraints of Anglo and Anglo-Irish society and expectations, even conspiring with the French to invade Ireland. This is apparent even in O'Toole's presentation of Sheridan's elopement with Eliza Linley.

As other biographers, O'Toole allows that Sheridan loved Eliza, that he performed the role of the gallant protector because of the truthfulness of his emotions. Through the course of his narrative, however, there are intermittently unmistakable references to Sheridan's blooming political agenda. Before describing the events surrounding the elopement, O'Toole devotes some time to Sheridan's writing collaborations with Nathaniel Halhed, Sheridan's good friend from Harrow school, when they first endeavored to make money at writing plays. Although their first attempt, *Jupiter*, is now lost except for excerpts included in Moore's biography, O'Toole is most concerned with the contrasting writing styles omnipresent in the text. For O'Toole, the styles reveal the divergent political futures of both young playwrights: "their different approaches to language would, in less than twenty years, lead to their engagement on opposite sides in one of the greatest political conflicts of the day—the impeachment of Warren Hastings" (46). While this chapter ends by asserting that the "young Irishman" Sheridan remained in Bath because of Eliza, this overt political reference inherently influences our reading of the subsequent chapter, which presents the elopement episode.

After introducing the family of the Linleys and narrating Eliza's entanglements with Long and Mathews, O'Toole questions the true extent of Sheridan's infatuation by noting his sister's surprise at his "startling confession." O'Toole muses that "nothing in his previous behaviour had suggested he was lovestruck," given that he had acted as the "go-between" for Halhed, who had already professed his attraction to Eliza. Sheridan, according to O'Toole, probably had romantic feelings for Eliza, but his declaration "may not have been entirely divorced from his feelings of rivalry with his brother . . . who had been deeply in love with Eliza since they had first met." The implication of Sheridan's true ambitions becomes unmistakable when O'Toole compares the two sons: Charles "was afraid of provoking his father's displeasure" whereas Richard "had an opportunity to prove himself a better man than his brother. . . . And, he could, at the same time, break free from his father." This distinction between the two brothers contributes to the progression of Sheridan's figure as a political romantic, one who will always seek ways to disrupt class expectations. In O'Toole's narrative, Sheridan's sudden pursuit and capture of Eliza presents "a dramatic declaration of independence" (55–56), one in which the young writer establishes a pattern of self-reliance and self-promotion.

Whereas Oliphant's biography establishes economics as the over-arching motivation behind Sheridan's pursuit of Eliza, O'Toole emphasizes the political nature of their romance, which is most apparent in his discussion of Sheridan's duels with Matthews. Following "The Language of Love," O'Toole presents in the next two chapters—"Gentleman and Players" and "The Great Gate of Power"—a figure consistently mindful of his lack of political and cultural agency. O'Toole asks, "Why did Sheridan risk his life with Mathews a second time?" when it appears that "He had everything to lose and nothing to gain." Although the first duel arose somewhat understandably out of his love for Eliza, the second duel arose only in conjunction with Mathews' insult in the *Bath Chronicle*, "'I cannot longer think he [Sheridan] deserves the treatment of a gentleman.'" O'Toole explains that Sheridan never intended to follow through with a second duel with Mathews, for both men seemed content to drink together to work out their differences. When Sheridan read the exact text of Mathew's insult, however, he determined to defend his honor. Like his courtship of Eliza, this was an opportunity for Sheridan to elevate his own cultural standing, which, for O'Toole, is inherently a political opportunity—"[i]f [Sheridan] was to beat the system, he had first to be able to enter it"—and one that relates to Thomas Sheridan's earlier attempts to be seen as a "gentleman." By dueling Mathews a second time—and being almost mortally wounded—Sheridan, according to O'Toole, attained the status of being a "gentleman." That the elopement episode attains political significance for O'Toole becomes very clear when the biographer concludes, "[i]n [Sheridan's] mind at least, he had confounded the ordained social order of eighteenth-century England" (66–67, 73).

The elopement episode is simply an early step in Sheridan's political progression, however, for he would most "confound" the system later as a radical Whig M.P., as first evidenced during the Hastings Trial. Contrasting Oliphant and Sichel, O'Toole affirms Sheridan's passion—as opposed to empty political posturing—for righting the wrongs of English imperialism. Citing a speech in 1784, four years before the Hastings trial, O'Toole proves that Sheridan was already critical of the East India Company for "itself becoming a new source of autocracy in Britain" and had "sympathy for India itself" and a "loathing for Hastings" (214). Although Sheridan's rhetoric was brilliantly performed, it was nonetheless informed by a man consistently motivated to shed light on the "oppressed multitudes" of a country effectually raped—"sacrificing female dignity"—by English capitalism (218). Fittingly, O'Toole's most deliberate description of Sheridan's speeches appear in a chapter titled "The Rights of Man," where the biographer again emphasizes the political import of Sheridan's motivations. Whereas one would assume that a speech before the House of Lords is conspicuously political, given the rhetorical focus of other biographies, O'Toole's assertion of Sheridan's political radicalism is distinctive. To O'Toole, Sheridan continually attacks British self-aggrandizement: "he [Sheridan] satirizes two of the commonplaces of British imperialism—the notion that British rule has a civilizing effect and the idea that British mastery of other races is God's will"; "Sheridan quickly returned to his attack on the reality of sacred British values in India"; and "[i]n assaulting the sacred symbols of British rule, Sheridan went so far as to reverse the meaning of the British flag itself." Contrary to those who assert the speeches are disingenuous presentations of theatrical spectacle, O'Toole argues that Sheridan "brought his own deep-rooted concerns to bear on a world of which he had no direct knowledge" and his speeches look "forward to his great polemics of the 1790s" (227–31). Whereas other biographies note the reactions of the more prominent Members of Parliament—Pitt, Fox, Burke—O'Toole poignantly notes that radical thinkers like John Wilkes and Sir Philip Francis praised the speech as well (221). In his final estimation, it is Sheridan who deserves some credit for contributing to the eventual reverence for human rights that exist in present-day political discourse. The Hastings trial "appears as a great moment in the history of international law. The idea on which Sheridan relied—the universal nature of human rights and responsibilities—would not be fully elaborated until the twentieth century, but they were at least given powerful expression at the heart of an imperial power" (230).

Understanding the political thematic focus of his work, it is fitting that O'Toole chooses to close his biography with the reference to William Godwin's visit to Sheridan's grave. Godwin, like O'Toole, remembers a man who "had done all in his power to create a Britain that valued freedom over conquest and an Ireland that was stultified neither by Catholic tribalism nor by Protestant claims to ascendancy" (471). O'Toole thus suggests yet another interpretive figuring: Sheridan was not so much a sentimental wit or arriviste as he was consistently a man concerned with the rightful distribution of political power.

We have here briefly discussed how the spectacular flashes of Sheridan's life have no doubt encouraged the consistent biographical refashioning of his character. Examining the evolution of his biography, we encounter a Sheridan who is difficult to define, despite the innumerable attempts; he appears less of a historical figure and more of a hermeneutical signifier of the biographer's moral intention. Moore's and Oliphant's biographies became the standard accounts of the nineteenth century, both competing to estimate the value of Sheridan's contributions: Moore's presents the romantic Sheridan, full of passion and wit; Oliphant's, the vapid Sheridan, possessing only a modicum of ability and more concerned with social preferment and hierarchical status. Both biographies went through numerous printings, even while others presented "new" evidence from Sheridan's life. Sichel's biography is significant for our purpose because it represents an early twentieth-century attempt to avoid transparent moral evaluations, presenting a detached wonder at the spectacle of Sheridan's life and accomplishments. Most recently, O'Toole's biography reflects the influence of the recent postcolonial period of Sheridan studies as he deliberately and meticulously documents the Irish-radical underpinning of Sheridan's entire life and works.[24] Like Moore's, Oliphant's, and Sichel's works, O'Toole's work thus occupies an important place in Sheridan's biographical history by suggesting a new twenty-first century prism for viewing the complicated life. Taken together, these four biographies unveil the contradictory nature of Sheridan's enigmatic figure. Moving forward, the future of Sheridan studies will be unavoidably influenced by these competing biographical hermeneutics, as scholars negotiate the many lives of one writer and the perils of reconciling the perplexing relationship of the works to the man.

Notes

1. Lord Byron, *Letters and Journals*, ed. Rowland E. Prothero, 6 vols. (London: J. Murray, 1922–24), 6:45.

2. Edward Halim Mikhail, *Sheridan: Interviews and Recollections*, (New York: St. Martin's Press, 1989), ix.

3. Linda Kelly, *Richard Brinsley Sheridan: A Life* (London: Pimlico, 1998), 309; Fintan O'Toole, *A Traitor's Kiss: The Life of Richard Brinsley Sheridan, 1751–1816* (New York: Farrar, Straus, and Giroux, 1998), 471–72.

4. For example, R. Crompton Rhodes's *Harlequin Sheridan: The Man and the Legends* (Oxford: Blackwell, 1933) focuses on Sheridan's contemporary reputation, paying only brief attention to the famous plays. On the other hand, Jack Davis Durant's *Richard Brinsley Sheridan: A Reference Guide* (Boston: G. K. Hall, 1981); and James Morwood's *The Life and Works of Richard Brinsley Sheridan* (Edinburgh: Scottish Academic Press, 1985) appear to wrestle the playwright away from the man, structuring their chapters explicitly around Sheridan's main dramatic works.

5. The bibliographical data prior to 1980 included in this article derives mostly from Durant's helpful bibliography, *Richard Brinsley Sheridan: A Reference Guide* (1981).

6. Paula R. Backscheider, *Reflections on Biography* (New York: Oxford University Press, 1999), 3, 100.

7. Thomas Moore, *Memoirs of the Life of the Right Honourable Richard Brinsley Sheridan*, 5th ed. (London: Longman, Rees, Orme, et al., 1826); Margaret Oliphant, *Sheridan: English Men of Letters* (New York: Harper and Brothers, 1887); Walter Sichel, *Sheridan: From New and Original Material; Including a Manuscript Diary by Georgiana, Duchess of Devonshire* (Boston: Houghton, 1909).

8. Throughout this essay, I will note many biographies that share similar viewpoints with these four primary texts. Moore's *Memoirs*; Oliphant's *Sheridan: English Men of Letters*; Sichel's *Sheridan*; and O'Toole's *A Traitor's Kiss* biographies are unique, however, for they were extremely popular, represent important shifts in Sheridan's biographical history, and were highly influential on later biographies. In terms of the most recent treatments, O'Toole's *Traitor's Kiss* presents more directly another emerging trend in Sheridan studies—the playwright's position within a postcolonial hermeneutic. This is in contrast to Kelly's biography, *Richard Brinsley Sheridan*, which efficiently chronicles the multifarious aspects of Sheridan's life but does not venture into much previously unchartered territory.

9. John Watkins's is the first biographical account. A political rival of Sheridan's, Watkins uses Sheridan's life as a warning to others about the perils of imprudence. He also raises the possibility that Sheridan stole the plot for *The School for Scandal* from a daughter of a merchant on Thames Street. (See John Watkins, *Memoirs of the Public and Private Life of the Right Honourable Richard Brinsley Sheridan, with a Particular Account of His Family and Connexions*, 2nd ed. [London: Henry Colburn, 1817]; and Richard Brinsley Sheridan, *The School for Scandal*. Edited by Cecil Price. [Oxford: Oxford University Press, 1971]).

10. According to Durant's bibliography, *Richard Brinsley Sheridan: A Reference Guide,* a 5th ed. of Moore's biography already appeared before 1827; multiple reprintings appeared throughout the nineteenth century, including 1853, 1858, and 1882 (in New York).

11. Moore, *Memoirs,* 1:v. This and all subsequent references are taken from the 5th ed. (cf. n 7) published in 1826.

12. Oscar Sherwin's is the twentieth-century biography most like Moore's, setting Sheridan's life—his accomplishments and misadventures—against the backdrop of the late eighteenth century: "the Georgian era is a carnival of the animal man in which leading roles are played by Sheridan and his circle" (Oscar Sherwin, *Uncorking Old Sherry: The Life and Times of Richard Brinsley Sheridan* [New York: Twayne, 1960], 38).

13. Like Moore's *Memoirs*, Oliphant's biography, *Sheridan*, was extremely popular, going through five printings before 1909 (Durant, *Richard Brinsley Sheridan: A Reference Guide*).

14. This and all subsequent references are taken from Oliphant's *Sheridan* (cf. n 7). Lewis Gibbs presents an image of Sheridan similar to that of Oliphant. Although his career may be separated into three phases, all were marked by a constant propensity to accrue debt. Although Gibbs is not as critical as Oliphant, his work laments that Sheridan's accrual of debt exemplifies how a "kind of conduct which makes the greatest talents useless" (Lewis Gibbs, *Sheridan: His Life and His Theatre* [New York: William Morrow, 1948], 107–8).

15. Madeleine Bingham similarly sees Sheridan as a figure, like his father and grandfather, desperate to rise in class and become a gentleman. Thus, he stopped writing plays—the one profession where he may have surpassed all others—and chased political preferment the majority of his life. Madeleine Bingham, *Sheridan: The Track of a Comet* (New York: St. Martin's Press, 1972).

16. Many biographers focus more deliberately on Sheridan's education and schooling. Oliphant's work, to be sure, never intends to be comprehensive; however, in proportion to her treatment of other periods of Sheridan's life, the quickness of her narrative before the elopement episode is striking (Oliphant, *Sheridan*).

17. Issues of class appear in multiple biographies. Many, including Walter Sichel, assert that the Sheridans believed themselves to be above the Linleys in terms of social status (Sichel, *Sheridan*, 319).

18. While others suggest that Sheridan longed for public office early in his life, Oliphant perceives a paucity of evidence for such a contention: "[h]e had shown no particular inclination towards public life in his earlier days; no resort to debating clubs. . . . Oratory, in all probability, had been made odious to him by his father's unceasing devotion to his system" (Oliphant, *Sheridan*, 119).

19. This and all future references are taken from Sichel's *Sheridan*, cf. n 7.

20. Alice Glasgow employs a similar hermeneutic in her biography, narrating Sheridan's life as a play with many styles of performance. Chapter titles are illustrative—"The Setting," "Puppet Promenade," "Elopement a Trois"—of her emphasis on Sheridan's spectacular life (*Sheridan of Drury Lane: A Biography* [New York: Frederick A. Stokes, 1940]). In her 1931 biography, Eliza Marian Butler likewise emphasizes the numerous flashes of Sheridan's life, how he sought these moments throughout the early part of his life. More like Oliphant, however, Butler bluntly criticizes Sheridan for consistently avoiding responsibility for his actions: "He had desire that evanescent glory to the exclusion of everything else" (*Sheridan: A Ghost Story* [New York: Richard Smith, 1931], xii).

21. Contrasting Oliphant's perspective, Sichel removes any economic motivation from Sheridan's ambitions, noting that Charles Sheridan abandoned his pursuit of Eliza because "Miss Linley was poor, and a performer; old Sheridan, proud and ambitious for his sons. Charles would not hamper his future" on such a "ridiculous attachment" (Sichel, *Sheridan*, 335).

22. This is an important distinction from Moore's biography, *Memoirs*, which focuses on Sheridan's wit as opposed to effect of Sheridan's performance.

23. This and all future references are taken from O'Toole's *A Traitor's Kiss*, (cf. n 7). O'Toole's assertion contradicts Oliphant's argument, which asserts that writers like Goldsmith and Sheridan were Irish in name only: "Sheridan was so little of a Irishman in fact that there is not, we think, a single trace even of a visit to his native country" (Oliphant, *Sheridan*, 117).

24. The most recent entry on Sheridan in the *Dictionary of National Biography* has a distinctly Irish bent, focusing on the aspects of Sheridan's character exposed by O'Toole's *A Traitor's Kiss*. A. Norman Jeffares' entry ventures to conclude, "O'Toole's sparking account of the ramifications of Sheridan's political career is particularly searching" (*Oxford Dictionary of National Biography*, s.v. "Richard Brinsley Sheridan (1751–1816), by A. Norman Jeffares, http://oxforddnb.com (accessed June 2, 2011).

2

SHERIDAN'S EARLY STYLE

Robert W. Jones

THIS ESSAY CONSIDERS Sheridan's published writings up to the time of his marriage in April 1773. Although the great triumph of *The Rivals* did not come until the spring of 1775, Sheridan had made several forays into print by the time he attempted to settle down to married life in East Burnham. The canon of Sheridan's early poetry includes "The Ridotto of Bath" (1771) and *Clio's Protest; or, the Picture Varnished* (1772) as well as shorter love lyrics, including "Uncouth is the moss-covered stone" and "To the Recording Angel." The poems are lively and engaged pieces, often prompted by events in Bath's fashionable circles as well as in his own life. Sheridan also worked with his former school fellow Nathaniel Brassey Halhed to translate the *Love Epistles of Aristænetus* (1771), a daring and ambitious undertaking given the erotic content of the Greek original. This is a substantial body of work, all of it completed before Sheridan was twenty-two. Had Sheridan never ventured into print again, he would have been best remembered for having fought two duels with Thomas Mathews. Although there was some romance in the affair, as the combatants were rivals for Elizabeth Linley's affections, both duels were truly brutal fights (they fought finally with the "pointed ends" of their broken swords).[1] Having survived serious injury, Sheridan was accused of having acted in a "vaunting manner," a style at once aggressive and ungentlemanly.[2] Although Sheridan denied the charge, his biographers have since struggled to rationalize his violent conduct. Thomas Moore found writing his account of Sheridan's duels tremendously difficult, lamenting the violence of youth even as he aimed to exonerate his protagonist.[3] A "wild mêlée" is Fintan O'Toole's description of the second duel, while Madeleine Bingham derides it as a "simple fight between two males about a female." Although Bingham and O'Toole claim that the duels with Mathews laid the foundation of Sheridan's later public fame—a reputation exploited successfully in *The Rivals*—both find his conduct antithetical to his later sophistication.[4]

There can be little doubt that Sheridan could be an aggressive and assertive young man, forever keen to best his social and sexual rivals. It was a temperament that honed and pointed his initial forays into public life. Sheridan's first published poem "Hymen and Hirco: A Vision" was an attack on Walter Long (an aged suitor for Miss Linley's hand). Sheridan represents his rival as a snoozing dotard whose flabbiness makes him incapable of satisfaction. Represented with a "well-stuffed paunch" and "soul so mean," poor Long is the butt of a young man's scornful fun:

> Desist, old man! Give credit to your years:
> Thy lazy blood rejects the am'rous storm:
> 'Tis callous to the whip your fancy rears,
> Which only tickles, while it cannot warm.[5]

The aggression evident in "Hymen and Hirco" is far from exceptional. Sexual jealousy and rivalry are central to Sheridan's first efforts. Other early poems offer similarly edgy reflections on the nature of love and desire. One of the best of the poems in the *Aristænetus* is "Epistle XXVIII: The Rival Friends," a lover's lament on losing "his lover to a friend." Elizabeth Linley was probably the woman in question, as Moore and others have been quick to point out.[6] But aggression is evident everywhere in Sheridan's youthful writings: *Clio's Protest* challenges another poet, mocking his efforts while seeking further confrontation, as if dueling was always his preferred mode.

It is not enough to appreciate these clashes biographically. We need to be more sensitive to the apparent failings of Sheridan's youth but also to the complexity of his "vaunting manner." The phrase is instructive, capturing something of the young man's presumptive ambition, his lack of irony or self-awareness, but also his intrusive style. Style is perhaps always assertive: an intrinsic combativeness which manifests itself as an assertion of the will, not least as a desire to impress, to come down on others, as on the page. For Jacques Derrida, style is a process of continuous cutting and breaking. He writes, "in the question of style, there is always . . . some pointed object. At times this object might only be a quill or a stylus. But it could just as easily be a stiletto or a rapier."[7] Pricked by Derrida's comparison of sword and pen, this essay explores Sheridan's clashes with others and the aggressive nature of his first works. Hereafter "style" will be taken to encompass not just the attainment of a certain level of proficiency—though this is important—but the accomplishment and inscription of a personal presence. More specifically, my argument addresses the disturbing qualities of his early style, indeed the style of youth (and of youthfulness) to which it is closely allied but never completely reduced.

To broach this topic is to enter something of a critical vacuum and not only in Sheridan studies. Early work, even by recognized writers, is rarely discussed directly, still less regarded as a separate category. Some work has been undertaken on the nature of distinctive writing, notably by Richard Marggraf Turley in relation to Keats, but the meaning and purpose of early style is too little considered.[8] When considering early style, it is important to resist the crude label of "juvenilia," which reduces the youthful tendencies of early work to the facts of age or chronology and as such must rely upon the dubious perspective of hindsight. Judgment consequently rests solely on the question of immaturity, as if maturity were inevitable.[9] We might feel reading an early poem, such as Wordsworth's school-boy effort "Anacreon, Ἄγε ζωγράψου' ἀρίτε, Imitated," that there is something jejune in its challenge to Sir Joshua Reynolds. More so its invocation of a woman whose beauty exceeds the painter's but not the poet's art. Wordsworth's pleasure in the white neck and rosy lips of his imagined inamorata seems callow and his superiority over Reynolds claimed rather than earned.[10] The case becomes more complex when the focus shifts to Sheridan's nearer contemporary Thomas Chatterton. Dead before he was eighteen, Chatterton's work is potentially all juvenilia. However, his verse, especially the more sophisticated of the Rowleyan pieces, deftly invests existing forms, permitting new directions and ideas to emerge. However, his work is perhaps is most intriguing when it convinces least. His "Ode to Miss Hoyland" is a case in point, a lyric that seems both anxious and too cockily assured. Throughout the poem knowledge appears willed or contrived, especially in sexual matters, suggesting that the poet's thoughts have run ahead of his actual experience. But this is what is most impressive about the poem. The gap between ambition and realization, never entirely unwilled, allows the fragility of desire to speak more eloquently.[11] As these comparisons suggest, early style is about striking a pose and striking others in order to create a space in which to write. The isolation of "early style" as a distinct formation can help us to understand Sheridan's motives, words and actions more clearly. More specifically, the term can describe Sheridan's first works in terms of the intrinsic qualities they display, while also denominating its adversarial relationship, not just to later life or works, but to the context in which it was produced. Like the "vaunting manner" of his dueling days, Sheridan's early style is aggressive but self-fracturing; it is impetuous but in the end promises more than it delivers. Demanding attention and distinction, it really seeks acceptance and friendship.

I

Amongst the most arresting of Sheridan's early works is "The Ridotto of Bath," which appeared in the *Bath Chronicle* in October 1771.[12] Written from the perspective of a servant, Timothy Screw (who writes confidentially to his brother and fellow servant, Henry), the poem describes the lavish social gathering which opened the New Assembly rooms. Screw is an experienced observer of the social scene, opening his epistle: "At many grand Routs in my time I have been" but his presence has been required to serve others and not for his own pleasure (119). Consequently his perspective is nicely complicated: at once worldly and yet not of the *beau monde*, he is in a place to judge but never in a position of authority. Sheridan would seek a similar effect in the opening scene of *The Rivals*, when Fag assures Thomas the coachman that Bath is a "good lounge" before complaining that "their regular hours stupefy me."[13] The decorousness which oppresses Fag is scarcely visible in Sheridan's anarchic poem. Although the ridotto is controlled by "Marshall Wade," whose edicts Screw records, it is hopelessly unruly: "Variety," Screw notes, "ever marks a *Bath* ball":

> For here no dull level of rank and degrees,
> No uniform mode, that show all are at ease;
> But like a chess table, part black and part white,
> 'Twas a delicate checquer of *low* and *polite*
> The motley assemblage, so blended together
> 'Twas Mob, or Ridotto, 'twas both, or 'twas neither. (120)

In another context the image of a chess board might indicate the certainty of opposites and the possibility of tactics played out according to known rules, but in Bath it is merely "chequered." The heterogeneity of Bath society is emphasized when Screw describes the appearance at the ball of several lower-class women: named "Brussels," "Tape" and "Trinket," they are far from fine ladies. Screw affects to be disgusted by such a confluence of tailors and seamstresses but appears tolerant enough to offer an explanation: "From Bristol too came many dames of high breeding;-/ *Seven Shillings* was *money*—but then there was feeding" (*Poems and Plans of Richard Brinsley Sheridan*, 121). Screw's ironies complete a sense that Bath society is confused and deceptive, becoming a frantic and unseemly spectacle in which order is sacrificed to a presumptive carnival.

Although the poem anticipates Faulkland's complaints about the evils of public assemblies, there is nothing immediately novel or prescient about "The Ridotto of Bath."[14] Satires on Bath were common by 1770: witness Christopher Anstey's verse epistle *The New Bath Guide or Memoirs of the B—r—d Family* (1766), from which Sheridan may have taken inspiration. The verse epistle was well-established by the 1770s as an effective means by which the false refinements and moral blandishments of the "culture of politeness" could be mocked.[15] It is the extent and nature of the mockery that makes Sheridan's work distinctive. Like the poets of his grandfather's generation, Sheridan eschews the geniality of the Horatian mode for something more demanding. Screw's sideways perspective is partly responsible for this effect, but Sheridan's ferocity arises mostly from his antipathy to the social chaos he perceives at the ridotto, a disorder which threatens to exceed the formal constraints of the verse.

The fun starts with the arrival of the food. Bath society amazes Screw with its haste and appetite. A veteran of many London gatherings, Screw is shocked when guests snatch at dishes and spill their food. Each guest, he reports, "cramm'd while he was at table, / And then carried off all he could from the table." One drinks "like an Otter," another "ate like her lap dog." Screw watches in horror as food is trampled underfoot, and mixed into wigs and hair, as West Country citizens gorge themselves in the effort to get their money's worth (*Poems and Plans*, 122). The result is a sticky and bespattered anarchy of rich dresses and semi-masticated food, a chaotic scene recalling the worst dregs of Georgian society.[16] An apotheosis of sorts is reached in the mindless conversations of the dancers as they sway full-bellied and empty-headed across the Assembly Rooms:

> In ev'ry room—*folly, confusion,* and *pother*;
> With unmeaning questions, of "which room is hotter?"
> And, "madam, pray how do you like the *Rudotter?*"
> "To see Captain *Plume* dance—sure none can dislike him—"
> "Wade's picture I think is *purdigiously* like him—"
> "Do you dance, Sir, to night? "No Ma'am I do not:"
> "I don't wonder at it, 'tis *suffoking* hot." (*Poems and Plans*, 123)

The final flourish is surprising, even in such vibrant verse. Sheridan clearly meant it, as the stress in the line and the earlier attempt at drawling speech—"*purdigiously*"—confirms (*Dramatic Works*, 123). The pun is testimony of his daring and, arguably, the innocence of some readers, the editors of the *Bath Chronicle* included. Needless expletives are often cited as a marker of the juvenile mind, but in this case bad language introduces something more intriguing. The complaint about the heat is a rare concession from the parvenus of Bath of the discomfort their antics generate, creating a moment of unexpected sympathy between the reader and those the poem portrays. The poem certainly reflects on the ambiguities generated by commercialized leisure. Eighteenth-century readers would recognize much of the frenzied activity Sheridan describes as part and parcel of the fashionable social gatherings—notoriously routs and masquerades—reports of which filled the pages of magazines and newspapers.[17] Viewed positively, Sheridan's description of the Bath ridotto recalls Hogarth's unfinished *The Dance* (1745; Tate Gallery) in its exuberant and hectic performance. Later Hogarth would make the execution of a country dance a figure for taste and beauty.[18] Sheridan's vision, however, is less assured and less confident. As a satirist, he cannot see the "*amicable Collisions*" which, for the Earl of Shaftesbury, defined politeness; rather, the Bath crowd bump against each other in a chaotic and unbeautiful way.[19] Sheridan's poem has, therefore, a complex relationship to politeness, at once seeming to demand an adherence to rules of polite behavior, while at the same time reveling in their failure.

Sheridan continued his efforts to puncture the polite forms of Bath society in his next publication, *Clio's Protest: or the Picture Varnished*. The poem was written in response to Richard Fitzpatrick's *The Bath Picture; or, a Slight Sketch of its Beauties in 1771*.[20] Fitzpatrick's work is little more than a verse catalogue of the fashionable young women then prominent on the Bath social scene. Physical and social attributes are cloyingly relayed; as in his description of Miss Jennings: "What eyes! And what lips! and what hair! / Such a mouth too—what a pleasure to kiss!" (2). More of the same follows. There is little to be said about such verse; indeed to describe it as a "slight sketch" is to be more than fair. Despite its flimsiness, *The Bath Picture* provoked a reply from Sheridan that is unrelenting in its assault on the poem and its author. As with his attack on Long, Sheridan unpacks his rival step by step in order to prove that "True *Dullness* breathes in ev'ry line." Spelling, meter, rhyme and diction are all execrated. The description of the women, he complains, is too effusive: "Ev'ry *Goose* with him's a *Swan*" (6). Miss Jennings is the first recipient of his critical gaze:

So enter *J-nn-gs* in the van:
Behold she comes in beauty's state;
(The hobbling verse proclaims her gait)
Hark, what a general *buz* is spread!
(Tho' only with a single *z*)
The nymph, unconscious that we raise
This *buzzing buzz* to *buzz* her praise
Or skill'd that consciousness to hide;
Ne'er shews the smallest scrap of pride.
But we still buzz her noble size;
Her *pretty hair*, and *pretty eyes*;
And *pretty* brows those eyes to suit;
And *pretty*—God know what to boot:
Till *echo*, charm'd at beauty's reign,
With double *buzz* repeats the strain. (7–8)

The *Bath Picture* included the unfortunate couplet: "When the elegant *Jennings* appears, / What a buz thro' the room do they raise." It is clumsy, but the missing letter was surely accidental (2). The printer's error licenses Sheridan's delight in emphatic repetitions: "*buzzing buzz* to *buzz* her praise"; elsewhere he picks up and deliberately exhausts the weak epithet "*pretty*," splashing it across his lines until the word is utterly meaningless. He continues in this vein, not sparing the women or the poet, when he writes (of Miss Calder): "I hope thy *real* feet are fleeter / Than those you halt upon in metre" (9). The comment is an aggressive assertion of metrical superiority. It is also, consciously and deliberately, a dispute about the presentation of women in poetry. The women of Bath are fought over by two unyielding volunteer laureates more interested in the force of their verbal sparring than the feelings of those they depict. Such male-to-male conflict accords with what Eve Kosofsky Sedgwick terms homosocial competition. In these terms, *Clio's Protest* is a sally in a poetic duel which, though it claims to defend women from the attentions of a poor poet, soon neglects them for the sharper pleasure of attacking a rival.[21]

The effect of this verse altercation is impolite and rather ungallant. Sheridan savages his fellow poet's efforts regardless of the women whose lives and bodies are conscripted into their dispute. He is certainly at his best when mocking his rival's pretentions. He appears less sure-footed when attempting to exceed him. The lines below refer to Lady Margaret Fordyce to whom Sheridan had dedicated his efforts;

the *Bath Picture* had given her merely a "dimpling sweet smile." This weak compliment allowed Sheridan to hasten to her defense:

> And could you really discover,
> In gazing those sweet beauties over,
> No other charm, no winning grace,
> Adorning either mind or face,
> But one poor *dimple* to express
> The *quintessence* of *Loveliness?*
> —Mark'd you her check, of rosy hue?
> Mark'd you her eye, of sparkling blue?
> That eye, in liquid circles moving!
> That check, abas'd at man's approving!
> The *one*—Love' arrows darting round;
> The *other*—blushing for the wound. (10–11)

It is difficult to see these lines as much better than those they oppose. The image of Lady Margaret's eye "in liquid circles moving" is particularly unfortunate. The intention presumably was to capture something like James Thomson's depiction of Lucinda's "shining moisture" in *The Seasons,* but the line more convincingly evokes the central figure in Hogarth's *Gin Lane* (1751), whose eyes really are afloat.[22] The wayward image is indicative of a noticeable strain, an all-too obvious effort on Sheridan's part to prove his worth by addressing the beauties of women. Like his adversary, Sheridan appears presumptive and unkind; some of his later comments—upon "*good Mrs. D—x*" especially—are cruelly censorious, mocking her as a doughty rustic wife. Other women, such as Miss Cheshire and Miss Nurse, are similarly sneered at and their faults exposed (12–13, 17).

Clio's Protest is at once unsettling and unappetizing. The poem veers between accounts of women as duplicitous or simply unattractive and equally aggressive claims for the author's greater style. Laced through this weft of abuse is a finer thread, which hints at the emptiness lurking beneath fashionable ennui: "For Modern beaux," Sheridan concedes will "scarcely spare / More time to reading than to pray'r" (11). The sentiment informs Sheridan's final advice:

> —Henceforward satire guide your pen;
> But spare the women—lash the men.
> Tho' possibly your Muse may stare,
> To find such little diff'rence there;

So oft her verse would strike, in common
The *flirting Man*, and *rakish woman*. (16)

Sheridan's sense of his own masculinity is brought to the fore in these lines, as it is
when he complains of the "skipping *Wagtail*" and "grinning *Witwould*"—the latter
is one of the fops in Congreve's *The Way of the World*. As the young poet warms to
his theme, he attacks various other men on the Bath scene, beating them all down.
This is indeed a "vaunting manner," an assertion of masculine style achieved by
making verse a form of dueling. In this spirit, the poem looks forward to fights
to come, seeming to encourage conflict: "deal the same with me," he challenges
his rivals. But even as his adopts this braggart style, Sheridan appears to unpick it,
for as soon as he throws down the gauntlet he disregards it. Such altercations, he
claims, are characteristic of "schioliasts in verse" and perhaps of no matter. He even
teases his opponent by asking him to "*praise* me in your next." Sheridan's hopes
of praise were unfulfilled. *Clio's Protest* provoked *Pindar's Answer*, which took a
retaliatory delight in mocking his portraits of Jennings and Fordyce (20, 23–24).

II

Clio's Protest and "The Ridotto of Bath" are satires written by a young man keen
to attract notice and with a fine eye for a chance to shine. A more interesting
project is the translation of *Aristænetus*, on which Sheridan collaborated with Halhed. The precise circumstances of their joint project are not entirely clear, as only
Halhed's side of the correspondence survives. Fortunately, Halhed's letters reveal
a great deal about the ambitions and anxieties of two young authors. A number
of projects seem to have been conceived both before and during the work on the
translation: some bawdy stories, a classically themed farce and a miscellany, for
which Halhed recruited contributors at Oxford. There is no immediate way to
characterize such diverse offerings, though each seems designed to be provocative.
Moore thought them all regrettable.[23] What is striking, nonetheless, is both the
boldness of their shared intent and their interdependence as writers. Although the
surviving letters give the impression that Halhed was the chief progenitor, others
actively seek the assistance of Sheridan in ways which cast his role as significant:
"I am never so happy as when I know you are altering anything of mine, for on
the word of a brother poet I feel but too sensibly how little [my] abilities can do
. . . Pray add and correct whatever you like: for I have some time had full belief
and confidence that every correction of yours would be an emendation, and every

addition a new perfection."[24] Without Sheridan's side of the correspondence, it is hard to know for certain the precise nature of his role, but it is surely significant that the "Preface" (which seems to have been more Sheridan's responsibility) is signed "H.S." (xii).[25] Despite this declaration of joint authority, critics and biographers have tended to divide the *Love Epistles* into those by Halhed, which are generally deprecated, and those by Sheridan which are sometimes praised. The decision rests in part on distaste for Halhed, whose later career is at best ambiguous, and a proleptic appreciation of Sheridan's great talents. Acknowledging their relationship, the remainder of this essay treats the translation as an equal collaboration.[26]

Sheridan and Halhed's decision to translate Aristænetus, a later Greek prose writer, into English verse reflects both their youth and their ambition, not least because they had selected a writer with a distinctly awkward and unlikely pedigree. Greek culture was widely admired during the eighteenth century: Homer, Pindar and Theocritus were appreciated for their simple, unadorned and passionate verse. However, Greek literature was thought to have decayed irretrievably by the fifth century when the *Love Epistles* were written. Aristænetus's erotic pastorals seemed to support this general claim. To make matters worse, the *Love Epistles* appeared to be merely a synthesis of earlier writers' work, a fact that led some critics to doubt that Aristænetus had ever existed. Sheridan and Halhed had therefore selected as the basis for their collection of poems an obscure Greek prose writer who was known, if he was known at all, as the mere compiler of indecent erotica.[27] Some confession of these problems was required in the Preface, where they wrote that Aristænetus's work is: "terse, elegant, and very poetical, both in language and sentiment: yet pleasing as they are, they have scarcely anything original in them, being a cento from the writings of *Plato, Lucian, Philostratus*, and almost all the ancient Greek authors." It was possible, however, to commend the taste which had led to such a compilation and to understand that selection as possessing refinement in its own right (vi). Elegance and refinement are adopted as the keynotes of the preface, as the young authors attempted to justify their decision to translate prose into poetry. The "languid formality of an English *prosaic* translation" is discounted as unsuitable for the elegant and witty Aristænetus. Another English writer—the "ingenious *Tom Brown*"—had attempted such a work, but they derided his contribution as inelegant (viii).[28] Instead their work would raise English verse by introducing the natural elegance and simplicity of Greek writing; indeed the requirements of the task demanded that they employ not one, but several modes and meters, introducing new words when the original resisted translation (x–xi).

Sheridan and Halhed were unaware of (or chose not to mention) another prose translation of Aristænetus. Published in the 1716, *Letters of Love and Gallantry* was a deliberately titillating volume. Its title page promised in leaden verse that "This Book will show / How Women lov'd a thousand Years ago."[29] Where *Letters of Love and Gallantry* was unabashed, Sheridan and Halhed affected sentiment and assured readers that they had modified their *Aristænetus* to avoid both the "indelicate" and "indecent" (ix). This statement was hardly candid ("treacherous" is Moore's term for their evasions). Halhed and Sheridan gave their readers a collection which included several poems reveling in the depiction of sexual longing, nudity and physical pleasure. The first poem in the volume describes the writer's mistress in lavish terms. Like the young Wordsworth, Halhed and Sheridan are supremely confident of their ability to describe a truly beautiful woman (3–4). There is nothing coy, either, about their representation of her "heavenly frame":

> How beautiful she looks, when drest!
>> But view her freed from this disguise,
> Stript of th' unnecessary vest—
>> 'Tis Beauty's self before your eyes! (5)

Offering her body to an eager gaze, the woman seems both irresistible and unresisting. This is dramatic in itself, but the energy—the "style" in Derrida's sense—lies with the male gaze as it penetrates. As it performs this act of undressing, the poem exhibits an obvious, even embarrassing, enthusiasm. Halhed and Sheridan seem all too assured of their daring as well as their technique. As the two young translators continue, they get even more excitable:

> But how shall I describe her breast!
>> That now first swells with panting throb
> To burst the fond embracing vest,
>> And emulate her snow white robe. (6)

The poem, along with many others in the collection, needs to be seen as an exploration of the possibilities of the pastoral. David Fairer has noted how the pastoral served as a space for experimentation, especially for younger poets, who found its "malleable" form usefully open and suggestive. Pope, Collins and Gray were all pastoralists in their youth. The pastoral was also highly amenable to erotic, even pornographic appropriation.[30] Alive to the possibilities of this countertradition, Halhed and Sheridan make their pastoral more sexually charged than their predecessors. Through the collection, a succession of different sexual encounters are essayed and even consummated. In one poem a young singer seduces two women at once; in others women deceive their husbands to spend more pleasurable time with their lovers; elsewhere the sexual sophistication of actresses is both feared and desired without ever quite losing the pastoral's foreclosure as a special realm (11–15, 35–38, 157–60).

The importance of the pastoral as an erotic mode is most evident in the third epistle, "The Garden of Phyllion," from Philoplatanus to Anthocomé. Incidentally, the poem is the verse most confidently assigned to Sheridan by Moore, who cited an error in the Greek translation as the grounds for denying Halhed credit. The letter also appears in prose form in the *Letters of Love and Gallantry*. Halhed and Sheridan, even allowing for their use of somewhat languid verse, write at greater length and with more explicitness than their predecessor.[31] The poem describes a pleasure-filled afternoon spent with the lovely Limona. The location for their tryst is lavishly described with "rich perfume" and "fruits nectareous" adorning the secluded garden (16). The sumptuous landscape foretells the lovemaking that follows:

> Aloft each elm slow wav'd its dusky top,
> The willing vine embrac'd the sturdy prop:
> And while we stray'd the ripen'd grape to find,
> Around our necks the clasping tendrils twin'd. (17)

The images of clustering and interlacing are worked through a long passage of fruit picking as Limona provocatively chooses fruits for their sweetness, disdaining those she finds "immature." After watching some villagers gathering and pressing grapes, the Limona and Philoplatanus pass through a thicket beyond which is a stream where they bathe:

> We bathed—and while we swam, so clear it flow'd,
> That ev'ry limb the crystal mirror shew'd.
> But my love's bosom oft deceiv'd my eye,
> Resembling those fair fruits that glided by;
> For when I thought her swelling breast to clasp,
> An apple met my disappointed grasp. (20–21)

Despite the comic bathos, the poem delights in the revelation of the body, lingering as Limona's blushes are echoed in the water that laps her body. The consummation of their passion is pure delight: "And we *did* kiss, my friend, and *love* was there, / And smooth'd the rustic couch that held my fair" (25). Such an evocative, sensual lyric recalls the eroticism of what Jeffrey N. Cox terms the Cockney classicism of second-generation Romantic poets. According to Cox, the project of Cockney classicism was to "ground the ideal in the real," which meant evolving an aesthetic of play, anticipation, fear and longing. Owing a debt to Winkelmann, Keats and others made classicism sensual and erotic. Their classical bodies are not cold marble, but warm to the touch.[32] Throughout their *Aristænetus*, Halhed and Sheridan follow a similar trajectory; indeed although the pleasures of vision—specifically, of seeing beautiful women—often seem paramount, the moment is generally elaborated though other senses, also including taste and smell: "A leaf I bruis'd—what grateful scents arose!" (17).

Unabashed in its enjoyment of erotic, the "Garden of Phyllion" closes with Philoplatanus declaring that he will enjoy the pleasures of Limona again, while assuring Anthocomé that his turn will come (26). Elsewhere in the collection, the young poets find more conflict and grounds for anxiety, but their impetus is still towards beauty's disclosure and the revelation of sexual possibilities. In "The Disappointment," for example, Cyrtion tells Dictys of an incident that occurred while he was fishing. As he cast his line a young maid approached and asked him to mind her clothes while she bathed: "'Yes, Yes,' I eagerly replied, / 'In hopes her naked charms to spy.'" His eager, breathless response is succeeded by a similarly excited description of her naked body:

> Bright polish'd arms, a neck of snow,
> Through lovely locks of lovely jet were seen;
>   Which by their blackness seem'd to throw
>   An added lustre on her skin
> Two rising globules at her breast,
>   Whose swelling throb was such,
> They seem'd upheaving to be prest,
>   And sued impatient for the touch. (46–47)

The description owes something to eighteenth-century descriptions of the *Venus de Medici*, which, as John Barrell has argued, frequently make the act of looking coincident with the experience of touch.[33] Although he can only imagine touching her as he stands on the shoreline, Cyrtion watches "each pressing wave" surround her body. The waves serve as surrogates for his hands, promising possession but delaying gratification as the poem builds toward a sexual climax. However, when the woman emerges from the water, she is embarrassed and resentful. Surprised by Cyrtion's declaration of passion, she breaks his rod and throws his net and catch away, leaving him to regret: "The fish I'd caught, and her I lost" (48–49).

"The Disappointment" is only one of several poems in which the promise of gratification is either deferred or destroyed by clever, angry or otherwise unsympathetic women. In the fourteenth epistle the reader learns of a maid who rejects a suitor because he offers music rather than money. Her cold disdain is most clearly realized when she chides her lover for his naiveté: "'your aim is beauty, sirs, and mine is . . . gold'" (101, 105). The idea is extended and more clearly eroticized in the twenty-first epistle, "Cruel Compassion"; a "whimsical account of a lover and his mistress, who admitted him to every favour but the last," according to their translators' note (135). The woman appears initially to be generous and to offer herself freely, allowing kisses and even her breasts to be touched (providing she is dressed), but such freedoms are offered only with "a view to beguile," leaving the youth enticed and frustrated:

> —Thus pines the poor victim away,
>   Forc'd to nibble and starve on a Kiss.—
> Serv'd worse than e'en eunuchs—for they
>   Can never feel torture like this. (137)

These lines are suffused with a crisis of masculine pain and doubt. Never as brazen or angry as the Earl of Rochester's "Imperfect Enjoyment," or as fearfully sensuous as Keats's "La Belle Dame sans Merci," the poem nevertheless conveys a sense of deeply felt adolescent longing, one haunted by a fear of rejection and disappointment. Fear of being spurned and even unmanned by rejection (like a eunuch) recurs in several poems. In Sheridan's unpublished occasional verse of this period there is a similar but more gently expressed apprehension. While the poems of his courtship with Elizabeth Linley—especially "Dry Be That Tear, My Gentlest Love" and "To the Recording Angel"—seek to win her over and to gain her confidence, there remains, for all his proffered tenderness, an anxious and abiding sense that his love may be wasted or lost.[34]

In the *Aristænetus*, this pensive feeling is most concretely realized in the final epistle, "The Rival Friends," a verse written by a lover "resigning his mistress to his friend" (167). The poem is arguably the most sophisticated piece in the collection and displays a confidence and elegiac calm not found elsewhere in their work. Where "Hymen and Hirco" visited contempt upon on an aged rival living out the "dross of manhood's strength," "The Rival Friends" acknowledges the potency of the victor:

> My vows are scorned, and all my gifts forgot:
> A happier rival must her power defend;
> And in that rival, I have lost a friend! (169)

As he describes his plight, the twice-forsaken lover represents himself as downcast and made hopeless by the "pangs of baffled love." He paints a picture of his grief that rebukes his friend through its image of a wounded and broken man:

> My life has lost its aim! That fatal fair
> Was all its object, all its hope and care;
> She was the goal to which my course was bent,
> Where ev'ry wish, where ev'ry thought was sent;
> A secret influence dart'd from her eyes,—
> Each look, attention! And herself the prize. (172)

These lines with their reference to "secret influence" and darting eyes rehearse the usual poetic clichés of enraptured love, but do so in order to elaborate an image of a much-injured pride. On one level the lines instance the defeat of style, in so far as they reveal a wounding, not a striking, one that discloses the vulnerability of the male gaze rather than its conventional acquisitiveness.[35] On another level, however, the image of the disregarded friend aims to prick consciences through its simultaneous demand that both injury and justice be acknowledged. The volume therefore concludes with a different tone through which style functions not as a point of aggressive contact but as a way of resolving the tensions of life that are both amorous and social.

Halhed imagined that *Aristænetus* would appeal to his fellow students at Oxford; though he also feared that publication would mean that he was teased and abused. It is perhaps easy to see why.[36] The easy eroticism of some poems, such as the second—"The Pleasing Constraint"—which ends with a man taking two women, is presented alongside lyrics which praise the beauty of women and depict it sensually. But the collection is not entirely in this mode. Although poems view women appreciatively and excitedly, others pieces such as "The Haughty Beauty" and "Excuses" regard women with suspicion or fear them as the withholders of pleasure (117–20,121–24). The result is a volume that shifts, not always confidently, between poems of sexual experience and sexual doubt. Running through the venture, however, is a boyish delight in at least the prospect of sexual pleasure. This is most evident in poems such as the twelfth epistle, which offers a defense of libertinism that extends to the sexual freedom of women: "Love shall make amends for all" (90). The tone of these variously Pindaric and Anacreonic lyrics appears indicative of the bawdy sub-culture, which, as Vic Gatrell has argued, challenges the eighteenth-century culture of politeness. Halhed's letters reveal that he at least was conversant with the attractions of such literature, as when he glibly tells Sheridan of an undergraduate life spent in "idleness, company, drunkenness, singly or altogether" but nonetheless promises "another of my *Bags and Tales*."[37] Halhead has in mind the loosely erotic work of John Hall Stevenson, whose *Crazy Tales; or Fables for Grown Gentleman* (1762) enjoyed an underground popularity in the mid-century. While Halhed and Sheridan abandoned their plan to imitate Hall Stevenson's work directly, their *Aristænetus* retains echoes of that earlier project, especially when depicting women who steal away from husbands or the intimate possibilities of chance encounters. They are perhaps rather Sternean in their treatment of desire and sex, often delighting in an erotic of incompletion when pleasure is teasingly deferred. Such provocative ambitions secured the young poets some decidedly mixed reviews. Although the *Critical Review* praised their efforts as translators, the libertinism of the collection caused the reviewer to wish the "English *Aristænetus*" had paid "more regard to the moral sentiments of his readers."[38] But he wished them well, providing that they did not pursue their views in practice. The *Critical's* tolerance was not evident in the *Hibernian Magazine* still less in the *Monthly Review*, which warned its readers against wasting time on "trash such as this." What these journals did not like was the immoral and scandalous tendency of a work, a habit of mind what the *Aristænetus* often exhibited with a deliberate and youthful insouciance.[39]

III

Halhed and Sheridan intended to push boundaries and to penetrate hypocrisies, just as Sheridan intended to punish lapses of taste and talent in his peers. Their style was one of provocation, but it is a curiously conflicted, as well as youthful, approach and as such requires further thought. As we have seen, Sheridan's first literary writings were marked by a delight in attack, mockery and satire. Like his conduct as a duelist, Sheridan's first works exhibit a "vaunting manner." Sheridan assails Walter Long in "Hymen and Hirco" and Richard Fitzpatrick in *Clio's Protest* no less than he had Thomas Mathews on Kingsmead Fields. On that occasion, Mathews's second accused him of an ungentlemanly and inept desire to "run in" on his opponent, as if violence was all he sought. Perhaps the same is true of his early verse, as his desire for combat is everywhere apparent.[40] His willingness to enter the fray is detectable (even if he has to stage the provocation first) in what is probably Sheridan's first attempt at a foray into print and politics, his draft letters to the editors of the *Public Advertiser*, where a desire to coruscate the poor style of his opponent dominates all others.[41] The desire to provoke a response recurs in all his early writings, and we ought to include the first unsuccessful version of

The Rivals in that appraisal. The will to conflict, to best rivals of whatever kind, gave Sheridan a style (and sometimes a mere pose) which gave him terrific license, building his confidence and encouraging his more satiric endeavors.

However, if style is always a matter of cutting and breaking, as Derrida claims, then it is important to distinguish between those who wield their stilettos expertly and those who merely enage in a "wild mêlée" with "pointed ends." Style is something which needs to be achieved. The question of style, its meaning and its force, has been illuminated by Edward W. Said in his posthumous collection, *On Late Style*. For Said, late style, which is not related to maturity or simple lateness—though it might coincide with either—is a mode of controlled intransigence, characterized by a refusal to resolve contradictions: a refusal of order designed to foreground the work's own discordant processes. But while late style refuses harmony it is full of memory. It is this precious quality which makes it unique and strangely wise.[42] Said's perceptive work can help us clarify the nature of Sheridan's early style, as a similarly combative but less immediately meritorious mode. Where Said's late style foregrounds discordances with a mature if disconcerting candor, Sheridan's first works confess them unwillingly. Anxieties spill out, doubts about potency, women and about the poet's place in the world return repeatedly. The idea that lovers or friends may desert or disappoints recurs in the early canon. Sheridan's masculinity and sexuality—his "style" of manliness—is asserted rather than really proven. The traces left by these barely repressed doubts frustrate the bravado enacted elsewhere. For all its self-conscious rage and anxiety, Sheridan's early style is not simply the reverse of late style as Said understood it. It is more striking than the simply infantile, and more ambitious. Although it aspires to intransigence and rebellion, it undermines its own claims with a more emphatic desire to belong and to be loved. Sheridan's earliest work is rich in these conflicting aspirations.

Notes

1. *Morning Chronicle*, London: William Woodfall, July 8–9, 1772; *London Evening Post*, London: John Miller, July 2, 1772).

2. Thomas Moore, *Memoirs of the Life of the Right Honourable Richard Brinsley Sheridan*, 5th ed. (London: Longman, Rees, Orme, Brown, and Green, 1826), 1:65–67.

3. Richard Brinsley Sheridan, "To William Barnett" [1773], in *Letters of Richard Brinsley Sheridan*, ed. Cecil Price, 3 vols. (Oxford: Clarendon Press, 1966), 1:73–76; and Moore, *Memoirs*, 1:65–67. See also Robert W. Jones, "A Matter of Honour: The Duel in Thomas Moore's *Life of Richard Brinsley Sheridan*," *Journal for Eighteenth-Century Studies* (forthcoming 2012).

4. Fintan O'Toole, *A Traitor's Kiss: The Life of Richard Brinsley Sheridan, 1751–1816* (London: Granta, 1998), 58–62; and Madeleine Bingham, *Sheridan: The Track of a Comet* (London: Allen and Unwin, 1972), 78–81, 87–92.

5. The poem was published in the *Bath Chronicle* (May 9, 1771). See Cecil Price, "Hymen and Hirco: A Vision," *Times Literary Supplement* (July 11, 1958), 396. See also James Morwood, *The Life and Works of Richard Brinsley Sheridan* (Edinburgh: Scottish Academic Press, 1985), 21–22.

6. Aristaenetus, Nathaniel Brassey Halhed and Richard Brinsley Sheridan, *The Love Epistles of Aristænetus: translated from the Greek into English Metre* (London: J. Wilkie, 1771), 167–74. Subsequent references to this work will appear in the text; Moore, *Life of Sheridan*, 1:24–25.

7. Jacques Derrida, *Spurs: Nietzsche's Styles*, trans. Barbara Harlow (Chicago: University of Chicago Press, 1981), 37–38.

8. Richard Marggraf Turley, *Keats's Boyish Imagination* (London: Routledge, 2004).

9. See Chris Baldick, "Juvenilia," in *Oxford Concise Dictionary of Literary Terms* (Oxford: Oxford University Press, 2001), 132–33.

10. William Wordsworth, *Early Poems and Fragments, 1785–1797*, eds. Carol Landon and Jared Curtis (London: Cornell University Press, 1997), 362–69.

11. Thomas Chatterton, *The Complete Works of Thomas Chatterton: A Bicentenary Edition*, ed. Donald S. Taylor, in assoc. with Benjamin B. Hoover, 2 vols. (Oxford: Claredon Press, 1971), 1:158–59. The question of youth and juvenilia is rarely discussed in Chattertonian circles. The issue is touched upon, however, in *Thomas Chatterton and Romantic Culture*, ed. Nick Groom (Basingstoke: Macmillan, 1999).

12. Richard Brinsley Sheridan, "The Ridotto of Bath," *Bath Chronicle* (October 10th, 1771); the present essay cites the version printed in *Poems and Plays of Richard Brinsley Sheridan*, ed. R. Crompton Rhodes, 3 vols. (Oxford: Basil Blackwell 1925), 3:119–23. Page numbers appear parenthetically hereafter.

13. Richard Brinsley Sheridan, *The Dramatic Works of Richard Brinsley Sheridan*, ed. Cecil Price (Oxford: Clarendon Press, 1973), 1:79.

14. Sheridan, *Dramatic Works,* 1:94.

15. See David Fairer, *English Poetry of the Eighteenth Century, 1700–1789* (London: Longman, 2003), 21, 26–27, 60–62.

16. See Peter Stallybrass and Allon White, *The Politics and Poetics of Transgression* (London: Methuen, 1986), 80–124.

17. See Terry Castle, *Masquerade and Civilisation: The Carnivalesque in Eighteenth-Century English Culture and Fiction* (London: Methuen, 1986); and Gillian Russell, *Women, Sociability and Theatre in Georgian London* (Cambridge: Cambridge University Press, 2007).

18. William Hogarth, *The Analysis of Beauty. Written with a View of Fixing the Fluctuating Ideas of Taste* (London: J. Reeve, 1753), 137–38, 147–50.

19. Anthony Ashley Cooper, Third Early of Shaftesbury, *Characteristics of Men, Manners, Opinions, Times*, ed. Philip J. Ayres, 2 vols. (Oxford: Clarendon Press, 1999), 1:39.

20. Both poems were later published together as Richard Brinsley Sheridan's *The Rival Beauties: A Poetical Contest* (London: W. Griffin; Bath R. Crutwell, 1772). All quotations are from this edition.

21. Eve Kosofsky Sedgwick, *Between Men: English Literature and Male Homosocial Desire* (New York: Colombia University Press, 1985).

22. James Thomson, *The Seasons*, ed. James Sambrook (Oxford: Clarendon Press, 1981), 29.

23. Moore, *Life of Sheridan*, 1:26–28.

24. Nathaniel Brassey Halhed, undated letter to Sheridan, in *Letters from Mr. N. H. Halhed to Mr. R. B. Sheridan* (Frampton: privately printed, 1872), 13.

25. Halhed advised Sheridan on the contents and style of the Preface, but seems to have left the actual writing of it to his collaborator. See Halhed, *Letters from Halhed to Sheridan*, 16, 23–24.

26. See Moore, *Life of Sheridan*, 1: 23, 29–31; and O'Toole, *Traitors Kiss*, 46. For a contrasting view, see Walter Sichel, *Sheridan, From New and Original Material; Including a Manuscript Diary by Georgiana, Duchess of Devonshire*, 2 vols. (London: Constable, 1909), 1: 289–94.

27. See Moore, *Life of Sheridan*, 1:28; John Watkins, *Memoirs of the Public and Private Life of the Right Honourable Richard Brinsley Sheridan*, 2nd ed., 2 vols. (London: Henry Colburn, 1817), 1:217; and *Monthly Review* (December, 1771), 511.

28. See Thomas Brown, *The Works of Thomas Brown, in Prose and Verse; Serious, Moral, and Comical*, 2 vols. (London: B. Bragg, 1707).

29. *Letters of Love and Gallantry, written in the Greek by Aristænetus* (London: Bernard Lintot, 1716).

30. Fairer, *English Poetry*, 79–82, 88–89. See also Karen Harvey, *Reading Sex in the Eighteenth Century: Bodies and Gender in English Erotic Culture* (Cambridge: Cambridge University Press, 2004); and Julie Peakman, *Mighty Lewd Books: The Development of Pornography in Eighteenth-Century England* (Basingstoke: Palgrave Macmillan, 2003).

31. Aristænetus, *Letters of Love and Gallantry*, 18–21.

32. Jeffrey N. Cox, *Poetry and Politics in the Cockney School: Keats, Shelley, Hunt And Their Circle* (Cambridge: Cambridge University Press, 1998), 168–82, 184.

33. See John Barrell, "'The Dangerous Goddess': Masculinity, Prestige, and the Aesthetic in Early Eighteenth-Century England" *Cultural Critique* 12 (1989): 101–31.

34. Sheridan, *Poems and Plays*, 3:229, 231; and Moore, *Life of Sheridan*, 1:33–38.

35. See Edward Snow, "Theorising the Male Gaze: Some Problems," *Representations* 25, no. 1 (1989): 30–41; and Lynda Nead, *The Female Nude: Art, Obscenity and Sexuality* (London: Routledge, 1992).

36. Halhed, *Letters from Halhed to Sheridan*, 5–6, 18; Vic Gatrell, *City of Laughter: Sex and Satire in Eighteenth-Century London* (London: Atlantic Books, 2006).

37. Halhed, *Letters from Halhed to Sheridan*, 3.

38. *Critical Review*, London: Archibald Hamilton (September, 1771), 208.

39. *Critical Review* (September, 1771), 208; *Hibernian Magazine or, compendium of entertaining knowledge*. Dublin: T. Walker (September, 1771), 424; *Monthly Review*. London: R. Griffiths (December, 1771), 511.

40. Moore, *Life of Sheridan*, 1:65.

41. Sheridan, "To the Editors of the *Public Advertiser*," (1769), in *Letters from Halhed to Sheridan*, 1:3–11.

42. Edward W. Said, *On Late Style: Music and Literature Against the Grain* (London: Bloomsbury, 2007), 7–9, 12–14.

3

THE LITERARY ORIGINS OF
SIR LUCIUS O'TRIGGER

David Haley

RICHARD BRINSLEY SHERIDAN'S first play, *The Rivals* (1775), was a brilliant success—on its *second* night. At its début, the comedy was greeted with some enthusiasm, but it was also loudly booed by parts of the audience, prompting the novice playwright to take the unusual step of withdrawing it. Eleven days later, with its roles recast, Sheridan's revised and pruned version of *The Rivals* reopened to universal acclaim of the kind it has enjoyed ever since.

From the critical notices, and from the author's preface to the revised play (which was in print within two weeks), we know that much of the initial protest focused on the role of the "stage Irishman," Sir Lucius O'Trigger. His part, as originally written and acted, was jeered as a farcical caricature by most of the audience, while an indignant faction denounced it for a libel. Sheridan revised (and recast) the part to produce the genteelly menacing duelist who even today has the power, if his role is properly acted, to animate a performance of *The Rivals*.

The goals of the following essay are to determine when Sheridan may have begun working the materials of his own duels into his playscript for *The Rivals*; to examine the play's reception in the light of the author's prefatory account; and finally, to show his indebtedness to a seventeenth-century play featuring the prototype of Sir Lucius O'Trigger.

I

Exactly when Sheridan began to write his maiden play remains something of a mystery. *The Rivals* premièred at the Theatre Royal on 17 January 1775. It had been put into rehearsal only two months earlier, according to Sheridan's letter to his father-in-law disclosing that he had found a producer for his draft:

> There will be a *Comedy* of mine in rehearsal at Covent-Garden within a few days. I did not set to work on it till within a few days of my setting out for *Crome*, so you may think that I have not, for these last six weeks, been very idle. I have done it at Mr. Harris's (the manager's) own request; it is now complete in his hands, and preparing for the stage. . . . I had not written a line of it two months ago, except a scene or two, which I believe you have seen in an odd act of a little farce.[1]

Sheridan and his wife had visited Croome Park that summer, so he would appear to have begun *The Rivals* in September 1774, after returning to London from Worcestershire. He must have completed the play over the next "six weeks" in a characteristic burst of concentrated writing.

Thirty-one years later, however, when the play was revived and acted privately in his honor around Christmas 1805, Sheridan claimed he wrote it before 1774. In a letter to his wife, he confessed that watching the performance made him "very nervous[;] I don't mean the writing or sentiments of the Play but the recollection of the Days, when, just past twenty one, I wrote it."[2] Since he had completed his twenty-first year in September 1772, Sheridan, on this later occasion, was dating the composition of *The Rivals* a full two years antecedent to its first rehearsal. That would mean he began the play not in the fall of 1774 but in the fall of 1772, when he had been exiled by his father to Waltham Abbey in Essex. Thomas Sheridan wanted his son to forget about Elizabeth Linley and his duels with her importunate suitor, Mathews, and to use his leisure to read the law in preparation for enrolling at the Middle Temple. His later recollection of his condition during this period—the nine months between his nearly fatal duel in July 1772 and his marriage to Elizabeth the following April—still made the fifty-four-year-old Sheridan "very nervous."

To reconcile these inconsistent accounts, we need to examine what Sheridan meant by saying he had written a *play*. The manuscript he put into the hands of the manager, Harris, in November 1774 had a disappointing première two months later and was immediately withdrawn so the author could make changes. Eleven days afterwards, on 28 January 1775, a much-revised and shortened version of *The Rivals* was presented. This is the version that Sheridan immediately published and that he saw performed thirty years later, conjuring up the troubling circumstances in which he had originally tried to construct a narrative of what had befallen him and Eliza in the first half of 1772. If he confused their experience with the various newspaper accounts of it, that was because Sheridan looked back upon the events of 1772 as moments in the ongoing narrative of his life. In that broad retrospect, it is possible that his first comedy had become merely another in the series of episodes that combined to make up the grand epic—or mock-epic— that Sheridan never ceased to revise.

The "play" that he remembered writing in the fall of 1772, therefore, was probably not much more than a dramatic sketch, a project along the lines of the juvenilia printed in the memoir by his first biographer, Thomas Moore.[3] No dramatic writings from his months at Waltham Abbey survive, but two letters by Sheridan—one written in July 1772 and the other drafted before February 1773—reveal him still preoccupied with the duels on which he would model the climax of *The Rivals*.[4]

The first letter, written while Sheridan was recovering from the wounds re- ceived from Mathews in the later duel (a bloody and allegedly drunken scuffle at Bath), is addressed to one Captain Knight who had been Mathews's second in the London duel two months before. Sheridan relates how a Mr. Barnett, "on the eve- ning preceding" the Bath duel, while acting as Mathews's second, demanded that he endorse "a paper to me written by Mr. Mathews" purporting to give a full account of their three-months' quarrel. (Sheridan's refusal to sign it triggered their duel near Bath the next day.) The convalescent now tells Knight that he had hitherto ignored the false reports Mathews was spreading of their London duel, but on being shown the paper he was alarmed to find Mathews's falsehood "seemingly authenticated by Mr. *Knight's* name being subscribed to it." He insists that Knight, at the very least, owes it to him to confirm or deny five allegations concerning the London duel. Couched as questions, allegations two, three, and five read as follows:

> Did Mr. Mathews *not beg* his life?—He insinuates he did not.
> Did I break his sword *without warning?*—He affirms I did it without warning, on his laying it on the table. . . .
> Did Mr. Mathews give me the apology as a point of generosity, *on my desisting to demand it?*—He affirms he did.[5]

These affirmations and denials concerning the original duel in London point to the strong likelihood that Sheridan, despite his promise not to reveal Mathews's capitulation, found his status as a gentleman enhanced by all the gossip about his triumph. Once it was brought home to Mathews that his rival's heightened status had come at the expense of his own reputation, Mathews had no recourse other than to deny the reports of his baffling. However generously Sheridan imagines himself to have behaved at the London duel, his subsequent conduct was not magnanimous enough to conceal his rival's humiliation. A more confident victor, by carrying himself superior to the loser's insults, might have been able to rob them of their sting.[6]

Six months later Sheridan was still trying to frame the narrative in such a way as to make his conduct appear consistently honorable over the course of their quarrel. In a second, unsent letter on the subject, drafted during his sojourn in Essex and nominally addressed to Barnett, Sheridan takes up yet another account, an "Exact Narrative" of the Bath duel that Mathews's second had composed at his request and that Sheridan's own, less experienced second, Paumier, reportedly had verified. Sheridan subjects this narrative to a hairsplitting analysis of what he says are its inconsistencies:

> The first Point in Mr. Barnett's Narrative that is of the least consequence to take notice of, is where Mr. M. is represented as having repeatedly signified his Desire to use Pistols prior to swords from a conviction that Mr. Sheridan would run in upon him and an ungentlemanlike scuffle probably be the consequence. . . . As this insinuation bears an obscure allusion to a past transaction of Mr. M.'s [i.e., the circumstance that Mathews had begged his life when Sheridan disarmed him in their London duel] I doubt not but He will be surprised at my indifference in not taking the trouble even to explain it. However I cannot forbear to observe here, that had I, at the period which this Passage alludes to, known what was the Theory which Mr. M. held of *gentlemanly scuffle*, I might possibly have been so unhappy as to have put it out of his Power ever to have brought it into practice.[7]

By referring to the London duel (which Barnett of course did not witness), Sheridan hints that Barnett may have been imposed on by Mathews, who—as Sheridan relates in the July letter to Knight, cited above—pretended that his apology to Sheridan was given "as a point of generosity" and not because it was forced from him. The insinuation is clever. Sheridan was discovering how he might use wit to divide his opponents and, at the same time, was beginning to exaggerate the absurdities of their monolithic honor code. Eventually he would figure out how to reduce the whole murky ordeal to a grotesque farce.

By 1773, then, Sheridan had very likely wrought from the materials of his own experience several dueling scenarios, some of them dressed in witty repartee, but he had not yet formed these inchoate scenes into what he later called a *play*. He had discovered that his talent for caricature and for grotesque dramatization, already evident in his juvenilia, might be applied to his own life.

The discovery was fairly momentous, in that it adumbrated to him a public career that should make him independent of his father's plans and profession. Sheridan audaciously affirms his newfound independence in a letter of February 1773 to Grenville, an aristocratic friend who had been his father's pupil. In a previous letter, Grenville had "talk[ed] most profanely of certain *Spheres in which God has placed us.*" In replying, Sheridan "violent[ly]" spurns the notion that

> God could ever have intended individuals to fill up any particular Stations in which the accidents of Birth or Fortune may have flung them. . . . *The Station* in which it has pleas'd God to place us, (or whatever the words are) is not properly interpreted. And as God very often pleases to let down great Folks from the elevated stations which they might claim as their Birthright, there can be no reason for us to suppose that He does not mean that others should ascend etc. etc.[8]

Sheridan has no patience with the doctrine that we ought to seek guidance from a Providence that is fixed and inalterable. He has in mind a riskier, more liberating scenario—for "he had diced with death and won," as a recent biographer puts it.[9]

With its bold disavowal of providential guidance, this letter marks an epoch in his life. After ironically recounting his father's latest plan to distance him still farther from any contact with Mathews or Eliza by removing him from Essex into Yorkshire to continue his law studies, Sheridan writes: "I have some reason to suppose He has re-altered his mind. But it is a matter of little moment to me, as I can sincerely say that it is very indifferent to me what the Latitude of the Spot of Ground is where I am to eat drink and Sleep. My sole Idea is to qualify myself so that it shall not be indifferent [i.e., a matter of indifference] to the place where I hope to do something more." Over the coming months, he made good on this boast that he could thrive under restraint, so confident was he of attaining the elevated station or "place" where he might pursue his ambitions. In April, he enrolled as a student at the Middle Temple, and the next week he and Eliza were married.

II

The sprawling manuscript play Sheridan completed eighteen months later was a medley of disparate fragments provisionally stitched together. Some elements of *The Rivals* had already appeared on the stage, such as the character of Mrs. Malaprop with her perverse volubility, which Sheridan thought his father-in-law might have recognized from "an odd act of a little farce."[10] Critics of the new play pounced on superficial resemblances to familiar types in the characters of Jack Absolute ("a second *Atall*, or *Double Gallant*"); Bob Acres ("a second Tony Lumpkin"; Lumpkin's role had recently been played by John Quick, who now created Acres); Sir Anthony Absolute (echoes Congreve's Sir Sampson Legend); Lydia Languish (sister to Coleman's Polly Honeycombe); and Sir Lucius O'Trigger (copied from Cumberland's popular "stage Irishman," Major O'Flaherty). In addition to these five personae whose counterparts Sheridan no doubt had seen in contemporary performances, he imported the romantically unstable character of Faulkland from his mother's novel, *Memoirs of Miss Sidney Bidulph* (1761).[11]

In theatrical history, "stage Irishman" refers to a type that first appeared in the person of Teague, a simple-minded footman utterly devoted to the Cavaliers in Sir Robert Howard's *The Committee* (1664). When he hears that the oppressed Cavaliers' estates are forfeit to the Commonwealth because they have refused to "take the covenant," Teague steals a copy of the Covenant from a bookseller and proudly presents it to his masters. Like Teague, subsequent Irishmen on the stage speak with a Hiberno-English brogue and are marked by their impulsiveness and generosity of spirit that makes them incapable of prudential calculation. After the Williamite wars of 1689–1691, the stage Irishman was often a military officer whose British loyalty obliged him to fight against fellow Catholics, like Cumberland's Major O'Flaherty; or he became a fortune-hunter like Sir Lucius O'Trigger. Sheridan's initial model for the type would have been Captain O'Blunder, the hero of a farce, *The Brave Irishman*, by Sheridan's father. Captain O'Blunder, a huge man who wields a shillelagh, has come to London to woo the daughter of a rich tradesman. Despite his rough appearance and his "potato face," he understands his place as a gentleman and behaves with greater dignity than his rivals. He not only wins the daughter's love, but magnanimously provides a dowry for her maid so she can be married to his unsuccessful rival.

When the play was withdrawn after the first night and revised for its reopening with an entirely new cast on 28 January, most of the criticisms vanished. Nevertheless, Sheridan felt defensive enough about such more or less demonstrable, yet insignificant, borrowings to add a preface to his successfully revised play, which was soon in print. In this preface, the author insisted that his maiden effort was the spontaneous offspring of his own invention. He concedes that many errors arose "from my being by no means conversant with plays in general, either in reading or at the theatre." But he also believes his theatrical naïveté gave him a real advantage:

> In one respect, I did not regret my ignorance: for as my first wish in at-
> tempting a Play, was to avoid every appearance of plagiary, I thought I
> should stand a better chance of effecting this from being in a walk which
> I had not frequented, and where consequently the progress of invention
> was less likely to be interrupted by starts of recollection: for on subjects
> on which the mind has been much informed, invention is slow of exert-
> ing itself.—Faded ideas float in the fancy like half-forgotten dreams;
> and the imagination in its fullest enjoyments becomes suspicious of its
> offspring, and doubts whether it has created or adopted.[12]

For a novice author, this is a very confident manifesto. He has coolly appraised his dramatic talent and has discovered that his genius thrives on experience (bi-ography) rather than on theatrical commonplaces (plagiarism). He adds that he relies implicitly on the judgment of the public, who damned the original play and applauded its revision. By posing as a gentleman amateur, or by affecting the *sprezzatura* that he admired in Sir Philip Sidney, Sheridan disarms his critics and encourages his readers to enjoy his play instead of trying to uncover its sources.[13]

This candor cuts two ways, however. A large part of the audience's enjoy-ment lay in having their curiosity gratified—namely by feeding their hunger to know more about this chivalric young Irishman and the fair singer whom he, in Milton's words, had "brought like Alcestis from the grave, / Rescued from death by force, though pale and faint." While Sheridan in his preface congratulates the audience on recognizing the novelty of his play, he says nothing about the expecta-tions they brought to the playhouse: expectations raised, for example, by Foote's *The Maid of Bath* (1771), which had already sensationalized the cruel situation of one Kitty Linnet, who was besieged by the unwanted attentions of Major Racket (standing for Captain Mathews) and was falsely promised marriage by a wealthy old lecher (William Long, to whom Thomas Linley contracted his daughter in exchange for a large settlement; a *senex amans* arrangement that Sheridan would exploit later in portraying the uneasy match between Lady Teazle and Sir Peter).

And it's unlikely that either the author's imagination or that of his audience would "doubt whether it ha[d] created or adopted" the notorious rivalry between Sheridan and Mathews, which had become a staple of gossip. On the day of *The Rivals'* début, one newspaper cautioned: "It having been reported, that the story of the new comedy of The Rivals was not a fictitious one, we have the authority to assert, that such a report is entirely void of foundation, and that there is not the slightest local or personal allusion whatever throughout the piece."[14] In portraying Lydia's fantasies of eloping with Ensign Beverley or Faulkland's testing of Julia's loyalty to a murderer, Sheridan certainly was not expecting his lurid escapades to fade from memory and "float in the fancy like half-forgotten dreams." On the contrary, the audience could not appreciate the author's *invention* without being generally *informed* of his biography.

The basic axiom of the preface—that comedy's sole aim is to delight and not to edify the audience—is echoed in couplets from the prologue that Sheridan wrote for the tenth performance:

> Can our light scenes add strength to holy laws?
> Such puny patronage but hurts the cause;
> Fair Virtue scorns our feeble aid to ask,
> And moral Truth disdains the trickster's mask. (lines 41–44)

The speaker—Mrs. Bulkley, cast as Julia—is pointing to the sculpted figure of Comedy, who struggles to preserve humor from the ravages of sentimental drama. Comedy cannot expect assistance from "Virtue" or "moral Truth," for these are the servants of Tragedy; as such, they disdain to mingle on the boards with their bastard simulacra from the humorless plays in fashion. When Comedy pretends to stand for virtue or "moral truth" (a pretense the infamous Joseph Surface would immortalize), she too becomes a mere simulacrum. Comedy, in order not to appear overbearing, should always mock herself, as the heroes of sentimental drama are never allowed to do. And she must avoid the taint of edification, mindful that her "light scenes" *cannot* "add strength to holy laws."

Like Goldsmith, Sheridan sought to restore laughter to comedy, but he lacked Goldsmith's easy command of the natural "humors" that lend vitality to rustic characters such as Tony Lumpkin or Hardcastle's servant Diggory. That this deficiency of "humors" is not just the effect of a more polished urbanity can be proved by comparing Sheridan's "humors" with those in Congreve. Sheridan realized that many of Congreve's "humors," and most of Vanbrugh's, were simply too coarse to give delight to a refined, modern audience. Avoiding—at least at the outset—tragedy with its personae embodying "moral truths," Sheridan hit upon his signature device of self-caricaturing figures. His characters are not so much "humors" as parodies of "humors." The self-conscious audience he inherited was less attentive to nature in the raw than to nature refined, and the easiest way to make them laugh was to exaggerate their refinement until its representation became so grotesque that it no longer seemed to be part of themselves.[15]

Missing from Sheridan's light, gregarious comedy is the strong element of Jonsonian satire that informs Restoration plays such as Wycherley's *The Country Wife* (1675) or Congreve's *The Way of the World* (1700). Sheridan's society had become too polite, or too benevolent, to appreciate satire ostensibly meant to correct its affectations. Sheridan allows audiences to enjoy his parody without fearing that the mockery may be turned against them. Except for parts of *The Critic* (1779), his comedies do not make the audience itself the object of scorn. When, however, Sheridan does take aim at affectation, which is the perennial target of urbane satire, his practice is to make the affectation increasingly grotesque until the audience grows uneasy from anticipating the inevitable exposure. Examples are the affectation of knowledge or wit by Mrs. Malaprop, by Puff in *The Critic*, and by Isaac, the duped suitor in *The Duenna* (1775); or affectation of a false role by Jack Absolute (as Beverley), by Mrs. Malaprop again (as "Delia"), by Sir Oliver (as Premium), and by the Duenna, Margaret (when she pretends to be her mistress); or finally, the vulgar affectation of concealing one's discreditable motives, as Lady Teazle and Joseph Surface are frantically doing until the screen falls. In satirizing this last, virtually universal affectation, Sheridan on rare occasions suspends the entertaining comic laughter just long enough for us to experience "moral truths." What we glimpse at these moments is not quite tragic loss, perhaps, but something very near to it: the real possibility of betrayal.

In his preface written after *The Rivals* successfully reopened, the young author makes an implicit pact with the audience. He credits them with having vindicated his unique experiment of withdrawing a faulty play so it might be revised. Their critical judgment pointed him the way to succeed, and he hopes that they may continue to act at premières "as a candid and judicious friend attending, on behalf of the Public, at his last Rehearsal. If he can dispense with flattery, he is sure at least of sincerity." In this preface—which, apart from his prologues, was to be the sole occasion on which he addressed the public in his character of playwright—Sheridan pretends absolutely to dissociate himself from any personal interest in the play. *The Rivals* exists only in the theater, and there the audience presides. Regarding the passages that had been booed on the first night, he says,

> I confess, that if I felt any emotion of surprise at the disapprobation, it was not that they [i.e., particular passages] were disapproved of, but that I had not before perceived that they deserved it. As some part of

the attack on the Piece was begun too early to pass for *Judgment*, which is ever tardy in condemning, it has been suggested to me, that much of the disapprobation must have arisen from the virulence of Malice, rather than severity of Criticism: But as I was more apprehensive of there being just grounds to excite the latter, than conscious of having deserved the former, I continue not to believe that [i.e., the disapproval sprung from malice?] probable, which I am sure must have been unprovoked.[16]

The last sentence sounds confused. If Sheridan neither deserved nor provoked malice with his play, then the early and uncritical attack on *The Rivals* was probably not malicious. Yet he adds in the next sentence that even if he knew whence this (improbable?) malice came, "it would be ungenerous to retort; no passion suffers more than malice from disappointment."[17]

Sheridan is being disingenuous. What prompted him to come forward with this public account after his play had already gained the unanimous approval of its best judges? He scorns to provide "an Address to the Closet" that might imply his "consciousness of the weakness of the cause." His preface, he admits, would be redundant were it not for the unusual circumstance that the play had nearly flopped at its première and had been withdrawn. But now it has reopened to unqualified praise; why should the author wish to dwell on its faults—the play's length, the unlucky casting of its parts, the author's inexperience and alleged plagiarism—when these had all been amended or proven illusory?

The answer, I believe, is that Sheridan feared his character of Sir Lucius O'Trigger was liable to being misconstrued, along with the dueling scene that concludes the play. He worried that his caricature Irishman would seem a provocation to Mathews—or, more likely, to Mathews's friend Barnett, who evidently was still trying to get satisfaction from Sheridan thirty months after the final duel at Bath. Three days after the première, in the *Morning Post* for 20 January, "A Librarian" rebuked "Mr. B——d" for trying to "create a prejudice against the performance by every mode that malevolence could suggest." Barnett's vociferous protests must have fueled the "pretty warm contest towards the end of the last act" reported by *The Town and Country Magazine*; that would explain the "virulence of Malice" which Sheridan remarks in his preface. Everyone in Bath knew the story of how Barnett had goaded Mathews into the repeat duel, and how, acting as Mathews's second, Barnett had delivered a sealed challenge to Sheridan's sister Alicia, telling her it was "an invitation" for her brother Richard. No doubt Barnett, hearing reports that he was to be traduced in *The Rivals*, got up a faction capable of protesting and bearing witness to this latest, theatrical slur upon his honor.[18]

That brings us to another ambivalence in the preface, the author's apology for having overdrawn and exaggerated the character of Sir Lucius O'Trigger. Ignoring the biographical circumstance that Sir Lucius grew out of his quarrel with Mathews, Sheridan now claims to be delighted that the audience repudiated his undignified caricature and forced him to refashion his stage Irishman into a more just likeness:

> It is not without pleasure that I catch at an opportunity of justifying myself from the charge of intending any national reflection in the character of *Sir Lucius O'Trigger*. If any Gentlemen opposed the Piece from that idea, I thank them sincerely for their opposition; and if the condemnation of this Comedy (however misconceived the provocation) could have added one spark to the decaying flame of national attachment to the country supposed to be reflected on, I should have been happy in its fate; and might with truth have boasted, that it had done more real service in its failure, than the successful morality of a thousand stage-novels will ever effect.[19]

No matter what really provoked the booing of the original Sir Lucius O'Trigger—and one may note that "misconceived . . . provocation" also covers Barnett's vociferousness—Sheridan now maintains he could actually "have been happy in [the play's] failure," for that failure caused the public to acknowledge the true manners (mores) of an Irish gentleman. Here is "moral truth" with a vengeance. Sheridan goes so far as to claim that his biographically derived and morally flawed portrait of Sir Lucius worked a greater effect on the audience "than the successful morality of a thousand stage-novels." With this argument based on "moral truth," the author of the preface abandons the comic world of "light scenes" and the "trickster's mask" mentioned in the prologue. Against the specious glory of the theatrical world and his sudden rise to fame, Sheridan is prepared to stake the honor of an Irish gentleman.[20]

O'Toole notes that a greater embarrassment to Sheridan about this time may have been his father. Thomas Sheridan "had returned, to some acclaim, to act at Covent Garden for the first time in fourteen years."[21] There is some evidence that Thomas, always ready to emulate his younger son, tried to capitalize on Richard's success by reviving his own farce from the 1750s, *The Brave Irishman* (see above). Sheridan's initial version of Sir Lucius O'Trigger was much closer to Thomas's coarse and overdrawn hero, Captain O'Blunder, and Sheridan's greatest improvement to *The Rivals*, as everyone agreed, was the makeover of his stage Irishman.

In revising his farce sometime in 1775 or 1776, Thomas evidently took his cue from his son. An undated revision of *Captain O'Blunder: or, The Brave Irishman* bearing the imprint "London, printed, and Dublin, re-printed, and sold by the booksellers" is in the National Library of Ireland.[22] Its title page continues: "A farce. As it is acted at the Theatre-Royal in Smock Alley. And now in rehearsal at the Theatre in Covent Garden. By T–s S–n, Esq." The text, which includes a preface as well as a prologue addressed to an Irish audience, is a revision of the previous (1771) London edition of this farce that had not been altered since its publication in 1755. Except for a few topical updatings (such as the opening allusion to the Royal Marriage Act of 1772), nothing has been added, but the hero's Irish dialect, harking back to the 1750s when Thomas Sheridan staged the play at Smock Alley, has been pruned to make Captain O'Blunder sound more like an English gentleman and his manners have been refined precisely along the lines of Sir Lucius O'Trigger. Thanks to this transformation, Captain O'Blunder now deports himself in London with a dignity that could only make his countrymen proud, as the preface and prologue both aver.

III

Having canvassed the questions of when *The Rivals* was written and how it was received, we can revisit the author's claim that his "first wish in attempting a Play, was to avoid every appearance of plagiary." Sheridan means that, rather than imitate plays he has read or seen, he chose to make a play out of materials that he could not *recollect* either from stage or from page. By following that tack he could better achieve novelty, because "the progress of invention was less likely to be interrupted by starts of recollection." This preface, written close on the success of the revised play, was dropped from subsequent editions of *The Rivals*—presumably because Sheridan did not wish to bore readers with his candid assessment of the play's initial failure.[23]

Or it's just possible that, once the first flush of triumph had faded, the young playwright was interrupted by one of those "starts of recollection" that gave the lie to his boast of having eschewed "plagiary." For the evidence is quite clear that Sheridan wrote *The Rivals* with the 1673 Folio of Sir William Davenant's *Works* near at hand. Whether he found this volume at Waltham Abbey in 1772 or discovered it two years later in the archives of the Drury Lane Theatre (which Davenant himself had originally managed), Sheridan drew freely on the Folio: not only for its prototype of Sir Lucius, but also for the situation of a whimsical heiress who makes quixotic demands on her favored suitor; for the rivalries between him and three other suitors (who are fooled by the heroine with the help of two more women); and for the duel that climaxes the play's tenuous plot.[24]

Davenant's *News from Plymouth* (1635) is a whimsical bagatelle written evidently to exploit nationalistic pride in England's East India seamen who had skirmished with the Dutch at Amboyna. (A Dutch captain and his turncoat English skipper, the only villains in the comedy, undergo public baffling—like Mathews and Bob Acres.) Lady Loveright, a wealthy heiress who likes to assert her independence, has taken lodgings at Plymouth where she secretly plans a rendezvous with her fiancé, who is returning from service at sea—a service she enjoined upon him as a condition of their marrying, along with the further condition that he completely divest himself of his wealth. While awaiting his ship, she amuses herself by receiving the addresses of Seawit, the cleverest and the most courtly of three fortune-seeking "Sea-Captains" who are windbound at Plymouth. This slightest of plots hinges entirely on the fickle wind and the willfulness of Loveright: the play ends when a Boatswain enters to break up the assembled characters and their barely thwarted duel with his cry, "Aboard, aboard, the Wind stands fair" (V.33).

News from Plymouth, like Davenant's later, Restoration comedy, *The Playhouse to be Let* (1663), is written with a high-spirited insouciance that must have appealed to Sheridan. The perspective in which Davenant represents Plymouth and its provincial inhabitants mirrors the viewpoint of amused, slightly condescending courtiers on vacation. The idle Captains and other genteel sojourners, much like the visitors to Sheridan's Bath, pass their time in gossip, light intrigue, and the cultivation of "humors." The main action, such as it is, revolves around Loveright's flirtation with Seawit, whom Loveright's niece tries to seduce for herself when she realizes that her aunt does not love him. Seawit comes to suspect he is being fooled by both women, and, when he confronts them, he is overheard and challenged by Loveright's jealous fiancé. Exactly as happens in *The Rivals*, their duel is interrupted by the alarmed women who, in this extremity, freely avow their true love. The garrulous "humor" of another character, Sir Solemn Trifle, generates its own subplot: Trifle, who with his team of clerks dispatches forged news by way of "courants" and "gazettes," offers to help one of the Captains by publishing a rumor that Lady Loveright has contracted herself to him.[25]

The strongest "humors" of the play, however, are on display in its cynosure, the honor-obsessed, Staffordshire squire Sir Furious Inland, who lives only for quarreling. When he invented this frighteningly original figure, Davenant was not trying to create another *miles gloriosus* such as Pistol or Jonson's Bobadill. Rather, he was tapping into English mythology with its Green Man or *woodwose*—a type of wild forest-dweller possessed of supernatural energy, like the Savages in Spenser's *The Faerie Queene* or the Wild Man in the play of *Mucedorus*. Seawit has taken the young squire into his charge with the vague purpose of civilizing him (Davenant's word "inland" inverts the sense it carried in *As You Like It*, where Rosalind credits her uncle with being "an inland man, one that knew courtship"). Seawit describes this curiosity to Lady Loveright:

> *Loveright*: What kind of man is that Sir Furious Inland—your charge, I think they call'd him?
>
> *Seawit*: He's a gentleman of fair descent and ample means, but subject to their disease of quarreling; his sword hangs still too near his right hand. He loves fighting above all pleasures, and is more delighted with the dangers of a duel than the honor of having had the better. He was trusted by some of his noble kinsmen to my care, in hope the discipline of the war might tame him. I have done little good upon him yet; his mettle will not bow.[26]

This description heightens the comic interest by making us anticipate Sir Furious's introduction at Loveright's provincial demi-court. When we first meet him in person, he has just escaped from the ship and the Boatswain who was superintending him:

> *Seawit*: Who Hath chaf'd my little Libyan lion thus Into a foam? Methinks thou look'st as thou did'st come from slaughter, and from prey.
>
> *Inland*: A rogue vex'd me as I pass'd through the high street.
>
> *Seawit*: How, my dear charge?
>
> *Inland*: He asked me what a' clock it was.
>
> *Seawit*: Was that offence?
>
> *Inland*: Death! Do I look like a watchmaker, am I bound to take charge of the hours, and give every rogue intelligence how they pass?
>
> *Seawit*: Well, and how did you proceed?
>
> *Inland*: I beat him. (II.11)

In passages like this, Sheridan found a whimsical delight in caricature akin to his own genius. Although Davenant's "humors" characters bear the rough stamp of the old Jonsonian way of writing, Sheridan might—with a little scouring of their language and some polishing of their manners—give them the grotesque charm to which a politer, eighteenth-century audience was accustomed. In any event, Sheridan absorbed every detail of this wild young squire's "humors." In the next scene (III.i), after we meet him, for example, Sir Furious and Seawit encounter a group of sailors just landed, including their Dutch-speaking Captain and Loveright's fiancé. When the new arrivals propose a health to the king, Sir Furious is outraged. "How! A butter-box? He pledge the king's health, being an alien, before his natural subject? On our allegiance, we must not suffer it." Here is where Sheridan got the idea for O'Trigger's artificial quarrel with Jack Absolute, whom he accuses of having "put a jest on me lately, at the expence of my country."[27]

An even closer borrowing from Davenant's text may be seen in the original dénouement of *The Rivals*. When his duel with Jack is interrupted, O'Trigger shows the letter that, he supposed, came from his antagonist. Bob Acres sees that the letter is actually the challenge that O'Trigger penned for *him*. Acres had addressed it to "The Lover of Miss Languish" and his servant had mistakenly delivered it to O'Trigger himself, who glanced at it and—implausibly—without recognizing his own hand, assumed the note was from Jack confirming their dueling appointment. He fails to appreciate the comedy of his situation and erupts when he is told, "Sir Lucius, then, you have Challeng'd yourself."

> *Sir Luc*: Challeng'd myself!—Hell and Fury, Sir, what do you mean? 'Sblood! I would resent an affront from myself, as soon as from another Gentlemen. And if my Honour were concerned in it, my right hand should measure swords with my left! How dare you laugh.[28]

This extravagant speech, which Sheridan cut (along with Lucy's naming Jack to O'Trigger as his rival) from the revised Act V, was clearly inspired by Davenant's central scene where Inland urges the Captains to quarrel. It begins with Seawit introducing Sir Furious to Lady Loveright:

> *Seawit*: Why, how now, Charge? Struck dumb? You have no more Compliment than a fish. Go, speak to her.

> *Inland*: You'll give me leave to rub my elbow first, In sign that I am taken. All Staffordshire Cannot show her fellow.

> *Seawit*: Come, your address! An old haberdasher Hath as much courtship. Do but speak to her!

Inland: Madam, have you any quarrels?

Loveright: Sir,
I deserve not any, for I do no wrong.

Inland: Right or wrong, that's not the business. If you
Have none, dispatch and make some; as many
As you please, too. I'll fight 'em over and over. (III.15)

Inland's "humors" are protracted into a kind of play-within-a-play, with Loveright and Seawit doing the commenting. Sir Furious takes aside Loveright's other two suitor, Captains Topsail and Cable, and chides either of them in turn for squabbling in her presence.

Inland: How dare you, sir, appear before this lady,
That lately in her presence were so rude?

Topsail: Sir, I have ask'd her pardon, and am reconcil'd.

Inland: How! Reconcil'd a quarrel without blood?

Topsail: You must consider, sir, 'twas with a lady.

Inland: No reconcilement can be made with honor
Till one or both have bled for it, be the defendant
Man, woman, or child.

Topsail: These are new sword-cases, but I shall learn. (III.16)

Pretending to be superior to these insults witnessed by Loveright, Topsail and Cable play along with the squire's crude "humors" by instructing him in the niceties of dueling. "You are my noble second, and my friend," Topsail tells Sir Furious, sending him to challenge Cable, who retorts, "Troth I am sorry that his choice / Could find no other bearer than yourself, / For you are he I had design'd *my* second." Sir Furious gladly accepts the office and "*beckons Topsail aside.*" (This, the only stage direction, helps us to visualize the farce being acted out before Loveright and Seawit.)

Topsail: How, Sir Furious! why, you are mine!

Inland: Sir, I am any man's that will fight, and you
Had best agree both upon a meeting,

And fall to't handsomely without satisfaction.
I'll have no satisfaction, 'tis a base word
And fitter for the bottom of a bond
Than for a soldier's mouth. (III.16)

Realizing he must intervene before things are carried too far in Loveright's presence, Seawit takes Sir Furious aside:

Seawit: Dost thou hear, Charge. If they should fight it out after the French way, where the seconds must encounter too, how will you find an opposite?

Inland: I thank you for that question, Governor. But now I think on't, you may choose which side you please, and we'll fight two to two! (III.17)

At this point, Loveright appeals to Seawit. "I must entreat some privacy / And truce among these men of wrath, and their / Bold second for an hour. You'll procure it?" Seawit bids Sir Furious entertain the rival Captains, promising to join them "e're you can pledge / Two ramekins of wine." Left alone with the Captains, Sir Furious now proves himself quite the adept in this new art of the duel and undertakes to instruct *them* how to quarrel honorably:

Inland: Gentlemen, no words here. Besides, it is
My governor's request I lead you both
Where we may drink together, and appear
Not like to things enrag'd with malice, but
Provok'd to battle by our *honor*.
Those I take to be his words. He'll meet us strait. (III.33)

In this scene, Davenant's young wild man learns civility by discovering the dueling code that prescribes rules for exercising his quarrelsome "humors." He is becoming an English gentleman, jealous of his honor and a stickler for punctilious form in the duel. He's not unlike the officious Barnett, watchful of his reputation lest Sheridan mock him in the figure of Sir Lucius O'Trigger; or unlike Sheridan himself, insisting that Mathews drink with him before their final duel.

Despite its title, *News from Plymouth*, like all five of Davenant's plays performed before 1635, was adapted to the courtly taste that the King's Men sought to gratify. Davenant's prologue and epilogue link the play to its audience. The prologue apologizes to the "Noble company" (i.e., nobility) among them for presenting the "humble theme [of] a few Seamen, wind-bound in a port." In the epilogue, Sir Furious steps forward to warn the audience that they

> had not best
> Believe my rage or Humour so oppress'd
> I'th' heat of the last scene, as that you may
> Freely, and safely too, cry down our play; (1–4)

for if they do, he'll cudgel them for enemies who "lay sad plots to beggar the King's Men."

The relation between Sir Furious and his audience, whose mores reflected the court of Charles I, allowed Davenant to transform his wild man into the king's soldier all in the space of five acts. In learning to channel his fierce "humors" into the court's code of honor, Sir Furious rejuvenates that code. In this way, the mores (or "moral truths") of the court are reinforced by the spectacle of the wild man tamely subjecting his savage strength to a woman's direction while his dangerous honor shields (and thereby enhances) her beauty. Yet as the epilogue shows, Sir Furious Inland's audience took this honor more lightly—and at the same time regarded it more highly—than would the audience of Sir Lucius O'Trigger.

Either of these quarrelsome knights is reconciled to his society by a final dueling scene. The contrast between the two endings is instructive. When Lydia, meaning to disabuse Sir Lucius, pledges herself to Jack, Jack realizes "there must be some mistake." He apologizes to Sir Lucius for having inadvertently affronted his patriotism; but he stands ready to make good his claim to Lydia. Sir Lucius shakes hands with him, saying "an affront handsomely acknowledged becomes an obligation. And as for the Lady—if she chuses to deny her own handwriting here / . . . . When he is told by Mrs. Malaprop that he has been paying court to *her* ("You Delia?—pho! pho! be easy"), Sir Lucius cynically owns that he's been deceived (cynically, because he played the fortune-hunter himself): "To shew you I'm not ungrateful, Captain Absolute: Since you have taken that lady from me, I'll give you my Delia into the bargain" (*Dramatic Works*, 1:144). Self-betrayed, Sir Lucius in effect gives up all his pretensions to courtship and honor as if they were of no more significance than a lost wager.

Sir Furious, by contrast, would put his life at risk before he'd betray his honor. In the final scene of Davenant's play, when the ladies have interrupted the duel and begun their explanations, Sir Furious bursts excitedly upon them: "None kill'd yet? / I've heard of the quarrel, and I *will* make one—/ I care not on which side." Lady Loveright begs them to "Quiet this storm, and I will give you reason / For what we do, or have done." Thereupon all three of her suitors, joined by her fiancé, gang up against Sir Furious to chastise his insolence. Even though they threaten him with their swords, however, Sir Furious refuses to give ground: "Cow me with odds? Were your number ten times doubled, / I would not budge. Ladies, stand fair, you shall / Perceive I am not aw'd, nor tongue-tied." Sir Furious is no mere braggart soldier (*miles gloriosus*), as the suitors now realize: "Sure the Devil's in him . . . [We] must take another course." Each of them, starting with Seawit, then recants and salutes Inland as their leader: "Thou shalt be / Our Admiral, and kill the King's enemies / By dozens; be but reconcil'd!" "I am," Inland replies. The ladies then make their pledges to their lovers, whom they encourage, along with Sir Furious, to fight for the king (V.32).

This courtly ending leaves one quite unprepared for Sheridan's rude finale that heaps ridicule on the dishonored Mrs. Malaprop. Seeing her rejected in turn by Sir Lucius, Jack, and even the cowardly Bob Acres, the refined audience must wince at the collapse of civility. Sir Anthony makes a half-hearted attempt at gallantry: "Come, Mrs. Malaprop, don't be cast down—you are in your bloom yet." But the undeceived lady has lost her stomach for chivalry. "O Sir Anthony!—men are all barbarians."

Sheridan might admire these mores and the honor that nourished them, but he could not recreate them on the eighteenth-century stage, much less adapt them to his own biography. The Caroline court and Davenant's audience had been supplanted by audiences whose mores had become increasingly denatured even as they were ceaselessly and unsparingly refined. To Sheridan's audience, Jonson's and Davenant's "humors" seemed more embarrassing than mirthful, even when those "humors" were filtered through urbane plays like Congreve's.

Believing profoundly as he did that honor was the root of gentility, Sheridan tried to embody this "moral truth" in a stage Irishman. But O'Trigger's society, in contrast to Sir Furious Inland's, no longer required honor to protect its women or its bonds of friendship. For Sheridan and his society, the honor that counted most was public and directly related to the nation's interest. Fifteen years later, Burke would lament that chivalry died with the French Revolution. On that issue, however, Sheridan the public servant would break with his fellow Irishman, holding instead that the political cataclysm signified chivalry's *replacement* by the greater honor of the people. What really died in 1789 was the proud and ultimately self-glorifying honor of men like Sir Lucius O'Trigger. That honor, which had nearly cost Sheridan his life, was best confined to the stage, where it could be preserved for the idle mockery of posterity.

Notes

1. Letter to Elizabeth's father Thomas Linley dated November 17, 1774. See Richard Brinsley Sheridan, *The Letters of Richard Brinsley Sheridan*, ed. Cecil Price, 2 vols. (Clarendon Press: Oxford, 1966), 1:85, hereafter referred to as Sheridan, *Letters*. See also n10: Price thinks the "little farce" was probably Sheridan's adaptation of his mother's unpublished play, *A Trip to Bath*, whence Sheridan derived Mrs. Malaprop.

2. Letter dated December 25, 1805 (Sheridan, *Letters*, 2:251). Sheridan is addressing his second wife, Esther (or "Hecca") Ogle, who was born the year *The Rivals* appeared. Eliza had died in 1792. In letters written in the last decade of his life, Sheridan uses the word "nervous" to mean depressed.

3. Thomas Moore. *Memoirs of the Life of the Right Honourable Richard Brinsley Sheridan*, 5th ed., 2 vols. (London: Longman, Rees, Orme, Brown, and Green, 1826). Copious extracts from the juvenilia are printed by Walter Sichel, *Sheridan, From New and Original Material; Including a Manuscript Diary by Georgiana, Duchess of Devonshire*, 2 vols. (London: Constable, 1909).

4. Sheridan, *Letters*, 1:30, 73. Sheridan and Mathews fought twice in two months. At their first duel, in London on May 4, 1772 Sheridan had disarmed his antagonist and obliged him to retract the slurs he had posted in the Bath newspapers the month before, when it transpired that Sheridan, mainly to help Eliza escape from Mathews's attentions, had escorted her to France. After the retraction appeared in *The Bath Chronicle* on May 7, 1772 (it is reproduced by R. Compton Rhodes, *Harlequin Sheridan: The Man and the Legends* [Oxford: Basil Blackwell, 1933], 42), Mathews was persuaded by Barnett, a stickler for gentlemanly honor, that he had to challenge Sheridan and repeat their duel in order to prove that the retraction was not an act of cowardice. Barnett accompanied Mathews to Bath as his second and "was the bearer of the Challenge which he had the cruelty to put into Miss [Alicia] Sheridan's hands, saying it was an invitation for her brother" (Sheridan, *Letters*, 1:30). Sheridan had already spared Mathews's life and was under no obligation to meet his antagonist a second time. Nevertheless, he was either too diffident or too generous to reject Mathews's specious plea that Sheridan had violated the dueling code by breaking the sword that he took from his submissive opponent in their London duel. Both in his July letter to Knight and in the subsequent letter that he drafted (but never sent) to Barnett, Sheridan is clearly anxious to forge a competing narrative to the several accounts broadcast by Mathews.

5. Sheridan, *Letters* 1:30, 33.

6. Fintan O'Toole, *A Traitor's Kiss: the Life of Richard Brinsley Sheridan, 1751–1816* (London: Granta, 1997), argues that Sheridan consented to the repeat duel because he felt defensive—less on the score of his Irishness than because he was the son of an actor. "Richard would certainly have been well aware of what his father had to go through in order to defend his right to be recognized as a gentleman [four years before Richard was born Thomas was grossly insulted in Dublin by a clique of "Gentlemen" while acting at Smock Alley]. Mathews's public declaration that he did not deserve 'the treatment of a gentleman' was much more than a mere personal insult. It threatened to undo what his parents had achieved in the past and to undermine his own future" (68).

7. Sheridan, *Letters* 1:75. In a letter dated January 4, 1773 to his friend Grenville, Sheridan decries Paumier's rumored perfidy and says he wishes he "had it in my power to have given you some less confused account of the late affair at Bath. But I am still very uncertain; and am really so much

disgusted with the whole set of them on both sides, that I believe I shall grow very indifferent about their machinations" (70).

8. Sheridan, *Letters* 1:77.

9. O'Toole, *A Traitor's Kiss* 70.

10. Sheridan, *Letters* 1:85. The farce is *A Trip to Bath*; see n1.

11. Ibid., 1:85. In his Preface to the first edition (published in 1775), Sheridan says that the ms. he put into "Mr. Harris's hands . . . was at that time at least double the length of any acting comedy.—I profited by his judgment and experience in the curtailing of it." My quotations and paraphrases of the Preface, the play, and its earliest critics are all based on *The Dramatic Works of Richard Brinsley Sheridan*, ed. Cecil Price, 2 vols. (Oxford: Clarendon Press, 1973), 1:70; (Preface), 42, 44, 99, 52, cited hereafter as Sheridan, *Dramatic Works*. For the derivation of Mrs. Malaprop from Frances Sheridan's Mrs. Tryfort, see n1 above.

12. Sheridan, *Dramatic Works* 1:70.

13. Sheridan, *Dramatic Works* 1:70. He flatters the audience by saying they perform the office of "a candid and judicious friend." For Sheridan's appreciation of Sidney, see Sheridan, *Letters* 1:66.

14. Ibid., 1:40. Another newspaper reported after the première that "it was believed by the friends of the author that it would meet with opposition from a certain quarter, as it was thought by many to have a close connexion with a certain affair at Bath, in which the celebrated Miss Linley (now Mrs. Sheridan) was the subject of rivalship; but they appear to have been mistaken. . . . After a pretty warm contest towards the end of the last act, it was suffered to be given out [i.e., repeated] for the ensuing night" (ibid.). O'Toole thinks Sheridan himself inspired the disclaimer that appeared on the opening day (*A Traitor's Kiss*, 92).

15. Commenting on the revision of Vanbrugh's *A Trip to Scarborough*, Jack Durant notes that in addition to Sheridan's "emasculation of Vanbrugh's language," one finds that "Sheridan sidesteps all the major issues of Vanbrugh's play: its close analysis of human sexuality, its tough satire against aristocratic preferment and clerical profligacy, and its indictment of the laws of primogeniture. All this content Sheridan sacrifices to high moral scruples on the one hand and low buffoonery on the other. He was right to upbraid himself years later for meddling with Restoration comedy." See Jack Davis Durant, *Richard Brinsley Sheridan* (Boston: Twayne Publishers, 1975), 134–35.

16. Sheridan, *Dramatic Works* 1:70

17. Sheridan, *Dramatic Works* 1:70. Compare the report above (see n14). Four years later, in *The Critic*, Sheridan will again dissociate himself from his play, not by adding a preface but by employing the device of the play-within-a-play. Either expedient is calculated to disarm potential critics, demonstrating that they have been anticipated by an author who is his own severest critic.

18. Ibid., 1:40; see above, n4 and n14. Barnett's name was sometimes spelt Barnard; hence the abbreviation by "A Librarian." For Barnett to claim that he was slandered in the person of Sir Lucius, he would have to argue that the cowardly Bob Acres stood for Mathews—an identification that could not redound much to the credit of either man.

19. Sheridan, *Dramatic Works* 1:70

20. Ibid., 1:71. In chap. 10 ("Beastly Pimping Actors"), O'Toole examines Sheridan's ambivalent feelings about the stage and his dependence on it. He wrote to his father-in-law to dissuade Linley

from allowing Eliza's younger sister, Mary, to accept Garrick's invitation to act at Drury Lane, declaring at the time (May or June 1775): "No Gentleman of Character and Fortune ever yet took a Wife from behind the Scenes of a Theatre" (Sheridan, *Letters*, 3:298). O'Toole remarks that "he might have added that no gentleman had a sister-in-law on the stage either" (*A Traitor's Kiss*, 84).

21. O'Toole, *A Traitor's Kiss*, 110.

22. Sheridan, Thomas. *Captain O'Blunder: or, The Brave Irishman*. Dublin, no date. This item is in the National Library of Ireland, ESTC Number T212766.

23. Sheridan, *Dramatic Works* 1:70, 60 (for the notices, which appeared in the *London Chronicle* within two weeks of the January 28, 1775 reopening).

24. The quotations that follow come from the facsimile reprint of *The Works of Sir William Davenant* (first published in London, 1673 in 2 vols.; reissued New York: Benjamin Blom, Inc., 1968). Because the 1673 folio divides the play into acts but not into scenes—except for acts 1 and 2 (each of which is broken into two scenes)—I have inserted after each quotation the folio page number where it may be found.

Besides these four elements from Davenant's play that I've noted (and will discuss below), Sheridan found also in the folio the nucleus of a scandal industry foreshadowing the arts of Lady Sneerwell and Snake, as well as the methods of Puff (in *The Critic*). Moreover, the first act of Davenant's *The Playhouse to be Let* may have inspired the opening of *The Critic*—about which Sheridan would later remark that "he valued the first act more than anything he ever wrote" (Sheridan, *Dramatic Works*, 2:468).

25. Act IV.8. Sir Solemn Trifle's usual forgeries trade in international politics, but his offer to slander Lady Loveright shows him a master of local scandal as well. Davenant was of course writing before the advent of periodical newspapers, and his obvious model was Ben Jonson's *The Staple of News* (1625). At the Restoration, Davenant was granted one of the two royal patents for theaters in Covent Garden and Drury Lane, where he revived and adapted the plays of Jonson and Shakespeare. Dryden portrays him under the "feigned name" of Eugenius, one of four gentlemen who debate the merits of English and foreign drama in *An Essay of Dramatick Poesy* (1667). For more on Davenant's influence on the drama after 1660, see my *Dryden and the Problem of Freedom: The Republican Aftermath, 1649–1681* (New Haven, CT: Yale University Press, 1997), chap. 5.

26. *News from Plymouth* II.8. The Folio prints these lines as verse; I've restored them, and similar passages below, to prose and modernized the punctuation.

27. Sheridan, *Dramatic Works*,1:117. This patriotic quarrel is one of Sheridan's revisions; originally, Sir Lucius challenges Jack Absolute because Lucy, knowing that he thinks "Delia" is Lydia's nom de plume, told him Jack was his rival for "Delia's" affections. Hence the confusion described in the next paragraph.

28. Sir Lucius's speech is quoted from the edition based on the Larpent MS., which is an official copy, prepared for the Lord Chamberlain's license, of *The Rivals* as originally acted. See Sheridan's *The Rivals, a comedy. As it was first Acted at the Theatre-Royal in Covent-Garden*, ed. Richard Little Purdy (Oxford: Clarendon Press, 1935), 112. This excised speech reveals the kind of personal caricature that must have drawn loud protests from Barnett and his faction on opening night.

4

REFLECTIONS UPON MAINTAINING A
COMPETITIVE EDGE

The Duenna and Her Peers at Drury Lane

Mita Choudhury

[T]hey were to work together at Drury Lane for the next quarter of a century, their lives running strikingly parallel outside the theatre as well as in. Each was a brilliant performer, she on stage, he both in Parliament and in society; and both dazzled the watching world by taking risks, as good performers do. They were not such different creatures as he liked to think, and must at times have recognized their kinship. Their Irish background gave them a first point in common; both disliked it, but it was inescapable.[1]

Claire Tomalin has thus compared the actress Dorothy Jordan to Richard Brinsley Sheridan, an unlikely coupling—despite the "dazzle" associated with their names—but one that might also be used to explain some of the difficulties of assessing Sheridan's legacy almost two hundred years after his death. Even the soberest of retrospections succumb to the dazzle. Whether Jordan benefits from Tomalin's comparison is debatable, but Sheridan is well served because he appears from this perspective to be precisely the sort of brilliant maverick that he so wanted everyone to recognize and to reward. Undergirding Tomalin's compliment and implied in it is a reference to the inflexible social stratification very much in place in the late eighteenth century. Inherent in this comparison, simultaneously, is the relish with which postmodernity rejects such archaic notions of order and hierarchy and champions the cause of those who managed to shake the foundations.[2] To press this point further, one could also argue that the quintessential outsider with talent and grit, a "character" such as Jordan or Sheridan, is uniquely suitable for challenging the foundations of existing socio-political hierarchies.[3]

Theirs was a world where power and privilege were still anchored by money and title, with the mercantile-colonial new money fueling the same infrastructure and pledging allegiance to the same old and still-potent hierarchies. Among Sheridan's memorable characters, Isaac Mendoza and his lackey, Don Carlos, are unique because the plot of *The Duenna* (1775) is forced into integrating these outsiders (not just outcasts like Charles Surface) and naturalizing them within the otherwise typical complications in comedy. Inevitably, in the context of the 1770s, the privilege of endowing respectability, say, to a recent convert to Christianity, lay more often than not in the hands of those who resisted the idea of assimilating an outsider whose identity is awkwardly positioned somewhere "between the Old and New Testament."[4] The search for novelty was thus preempted by a resistance to the same. This essay is premised upon two facts related to Sheridan studies that should have been tagged as remarkable, if not baffling, but have not: the fact that Sheridan's most successful comedy (if success is defined as impact during the first season) has received the least critical attention.[5] Additionally, this criticism has focused almost exclusively on a character that is rejected from the framework of the happy ending, Isaac; indeed, the happy ending is predicated upon the elimination of this destabilizing factor, this diminutive outsider of Falstaff proportion. This essay also argues for the need of a fresh analytic trajectory that accommodates the dialectical tensions between the two principal theatrical venues circa mid-1770s to show, for instance, how Drury Lane responded—in a remarkable blend of serendipity and contingency—to the unexpected success of *The Duenna* at Covent Garden.[6]

"*The Duenna*, considered as a whole, is the most perfect opera in our language." Few disagreed with this assessment by William Oxberry, but there were two constraining factors in this "most perfect opera": the operatic or singing parts had to be molded seamlessly into a typical comedy *and* assigned to actors who could efficiently carry these parts.[7] The perfection is generally explained in terms of its tight three-act structure and streamlined plot—its formal parameters, in other words. The generic tag that most frequently described *The Duenna* was comic opera—though "play" was also used, as it is now, because this tag elides the differences related to structure, position in entertainment sequence (depending upon whether it was a main piece or an after piece), and so on. A "play" can then be qualified in a number of ways to accommodate both its immediate and its long-term impact, as Mark S. Auburn has done in the following assessment of Sheridan's works: "He had written and had helped to produce two *enormously popular plays* (my emphasis), *The Rivals* (January 1775) and *The Duenna* (November 1775), at the Theatre

Royal in Covent Garden." And "Sheridan gave two *great plays* (my emphasis) to Drury Lane, *The School for Scandal* (May 1777) and *The Critic* (October 1779), several entertainments, and one political spectacle, *Pizarro* in 1799."[8] Auburn's purpose here is rightly to situate Sheridan as the most successful playwright in the late eighteenth century. Moreover, the demarcation in his assessment between the plays that are popular and those that are great (an assessment with which I entirely agree) points perhaps to a more historically prevalent and thus deeply entrenched series of demarcations: between a traditional five-act structure and (what might be considered as) the new-fangled three-act structure; between straight comedy and comic opera (with large doses of farce); and between traditional characters/ predictable outcomes and non-traditional characters/ unpredictable outcomes.[9] The question of why the "popular" is not necessarily the best qualified to be considered "a great work" has more to do with traditsion, heritage, and history than with the particularities and the contingencies of the specific play's intrinsic merit or performance history. A popular play, therefore, could be judged by traditional standards and found to be deficient, which is not exactly the case with *The Duenna*.

The popularity of *The Duenna* is, of course, assessed in terms of the number of nights it was performed in the first season and, based upon the number of seats and the overall capacity of the theatre, one could also come up with a rough calculation of the numbers of spectators who saw a particular play in a given season. The reasons for the success of this comic opera or its popularity, however, had nothing whatsoever to do with originality, and this point has been made repeatedly—most memorably by Charles Dibdin because he is considered to be a hostile witness.[10] But if there was any animosity between Sheridan and Dibdin, it is absent from this overall assessment of Sheridan's works:

> Sheridan, a man of most commanding talents, would have stood inferior to very few writers, on this or any other similar list, had his time been entirely devoted to the theatre; for, in that case, as genius loves to spread and expand, and seldom satisfies itself with adopting when it can have opportunity of traversing the wide range of invention, the public would no doubt have seen original tragedies and comedies, such as might have served as models for the imitation of authors not so happily gifted, instead of scenes, hints, and circumstances, most ingeniously wrought together indeed, but as far as any thing on the stage from originality.[11]

I find this to be a very fair assessment that provides an appropriate framework for analyses of individual plays by Sheridan, for each of which Dibdin provides a succinct commentary. It was Dibdin who first provided exact citations pointing to the extent of Sheridan's continental borrowings in *The Duenna*: In Molière's *Le Sicilien, ou l'Amour peintre* (1667) and in *Il Filosofo di Campagna* (Baldasarre Galuppi, composer, and Carlo Goldoni, librettist, 1754), he said, "every circumstance is to be found from the serenade in the first scene to the marriage in the last" (Ibid., 5: 298). Furthermore, Dibdin noted that "Father Paul is (Jean-François) Marmontel's *Philosophe soi-disant*, who, as he sits at a feast and enveighs [*sic*] against gormandizing, actually says, as he entreats a lady to help him to some nicety at table, 'Can't we be satisfied with the wholesome roots of the earth?' and laments, after drinking a glass of Burgundy, that people will not be content, like our forefathers, 'with the chrystal stream'" (5: 297–98).[12] In conclusion too, Dibdin comes across as a seasoned critic: "As to the dialogue of this piece it is lively, pointed, and pertinent. It has not the ease of Vanbrugh, the neatness of Farquhar, nor the wit of Congreve, and yet it has something of them all. It is managed with the cunning of a painter who does not imitate any particular artist, but who copies the school" (5: 299–300).

The evidence regarding Sheridan's extensive borrowings is incontrovertible even when the circumstances of his acquiring such familiarity with these French and Italian sources remain a mystery: when did he have the time to study Molière and Italian opera, let alone to borrow so strategically as to enhance the comic effects of (in this case) several important scenes in *The Duenna*? Instead of dwelling on Sheridan's mystery years—important though this may be in any consideration of *The Duenna* because of the presumed dates of its composition—the focus of this discussion will be on the unique elements that account for the popularity of the comic opera: Isaac Mendoza and Don Carlos. In addition to the music in the piece, it was the character of Isaac that received the greatest attention—albeit, mostly in the context of how he was first conceptualized and how his role was subsequently revised and streamlined, with a ripple effect upon the role of his lackey Moses, later renamed Carlos. Dibdin's analysis of Isaac underscores the creative and arguably original feature of the comic opera: "The aside speeches of Isaac, shewing before hand, and without his knowledge how easily he is himself to be taken in by his different attempts to cheat others, convey the most artful species of anticipation that ever was practiced, and shew a judgement of theatrical effect, powerful, new and extraordinary" (5: 300). Coming as this does from Dibdin, "powerful, new and extraordinary" are particularly strong recommendations of Sheridan's "judgment of theatrical effect." Equally important, even as early as in 1788, Dibdin saw Isaac as a precursor of what Sheridan would later become—but this affinity was, he says, the result of unconscious artistry, created "without his knowledge."[13] It is in this segment of the critique of *The Duenna* that Dibdin reveals his animosity toward Sheridan, although the view is no different from the views of a significant segment of Sheridan's political and theatrical constituencies, beginning as early as the 1780s, but particularly potent post-1800.[14]

The comic intrigue in the plot unfolds in Spain and is launched by Don Jerome's insistence that his daughter, Louisa, marry a man of considerable means: his choice, Isaac Mendoza. The stereotypical patriarch is clear about his plans, and he has reasons for his sense of urgency: "I'll suffer no more of these midnight incantations, these amorous orgies that steal the senses in the hearing, as they say Egyptian Embalmers serve mummies, extracting the brain thro' the ears; however, there's an end of your frolics—Isaac Mendoza will be here presently, and tomorrow you shall marry him" (I.iii.236).[15] However, Louisa is in love with Antonio and Isaac is not only a Portuguese, but he is also a dubious convert to Christianity—objections that both Louisa and her brother put forth to their father thus:

Ferd: He is a Portugueze in the first place.

Jerome: No such thing, boy, he has forsworn his country.

Louisa: He is a Jew.

Jerome. Another mistake: he has been a christian these six weeks.'

Ferd: Ay, he left his old religion for an estate, and has not had time to get a new one.

Louisa: But stands like a dead wall between church and synagogue, or like the blank leaves between the Old and New Testament. (I.iii.237)

The impediment standing in the path of the lovers must be removed by the following: Isaac must be duped into marrying an ugly (inevitably) old spinster, the duenna—who appears to him disguised as Louisa—and he must simultaneously be discredited due to his tenuous links to both state (Spain) and religion (Christianity). Moreover, as Ferdinand underscores, "the remarkable part of his character, is his passion for deceit, and tricks of cunning." And Louisa forecasts the dénouement when she says "the fool predominates so much over the knave, that I am told he is generally the dupe of his own art." The duenna acquires some authority, if not prestige, by striking the following bargain with Louisa: "[I]f we succeed, you resign all right and title in little Isaac the Jew, over to me." Louisa's response

Figure 4.1   *Michael Leoni as Carlos and Isabella Mattocks as Louisa,* artist unknown. Courtesy of TCS Prints 44, Harvard Theatre Collection, Houghton Library, Harvard University.

indicates that the duenna's physiological and social limitations are not tied to her future prospects: "I shall wish you joy most heartily. He is twenty times as rich as my poor Antonio" (I.iii.236–37). The defects of Isaac's birth (his liminal social status, his diminutive form) are thus linked to his character, while the defects of the duenna's physiognomy present no hindrance to future happiness, except for the ridicule she is subjected to in the comic opera's most effective scenes. These two characters are not entirely equal in terms of defect because the scales are tipped slightly in favor of the duenna.[16]

The facts about the Moses-Carlos character are as follows: In the original version, Carlos was still Moses and, as Thomas Moore noted, "[t]he greater part of the humor of Moses here was afterwards transferred to the character of Isaac."[17] Moore's *Memoirs* provides the (only extant) "original state" of the Isaac-Duenna scene, which was substantially edited out to reduce the burden of Carlos's speaking role in act 2, scene 2, to roughly five truncated queries or exclamations such as "Why she's dam'd ugly" (Price, 1: 195). This reduction in role was designed to accommodate Michael Leoni's limited ability to speak in English and his superior talent as a singer. The plan of the overall piece did not undergo any substantial changes, according to Moore: "It does not appear, from the rough copy in my possession, that any material change was made in the plan of the work, as it proceeded" with the one exception. "Carlos was originally meant to be a Jew and is called "Cousin Moses" by Isaac, in the first sketch of the dialogue; but possibly from the consideration that this would apply too personally to Leoni, who was to perform the character, its designation was altered." The name-change was necessitated by the fact that Leoni was Jewish; the modification in the role was necessitated by the twin considerations of Leoni's shortcoming (command of the English language) and strength (talent for singing). There was one more significant accommodation: About the initial run of the opera, Moore pointed out that it "was acted no less than seventy-five times during the season, the only intermissions being a few days at Christmas, and the Fridays in every week;—the latter on account of Leoni, who being Jew, could not act on those nights."[18] Particularly remarkable is the fact that performances of the play were suspended on Fridays on account of Leoni's—one actor's—religious engagements on that day. This fact, embedded in the performance history of *The Duenna*, points to two specific theatrical trends in the period, with roots that go back to the early part of the century: the bargaining power of foreign performers, as well as the greatly evolved state of business practices, which necessitated what we now call "reasonable accommodation."

Michael Leoni was actually Myer Lyon, a German Jew, who, the *Biographical Dictionary* informs us, was trained to be a reader in a synagogue in Frankfort on the Main.[19] Word of his talent reached the ears of the German Jewish community in London and he was immediately recruited to sing at the synagogue in Duke's Place, where he impressed everyone.[20] Subsequently, his introduction to the Earl of Sandwich and David Garrick paved the way for his transition from religious to secular singing. Indeed, the music for Garrick's *The Enchanter; or Love and Magic* was written by J. C. Smith to introduce Leoni to the London theatrical audiences circa 1760. But it was when he replaced George Mattocks to sing Arbaces opposite Mrs. Mattocks, who played Arbanes in T. A. Arne's opera *Artaxerxes* (1762), that Thomas Harris, recognizing the full force of Leoni's talent, recruited him to appear in the role of Carlos in *The Duenna* at Covent Garden. In 1775, he might still have had obligations to sing at the Duke's Place synagogue on Friday nights. The original Isaac was played by John Quick—who was enormously successful as Tony Lumpkin in *She Stoops to Conquer*—a veteran comic actor with a thirty-one–year career at Covent Garden.[21]

In her *Remarks*, Elizabeth Inchbald observed that "the author did not receive undivided praise for its success:—Musicians had their share, and certain singers of the most forcible attraction." Inchbald aligns herself with the author in this case and argues cryptically that neither authors nor domestic actors had the bargaining power of foreign performers. About Isaac, Inchbald's comments are perhaps the most puzzling, since here too she says far less than what she implies and leaves to the readers' imagination: "The comparing of Isaac's neuter faith to the blank leaf between two scripture doctrines, is, indeed, the happy conception of a very extraordinary imagination; but as this brilliant sentence stands in the dialogue unrivalled, without companion, or comparison with any other in the play, it has more the appearance of some other writer's wit, than that of the ostensible author."[22] In his *Remarks*, William Oxberry noted the following "defect . . . in the character of Carlos, who is not sufficiently connected with the other parts of the story. He seems like a stranger, who, in spite of all his efforts, his bustling assiduities, and a word occasionally thrown in, still remains an isolated intruder."[23] As an actor and the author of *A Mogul Tale* (1784), Inchbald was no stranger to the business of incorporating into effective plots all sorts of odd and alien characters and situations. Oxberry too was fully aware of the contingencies of the theatre where casting frequently shaped character (particularly in new pieces)—as the two additional examples in this discussion will further illustrate. But his comment is also worth dwelling on, if only because one must question the need for a character such as Carlos, which leads to a consideration of whether Isaac could have communicated the same ideas by himself without the aid of a lackey. Sheridan was clearly aware of this alternative trajectory with sharper focus on the principal target of satire because he "transferred many of the lines from Moses to Isaac." In any event, Sheridan was not preempting critiques such as the one by Oxberry; rather, he was tailoring very meticulously both the "outsider" characters to meet the contingencies of casting, determined primarily by Thomas Harris and based upon Harris's clear understanding of what would ensure box-office success: music. Music had become the single-most definitive and determining factor in the success of a comedy in this period.[24] This was not the case in 1728, when John Gay's *The Beggar's Opera* was first launched—a point worth keeping in mind, since *The Duenna* is so often compared to Gay's *Opera*.[25]

Echoing the sentiments of Dibdin and others, Inchbald expressed the consensus opinion that "little Isaac, the Jew seems to be a character wholly original."[26] But the musical parts of the play presented a challenge to Sheridan, who repeatedly asked Thomas Linley, his father-in-law, for help. The urgency communicated in the letters indicates that Sheridan was out of his depth when it came to the songs in the "opera," and committed to follow the directives of Thomas Harris, who had already decided after the success of *Artaxerxes* that Leoni had to have a critical role in *The Duenna*. "[U]nless you give us three days in town, I fear our opera will stand a chance to be ruined." Thomas Moore's date for this letter is October 1775, which indicates that rehearsals were not only limited, but precariously close to the premiere of the play in November. "Harris is extravagantly sanguine of its success as to plot and dialogue, which is to be rehearsed next Wednesday at the theatre. They will exert themselves to the utmost in the scenery, etc., but I never saw any one so disconcerted as he was at the idea of there being no one to put them in the right way as to music."

In the next extant letter to Linley, also dated October 1775, Sheridan continues to communicate a sense of urgency since, clearly, Linley had yet to arrive in London for the musical rehearsal: "The truth is, that what you mention of my getting a master to teach the performers is the very point where the matter sticks, there being no such person as a master among them." In fact, even at this late date, Linley had never heard the baritone sing, even though he had been asked to compose the music for a very specific character, Carlos. More importantly, Linley did not know the specific dramatic situation within which Leoni's singing parts had to be incorporated: "[Y]ou must excuse my impertinence in adding an idea of the cast I would wish the music to have; as I think I have heard you say you never heard Leoni; and I cannot briefly explain to you the character and situation of the

Figure 4.2. *Mr Quick as Isaac Mendoza in The Duenna*, pen and brown ink, by Robert Dighton, English, 1752–1814. Courtesy of The Art Archive / Garrick Club / Art Resource.

persons on the stage with him." A month before the opening, the composer had little to no idea about the context for his composition. Sheridan's letter to Linley, dated November 2, indicates that the latter had yet to arrive in London.[27]

The review of *The Duenna* in the *Morning Chronicle* on November 29, 1775 described succinctly the immediate effects of the success of Sheridan's new comic opera at Drury Lane:

> Among the various instances of national inconstancy that occur almost
> every hour in this strange metropolis, none has surprised me more than
> the sudden partiality of the Town to Covent Garden Theatre, and their
> ungrateful desertion of poor old Drury-Lane: Mr. Garrick, with a spirit
> undiminished by age, has beautified and adorned his playhouse, and
> made it the prettiest Assembly room in the whole Town. He himself
> performs the best parts three or four times a week; and yet this new song
> thing, the *Duenna*, brings crowded houses to Covent-Garden, and leaves
> Roscius almost in utter solitude,—I know the general taste for musick
> may be alleged as an explanation of this phaenomenon. But surely the
> wit of Shakespear, and the incomparable humour of Ben Johnson,
> should still retain the admiration of every sensible Englishman.[28]

As always, the reviewer summons the "great works" of the English theatre in the
cause of resistance to the new-fangled and the outré that threatens the box office
at the competing theatre, Drury Lane. A number of Shakespeare and Jonson plays
were indeed in production at the time. But this reviewer forgets that the "incomparable humour of Ben Jonson" was not sufficient; bear-baiting was also very
popular when Jonson's plays were first produced, and continued to be a big draw
throughout the seventeenth century. What was Garrick's response to this surprising desertion of Drury Lane? According to Moore,

> In order to counteract this great success of the rival house, Garrick found
> it necessary to bring forward all the weight of his own best characters;
> and even had recourse to the expedient of playing off the mother against
> the son, by reviving Mrs. Frances Sheridan's comedy of *The Discovery*,
> and acting the principal part in it himself. In allusion to the increased
> fatigue which this competition with *The Duenna* brought upon Garrick,
> who was then entering on his sixtieth year, it was said, by an actor of the
> day, that "the old woman would be the death of the old man."[29]

In late November, when *The Duenna* was first performed, Garrick must have
been particularly peeved by the accolades it received because he too had written a
farce—albeit a much shorter one—to accommodate a Jewish singer. And he, too,
had given her the sort of role that he thought would accommodate precisely the
current taste in the theatre: a visually striking Other, who had the added advantage
of being a pretty young female singer. On Saturday October 28, 1775, Garrick's
May Day; or the The Little Gipsey was produced as an afterpiece following the
performance of Nicholas Rowe's *The Fair Penitent*.[30] According to the prompter

William Hopkins, Garrick wrote this one-act piece "on purpose to introduce Miss Abrams (a Jew) about 17 years old. She is very small, a Swarthy complexion, has a very sweet Voice and a fine Shake, but not quite power enough yet—both the piece and the Young Lady were receiv'd with Great Applause."[31] But this applause was dwarfed by Sheridan's main piece, produced at the rival theatre just one month later. The irony was that Garrick had been introduced to Leoni much before Thomas Harris became so enamored of the young German émigré. Linley was the composer in *The Duenna*; Garrick had a composer just as renowned: the music for *May Day* (including the songs, choruses, and overture) was composed by Thomas Arne, who had been recruited by Drury Lane in 1774.

The advertisement for the published piece explains the marketing contingency of Garrick's *May Day* thus:

> The Author of this musical Farce, begs leave to inform the readers, if there should be any, that it was merely intended to introduce *The Little Gipsy* to the public, whose youth and total inexperience of the stage made it necessary to give as little dialogue to her character as possible, her success depending wholly upon her singing—This reason added to another, which is that the piece was produced at an early part of the season, when better writers are not willing to come forth, is the best apology the Author can make for its defects.[32]

When better writers are not available and almost the entire repertory in both theatres suffered from lack of novelty in endlessly recycled materials, Abrams, "a Jew," is summoned to play "the little gipsy." A musical farce (genre) is thus further enhanced by the foreignness of the gypsy (character) played by Abrams (actor) whose "[s]warthy complexion" provided just the right hint of the much-desired outré. A comparison between *May Day* and *The Duenna* would be akin to a comparison of apples and oranges. One was an afterpiece, the other a main piece. However, a *juxtaposition* of the two makes sense because the point I wish to make is that the demand for theatrical entertainment, such as it was in the latter half of the century and particularly toward the end of it, put enormous pressures upon the existing genres (five-act tragedies and comedies) as well as upon the content of the entertainment (with, of course, a corresponding pressure upon the managers, who had to recruit actors accordingly). Thus, the universality of comic situations and characters had to be revitalized with small, measured, and strategic incorporations of what I have characterized here as the outré.

Foreign accents, a propensity for opera, random stereotypes of Jews—just to use some random markers of Otherness—had very specific epistemological and social significance in the eighteenth century. In his discussion of the practice of sodomy in the eighteenth century, George Haggerty has pointed out that "[w]ith a few crucial exceptions, broadsides and fictional accounts describe sodomy in very general terms, not as a transgressive sexual practice that involves certain unspeakable activities, but rather as a set of specific habits of dress or personal hygiene, often a foreign accent or questionable religious leanings, and occasionally a taste for opera."[33] So, for instance, if Italian castrati are regarded as a sexual threat, it is not necessarily because of what they do but, rather, because of how they speak, behave, and *act*. Transgressive sexual practices are thus tightly bound with myriad codes of Otherness—so much so that certain habits and certain behaviors identified as symbols of transgression are automatically stamped as unspeakable. Dress and foreign accent might then be masks and the person with a foreign accent the masquerader, relegated to the realm of the abnormal in perpetuity.

Isaac Bickerstaff's *The Sultan; or Peep into the Seraglio* (1782) also assumes particular significance when positioned alongside *The Duenna* for a variety of reasons. By the time this afterpiece premiered at Drury Lane, the author had long disappeared from the London theatrical scene, to avoid being prosecuted for sodomy.[34] But his afterpiece was a big success, and one that benefitted both Garrick and Frances Abington.[35] Sir Joshua Reynolds's impressive portfolio of theatrical portraits of the period includes two of Frances Abington: "Mrs. Abington as the Comic Muse" (which complemented "Mrs. Siddons as the Tragic Muse") and also Abington as Roxolana, based upon Isaac Bickerstaff's rendition of *The Sultan*.[36] Several portraitists of the period saw Abington as the quintessential comic muse. Reynolds, reported to be her admirer, was no different in this respect from Cosway (who painted her as Thalia), and at least two other unknown artists who also saw her as the epitome of comedy.[37] In the Reynolds portrait of Abington as Roxolana, she is seen pushing aside the curtain and making an entry, which is presumably the one that she makes at the very end of *The Sultan*—an entrance that brings about the dénouement and establishes the superiority of this slave over her submissive counterparts as well as her master, the whimsical Sultan.[38] Roxolana is different, muses the Sultan, because although "[s]he's not handsome, that is, what is call'd a beauty; yet her little nose, cock'd in the air, her laughing eyes, and the play of her features, have an effect all together . . . yet, methinks, I have a mind to sift Roxolana's character; mere curiosity and nothing else."[39] By implication, Eastern conceptions of beauty are rejected and replaced by a liberated aesthetics-*cum*-sexual politics, even as Reynolds, Bickerstaff, and Garrick—the portraitist, the playwright, and the staging expert—orchestrate the transfer of power from the eponymous hero (a mere figure-head at best) to the real puppet-master masquerading as Roxolana, Frances Abington. I would like to argue that Abington-Roxolana represents one of the most organic and thus memorable fusions of character and actor on the late eighteenth-century stage. This composite is the visual focus, the elusive object of curiosity whose pursuit necessitates the peep, and facilitates the reification that repeated performance and portraiture produced.[40]

The success of this fusion of actor-character is best expressed in the fact that on Tuesday December 12, 1775, a performance of *Richard III* at Drury Lane was followed by an afterpiece, a farce written by Bickerstaff—but it is the farce that draws overwhelming attention. In terms of reception, then, the afterpiece becomes the centerpiece: not only immediately, at the unveiling, but also in subsequent accounts of it. The promise of undiluted entertainment at the end of the show was what ensured a box-office success. More importantly, it was Abington-Roxolana in the 1770s and Dora Jordan-Roxolana in the 1780s—in one of the most remarkable examples of branding—that catapulted this insignificant script onto an underserved pedestal of praise and prominence.[41] Roxolana is intractable from start to finish, and her arrogant claims—such as "Men were born for no other purpose under heaven, but to amuse us"—are critical punch lines that no doubt evoked laughter from an audience familiar with Abington's extra-theatrical persona, pedigree, and passage to stardom. Used to having subservient mistresses who are hardly distinguishable from slaves, the Sultan is stunned by Roxolana's surprise appearance and also by her spirited defense of her position, some of which goes as follows: "You are my master, it is true; but could the robber, that sold me to you for a thousand chequins, transfer my mind and inclinations to you along with my person?—No, Sir, let it never be said that the great Solyman meanly triumphed over the person of the slave whose mind he could not subdue." The response of the Sultan underscores once again the preoccupation with curiosity: "Tell me who you are; what species of inconsistent being, at once so trifling and respectable that you seduce my heart while you teach me my duty?"[42] The Sultan cannot fathom Roxolana's identity or the 'species' to which she belongs.

The curiosity of the British spectator and the presumed curiosity of an Eastern sultan find expression in a peep—a tantalizingly small, narrow, or fleeting ocular scope for discovery. Thus the curtain from behind which Reynolds's Abington emerges to challenge authority carries more metaphoric weight than the formulaic denouement of Bickerstaff's farce can reasonably be expected to support. On the one hand, the semiotic force of the masked Abington's "foreign-ness" carries the burden of forces well beyond the control of these players in this specific moment. On the other, Reynolds's Abington as Roxolana creates a permanent imprint in the public sphere, where the performance—now frozen in portraiture—becomes a "private" collector's item that ensures its posterity. It is this composite mask—or a masquerade of still and moving images—that finds place within a system of circulation that legitimizes not just the concept of a Western sultana (abstract and imagined) but also the memoirs of a woman of pleasure (real and imagined) whose performance, celebrity, and sexual notoriety demand a "peep into the seraglio."

The protean nature of this historical subject—Richard Brinsley Sheridan—raises practical and theoretical questions, some of which might be summarized as follows: how can a retrospective view—rejuvenated in the beginning of the twenty-first century by digitized access to printed materials from the period—accommodate the many constitutive narrative strands? And, to what extent should the realm of the literary be merged with the realm of the social or political, particularly in this case when the latter threatens the legitimacy of the former and creates a pre- and post-1780 divide? Biography enforces a chronology as well as a linearity that celebrates progression if not development. Thus, inevitably, biography becomes a grand narrative that casts the biographical subject as the protagonist of a textured, sublime, and transformative performance. The focus in this paper on some theatrical trends at Drury Lane and Covent Garden circa the mid-1770s disrupts the smooth continuum of the Sheridan story that is full of public spectacle and splashy grandiloquence, trimmed delightfully with rumors of private misdemeanors and nocturnal masquerades, that cannot eclipse the stories of his mismanagement of Drury Lane. Indeed, in every contributory facet of *The Duenna*—from composition to revision to rehearsal to further alterations to production—the twenty-four-year-old Sheridan emerges as a minor player and part-proprietor of a product that is, nonetheless, indelibly linked to his name.[43] Trends had something to do with competition, but Britain's global engagements at this time had also sensitized audiences to the presence of a much larger world, a world whose unmistakable impact on London can be seen in haphazard instances of a preference for a dark-hued actor, one (akin to members of the royal family) who could barely speak in English, or one dressed as a sultana. In addition, the "reception" of *The Duenna* provides a marvelous test case of the contemporary disjunction between the principles of criticism and the practice of performance. Experts, critics, journalists, and contemporary historians of theatre continued to assess merit by the yardstick of originality, even when originality was completely irrelevant and immaterial in performance. The trick was to figure out the best possible formula for box office success—and in this endeavor Sheridan was just as good as Garrick, Bickerstaff, Inchbald, Dibdin, Colman Jr., and many others. Criticism, grounded in history and heritage, and thus stable and disciplined if not inflexible, could never fully account for the success of a performance that was irrevocably contingent and thus volatile and unpredictable.

Notes

1. See Claire Tomalin, "Proprietor and Prince" In *Mrs. Jordan's Profession: The Story of a Great Actress and a Future King* (London: Viking, 1994), 56–68, specifically, 57.

2. Sir Francis Chantrey's sculpture of Dora Jordan is perhaps the most telling symbol of the institution of royal marriages in the late eighteenth century and how this institution dealt with what it perceived to be an aberration. King William IV may have been the monarch (in 1830), a patron of the arts, and he was also able to pay two hundred guineas to Francis Chantrey for undertaking a project of monumental importance to him, but he did not have any power to ensure that Chantrey's sculpture of a neo-classical Dora Jordan with her two sons would be placed in Westminster Abbey. The Royal Marriages Act, passed in 1772, was designed to bar members of the royal family from marrying without the king's consent. In any event, Jordan could not have married the Duke of Clarence with whom she had ten children. For details, see Tomalin, *Mrs. Jordan's Profession*, specifically 1–3, and also 68.

3. Both William Pitt and Charles James Fox (the latter a close friend and ally of Sheridan) were of wealthy and thus privileged backgrounds. If there was a common thread in the lives of the Sheridan family members, it was their constant battle to ward off economic disaster. Sheridan's sister, Betsy, put it best when she sent in March 1775 the following letter from London to her sister Alicia, who was then in Dublin:

   > I was the only person in the room who had no some consequence in life from fortune, rank or acknowledg'd abilities, I felt alone in the croud and could not wholly banish the mortifying ideas this consciousness necessarily brought with it. Yet the people were all civil and attentive to me, but I have no business among them. I never coveted the honor of sitting at great people's tables and every day I live I wish for it less. There can be no true pleasure derived even from the most delightful society unless you feel you have a right to your place in it.

   To the best of my knowledge, Sheridan never articulated his anxieties about class and money with as much candor and sensibility. The form of Betsy Sheridan's 'journal' was the same as Pamela's letters (detailed accounts of daily life crafted as epistles and addressed to a specific person) and facilitates thus a high level of transparency. See William LeFanu, ed., *Betsy Sheridan's Journal* (New Brunswick, NJ: Rutgers University Press, 1960), 43–44.

4. *The Duenna, A Comic Opera in Three Acts,* act one, scene 3, 13. See Sheridan, *The Dramatic Works of Richard Brinsley Sheridan*, ed. Cecil Price, 2 vols. (Oxford: Oxford University Press, 1973). All citations will be from this edition unless otherwise indicated.

5. It is worth noting, of course, that *The Duenna's* reliance upon music throughout its dramatization makes it pedagogically less attractive than Sheridan's other works.

6. See Mark S. Auburn, "Theatre in the Age of Garrick and Sheridan," in *Sheridan Studies*, eds. James Morwood and David Crane (Cambridge: Cambridge University Press, 1995), specifically 8.

7. The title page of the Oxberry edition is as follows: *Sheridan, The Duenna, An Opera; by Richard Brinsley Sheridan. With Prefatory Remarks.* The only edition existing which is faithfully marked with the stage business, and stage directions, *As it is performed in the Theatres Royal, by W. Oxberry* (London: Simpkin and Marshall, 1820). This is not an authoritative edition; however, the brief descriptions of costume deserve attention. The "stage business" as well as "directions" are minimal. Oxberry's "Remarks" are styled after Inchbald's *Remarks for the British Theatre*, and are important because he presents an actor's point of view, one that both overlaps and counteracts the assessments of Charles Dibdin and Elizabeth Inchbald, which I discuss here.

8. Auburn, "Theatre in the Age," 8.

9. Afterpieces had all sorts of structures, but the three-act main piece also became commonplace. A tragedy could have a three-act structure, such as Mariana Starke's *The Widow of Malabar*. Additionally, in the latter half of the eighteenth century, due to the paucity of new materials, a new afterpiece was frequently the main subject of critical attention, eclipsing the main piece, as the examples later in this essay illustrate. The success or failure of an evening's entertainment, in other words, could easily be determined by the novelty of the afterpiece as well as the star power that gives it additional luster. Cecil Price's edition of *The Dramatic Works of Richard Brinsley Sheridan*—the authoritative "collected" works—does not provide any differentiation based upon structure or genre. In volume 1, for instance, *The School for Scandal* thus follows *The Duenna* and Price's editorial intervention follows the same pattern in each case, beginning with "composition," moving on to "reception" and so on.

10. In her *Remarks for the British Theatre*, Elizabeth Inchbald expresses similar reservations: "The manner of Clara's stealing out for the Duenna is no doubt an excellent contrivance; but, unfortunately, it happens to be old; it occurs in the 'Country Wife,' and again in 'She Would and She Would Not,' and in about half a dozen French pieces." (Inchbald, *Remarks for the British Theatre (1806–1809)* [Delmar, NY: Scholars' Facsimiles and Reprints, 1990].)

11. See Charles Dibdin, *A Complete History of the English Stage*, 5 vols. (London, 1800), 5:294–95. In this *History*, Dibdin incorporated his earlier writings, as, for instance, from *The Musical Tour*, 1788. All citations to Dibdin will be from *A Complete History*, with page numbers in parenthesis.

12. In his discussion of the "reception" of *The Duenna*, Cecil Price—who used the 1794 edition of the text as the authoritative text—cites a big chunk from this segment of Dibdin's text (from *The Musical Tour*) and has the following variation: "[i]sn't there the crystal spring [drinks]?" Otherwise, Sheridan's version (in bits and pieces) in act 3, scene 5, is almost exactly the same as in Marmontel (which I am assuming to be true as do Price, Thomas Moore and others).

13. The date is important because Sheridan entered politics in 1780; thus Dibdin's assessment in circa 1788 could not have accommodated the full extent of Sheridan's political years.

14. Ugliness—moral, political, intellectual if not physical—would define Richard Brinsley Sheridan if we were to look at him through the lens of, say, William Cobbett or Edward Mangin.

Nature never cast the image of man in a more unlovely mould than when she formed Bardolpho; his countenance possesses all the characteristics of ugliness and bestial sensuality; in figure he is more ungraceful than a hog, and in his whole appearance scarsely less filthy and disgusting; but such is the fascination of his tongue, that he has persuaded a second lovely woman to unite her destiny with his. . . . People of England! Subjects of the best of kings! . . . You are now called upon to determine whether you shall be represented by the friends of anarchy, the abettors of sedition, and the practices of fraud, or by men whose political and moral honesty will consult the true interests of the nation, while they strenuously maintain the dignity of the throne! (15)

Anonymous, *The Imposter Unmasked; or the New Man of the People; with Anecdotes, never before published, Illustrative of the Character of the renowned and immaculate BARDOPHO. Inscribed without permission, to the superlatively honest and disinterested Man, R. B. S—R—D—N, Esq.* (London: Tupper and Richards, 1806), 15. See also William Cobbett, *The Political Proteus: A View of the Public Character and Conduct of R. B. Sheridan, Esq.* (London: Cox, Son, and Baylis, January 1804); and Edward Mangin, *A Letter to Thomas Moore, Esq., On the Subject of Sheridan's School for Scandal* (Bath: George Wood, 1826). The clue about authorship of this letter is provided by the following disclosure on the title page: "By the author of an essay on Light-Reading." The British Library catalog identifies the author as Edward Mangin.

15. "[M]idnight incantations" and "amorous orgies" involving Sheridan, Elizabeth Linley, Fox, the Price of Wales and others belong to what I consider to be Sheridan's "Duchess of Devonshire years." When Sheridan wrote *The Duenna* he might very well have fantasized joining this elite club but he was not yet a part of it. Any hidden references here to the admonitions of his father in the early 1770s would have to be assessed by a biographer.

16. In this context, note that the original version of the play that only Moore had seen presented a more harsh picture of the old spinster: "In the first act . . . (scene 3) where Jerome abuses the Duenna, there is an . . . unaccountable omission of a sentence, in which he compares the old lady's face to 'parchment, on which Time and Deformity have engrossed their titles.'" See Thomas Moore, *Memoirs of the Life of Right Honourable Richard Brinsley Sheridan*, 2 vols. (New York: Greenwood Press, 1968), 1:115.

17. Ibid., 1:114. Moore's second edition, which Cecil Price uses, was published in two volumes in London in 1825. Price reiterates the same after quoting at length from the Moore transcription of this early version and adds the following: "At some time in the process of rewriting, Sheridan transferred many of the lines from Moses to Isaac, yet only twenty-six of them in the above passage appear (in slightly altered form) in act 2, scene 2, of W. Fraser Rae's transcript of Sheridan's later manuscript of the play." See Sheridan, *Dramatic Works*, 1:196.

18. Moore, *Memoirs*, 1:112–113.

19. It is not known why Lyon changed his French-sounding name to an Italian one. Italian performers garnered huge salaries in the latter half of the century as in the first half; however, the antagonism toward them had perhaps subsided. See Philip Highfill et al., *The Biographical Dictionary of Actors, Actresses, Musicians, Dancers, Managers, and other Stage Personnel in London, 1660–1800*, 16 vols. (Carbondale: Southern Illinois University Press), 9:239–42.

20. This spectacular Ashkenazi synagogue was built circa 1690 at Duke's Place, north of Aldgate; it was modified and enlarged at least twice; and finally destroyed by the London Blitz of 1941.

21. I have not found any references to the "diminutive" form of John Quick. My guess is that the script of *The Duenna* marked the "Jew" in a way that the contingencies of casting could not necessarily support. For a biography of Quick, see Highfill et al., *Biographical Dictionary,* 12:217–25.

22. See Inchbald, *Remarks for the British Theatre.* By "some other," Inchbald may be referring to Congreve or Moliere, but she could also be referring to a shadow collaborator, someone who allowed Sheridan to masquerade as the author when in fact he was just a player. Inchbald and Sheridan were born in the same year and both were deeply immersed in interlocking social networks besides being important theatrical personages.

23. See Oxberry, "Remarks," in Sheridan, *The Duenna,* iii.

24. On November 29, 1775, "Verax" observed the following in the *Morning Chronicle*: "I cannot . . . doubt, that when Mr. Garrick appears in some of his best tragedy parts, he will meet with the usual reception an admiring nation has ever bestowed on his unparalleled abilities. In a few years . . . this bright luminary of the stage must yield to the common lott of mortality.—Let us suspend our love of Operas, till that melancholy period. I really think it will be mentioned as among the many instances of our degeneracy that we lost the favourable moment of beholding Garrick's Macbeth, Hamlet, and Lear, to listen to a little Spanish Opera, and indulge an unaccountable partiality for music." Quoted in Sheridan, *Dramatic Works*, 1:209.

25. The comparison is generally related to the number of performances in the initial run. In every other way, these two "operas" are markedly different. The physicality of the mock-scenes between Polly and Lucy do, however, refer to two foreign performers, Bordoni and Cuzzoni, and their public animosity toward each other. For a discussion of the xenophobic responses to foreign performers, see Mita Choudhury, "The Italian Incursions and 'English' Opera" in *Interculturalism and Resistance in the London Theater, 1660–1800 Identity, Performance, Empire* (Lewisburg, PA: Bucknell University Press, 2000), 35–60.

26. Inchbald, *Remarks for the British Theatre*, 4.

27. Of importance to this discussion are Sheridan's letters to Thomas Linley, dated October 1775 (2), October, 23–27, 1775 (1), and November 2, 1775 (1775). See Sheridan, *The Letters of Richard Brinsley Sheridan*, Cecil Price, eds., 3 vols. (Oxford: Clarendon Press, 1966), 1:86–93. These letters provide some of the most revealing examples of collaborative writing-composing process in late eighteenth-century theatre history.

28. Quoted in Sheridan, *Dramatic Works*, 1:209.

29. Moore, *Memoirs*, 1:112.

30. This is not to be confused with Charles Dibdin's *The Gipsies. The Gipsies: A Comic opera, in two acts. As it is performed at the Theatre-Royal in the Haymarket* (London: T. Cadell and T. Sherlock, 1778). Writing plays and farces was lucrative. "Garrick's income from the theatre in 1775–6 had been: as author, £400; as actor £800; as manager £500" (Price, ed. [who cites Moore], Sheridan, *Letters*, 1:97). See, also, Robert D. Hume and Judith Milhous, "Playwright's Remuneration in Eighteenth-Century London," *Harvard Library Bulletin*, 10, no. 2–3 (Summer-Fall 1999).

31. Quoted in Highfill et. al., *Biographical Dictionary*, 1:23.

32. See George Winchester Stone, Jr., in William Van Lennep, et al., *The London Stage: A Calendar of Plays, 1660–1800*, 11 vols. (Carbondale: Southern Illinois University Press, 1960), part 4, 129.

33. See George E. Haggerty, "Keyhole Testimony: Witnessing Sodomy in the Eighteenth Century," *The Eighteenth Century: Theory and Interpretation* 44, no. 2–3 (Summer-Fall 2003): 167.

34. Robert D. Hume and Judith Milhous, "Isaac Bickerstaff's Copyrights—and a Biographical Discovery," *Philological Quarterly* 83, no. 3 (Summer 2004): 259–73. Garrick's sponsorship of Bickerstaff's dramatic works produced scandalous results when William Kenrick accused Garrick of being a homosexual—a charge that seems absurd to us but not very easy for Garrick to handle at the time.

35. No one seems to know who exactly had the copyright to this afterpiece. Abington was the principal actor, but it is not known whether Garrick or Abington bought the rights to it for £40 or £50—which was then the top price for an afterpiece, according to Hume and Milhous, "Isaac Bickerstaff's Copyrights," 261.

36. Daniel O'Quinn and others have rightly pointed out that Bickerstaff's farce is an adaptation of Charles Simon Favart's *Solyman II* and also Marmontel's *Contes Moraux*. See O'Quinn, *Staging Governance: Theatrical Imperialism in London 1770–1800* (Baltimore: Johns Hopkins University Press, 2005), 17.

37. "Mrs. Abington as the Comic Muse" "hangs now at Waddesden Manor, Aylesbury, Buckinghamshire, as a part of the James A. De Rothschild bequest to the National Trust." See Highfill et al., *Biographical Dictionary*, 1:19.

38. The provenance of the original by Sir Joshua Reynolds is difficult, if not impossible, to trace because it is in a private collection. The National Portrait Gallery in London has a print of it. The original owner of this theatrical portrait might have been Sir John Eliot of Cecil Street in the Strand, as suggested by this advertisement for a catalog: *A Catalogue of Valuable Collections of Pictures,* "*Amongst which are a very fine Portrait of Mrs. Abington, by Sir Joshua Reynolds*"; etc. "*Which will be sold by auction, (by order of the executors) By Mr. Christie, At his Great Room in Pall Mall, on Thursday, April 19th, 1787.*" The British Library has a copy of this advertisement.

39. Isaac Bickerstaff, *The Sultan, or Peep into the Seraglio. A Farce, in two acts* (London: C. Dilly, 1787), 11.

40. Palmer as Solyman and Charles Bannister as Osmyn appear in supporting roles, the latter hired primarily to carry the singing parts for which he had become an invaluable asset to Garrick by circa 1775. Singing one of the airs, Charles Bannister echoes the obsession with Abington's nose: "Ali! Ali!/ Shall a cock'd up nose subdue,/ Him who never victor knew?/ Of Solyman be conquerer? / Soon, soon he will adore her;/ Laws! Customs! Prophet! Emperor!/ Will sink down all before her." See Isaac Bickerstaff, *Songs Introduced in the New Dramatic Entertainment, called The Sultan; or a Peep into the Seraglio* (London, 1787), 3.

41. While the 1775 performance of The Sultan at Drury Lane was cast with Frances Abington in the lead role, the 1787 performance was cast with Dora Jordan as Roxolana while Frances Abington appeared once again the same year as Roxolana on the competitor's stage at Covent Garden—this time at the age of 50.

42. Bickerstaff, *The Sultan, or Peep into the Seraglio*, pages 10 and 20. It appears that this print version of the play was based upon the 1787 performances at both Drury Lane and Covent Garden, but was probably the same as the one used for the 1775 performances at Drury Lane, which were toward the very end of David Garrick's management of the theatre.

43. I am not referring here to the issue of copyright. Donaldson v. Becket (1774) changed the established practice of the authors handing over their copyright to the publisher in perpetuity. Prior to the passing of this act, authors would receive immediate payment for their work while publishers stood to gain over time. However, even this was not always the case, as Milhous and Hume have argued in "Isaac Bickerstaff's Copyrights." Sheridan's play was written and produced after Donaldson v. Becket; and my interest here is less in legal rights of the author than about the reputation of the author and the perception of authorship.

5

SCHOOLS BEYOND *SCANDAL*, 1776-1800

Emily C. Friedman

B ETWEEN 1776 AND 1800 —at the end of Garrick's reign at Drury and the rise of Edmund Kean—the shape of Europe, the role of women in the public sphere, and even the size of London's patent theatres underwent renovation and reconstitution. The results often wore familiar faces, even as meaning was changed by new contexts and editorial flourish. In this spirit of adaptation, this paper will consider the most popular comedy of the late eighteenth century, Sheridan's *The School for Scandal* (1777), and the plays and prose pieces throughout the eighteenth century that bore the same title convention.

It is important to identify both the innovation and the conformity of any given text, and it takes little away from Sheridan's masterpiece to note its connection to a popular extant naming tradition. When one considers texts that adopted the "school for" title formula in this period, *The School for Scandal* was as much riding a trend as it is furthering one. True, the massive success of Sheridan's play led to a sharp increase in material following the "school for" naming convention.[1] But when it debuted on May 8, 1777, Sheridan's play appeared in the midst of large number of translations and original plays entitled along the "school for" formula, many of which would see multiple editions in the decades that followed. The plays promised all manner of education: schools for rakes and greybeards, wives and lovers, fathers and guardians, honor and arrogance. A play written and performed in America and transatlantically published also called *The School for Scandal* flew under the cover of the popular comedy to satirize the American Revolutionary War.[2]

Indeed, it was not only a theatrical trend: the "school for" formula expanded to encompass actual educational texts in "schools" for children, Christians, and happiness; translated texts were dubbed "schools" for good manners and marriage. Novels created multivolume "schools" for husbands, wives, tutors, widows, and fashion. It is tempting, given the dominance of Sheridan's play, to think of these other "schools" as part of a phenomenon cashing in on a popular play—a vogue which would show to be a mere flash in the pan. But both of these assumptions— first, that *The School for Scandal* was the source of many imitation "school for" plays, and second, that these plays centered around the decade after *The School for Scandal* debuted—I will show, are false.

What I wish to do here is to describe the many ways in which *The School for Scandal* can be understood within the context of the world of stage and print, through an examination of the other texts that traded on the "school for" naming convention. In the wake of Sheridan's success with *The School for Scandal*, the convention took on new life, used for political and for publicity purposes, to breathe new life into old plays as well as launch new ones. In addition to this theatrical tradition, I wish to highlight the sharp increase in prose fiction that also carried this title convention into the end of the eighteenth century, and indeed well into the nineteenth, an increase that might be understood as even more significant as a post-Sheridan explosion than the theatrical response.[3] *The School for Scandal*'s influence, when charted not by plot but by titles, reveals the larger cultural shifts around what it means to advertise a "school," moving from satirical send-ups of husbands and fathers to more insistent ones, with Sheridan's play serving as a turning point, containing both the earlier satirical comedic tradition and the sentimental education that will grow in strength thereafter.

Schools Before Scandal

Sheridan's play was not the beginning, but somewhere in the middle of the "school for" trend. Indeed, if one counts Molière's *L'École des maris* (1661) and *L'École des femmes* (1662) (which a few "school for" plays note as either an inspiration or otherwise indicate their awareness of), then the phenomenon's antecedents extend into the previous century. Many translations of Molière's plays can be seen throughout the century, and adaptations for English sensibilities followed, such as the 1735 farcical afterpiece based on Molière's *L'École des Femmes* that debuted under the name *The School for Women*.[4] Moreover, Molière's plays certainly inspired some of Sheridan and his cohorts' later plot choices, with their focus on older men whose desire for totally innocent/ignorant wives are thwarted by the natural cunning of the women they marry.[5]

The earliest such non-Molière play featuring a "school for" title in London appears to be the change of name of *The Professor Folly* to *School for Folly* a week into its run at Lincoln's Inn Fields.[6] In 1732, alongside the Molière adaptations and translations, *Female Innocence: or, A School for a Wife* was performed "at Mrs. Lee's great booth, on the bowling-green, Southwark, by comedians from the theatres."[7] Despite these titles in the early part of the century, it is not until the latter half of the eighteenth century that the title convention multiplied substantially.

The bulk of "school for" productions were plays that existed prior to *The School for Scandal*, and were dominated by two plays: Isaac Bickerstaff's *Lionel & Clarissa* (1768; by 1770 it appeared as *Lionel & Clarissa, or The School for Fathers*), and Hugh Kelly's *The School for Wives* (1773) both of which were performed at either Covent Garden, Drury Lane, or Haymarket nearly every year between their respective debuts and the end of the century.[8] In addition, Poet Laureate William Whitehead's *The School for Lovers* (1762) saw runs before and after *Scandal*'s debut, and Elizabeth Griffith's *The School for Rakes* (1769) was her most successful play, though it did not last into the post-*Scandal* performance seasons.

Even only counting works on the English stage, one can find as early as 1762 other "school for" play such as Whitehead's mildly successful *The School for Lovers* (1762), which made intriguingly complex claims to novelty. The play is derived from a French original, "formed on the plan" of Fontenelle's *The Will* (1751), which was "never intended for the stage, and printed in the eighth volume of his works."[9] Despite its status as an adaptation, the prefatory material of the 1793 edition nevertheless claims "this play may be considered as the model of the sentimental branch of the modern comedy" though it does admit of deficiencies of "wit and humor," which might "perhaps confine it forever to the closet."[10] The 1793 preface is largely disingenuous, as the play saw a healthy number of performances and was counted among Whitehead's successes.

The play is one that fits Jerry Palmer's notion that comedy (as opposed to farce) is often a genre that places a primacy on something beyond (or at least besides) the laugh and joke. As the preface braces us for, it is indeed populated by characters who, right down to the lowliest schemer, "are all distinguished by elegance of sentiment, purity of expression, and propriety of manners."[11] Three acts of the five consist largely of the hero and heroine, who have been betrothed for years, nobly renouncing one another for one reason or another. Interspersed is the subplot of Modely and Araminta, who play dim echoes of a bickering, jealous couple. Modely faithlessly flirts with the heroine Cælia for no reason other than boredom (and plot mechanics), and we are led to believe that he is reformed or about to reform at play's end, and that his future union with Araminta is now purified. It is all intensely contrived, and its appeal lies in its structural merry-go-round, but its epilogue, as with its title, implies a didactic turn:

> Where the fair dames who like to live by rule,
> May learn two lessons from the LOVERS School:
> While Cælia's choice instructs them how to choose,
> And my refusal warns them to refuse.[12]

Cælia's "choice" being no real choice at all, and Araminta's refusal being a mere postponement, an educational gloss on the play is improbable at best.

Isaac Bickerstaff's 1768 comic opera *Lionel and Clarissa*—which would be represented as *Lionel and Clarissa: or a school for fathers,* or simply *The School for Fathers,* after 1770—is not much more didactic, continuing the tradition of presenting rather than telling.[13] While Bickerstaff deemed it his best piece, *Love in a Village,* his reworking of Samuel Richardson's novel *Pamela,* was performed "ten times for once this piece is acted," as the prefatory material to the Bell's British Theatre edition (1791) notes. The author of the preface goes on to speculate as to why this would be so, and concludes that the answer must lie in the music, "for such Character and Writing as [the two plays] exhibit, seem tolerably uniform;—a severe critic might say uniformly terrible."[14]

The plot parallels two well-meaning fathers: the brash Colonel Oldboy and the more sensible Sir John Flowerdale. In the main plot, the titular Lionel is in love with Clarissa, the daughter of Sir John. Lionel has been educated for the church, and true to innumerable other sentimental heroes, is willing to nobly refrain from speaking his love because of his presumed social and financial unworthiness to aspire to Clarissa. Meanwhile, Colonel Oldboy, who eloped with his wife when they were young, is tricked into assisting the clever Harman into eloping with Diana Oldboy, the Colonel's spirited daughter. At the dénouement, Sir John reveals he has tested Lionel and Clarissa's love and obedience by pretending to favor another suitor for Clarissa, and convinces Colonel Oldboy to follow Sir John's example and celebrate the marriages of Lionel and Clarissa and Diana and Harman. Though the title promises a "school for fathers," only one father, Colonel Oldboy, is really "schooled," and even that is more of comeuppance for the audience's amusement than their edification.

As with Whitehead, Bickerstaff's pride in his work lies in a sense of its originality: "I had not borrowed an expression, a sentiment, or a character from any dramatic writer extant."[15] Such a claim is as inflated as it is odd, as the play in terms of plot it is as pure formula as its later title: to recount its love triangle, sentimental hero and heroine, obligatory supporting soubrette role, and other details would amount to not much more or less than many other plays. Indeed, the most striking deviation is the character of Mr. Jessamy, a hyper-educated coxcomb so effeminized that he cannot pair off at the resolution of the play. Frequently discussed as impotent, the play implicitly looks forward to his death to enrich his relatives, as he is an unfit heir to the estates he has accumulated. Nevertheless, the play was successful: as *Lionel and Clarissa*, the play saw ten productions in the last quarter of the eighteenth century, equally divided between Covent Garden and the Haymarket. Under the name *The School for Fathers*, the play saw an additional seven productions at Drury Lane in that same period.

Perhaps stemming from Whitehead's success, Elizabeth Griffith transformed Beaumarchais's *Eugénie* (1767) into her most popular play, *The School for Rakes* (1769), which was so successful that Griffith was able to enter her son Richard into the East India Company on its proceeds, an act that would end up ensuring her family's prosperity and her own comfortable old age.[16] This seems no surprise, for in the period the formula Griffith followed seems nearly foolproof: French source material altered for English tastes, coupled with the "school for" title that, as seen from Molière, Whitehead, Bickerstaff, et al., signifies more the focus of the audience's amusement rather than the group that will be preached to or instructed. Nevertheless, the play would not survive long on the London stages: while the play would see new editions in print into the 1790s, the play saw its last eighteenth-century performance on April 26, 1776 at Drury Lane, little more than a year before *The School for Scandal* would appear on the same stage.

The last of the pre-*Scandal* "school for" plays, Hugh Kelly's *The School for Wives* (1774) also played on the Drury Lane stage three years before *The School for Scandal* would debut on the same boards, and after *The School for Scandal's* debut *The School for Wives* would move to Covent Garden, where it was performed eighteen nights across nine different seasons, three times appearing within weeks of a run of *The School for Scandal*. Kelly's work is another good example of the strange game of influence and originality occurring amongst the "school for" plays. The preface to the 1774 text notes that "though he [Kelly] has chosen a title us'd by Molière, he has neither borrowed a single circumstance [from Molière] . . . nor to the best of his recollection from any other writer."[17] The preface goes on at some length about the originality of the piece, emphasizing its striking (in the author's opinion) balance between "sentimental gloom" and "excess of uninteresting levity," as well as its rehabilitation of the legal profession.

Frances Abington, who would go on to play Lady Teazle in *The School for Scandal*, here plays Miss Walsingham, who like, Lady Teazle, must defend herself in the play's epilogue. There the similarities end, as Miss Walsingham's story is not so much a battle of wits between a couple as it is a well-worn plot of misunderstandings and proper and improper suitors. The sentimental plot is between a married couple, the Belvilles. At the beginning of the play, Belville has just seduced a young girl, Miss Leeson, in the guise of an Irish stage manager who will make her a star, and he has not even consummated the affair before he sets his eyes on Miss Walsingham. His unsuccessful seduction is part of the humor of Miss Walsingham's larger plot, but his behavior becomes dangerous for him when his wife discovers his infidelity, and moreover he is challenged to a duel by Miss Leeson's brother.

Miss Leeson, a would-be actress whose "fort [sic] is tragedy entirely" but whose role in the play we witness is almost entirely comic, encapsulates in a line the dichotomy between the sly digs at the theatre and the sentimental plot which we are supposed to be invested in.[18] As she says to Lady Rachel Mildew, the playwright of "crying comedies" and "boarding school romps," Miss Leeson does like some comedies, namely the sort of sentimental comedy which the audience is witnessing: "some of the sentimental ones are very pretty, there's such little difference between them and tragedies."[19] Safely married off, Abington's character speaks the epilogue, which constructs the theatre as a place of learning—"an ancient college to instruct the town!" and indeed, the only place of learning available to women aside from "Cornelly's, and Almack's, our Universities!"[20] In a world where women must learn from places of leisure or not at all, the implication goes, it is a minor miracle that women like all-forgiving Mrs. Belville and the clever-but-chaste Miss Walsingham survive.

As with prior plays, where the "school" lies in these two plots is difficult to tell. Certainly, the minor character Lady Rachel is learning constantly, as she takes notes from the character's reactions for use in her "crying comedies." But the intention of blending didactic agenda with a dose of self-reflexive humor, while not very successful in Kelly's play, does provide an interesting combination for later plays—significantly *The School for Scandal*—to master.

After *Scandal*, Part One: Sheridian Commentary and Plot Adoption

Between the debut of *The School for Scandal* and the end of the century, six plays appeared under the "school for" title convention, seven at Drury Lane, and four at the Haymarket. Most plays on Sheridian titles did not aim to imitate Sheridan's plots, but built on an extant knowledge of Sheridan and his plays—a theme not limited to plays with parodic titles. Primarily such plays in the late 1770s reference *The Critic*, such as *The Critic Anticipated; or, The Humors of the Green Room* (1779), attributed to "R.B.S. Esq." but functioning as a scathing satire on Sheridan as despotic manager, a critique that would also appear in *The Critick; or A Tragedy Rehearsed, A Literary Catchpenny* (1780) and Leonard MacNally's *Critic upon Critic* (1788).[21] *The School for Scandal Scandaliz'd* (1779 York, 1780 Covent Garden), which Dane Farnsworth Smith attributes to John Philip Kemble, engages in the same debate over Sheridan, but takes the side of defense rather than critique.

The most direct use of *The School for Scandal*'s name are two political texts that take their names directly from Sheridan's play: John Leacock's American *The School for Scandal* (1779) and an anonymous Pittite *The School for Scandal* (1784). As David Francis Taylor has recently shown, the titles of Sheridan's popular comedies (*The Duenna, The Critic,* and *The School for Scandal*) were assumed by political authors, creating dramatized political pamphlets that flew under the title and formatting conventions of the stage. In the case of Israel Pottinger's *Duenna* (1776) and *Critic* (1779) and the 1784 *Scandal*, the texts themselves have absolutely no ties to the Sheridan originals other than that of title, and the contents of all such "parodies" were essentially politically unperformable: indeed, barely publishable.[22]

Leacock's *Scandal*, like the transformations of *The Critic*, does retain the character names of the original play, though each are transformed by cast lists that place political movers and shakers in each role: "Mr. King" (George III) as the venal but good-natured Charles Surface, Lord "Thane" (Bute) as his scheming brother Joseph, Lord "Sh—le—ne" (Shelburne) as the rescuing nabob Sir Oliver, Lord "Boreas" (i.e., North) as the moneylender Moses, and "Signor Frazerino" (William Fraser, editor of the *London Gazette*) as Snake. It was apparently successful enough to lead the *London Magazine* to warn readers of unthinkingly purchasing the Leacock *Scandal* as "Many persons have imagined that it was the celebrated comedy under that title written by Sheridan."[23] This was a very real danger in the 1770s and 1780s, as Sheridan did not produce an authorized version of *The School for Scandal* until 1799—over twenty years after its first performance, during which time unauthorized editions had been produced nearly every year in both Ireland and England.

Taylor and Farnsworth Smith both note that the direct title-lifting from Sheridan dies down markedly after the first few years of *The School for Scandal*'s debut, coinciding with Sheridan's increasing presence in Parliament, beginning in the 1780s.[24] However, echoes of *The School for Scandal*'s title would continue in more subtle—and more far-reaching—variants through to the end of the century.

After *Scandal*, Part Two:
Renaming and Timely Naming

In the wake of the success of *The School for Scandal*, plays not only assumed the title of Sheridan's play directly (as previously seen), but older plays also adopted a similar naming convention to rebrand themselves as part of *The School for Scandal* phenomenon. As seen earlier, Isaac Bickerstaffe's *Lionel and Clarissa* had long held the subtitle *The School for Fathers*. While the play would continue to see success as *Lionel and Clarissa* at Covent Garden and the Haymarket, on the Drury Lane stage it would be known exclusively by *The School for Fathers* title for the rest of the century, and all the subsequent editions of the play in print would carry *The School for Fathers* (either singly or with the "Lionel and Clarissa" title) on the cover.

Bickerstaffe's play was not the only one to see a shift in title to capitalize on the vogue for "school for" titles. Hannah Cowley's loose adaptation of Aphra Behn's *The Lucky Chance* (1687) was originally titled *The Mourning Bride*, but was resurrected and renamed *The School for Greybeards* (1786). In Cowley's case, the savvy renaming for the market is part of a career-long set of moves that echo, either in content or title, earlier theatrical hits: Cowley's *The Belle's Strategem* (1780) echoes George Farquhar's *The Beaux Stratagem* (1707), while her *A Bold Stroke for a Husband* (1783) recalls Susannah Centlivre's *A Bold Stroke for a Wife* (1717). What is striking about the appropriation of Sheridan's title is its relative youth. By turning from Farquhar and Centlivre's generation to Sheridan's, Cowley would seem to be highlighting the ways in which *The School for Scandal* has made its way into the repertory: to riff on its title is to believe it is as much a household name as the great Restoration comedies. The play had a run of nine performances—a very modest success compared to the blockbuster plays mentioned in this essay, but a success nonetheless. Such title changes were not necessarily raging successes, it should be noted. Richard Cumberland—like Cowley, no fan of Sheridan—also saw his play *The Country Attorney* (Haymarket 1786) renamed *The School for Widows* when it made its 1789 debut at Covent Garden. The play had a longer run at the Haymarket (six) than it would at Covent Garden (three).

The timely popularity of Sheridan's title was also exploited by political dramatists. Holcroft's *The School for Arrogance* débuted at Covent Garden February 4, 1791 and saw nine performances that year, then five in the 1793–1794 season, another two the following year, and single performances in 1796, 1797, and 1799. The next year, Thomas Dibdin's *The School for Prejudice, or Liberal Opinions* (1800) was also performed at Covent Garden. Still other plays would also capitalize on the naming convention and continue to do so well into the end of the century. Nor was this limited to the London stage: Edmund Eyre's *Consequences, or The School for Prejudices* (1794), announces on its title page that it has been performed in "Worchester, Wolverhampton, and Shrewbury"[25]—thus, even a play that can advertise only its success in a forty-mile radius in the west of England, over a hundred miles from the capital, still takes advantage of the "school for" convention.

Moreover, in the last decade of the eighteenth century, many plays saw print—many for the first time ever, or in many years. While Sheridan refused to produce an authorized print edition of his play until quite late in the century, numerous unauthorized editions were available almost immediately.[26] Close behind *School for Scandal* was, perhaps unsurprisingly, *The School for Fathers*. Holcroft's *The School for Arrogance* (1791) was published simultaneously with its theatrical debut. *The School for Wives* saw two new editions (1792, 1793), as did *The School for Lovers* (1793) and *The School for Rakes* (1795). Gotthold Lessing's *Minna von Barnhelm* was translated in 1786 and was first produced in London under the title of *The Disbanded Officer*, but a 1799 revival ran under the title *The School for Honor* (1799). The 1783 play *The Reparation* was repackaged and published (though not performed) as *The School for Libertines* (1800).

As part of that trend, the unperformed *The School for Ingratitude* (1798) seems to have been given that title exclusively for publicity, as its full title suggests:

"thou shalt not steal."
The School for ingratitude:
a comedy,
in five acts.
Presented—to a manager of Drury-Lane, in March 1797:
—Curtailed-by his Direction, and returned to him in May:
Finally—And after the Comedy, or Farce in Five Acts, called "cheap Living" (so like it, in many Points!-in one, so unlike it!) had been produced at Drury-Lane, Returned;—With a Note from A Prompter; which the Author has not perused—
—Further curtailments being avowedly reserved for the day which-ought to have come.[27]

It is hard to imagine anyone would have purchased the text otherwise, as the first forty pages of the text constitute an obsessive point-by-point comparison of the author's play and its resemblances to Frederick Reynolds' comedy *Cheap Living* (1797).

Beyond *Scandal*: Prose "Schools"

If the theatrical market for "school for" titles was buoyed but not begun by Sheridan's play, the effect on prose fiction seems, in some ways, even more substantial. It should first be noted that pre-*Scandal* prose fiction did not include "school for" titling practices as much as might be expected, given the didactic potential implied by the phrase. One might expect that "school for" titles would appear as didactic nonfiction works, and indeed a few titles appear to do so, such as "Michael Angelo's" *The Drawing School for Little Masters and Misses* (1774, 1777) and *The School for Marriage* by "Caesar Mussolini, professor of the Italian language" (1795). However, the handful that appear in the records suggest that the convention was not very firmly established among didactic works.

Three epistolary English "school for" fiction titles predate *The School For Scandal*: an anonymously authored epistolary *School for Wives* (1763), the anonymous *The school for daughters: or, the history of Miss Charlotte Sidney* (1771), and Treyssac de Vergy's *Nature: or, The school for demi-rapes* (1771). Like the immediate predecessors of *Scandal* on stage, these three novels date to the years of the 1760s and early 1770s, and all three novels connect themselves to the didactic and sentimental epistolary project followed by the novels Samuel Richardson and appear at the height of the sentimental mode, around the publication of Sterne's *A Sentimental Journey* (1768) and Mackenzie's *The Man of Feeling* (1771).

The School for Wives opens with a letter from the mother of a new bride worriedly seeking news of her daughter from the husband's sister. Unlike Molière's May-December marriages, the marriage is a love match only clouded by the husband Charles Goodwill's new friendship with Lord Rovewell and his "vile associates." His bride Clarinda is unable to speak for herself, but her sister-in-law Lucy Goodwill is more than willing to upbraid her brother and report on his conduct to his mother-in-law. While the title seems to allude directly to Molière's play of the same name, the substance of the short novel seems to owe a greater debt to Samuel Richardson's *Pamela in Her Exalted Condition* (1742), the sequel that examines Pamela's capacity for enduring the potential infidelity of Mr. B—after she has given birth to their first child, and also to *Clarissa's* (1748) scheming Lovelace as a model for the "bad influence" Lord Rovewell. Indeed, the novel even name-checks Richardson directly, as one of the characters is discovered reading *Sir Charles*

Grandison, leading to a discussion of a key subplot. In *Grandison,* the titular hero has a young ward, Emily, who falls in love with him. When it becomes clear that Sir Charles will marry the virtuous Harriet Byron, Emily leaves his house in order to more effectively conquer her inappropriate passion. Clarinda Goodwill artlessly asks Miss Charlotte Spendlove, who is suspected of being in love with Clarinda's husband, about Emily's case, and Charlotte tellingly reveals her sentiments by taking Emily's side. Clarinda is able to candidly ask "You are in love, my Charlotte, and you love—my husband," leading to an exchange that ends with the erring Charlotte collapsed in the arms of Clarinda.[28]

While the novel's title would seem to suggest that Clarinda must learn to be a better wife to her roving husband, the title seems to better function literally, as the text itself forms a "school" for the wives who read it and take the exemplary Clarinda as a model, and Charles Goodwill learns to better appreciate his paragon of a spouse. This is in keeping with the sentimental turn to the post-Richardsonian epistolary novel, which takes its didactic project literally. It should be noted that this is not uniform or even necessarily the dominant strain of Richardson-imitation. The *Monthly Review* patronizingly reviews *The School for Daughters* as formulaic of a particular sort of young, amateur, female novelist "regularly instructed and practiced in the school of love,"[29] and the *Critical Review* pithily notes, "We shall take particular care to keep our daughters from this School; or rather, this School from our daughters."[30]

Even more so, de Vergy's *Nature: or, The school for demi-rapes* (1771) is advertised as "a professed imitator of our Richardson" who has authored a novel "so agreeable, sentimental, and sensible . . . that were it not for the libertinism . . . we would not scruple to recommend it to such of our readers as have a taste fro this species of literary entertainment."[31] As might be divined from its title, the novel includes erotic scenes that reframe Richardsonian scenes, such as Pamela accidentally in bed with her would-be rapist Mr. B, and trace much more explicit female desire, as the heroine writes of "the consent her heart gave" as "Desire deadened" the voice of virtue.[32] While the novel ends with double marriage and reformation, the material within is far more vexed.

After *Scandal*: Fiction

After *The School for Scandal*, a number of works followed the "school for" naming convention while hewing much closer to the Richardsonian model than the Sheridian. Epistolary novels included multiple editions of *The School for Husbands*

(1776), as well as *The School for Tutors* (1788), *The School for Fathers* (1788), and Clara Reeve's *The School for Widows* (1791); and "oriental tale" outlier *The School for Majesty* (1780). It is important to note the primarily epistolary mode in which these novels were composed: the period of the 1770s and 1780s is also of course the height of the epistolary genre's popularity, and so novels designed to capitalize on the most lucrative part of the market would do well to adopt the form (in some cases, not wholly).[33] Moreover, the epistolary novel's emphasis on voice and audience would seem to make it a particularly useful crossover point—we can see attempts at this sort of crossover in earlier works such as Jane Collier and Sarah Fielding's *The Cry: A Dramatic Fable* (1754), which blends conventions of the theatre and the novel into a hybrid form. Like the "school for" plays that were extant pre-*Scandal*, many of the "school for" novels share similar moves and concerns, both as a group and as a subset of the overall market—in the majority of cases, the dominant sentimental mode popular from mid-century on.

Even the aforementioned outlier, *The School for Majesty*—which, at first, seems to have little to do with the epistolary sentimental project—appears to capitalize on an existing market, while branding with the more generic "school for" convention. A third-person novella dyed purple with exotic diction and faraway lands, it seems very much akin to Johnson's *Rasselas* (1759) in form. The novella, tells the story of Zomelli, the spoilt crown prince, whose life of listless ease is disrupted by an evil Genii who afflicts him with smallpox, allowing Zomelli's identical half-brother to ascend the throne as Zomelli is smuggled out and forced to find his own way through the world. In his struggle he learns that "the duty of princes" is to protect "the lower class against the over-bearing rich" (98). He is ultimately able, through the timely intervention of another king, to reclaim his throne and transform his kingdom into one designed for the benefit of its subjects. He is Rasselas returned to the Happy Valley, transformed definitely and empowered to rule justly.

Also brief, and perhaps the most overtly didactic fiction using this convention, is Charlotte Brooke's *The School for Christians* (1791) published as a children's book by subscription. The text is the closest any of the prose "school for" pieces comes to an actual school, written in dialogue between a father and son, to teach religious and ethical principles. It is one of the few places in post-Scandal "school" fiction that seems an empowered and generous paternal figure: in much of what will follow in my discussion, fathers and paternal figures are either absent, cruel, or hands-off.

The School for Husbands (1776) is an epistolary novel featuring two sisters: Lucy, the quiet sweet one, marries Dashwood, who only agreed to marry her to support his now-crazy-jealous mistress, Die (and their five-year-old son Ned). Die goes increasingly nuts (though pretty justifiably) as Dashwood dotes upon the sweet Lucy. Die ultimately tries to shoot Lucy, revealing all, but Lucy has known all along and still loves Dashwood, and Die is sent away to die (so to speak) in Bristol while Ned is raised by the Dashwoods. Bab, the "madcap" (though more rational, more committed to be reserved) loves Lord Charbury, who in turn believes himself pre-engaged to his ward Constantia, and marries her instead. Of course Constantia dies (of a fall), and not too long after (though still with misunderstandings) the two reveal their long-standing love.

The School for Tutors (1788) continues the epistolary trend of *The School for Wives* and *School for Husbands* earlier. In it, a young man Everard Villers returns from abroad, in love with a half-Irish woman who lives in Marseilles. While abroad, he had a correspondence that he believed was with his sister, but her letters were ghostwritten by her "plain" companion Henrietta "Harriet" Ottley. Like Harriet Byron before her, her letters to a female friend reveal her love for Everard. Everard discovers his French-Irish beloved is duplicitous (through a mis-sent letter), and is later "tricked" into revealing his love for Harriet by his father "proposing" to marry her himself. The short novel ends with letters from the tutor Francis Woodley with marital advice for the pair, concentrating on Harriet's ability to be the perfect wife for the spoilt Everard because she is devoted to his happiness. The novel's paternal tutor hovers over the novel like the benevolent patriarchal figures seen in various theatrical "schools," to contrast with tyrannical fathers.

Parental tyranny is still extant in these novels, however. *The School for Fathers; or, the Victim of a Curse* (1788) appears in the same year as *The School for Tutors* and seems to be the nightmare alternate world far removed from the similarly titled theatrical "schools" where bad fathers are appropriately punished, and virtue is rewarded. A young man, Harley, on his Grand Tour falls in with the family barely clinging to gentility. When Harley accidentally kills the brother of the family, he takes the surviving widow and her daughter Emily into his protection, and ultimately marries Emily. But Alfred himself is at the mercy of his father, who hears damning reports of Harley's conduct through his tutor. When Alfred travels with his new wife to beg for his father's mercy, he first sees his Aunt, who informs him of his father's death by apoplexy and his disinheritance. Alfred in turn dies, leaving Emily alone and pregnant, and she seeks protection in a distant relative, Mr. Nelson. That man educates Alfred and promises him a living, but dies before the living can be transferred. Thus, Alfred is doubly disinherited by both biological grandfather and adopted father figure.

The narrator then turns to Alfred's beloved Elwina and her own venal father, anticipating the conflicts with male authority (including brothers) that intrude upon the love story set up by the letters that follow. The narrative voice frequently makes the reader aware of future events (usually unhappy) in vague, ominous terms, and so when, after the first hundred pages, the novel becomes epistolary the reader is already primed for an unhappy end. Alfred and Elwina grow increasingly close through their correspondence, which only ends with the untimely death of Alfred. The novel then returns to first-person, and we discover that the narrator is a woman, Maria, who then reports the death of Elwina, surrounded by her contrite and grieving parents. Maria, Elwina's sole heir, uses the final pages of the novel to justify her writing and reemphasize the novel's connection to truth.

While not as directly excoriating in its narrative voice as *The School for Fathers*, Clara Reeve's *The School for Widows* (1791) is perhaps the most revolutionary nonetheless. Reeves' novel, like many of the others, is epistolary and focused on marriage, but from the other end, opening as an exchange between two widows. *The School for Widows* both contains and exists as an educational space for women of all ages and marital statuses, warning unmarried women of the dangers of the married state, while exemplifying ways that wives and widows can maneuver in the world. The educational aspects are more striking here, as widows educate other widows (and their daughters) in running a school, starting a shop, and other entrepreneurial feats. The novel ends with a *Millennium Hall*-like construction of a haven out of the former estate.

In this context, the last of the eighteenth century "School for" novels, Ann Ford Thicknesse's *roman á clef, The School for Fashion* (1800) seems to be the closest to *Scandal's* target, while daringly naming names and creating portraits of far more of the bon ton's vices than even those of Sheridan's Scandal School. Published by subscription and dedicated to "FASHION HERSELF" (vi) with a scathing critique of "her" power and corrupting influence, and promising in its introduction a novel compounded of "FACTS" (1) and "PLAIN TRUTH" (2), the thinly veiled memoir includes gossipy accounts of Euterpe's encounters with all manner of nobility and other upper class movers and shakers, including the Prince of Wales. Euterpe's options as a mistress as well as a marriageable woman are equally weighed, though with a veneer of middle class virtue (which is repeatedly referred to as irrelevant at the highest social rungs). The sentimental is wholly absent from this novel, and Euterpe's ambitious father is easily managed, hardly figuring at all in the machinations of various noble women and their potentially dangerous influence on the savvy Euterpe. That Thicknesse chooses to title her thinly disguised memoir as a "school" is both tongue-in-cheek and a homage to Sheridan, the son of her elocution teacher, Thomas Sheridan [34]

Conclusion

The School for Scandal's blend of sentimental and satire pointed directly at its audience are, by and large, a singular outgrowth from the thicket of formulaic responses that continued to take advantage of the marketability of the name for decades thereafter. Nevertheless, both *The School for Scandal* and other "school for" texts continue to coexist on the page and the stage throughout the end of the eighteenth century, a microcosm for a period that embraced the sentimental and the grand, the clever and the silly, and mixed tragedy and comedy on stages that were strikingly new and comfortingly formulaic.

So what does this mean for understanding *The School for Scandal* and its influence? From the cases of these plays and novels, we see that although *The School for Scandal* was not the first "school for" play, it would dominate the discourse and overwhelm other prior plays due to its sheer popularity, becoming a site of critique and commercial knock-off "brands." That said, it is important to recognize plays, like *The School for Fathers*, that flourished before and alongside *Scandal,* to note the ways in which *Scandal* incorporates elements from these earlier traditions. *Scandal*'s further inclusion of the sentimental then transforms the "school for" brand into one that becomes adopted in prose forms more strongly, primarily in epistolary novels that followed Richardsonian or other sentimental playbooks, while transforming the notion of "school" into texts that become spaces of discipline, rigor, and hopes of social transformation, alongside reports of scandal that might cause even Lady Sneerwell to blush.

Notes

1. Richard Brinsley Sheridan's *The School for Scandal* was the most-performed play of the late eighteenth century, performed 261 times by 1800.

2. John Leacock, *The School for Scandal. A Comedy* (London: S. Bladon, 1779), http://find.galegroup. com/ECCO (accessed May 24, 2012).

3. While this essay ends with 1800, editions of Sheridan's *The School for Scandal* continued to see print and performance, and plays and other works containing the title convention continued to be published: a ballad "The Weaver's Garland, or, a New School for Christians" (1800), *The School for Friends* (1806), *The School for Authors* (1808), *Chesterfield Travestie, or, School for Modern Manners* (1808, 1812), *Love's Victory or The School for Pride, a Comedy* (1825), *The School for Politics, a Dramatic Novel* (1854), *The School for Critics, a Comedy* (1868) and *School for Saints: part of the history of the Right Honourable Robert Orange* (1897).

4. William J. Burling, *A Checklist of New Plays and Entertainments on the London Stage, 1700–1737* (Rutherford and Cranbury, NJ: Farleigh Dickinson University Press, 1992), 171.

5. James Morwood deals with this at some length in "Sheridan, Molière, and the Idea of the School in *The School for Scandal*," *Sheridan Studies*, James Morwood and David Crane, eds. (Cambridge: Cambridge University Press, 1995).

6. Burling, *Checklist of New Plays*, 68.

7. Anonymous, *Female Innocence: or, a School for a Wife. As it is acted at Mrs. Lee's great booth, on the Bowling-Green, Southwark, by comedians from the theatres* (Southwark: G. Lee, 1732), http://galenet.galegroup.com/servlet/ECCO (accessed February 13, 2012).

8. All statistics concerning London theatrical productions are taken from Emmet L.Avery, et al., eds. *The London Stage, 1660–1800*, 11 vols. (Carbondale and Edwardsville: Southern Illinois University Press, 1960–1968).

9. William Whitehead, *The School for Lovers. A Comedy, by Wiliam Whitehead, Esq. Adapted for theatrical representation, as performed at the Theatres-Royal, Drury-Lane and Covent-Garden. Regulated from the prompt-books, By Permission of the Managers* (London: John Bell, 1793), http://galenet.galegroup.com/servlet/ECCO (accessed February 19, 2012), n.p.

10. Ibid., n.p.

11. Ibid., n.p.

12. Whitehead, "Epilogue," *School for Lovers,* 87.

13. With music by Charles Dibdin, who collaborated with Bickerstaffe on the opera.

14. Isaac Bickerstaff, *The School for Fathers; or, Lionel & Clarissa. A comic opera. By Isaac Bickerstaff. Adapted for theatrical representation, as performed at the Theatres-Royal Drury-Lane and Covent-Garden. Regulated from the prompt-book, By Permission of the Managers.* (London: John Bell, 1791), http://galenet.galegroup.com/ECCO (accessed February 19, 2012), ii.

15. Bickerstaff, *The School for Fathers*, iii.

16. Elizabeth Eger, "Griffith, Elizabeth (1727–1793)," *Oxford Dictionary of National Biography Online*, http://oxforddnb.com (accessed February 13, 2012).

17. Hugh Kelly, *The School for Wives. A Comedy. As it is performed at the Theatre-Royal in Drury-Lane. Embellished with an etching, by Mr. Loutherbourg.* 3rd ed. (London: T. Becket, 1774), http://galenet.galegroup.com/servlet/ECCO (accessed February 19, 2012), i.

18. Ibid., 33.

19. Whitehead, *The School for Lovers,* III.i.33.

20. David Garrick, "Epilogue" to *The School for Wives, Bell's British Theatre. Consisting of the most esteemed English plays* (London: Bell, 1797), http://galenet.galegroup.com/servlet/ECCO (accessed March 13, 2012).

21. Dane Farnsworth Smith and M. L. Lawhon, *Plays About the Theatre in England, 1737–1800: or, The Self-Conscious Stage from Foote to Sheridan* (Lewisburg, PA: Bucknell University Press, 1979), 100–7.

22. David Francis Taylor, "'The Fates of Empires': The American War, Political Parody, and Sheridan's Comedies," *Eighteenth-Century Studies* 42, no. 3 (Spring 2009): 379–95.

23. Sheridan, *The Plays and Poems of Richard Brinsley Sheridan*, ed. R. Crompton Rhodes, 3 vols. (New York: Russell & Russell, 1962), 3:343, quoted in Taylor, "'The Fates of Empires,'" 380.

24. Sheridan would of course continue to act as manager of Drury Lane until shortly after it burned down in 1809.

25. Edmund John Eyre, *Consequences; or, the School for Prejudice. A Comedy, of three acts. As performed at the theatres, Worcester, Wolverhampton, and Shrewsbury. By E. J. Eyre, Author of the Dreamer Awake; and the Maid of Normandy; or, the Death of the Queen of France, &c. Late of Pembroke College, Cambridge* (London: T. N. Longman, 1794), http://galenet.galegroup.com/servlet/ECCO (accessed February 13, 2012).

26. *The English Short Title Catalogue* lists 44 editions before 1800, the vast majority with Dublin imprints.

27. *The School for Ingratitude* ran to 183 pages in the 1763 edition.

28. Anonymous, *The School for Wives. In a Series of Letters* (London, MDCCLXIII [1763]), http://galenet.galegroup.com/servlet/ECCO (accessed February 15, 2012), 36.

29. "Art. VIII. *The School for Daughters.*" in Ralph Griffiths and George Edward Griffiths, eds., *The Monthly Review*, vol. 52 (London: R. Griffiths, 1775): 505.

30. Anonymous, *The School for Wives. In a Series of Letters.* (London: R. and J. Dodsley, 1763), http://galenet.galegroup.com/servlet/ECCO (accessed May 22, 2012).

31. Pierre Henri Treyssac de Vergy, *Nature: or, The School for Demi-rapes* (London: P. Shatwell, 1771), n.p.

32. Ibid., 55.

33. Franco Moretti graphs the rise and fall in new publication in each of three "hegemonic" subgenres (epistolary, gothic, and historical) in his *Maps, Graphs, and Trees: Abstract Models For A Literary History* (New York: Verso, 2007), 15–16. While his graphs do not factor in reprints and later editions, the graphs are still striking: for example, in 1776, 71 percent of all new novels were epistolary.

34. Sophie Fuller, "Thicknesse, Ann," *Oxford Dictionary of National Biography*, http://oxforddnb.com, (accessed February 24, 2012).

6

THE RULE OF *SCANDAL*

Sheridan in the Age of Wilde and Shaw

John Vance

RECENT THEATRE HISTORIANS have concluded that, although there was a "hesitant arrival of modernity" to the British stage, by the 1890s the London theatre scene was ready—even if reluctantly—to accommodate a series of changes that returned drama to the foremost place it held in Britain from the 1590s through the 1630s and again—after the Puritan interregnum— from 1660 to the end of the eighteenth century. These important changes included the renovation of existing (or the construction of new) London theatres, the doubling of contemporary works examined by the Lord Chancellor's Chief Examiner, the push back on censorship,[1] the dramatization of women's and other social issues, the campaign for a National Theatre, the acceptance of more challenging works for production (particularly after century's turn),[2] and the appreciation of Henrik Ibsen—either with stagings of *A Doll's House* and *Ghosts,* or in such critical estimations as Shaw's *The Quintessence of Ibsenism* (1891).[3]

Moreover in the 1890s, a group of actor-managers came to dominate the West-End theatre scene—John Hare, Charles Wyndham, George Alexander, and most significantly Beerbohm Tree at the Haymarket and Henry Irving at the Lyceum. (In 1895, Irving was the first actor ever to be knighted.) In addition to copyright laws protecting playwrights from 1891 on, some of the newer theatres were more intimate fan-shaped structures—unlike the huge and deep horseshoe-shaped houses, such as Drury Lane and Covent Garden—all accommodating a more realistic drama and a less declamatory and histrionic acting style. The days of the opening play, main-piece, and closing play were just about a thing of the past—with a single play comprising the evening or matinee performance.

Also by 1890, the older repertory system was by and large replaced by the long-run system, but of course the term was often more a wish than a reality. Plays had the goal of a four to six-week run, but they often closed after only a few days. Of the 235 new plays in the five theatre seasons from 1893–1897, only one-fourth ran long enough to be deemed successes.[4] Accordingly, managers still looked to box office receipts, and frequently staged adaptations of popular novels and the less grand but not necessarily less popular musical fare, some even lighter than the Gilbert and Sullivan offerings of the previous dozen years.[5] As for traditional comedy and drama, the first and second decades of the twentieth century continued to début dozens of new works. The bulk (whether British or European) were ephemeral of course, but some stimulated enough enthusiasm to secure a place in the repertory, and to enjoy frequent revivals in the years that followed. Rather than inhibiting attendance, the catastrophic First World War only made the theatre more necessary and popular than ever before.

Yet, for all their gazing toward and past the horizon of the new century, the London theatres frequently cast many a willing glance over their shoulders toward the classic English plays of the past.[6] Most notably, the London stage carried on a tradition of some two hundred years by devoting a good portion of each season to Shakespearean revivals.[7] From emerging theatrical stars to well-established luminaries like Irving, Tree, Robertson, Stella Campbell, Winfred Emery, and Ellen Terry, the London stage served Shakespeare masterfully, reviving several of the plays not seen in decades. Some later Victorians and Edwardians wished to see a more elaborately produced Shakespeare—with a pictorial emphasis and "authentic" costumes—while others reacted against this theatrical "excess," opting instead for cleaner and even abstract stagings.[8]

But Shakespeare did not command the exclusive attention of those wishing to stage or view a "classical" British play, for the period 1660–1800 was of considerable interest to the late Victorian and Edwardian theatre-going public. Yet with the exception of Sheridan's *The Rivals* (1775) and *School for Scandal* (1777) and Goldsmith's *She Stoops to Conquer* (1773), the record of London revivals or adaptations of Restoration and eighteenth-century plays staged from 1890 to 1909 is almost nonexistent—Robert Buchanan's *Miss Tomboy*, an adaptation of Vanbrugh's *Relapse* in 1890 and 1891 is about it.[9] Matters improved only slightly in the next decade, for we can only point to the single stagings of Hannah Cowley's *Belle's Stratagem* (1780) in 1913 and Farquhar's *Beaux Stratagem* in 1919. And Congreve's *Double Dealer* (1693) was revived for a two-performance run in 1916. As for *The Way of the World* (1700) and other major plays of the Restoration and eighteenth century (other than Sheridan and Goldsmith, that is), London would have to wait until the next decade to enjoy them.[10]

But the 1890–1919 period witnessed a series of newer plays *about* other literary works and literary and stage personalities from the years 1660–1800. For instance, the Restoration era was represented by Paul Kester's *Sweet Nell of Old Drury Lane*, which was staged in the first three years of the twentieth century (1900, 1901, and 1902) with two revivals in the next decade—from January 28 to May 4, 1912 (for 141 performances) and again from February 27 to April 3, 1915. The latter two runs featured as Nell Gwynne the effervescent Julia Neilson. Originally coached by W. S. Gilbert, Neilson was by now a veteran of Beerbohm Tree's company, an actress well known for her Shakespearean roles—especially Beatrice, Rosalind, and Oberon. Twenty years earlier, Neilson had been the original Lady Chiltern in Wilde's *An Ideal Husband*.[11] *Sweet Nell* was one of Neilson and her husband Fred Terry's signature pieces (he appeared as Charles II in both the 1912 and 1915 runs).[12] The famous Restoration actress was also the subject of *Nell Gwynne, the Player*, which appears to have had but one performance in 1908, and of Shirley and Landreck's *Nell Gwynne, the King's Favourite*, which ran at the Lyceum for 108 performances from February to May 1913 and starred Lauderdale Maitland—fresh from his silent film turn as Scott's Ivanhoe—as Charles II and Minnie Tittell Brune as Nell. San Francisco-born, Brune had acted with Junius Brutus Booth, Jr. (brother of the assassin John Wilkes Booth) and Roy Redgrave (grandfather of Lynn and Vanessa), and would appear in a number of silent films directed by Hal Roach and starring Harold Lloyd.

In addition, the Kingsway Theatre staged Christopher St. John's *The First Actress in 1911*, a short play about Margaret Hughes, who—by most accounts—was the first woman to appear on the English public stage (as Desdemona in December of 1660). Playing the part of Nell Gwynne in this production, which fancifully depicts Hughes's dream of the great actresses who would succeed her, was the inimitable Ellen Terry.[13] And there was also the frequently staged *Nance Oldfield*, which depicted Anne (or Nan) Oldfield, Colley Cibber's favorite actress. Taking the stage each year from 1891 to 1895 and also in 1898, 1900, 1901, and 1905, the most memorable of these performances, at the Lyceum, starred Ellen Terry as Nan.[14]

Audiences moreover enjoyed F. Frankfort Moore's *Kitty Clive*—about one of the mid-eighteenth century's leading actresses and vocalists, as well as a founding member of Garrick's company—which ran for three consecutive years from1895 to 1897 and then again for a single performance in 1915. And five years earlier the records show a single staging of *Peg Woffington's Pearls*, with Frances Weatherall as Woffington, the theatrical colleague of Kitty Clive and, of course, the live-in lover of David Garrick. Perhaps what is most noteworthy about this performance was the appearance of the famous Sybil Thorndike—then between tours of the United States.[15] As for Peg's lover, *David Garrick* by T. W. Robertson was the most popular play influenced by the eighteenth century. London productions were mounted in eleven of the twenty years between 1890 and 1910—with multiple runs in three of those years—and briefly revived in December of 1913 and January of 1918.[16] Owning the role of Garrick (except for the 1918 revival) was the noted actor and manager Charles Wyndham. Known earlier in his career for his excellent Charles Surface in *Scandal*, Wyndham was seventy-six when he performed his last Garrick in this production (1913).

Surely one of the most appealing depictions of Restoration and eighteenth-century personalities was the single matinee performance of *The Pageant of Drury Lane Theatre* on September 27, 1918. The "pageant" was constructed as a series of episodes and scenes—one of them featuring Charles II, Thomas Killigrew, and Samuel Pepys.[17] But more intriguing was another episode titled "On the First Night of Dr. Johnson's *Irene*"—featuring Samuel Johnson (played by Ells Dagnall), Joshua Reynolds, David Garrick, James Boswell, Oliver Goldsmith, Charles Macklin, Peg Woffington, Hannah Pritchard, and Susannah Cibber.[18] The cast was a sterling bunch—with noted *School for Scandal* veterans Ben Greet (as Charles Macklin) and Winifred Emery (as Susannah Cibber) headlining the bill. Nigel Playfair (Boswell) would soon become actor-manager of the Lyric Theatre and in 1923 would be highly influential in getting the first wireless Shakespeare broadcast to a grateful public. Gertrude Elliott (Peg Woffington) had earlier appeared as Ophelia in the 1913 silent film version of *Hamlet*—starring her husband, the acclaimed Shakespearean actor Johnston Forbes-Robertson.

Another of Samuel Johnson's acquaintances in the 1740s was the unfortunate Richard Savage, the subject of J.M. Barrie's (of *Peter Pan* fame) and Marriott Watson's unsuccessful *Richard Savage,* which had one performance at the Criterion Theatre in April of 1891. One might expect Samuel Johnson to have a cameo appearance in this work, but he doesn't. He does, however, show up in *The Rescue of Oliver Goldsmith*, with 16 performances in 1898—starring James Welch as Goldsmith and William Wyes as Johnson. But the best-known play featuring Johnson is unquestionably Leo Trevor's *Dr. Johnson* (1896), starring Arthur Bourchier—then in his mid-thirties—as Johnson, and Fred Thorne as Boswell. The play ran for 60 performances from April to July 1897, and for another 86 performances from

November 1899 to March 1900, and again with new cast members in 1902, 1903, 1905, and 1907.[19] In the next decade, *Dr. Johnson* appeared thirty-two times at His Majesty's Theatre in February and March of 1916. Now an experienced Shakespearean (and previously a Joseph Surface in *Scandal*), the fifty-two-year-old Bourchier reprised his Johnson to much applause.

As for Restoration and eighteenth-century plays themselves, Goldsmith's *She Stoops to Conquer* was extremely popular, having London stagings in 1890 (twice), 1895, 1898, 1900, 1906, 1909, and five additional runs in the decade of 1910–1919.[20] In several of those productions, the cast featured the charming and vivacious Winifred Emery (1862–1924) as Kate Hardcastle—the last time at age forty-four in 1906[21]—and Henry Kemble, the grandson of Charles, as Richard Hardcastle in 1890.[22] The 1915 production of five performances at the Royal Victoria Hall (or the Old Vic) was broadly spaced over a three-month period—from January to April—and featured Estelle Stead as Kate and William Stack as young Marlow.[23] The Old Vic revived the production later in 1915 and early 1916 for six more performances. Stack once more played Marlow, with Sybil Thorndike taking over the role of Kate Hardcastle. A year later, the Old Vic would revive *She Stoops* for yet another six performances, and then for nine more from January to March 1918, again with Thorndike as Kate and her brother Russell as Young Marlow. The male Thorndike was a novelist and a fine Shakespearean actor, showing considerable range in his depictions of Richard II, Claudius, Marc Antony, Touchstone, Caliban, Aguecheek, and King Lear. His sister Sybil played the Fool in that production of *Lear*, and Lady Macbeth to her brother's Macbeth in the 1922 silent film version.[24] Finally, the Old Vic offered the public eleven more performances beginning in December 1919, with Russell Thorndike now taking on the part of Tony Lumpkin.[25]

But other than Shakespeare, the most often-revived British playwright on the London stage between 1890 and 1919 was Richard Brinsley Sheridan. First, there were four recorded performances at the Old Vic of *St. Patrick's Day; or the Scheming Lieutenant* (1775) in March of 1917. *The Critic* (1779) received more attention in the 1910–1919 period, being twice staged—once in June of 1911, and for four performances six years later. Beerbohm Tree mounted the 1911 production and gathered a first-rate cast, including Sheridan alumni Arthur Bourchier, Cyril Maude, and Winifred Emery. The 1917 production starred Ben Greet as Don Ferolo Whiskerandos, Sybil Thorndike as Tilburnia, and Florence Saunders as Norah.

Although these totals are meager, we would expect a healthier number of *Rivals* performances from 1890 to 1919. After all, productions of *The Rivals* were frequently mounted in the earlier part of Victoria's reign, 1837 to 1885.[26] But the evidence suggests a precipitous decline of productions soon after: only one London performance of *The Rivals* in the decade of the 1890s at the Court Theatre for six weeks in November and December 1895, starring William Farren the younger as Sir Anthony Absolute.[27] As one reviewer remarked, the "sense is that the piece is flagging, losing its hold upon the public." Accordingly, the reviewer suggests that audiences go now while there is still a chance to see the play revived.[28] Sheridan's play fared slightly better at the beginning in the next decade, with seven performances at the Lyceum in March of 1900 and a substantial run immediately following at the Haymarket—eighty-three performances in all from the end of March through the middle of June of that year. The reviewer for *Athenaeum* believed the show was worth seeing owing to its "spirit and vitality" but added that the performances were often lacking in "distinction"—with the exception of Winfred Emery's Lydia Languish, which "remains bright and captivating."[29]

Although the reviewers were on the mark with their prediction that patrons "better see the play while they can"—for there were apparently no other revivals in the years 1901 to 1909—*The Rivals* made a bit of a comeback in the next decade, with productions mounted in 1910, 1915, and 1916. A single staging at the Lyric in 1910 starred Lewis Waller, a successful Shakespearean actor, as Captain Absolute, with Kate Cutler, earlier a very popular ingénue in musical comedy, as Lydia. The nine performances at the Old Vic—spaced from November 1915 to March 1916—however, had a first-rate cast: William Stack as Captain Absolute, Ben Greet as Bob Acres, and Sybil Thorndike as Lydia Languish. For the four performances in September, Sybil Thorndike remained as Lydia, Florence Saunders took the role of Julia Melville, and Arthur Fayne, who did Hardcastle in the recent run of *Stoops,* played to type as Sir Anthony Absolute. Although given but fourteen times in the decade, it was enough to stimulate a new appreciation of Sheridan's other comic masterpiece—and the 1920s would see *The Rivals* catching up with *Scandal* and *Stoops* as the most frequently staged comedy from the 1660–1800 period.

But without question, the one non-Shakespearean play that ruled in revival was *The School for Scandal.* In the first of Victoria's sixty-four years on the throne, and sixty years after the play's London début in 1777, we find *Scandal* performed fairly often in the summer of 1837. The casts for these performances were stellar, featuring William Farren as Sir Peter Teazle, Julia Glover as Mrs. Caution, and Madame Vestris as Lady Teazle. Farren (1786–1861) first appeared as Sir Peter in 1818 at the tender age of 32 and, throughout his career, had a major association with the role, whose comic demands Farren performed with remarkable ease.[30] The Irish-born Julia Glover (ca. 1779–1850), who claimed to be a descendent of the great Restoration actor Thomas Betterton, began as a Lydia Languish in late 1790s, going on to depict several Shakespearean roles, including Juliet, Imogen, and Lady Macbeth. At the time of this 1837 revival of *Scandal* she was in her later fifties—as Mrs. Caution.[31] The internationally known singer (she had sung Mozart's Cherubino in *Le nozze di Figaro*, for example), Lucia Elizabeth Vestris was forty when she depicted Lady Teazle in 1837. A year later she would marry one of Dickens's favorite actors, Charles James Mathews, and assist him in theatre management.[32]

London staged another revival with Farren and Vestris in the fall of 1839 and others with Julia Glover, right before her retirement, in 1846 and 1849. Other mid-century productions—at Drury Lane, Covent Garden, the Haymarket, Sadler's Wells, the Olympic, the Grecian, and St. James's—were mounted frequently, in 1840, 1844, 1845, 1850, 1854, 1855, 1861, 1864, 1865, and 1867[33]—with casts that included both the audience's favorites in the roles and those of lesser distinction.[34] Finally, the twenty-year period from 1870 to 1890 witnessed productions at the familiar venues of Sadler's Wells, the Globe, the Olympic, and St. James's, but now also at the Prince of Wales, the Adelphi, the Princes, the Strand, and the Vaudeville theatres.[35] Yet, the number of recorded performances of *Scandal* slips somewhat in this latter period—which may in some part be due to the death in 1861 of the favorite Sir Peter of his time, the elder William Farren.

The records reveal that during the late Victorian and Edwardian periods, however, no other play of the non-Shakespearean Renaissance, Restoration, or eighteenth century was more often staged than Sheridan's *School for Scandal*. One or more runs of the play were mounted in eight of the twenty years from 1890–1910. Only Shakespeare's *Hamlet* (sixteen seasons of the twenty), *Merchant of Venice* (fifteen of twenty), *Merry Wives of Windsor* and *Othello* (eleven of twenty) were produced in more seasons than was Sheridan's masterpiece, with *Julius Caesar* and *Taming of the Shrew* appearing in the same number of seasons as *Scandal* (eight). Therefore, London audiences saw Sheridan's comedy in more years than it did *Antony and Cleopatra, Lear, Macbeth, Measure for Measure, Richard III, Richard II, Midsummer Night's Dream, Twelfth Night, The Winter's Tale,* and *The Tempest.* Not surprisingly, Shakespearean revivals only increased in the second decade of the twentieth century. From 1910 to 1919, twenty-eight of Shakespeare's thirty-seven plays were given. Of those twenty-eight, only eleven had more separate production runs in the decade than did Sheridan's *School for Scandal*, which had seven—with *The Merchant of Venice* (sixteen), *Hamlet* (fifteen), *Julius Caesar* (eleven), *Taming of the Shrew* (eleven), *Twelfth Night* (ten), *Midsummer Night's Dream* (nine), and *Romeo & Juliet* (nine) claiming appreciably more impressive runs than *Scandal's* from 1910 to

1919. *Henry V* (eight) and *Merry Wives of Windsor* (eight) had only one more run than Sheridan's play, while *As You Like It* and *Othello* had the same number—with *Scandal's* being more frequently revived than the likes of *Coriolanus, Cymbeline, The Comedy of Errors, Henry VIII,* the two *Henry IVs, Richard II, Richard III, Winter's Tale, The Tempest, Macbeth,* and even *King Lear.*

Of the more contemporary plays, one can find less than a single handful that ran for more seasons during 1890–1910 than did Sheridan's play—one being the now obscure *Story of Waterloo*—with even Ibsen's *A Doll's House* appearing in the same number of seasons as *Scandal*—eight. And only two more contemporary plays topped *Scandal's* seven production runs between 1910 and 1919: Brandon Thomas's record-setting *Charley's Aunt* and J. M. Barrie's irresistible *Peter Pan* (both with ten). Finally, in the 1910–1919 period, *Scandal* had the same number of runs as Lady Augusta Gregory's Irish tragedy *The Gaol Gate* and Synge's *Playboy of the Western World,* and one more than Ibsen's *A Doll's House* (six). And not a single Wilde or Shaw play received the same number of productions in the decade than did Sheridan's *School for Scandal.* More specifically, from mid-January to early February of 1890, *Scandal* was given twenty-seven times at the Vaudeville Theatre, all evening performances except for three matinees. The cast included Winifred Emery as Lady Teazle, John McLean as Sir Peter, T. B. Thalberg as Charles Surface, and Cyril Maude as Joseph. Fred Thorne, who would play Boswell seven years later in Leo Trevor's *Dr. Johnson,* had the supporting role of Moses. One reviewer found the performance "unsatisfactory"—especially the men playing Joseph and Charles and shook his head at the "uncultivated style" of the dialogue. Yet Emery's Lady Teazle earned unqualified praise for being "bright, natural, and convincing"—with the reviewer predicting great successes for her in "bright comedy"—a most accurate prognostication, as it turned out.[36]

The following year found just the "Screen Scene" staged at the Lyric, with the captivating and notorious Lillie Langtry as Lady Teazle.[37] And then on February 19, 1891, there was a single matinee performance at the Adelphi, which is noteworthy because of several of its cast members. We find Hermann Vezin cast in the part of Sir Peter and Fred Thorne given a significant battlefield promotion—from Moses the year before to Sir Oliver Surface here. But this performance featured, as Lady Teazle, the most exquisite Mrs. Patrick Campbell—the irrepressible "Stella," who would become Shaw's most intense and long-lasting female interest and his first Eliza Doolittle in the 1914 London debut of *Pygmalion.* Campbell, then age 26, had not yet made her reputation on the London stage, having just débuted there the year before, but all indications were that she would soon be among the most sought-after actresses in the city.[38] This performance was followed six weeks later by the beginning of a forty-six-performance run at the Criterion. One reviewer reflected what surely was the consensus view: "[t]hat brilliant and ever popular comedy of manners"—"perhaps the most concisely written play in our language." In fact, the reviewer objected to the liberties taken with the original version. For instance, one scene in Lady Sneerwell's private room had been transported out to a crowded avenue of a "fashionable parade." This reviewer for the *Saturday Review* moreover found the Joseph Surface of Arthur Bourchier (who would play Samuel Johnson in Leo Trevor's later in the decade) "hopelessly unconvincing," and Mrs. Beere's Lady Teazle less than a rousing success, but had high praise for Charles Wyndham's Charles Surface and, of course, for William Farren as Sir Peter: "[h]e played it as it should be played."[39] Again, this is William Farren the younger—or junior—the second natural son of the elder William Farren, the Sir Peter of his era. The younger Farren (1825–1908) began to put his stamp on the part in 1882— then at the age of fifty-seven—and now for this 1891 revival at age sixty-six.

Augustin Daly "re-arranged" the play for the six-week engagement at the end of 1893. One reviewer found this effort at times appropriate "to suit the exigencies of the modern stage," but "when [Daly] proceeds, in a spirit of American squea-mishness to 'cover the legs of a piano,' it is time to protest." Entire passages were omitted; Moses was not permitted to say "damned disinheriting countenance" in referring to Sir Oliver's portrait. The reviewer growls that in America Daly can do what he likes with Sheridan, but "we in England pride ourselves on a robust and not a valetudinarian morality." He ends his assault with a hearty smack to the back of the head: "[w]e have not yet reached the time when Sheridan has to be treated like Wycherley." Of the cast—which included Arthur Bourchier as the other Sur-face brother (Charles), Violet Vanbrugh as Lady Sneerwell, and Ada Rehan as Lady Teazle (Rehan being "buoyant, ultra vivacious, and unconvincing"[40])—the review fully praises only the great Farren Junior as Sir Peter: he was "riper than ever"— "absolutely unsurpassable."[41] Following Daly's version, the more traditional text delighted audiences at the grand Lyceum for five weeks in June and July of 1896. Farren again portrayed Sir Peter with one of the brightest stars in the dramatic fir-mament—Johnston Forbes-Robertson as Joseph.[42] Fred Thorne was back as Moses, with Henrietta Watson as Lady Sneerwell. As Lady Teazle, we find the increasingly busy and utterly splendid Stella Campbell. A reviewer of this production noted of Farren: "[w]ho is to succeed him may well give us pause." The reviewer summarizes succinctly: *School for Scandal* is the "only English piece of its class that for stage purposes remains immortal."[43] Next came a short seven-performance run in July of 1898, which included a completely new cast, with the highly respected James

Fernandez as Sir Peter and Zeffie Tilbury as Lady Sneerwell.[44] This production was succeeded by six-performances in February of 1900—this time, with the popular Ben Greet as Sir Peter and Edith Wynne Matthison as Lady Teazle.[45] But the play received its usual royal treatment later that year at the Haymarket, first from June 19th to July 21st and then from October 16th to November 24th—seventy-nine performances in all, and the last under the rule of Victoria, who would die two months later. The reviewer for *Athenaeum* thought Sydney Valentine "one of the best Josephs to be recalled." The well-seasoned Cyril Maude played Sir Peter, which to the reviewer was "a fairly satisfactory rendering." Also appearing in the production was Henry Kemble as Sir Oliver Surface. But the highest accolades were reserved for the lovely Winifred Emery: "the best Lady Teazle that the present generation has seen." She was simply "beyond praise."[46]

Following these seventy-nine performances in 1900, *Scandal* took a fairly long hiatus—the next run (of five weeks) did not commence until early fall of 1907. Again, the cast was new, with Eric Lewis as Sir Peter, Lilian Braithwaite as Lady Teazle, and Viola Compton as Lady Sneerwell.[47] A reviewer reflected on traditional versus nontraditional approaches, which in this production did not "harmonize well": should we "permit our players to use their own intelligence unhampered by custom?" he asked. In this version, the actors playing Sir Oliver, Lady Teazle, Joseph Surface, and Sir Peter follow the "old school"—which the reviewer identifies as of a "customary breezy kind" with "full round, almost rasping tones, aiming at broad effects, yet underlining the smallest points." "Sheridan himself would have rejoiced," the reviewer concludes, "in Miss Braithwaite's Lady Teazle."[48]

The final production of the Edwardian period (1901–1910) ran at His Majesty's Theatre from April 7th to June 19th of 1909, with two further weeks of performances in July of that year—one hundred and one in all. And here we find (with Farren having died the previous year) Sir Peter played by the irrepressible Herbert Beerbohm Tree (1853–1917). Ensconced in the pantheon of great Shakespearean actors of the late nineteenth and early twentieth century—his Hamlet, Shylock, Petruchio, Malvolio, and Falstaff being particularly admired—Tree was also Shaw's Henry Higgins in the initial London performance of *Pygmalion* in 1914. During this period, Tree moreover assayed Marc Antony, Macbeth, Richard II, and Fagin in the stage adaptation of *Oliver Twist*.[49] The *Athenaeum* noted the difficulty in casting the revival, with the older and newer schools of acting co-existing, often with unhappy results: no production of this play can ignore tradition and let its actors "handle the piece as though it had never been presented before." Although "every revival is bound to be a compromise," several performances during this run just didn't suit. Crabtree was too over the top with his foppishness, and Lady Sneerwell was almost too "self-effacing" and "gentle" for an effective depiction. The reviewer thought Tree's Sir Peter half-way between the old and new schools, although "[n]o more personable Sir Peter has ever graced our stage." The reviewer did find Tree was a bit too young for the part, however (Tree was fifty-six), noting that Sheridan "hinted at a suggestion of senility" in Sir Peter—a debatable point, to say the least. As for the youthful Marie Lohr's Lady Teazle, he complains, "But, alas! Just as few actresses are competent enough to take up the part of Juliet till they are too old to look at it," so too with Lady Teazle, who in this production is "not merely a girl, but a child." Robert Loraine's Charles Surface (he of the new school) "can be praised almost unreservedly." Of the "modern touches" the reviewer finds most impressive the "softening down of the final speeches in the screen scene." Still—and this only demonstrates the reviewer's unsettled mind on this matter—an "actor has no right to defy Sheridan's own view of the character."[50]

The first of the post-Edwardian productions took to the boards in April and May of 1913, with Tree reprising his Sir Peter Teazle for the forty-seven performances: the last run of *Scandal* before the war.[51] Tree's Lady Teazle was twenty-one-year-old Phyllis Neilson-Terry, who had been quite busy with Shakespeare, portraying Viola, Rosalind, Desdemona, both Portias, and Juliet all between the ages of eighteen and twenty-one. Neilson-Terry came from impressive theatrical stock. Her father was the noted actor Fred Terry, and her mother the highly accomplished Julia Neilson, the Nell Gwynne in *Sweet Nell of Old Drury Lane* in the 1912 and 1915 productions. *The Athenaeum* observed that as Lady Teazle, Phyllis was "unusually young and fresh, hopelessly tantalizing, yet charming."[52] The reviewer moreover remarked that Philip Merivale as Joseph Surface "scored" often, but in the character's several private musings, he "unblushingly addressed himself point blank to the audience." Merivale was also an experienced Shakespearean, having done Cassio, Benedick, Othello, and Romeo—with Tree as his Mercutio in one production. In addition, *The Athenaeum* found Matheson Lang's Charles Surface "delightfully light-hearted" and "bubbling over with irresistible mirth," but criticized Lang's transformation in the play's final scene, which inappropriately bordered on "tragic seriousness." Canadian-born, Lang was one of the first stage actors to have a successful film career, which began with his 1916 depiction of Shylock.[53]

The School for Scandal next appeared on the London stage for a single matinee performance at Covent Garden in February of 1915, but with another outstanding cast. Tree again assayed Sir Peter, with the roles of Charles and Joseph Surface taken by Fred Terry[54] and Henry Ainley, who had also flexed his Shakespearean muscles recently as Cassius, Feste, Laertes, Bassanio, Malvolio, and Leontes.[55] And portraying Lady Teazle in this performance was Irene Vanbrugh—at the time forty-three, and some six years older than Constance Collier, who played Lady Sneerwell.[56] Vanbrugh was yet another Shakespearean veteran, appearing with Irving and other major actors of the age. But her major claim to fame was as the original Gwendolen Fairfax in Wilde's *The Importance of Being Ernest* some twenty years earlier.[57] What set this production of *Scandal* apart from the others was in the casting of Arthur Bourchier (a *Scandal* alumnus) and Henry B. Irving (the great Irving's son) as servants to Lady Sneerwell and Sir Peter Teazle respectively. And playing a servant to Joseph Surface was George Alexander, the famous actor-manager who, at the St. James Theatre in 1892 and 1895 first produced Wilde's *Lady Windermere's Fan* and *The Importance of Being Earnest*, as well as creating the roles of Lord Windermere and Jack Worthing. Taking the cameo parts of Lady Sneerwell's "guests" were the likes of Sydney Valentine, Arthur Holmes-Gore, Julia Neilson, and Lilian Braithwaite—the last, a former Lady Teazle (in 1907).[58]

The following month the Old Vic[59] staged another run with a new cast headlined by Leonard Shepherd as Sir Peter, Estelle Snead as Lady Sneerwell, and the previously mentioned William Stack as Charles Surface.[60] But this production would be marked by the introduction of Sybil Thorndike in the role of Lady Teazle. Thirty-three at the time, and having recently done turns as Shakespeare's Viola and Maria in *Twelfth Night*, Hermia and Helena in *Midsummer*, Kate from *Shrew*, Gertrude, Perdita, Miranda, Lady Macbeth, and Kate Hardcastle in *She Stoops,* Thorndike made her theatrical debut in a 1904 production of *Merry Wives*, and would from there tour the United States for the next four years, playing over one hundred roles. When she returned to Britain in 1908, Bernard Shaw spotted her while she was understudying the role of Candida, in his play of the same name. She would become a member of the Old Vic, and have immense success through the war years in Shakespearean and other classical roles. In 1924, she would take on Shaw's St. Joan, the role he wrote with her expressly in mind.[61] Thorndike would again appear as Lady Teazle in the four-performance run at the Old Vic in March of 1916, with Ben Greet as Sir Peter. (She had toured America with Greet's theatrical company after her 1904 debut in *Merry Wives*.) Greet, then 58, made his debut in 1883 (in *Cymbeline*), but was by now spending most of his time producing at the Old Vic, although he acted Bob Acres in the 1915 *Rivals* production. Having performed at Harvard and at Teddy Roosevelt's White House, Greet became the theatrical father of Sydney Greenstreet as well as of Sybil Thorndike.[62] The remainder of the March 1916 cast was excellent—William Stack as Charles, Katherine Carew as Lady Sneerwell, and Mona Maughan as Maria. Carew and Maughan were particularly busy in Shakespearean roles, with Carew shifting from parts such as Phoebe in *As You Like It* and Jessica in *Merchant of Venice* to Calpurnia and Lady Macduff—all between 1915 and 1916. Maughan demonstrated similar range—from Macduff's son and young Edward V in *Richard III* to Juliet, Titania, and the cantankerous Widow in *Shrew.* She also played the servant Lucy to Carew's Julia in the 1915 production of *The Rivals.*

The Old Vic brought *Scandal* back for another war-time run in September of 1916 and continued it in February of 1917—Greet and Thorndike again assaying Sir Peter and Lady Teazle, with Russell Thorndike as Joseph, Florence Saunders as Lady Sneerwell, and Mary Sumner as Maria. Now twenty-six, Saunders, as noted, was another well-experienced Shakespearean actor and veteran of *She Stoops, The Critic,* and *The Rivals.* And like Sybil Thorndike, Saunders would help fill-in for the male actors now off to war by playing Dick Wilkins in a 1917 *Christmas Carol,* as well as Lorenzo (*Merchant*), Valentine (*Twelfth Night*), and Silvius (*As You Like It*). Other than her turn as Lucy and Mrs. Dangle in *The Rivals* and *The Critic,* Mary Sumner depicted Lauretta in Sheridan's *St. Patrick's Day,* and a number of Shakespearean parts from Miranda to Desdemona. This production gave way to eight performances of *Scandal* at the Old Vic from January to early March, 1918. The cast was generally the same as the previous staging, with Ben Greet, Sybil and Russell Thorndike, and Florence Saunders reprising their roles. But Mary Sumner received a battlefield promotion to the part of Mrs. Candor, handing her Maria over to young Phyllis Fenton.

The decade's final (though first post-war) London staging of *The School for Scandal* ran at the Court Theatre from March 17 to May 24, 1919. Arthur Whitby—more recently a Polonius, Autolycus, and Toby Belch—took the role of Sir Peter, with Herbert Waring—the previous season a Malvolio—as Joseph Surface. Ironically, this Joseph was actually twelve years *older* than his Sir Peter. Twenty-two year-old Mary Grey, recently an Olivia in *Twelfth Night*, was Lady Teazle and twenty-seven year-old Leah Bateman performed Lady Sneerwell. This 1919 production ran for 63 performances and capped a decade in which Sheridan continued to rule as the most popular playwright in revival other than Shakespeare, with *Scandal* again the most frequently staged revived play of that era. And there was even a 1914 silent-film version directed by the American Kenean Buel.

As noted in the introduction to this book, the critical reception of Sheridan in the nineteenth and most of the twentieth century has been everything from genially kind to curtly dismissive. For theatre-goers at the end of the nineteenth and into the early twentieth century, however, the playwright's standing was little in question. Sheridan's *School for Scandal* (and soon enough *The Rivals*) informed every member of the London audience that he ranked at the very top of the playwrights plying their trade after Shakespeare. Was the frequent staging of *School*, then, primarily a matter of "the drama's laws, the drama's patrons give"? One should hesitate before answering yes, because during this period the theatres and their patrons seemed conscious not only that theatre had entered a stunningly new period, with acceptance of the new realism of playwrights such as Ibsen and Shaw, and with more contemporary plays demonstrating a staying-power rarely known in the nineteenth century. (Before Wilde and Shaw, what plays from that century are ever taught?) But there was also a renewed and vigorous sense and appreciation of Britain's dynamic theatrical past that goes beyond the understandable financial benefits of producing plays the public wished to see yet again. Playwrights and London theatres of the period, moreover, paid tribute to the vivacious age that preceded its own by writing and scheduling plays treating the leading theatrical, literary, and even historical figures of the Restoration and eighteenth century, from Nell Gwynne, Charles II, and the Earl of Rochester to David Garrick, Samuel Johnson, and even Sheridan himself. The productions of Sheridan's comedies, therefore, cannot be separated from the deliberate attempt to establish in the minds of London audiences Britain's glorious dramatic past. No longer would it be acceptable to think of that literary heritage as constituting only Shakespeare.

The best actors of their age brought their extraordinary talents to the service of Sheridan's work, and would continue to do so in the following decade. Without question, the reputations of Sheridan and eighteenth-century comedy were greatly enhanced by those who performed the roles of Sir Peter and Lady Teazle and Joseph and Charles Surface. *The School for Scandal* would maintain its lofty status on the London stage in the 1920s, but it would be joined by Goldsmith's *She Stoops to Conquer* in the frequency of revivals and almost be equaled by those of *The Rivals*. As a result, the sole monarchal rule of *Scandal* from 1890–1919 would soon give way to a sparkling literary triumvirate. But during a significant period in the history of the London theatre, Sheridan's comic masterpiece ruled supreme as the most frequently staged play of the Restoration and eighteenth century.

Notes

1. Even though works such as Oscar Wilde's *Salomé* (written in 1891) and Bernard Shaw's *Mrs. Warren's Profession* (1893) were denied public performances in the 1890s (the latter reaching the English stage in 1902; the former not until 1931), the fact that both works were initially intended for stage productions reflects the transformations soon to come.

2. For example, the opening of the reconstructed New Court Theatre (later Royal Court Theatre) in 1888 encouraged a different kind of drama to be written, staged, and read.

3. See, for example, Jean Chothia, *English Drama of the Early Modern Period, 1890–1940* (London and New York: Longman, 1996), 1–87; Richard F. Dietrich, *British Drama, 1890 to 1950* (Boston: Twayne Publishers, 1989); and Joseph W. Donohue, ed., *The Cambridge History of British Theatre. Vol. 2, 1660–1865* (Cambridge: Cambridge University Press, 2004); and Baz Kershaw, ed., *The Cambridge History of British Theatre, Vol. 3 since 1895*, 3 vols. (Cambridge: Cambridge University Press, 2004).

4. Chothia, *English Drama*, 27.

5. The considerable popularity of the operas of Verdi, Puccini, Wagner, Bizet, Mozart, Rossini, and Gounod is often underappreciated in discussions of London theatre at the turn of the century.

6. It shouldn't be surprising that one of the reasons revivals maintained their prominence on the London stage was that commercial managers were not always "adventurous in what they were prepared to stage." Actor-managers searched for plays that offered them choice leading parts: "[S]tars were what the public came to see" (Chothia, *English Drama*, 26).

7. Although the existing records inform us that the first years of the Restoration witnessed infrequent stagings of Shakespearean plays and adaptations, as the decades passed the number increased dramatically—with audience expectation of varied Shakespearean productions in the eighteenth century becoming commonplace. See Emmet L. Avery, et al., eds., *The London Stage, 1660–1800* (Carbondale and Edwardsville: Southern Illinois University Press, 1960–1968).

8. One example would be a bare stage production of Shakespeare's *Twelfth Night*. For more on the subject see Gail Marshall and Adrian Poole, eds., *Victorian Shakespeare: Theatre, Drama, Performance* (Basingstoke: Palgrave Macmillan, 2004).

9. Robert Buchanan had already given London his stage adaptations of Fielding's *Tom Jones* (1886) and Richardson's *Clarissa,* which ran for two and half months from early February to mid-April in 1890.

10. The list of Restoration and eighteenth-century London revivals from the 1920s includes George Farquhar's *The Beaux Stratagem* (featuring Edith Evans as Mrs. Sullen), which ran for 143 performances in 1927; John Gay's *The Beggar's Opera* in 1920, 1925, 1926, 1928, and 1929; George Colman the Elder and David Garrick's *The Clandestine Marriage* in 1928; William Wycherley's *The Country Wife* in 1924 and 1926, his *The Plain Dealer* in 1925, and his *Gentleman Dancing Master* in 1928. We also find productions of George Lillo's *The London Merchant* in 1927; John Dryden's

Marriage à la mode in 1920 and *The Rehearsal* in 1925; Thomas Otway's *Venice Preserved* in 1920 and 1928 and *The Orphan* in 1925 (with John Gielgud as Castalio); William Congreve's *The Old Bachelor* in 1924 and *The Way of the World* (featuring the brilliant Edith Evans as Millamant) for 158 performances in 1924.

All dates, cast lists, reviews, and other information for the years 1890–1919 come from J. P. Wearing's multi-volume *The London Stage: A Calendar of Plays and Players* (Metuchen, NJ: The Scarecrow Press, 1976, 1981, 1982, 1984). For other information about individual actors in the period see John Parker, *Who Was Who in the Theatre, 1912–1976: Biographical Dictionary of Actors, Actresses, Directors, Playwrights, and Producers of the English-Speaking Theatre.* Compiled from *Who's Who in the Theatre*, Vols 1–15, 1912–1972 (Detroit: Gale Research, 1978). Also useful is *Nineteenth-Century Theatrical Memoirs,* compiled by Claudia D. Johnson and Vernon E. Johnson (Westport, CT: Greenwood Press, 1982).

11. See Julia Neilson, *This for Remembrance* (London: Hurst & Blackett, 1940).

12. The 1912 *Sweet Nell* also featured Henry Hewitt as Rochester. Hewitt would later appear as Charles Surface in the 1930 film version of *The School for Scandal.*

13. Ellen Terry (1847–1928) was unquestionably one of the premiere Shakespearean actresses of the London Stage, partnering with Henry Irving for a string of memorable performances. Terry began her career at the age of eight, playing Mamillius in *The Winter's Tale* (with Charles Kean) and, as a child, would also act Puck and Fleance. At fifteen she would depict Titania and then go on to many of the great roles, including Lady Macbeth, Portia (*Merchant of Venice*), Beatrice (*Much Ado*), Juliet, Desdemona, Cordelia, and Viola. She would later turn her attention to the plays of Shaw and Ibsen. Terry appeared in several films from 1916–1922 and ended her stage career in 1919 as the Nurse in *Romeo and Juliet.*

14. Not yet known for his authorship of *Dracula,* Bram Stoker served as acting manager of the Lyceum for some of these performances.

15. Here we might also mention another, Louis Parker's *Mavourneen,* a new play which ran for 98 performances from October 1915 to January 1916. *Mavourneen,* which is Irish for "my darling," depicted among its characters the likes of Charles II, Samuel Pepys, Buckingham, and Barbara Villiers (Lady Castlemaine).

16. *David Garrick* (1864) was Robertson's first playwriting success. One of the most significant theatre personages of his time (the third quarter of the nineteenth century), Robertson acted, adapted Dickens novels for the stage, wrote more realistic and serious examinations of social ills as well as comedies, and directed his own work. He influenced the practical stagecraft applications of W. S. Gilbert, and his vision would be shared by later dramatists, most notably Shaw. See Maynard Savin, *Thomas William Robertson: His Plays and Stagecraft* (Providence, RI: Brown University Press, 1950).

17. Sydney Paxton, who played Pepys, was acclaimed for his Spettigue in Brandon Thomas's *Charley's Aunt*—and Langhorne Burton, as Charles II, had just appeared as Tom Jones in the silent film treatment of 1917.

18. Although Johnson was in the audience and Garrick, Cibber, and Pritchard on stage for the original February 1749 production of *Irene,* Goldsmith (then nineteen) hadn't yet settled in London and Boswell (age nine) was being tutored in Scotland by Dunn and Fergusson, still a full decade away from his first journey to London.

19. One of the new actors in these years was H. B. Warner—later to play Christ in Cecil B. DeMille's silent epic *King of Kings* and the drunken druggist in Frank Capra's *It's a Wonderful Life*.

20. That Goldsmith's masterpiece rivaled Sheridan's *Rivals* and *School for Scandal* for the most revived single play from the 1660–1800 period should not be surprising. The London theatres understood that they were establishing or at least solidifying a repertory of Restoration and eighteenth-century plays they could depend on for large and satisfied audiences and a healthy take at the box office. Goldsmith's *She Stoops to Conquer* had remained a favorite in the nineteenth century and any good comic actor would find it difficult to turn down a role in the play, especially considering that *She Stoops to Conquer* allowed the performers to more easily make the transition from play to play— that is, a Hardcastle could comfortably shift to Sir Anthony Absolute or Sir Peter Teazle; a Kate to Lydia or Lady Teazle; a Marlow to Jack Absolute or Charles Surface. Like the brilliant decade of the 1670s, which produced William Etherege's *Man of Mode*, William Wycherley's *The Country Wife*, and Aphra Behn's *The Rover* (although not fully appreciated in the 1890–1919 period), the 1770s was already notable for the triumvirate of comic masterpieces, *She Stoops to Conquer* (1773), *The Rivals* (1775), and *School for Scandal* (1777).

21. Also making her first stage appearance at the age of eight, Emery would join Irving's band at nineteen and tour America with the company. She would go on to play such roles as Beatrice in Beerbohm Tree's *Much Ado About Nothing*, Lydia Languish in *The Rivals*, Mistress Ford in *The Merry Wives of Windsor*, and, for Irving, Nerissa and Jessica in *The Merchant of Venice* and Olivia in *Twelfth Night*.

22. Winifred Emery's husband, the often-praised Cyril Maude (1862–1951), assayed the role of Hardcastle ten years later.

23. Three years earlier, Stead had lost her journalist father W. T. Stead, who was one of the ill-fated passengers aboard the *RMS Titanic*. Stack would go on to a very busy film career in the 1930s— including small parts in *The Last of the Mohicans*, *Tarzan and His Mate*, *Mutiny on the Bounty*, and *Gone with the Wind*.

24. Russell Thorndike had moved up the *She Stoops* pecking order, first playing the servant Diggory in the 1916 production. Much later he would have small film roles in Olivier's *Hamlet* and *Richard II* and appear as Captain Hook's genial accomplice Smee in ten revivals of *Peter Pan*.

25. Playing Kate in these performances was Florence Saunders, an experienced Shakespearean actress, having recently done turns as Phebe in *As You Like It*, Jessica in *Merchant of Venice*, Hippolita in *Midsummer Night's Dream*, Bianca in *Shrew*, and Constance Neville in the 1916 production of *She Stoops*.

26. During these years, William Farren was by all accounts a brilliant Sir Anthony Absolute, with Julia Glover as Mrs. Malaprop, and Madame Vestris as Lydia Languish in several runs at the Haymarket and Covent Garden. Taking on the role of Captain Jack Absolute in the 1884 production was thirty-one year old Johnston Forbes-Robertson—well on his way to becoming one of the leading actors—and greatest Hamlets—in the Age of Irving.

27. Interestingly, Sir Lucius O'Trigger was depicted by Brandon Thomas, author of one of the most adored plays of that decade and ever since: *Charley's Aunt*. Thomas (1850–1914) had been acting professionally since 1879. *Charley's Aunt*—in which he played Sir Francis Chesney—debuted in 1892 and went on to a record shattering 1,466 performances in its initial London run. See Jevan

Brandon-Thomas, *Charley's Aunt's Father: A Life of Brandon Thomas* (London: Douglas Saunders 1955).

28. *The Athenaeum A Journal of Literature, Science, the Fine Arts, Music, and the Drama* (London: Athenaeum Press, 1828–1921), November 16, 1895, 689–90.

29. *The Athenaeum,* March 31, 1900, 410.

30. The data for these pre-1890 Victorian performances (and those of *The Rivals*) comes from Donald Mullin, ed., *Victorian Plays: A Record of Significant Productions on the London Stage, 1837–1901* (New York and Westport, CT: Greenwood Press, 1987). For more on William Farren, see Carol J. Carlisle's entry "William Farren" in the *Oxford Dictionary of National Biography* (Oxford: Oxford University Press, 2004). Farren's father, also named William, played the role of Careless in the play's 1777 debut.

31. Thirteen years later she would take her final bows with an even more memorable Sheridan part— Mrs. Malaprop in *The Rivals*.

32. See Clifford J. Williams, *Madame Vestris: A Theatrical Biography* (London: Sidgwick and Jackson, 1973); and William W. Appleton, *Madame Vestris and the London Stage* (New York: Columbia University Press, 1974).

33. Noteworthy among these *Scandal* productions would be the 1850 staging, which again featured the admired William Farren as Sir Peter, but which also included his elder "natural" son Henry as Charles Surface, and his younger "natural" son William Jr. as Crabtree. There was also the earlier April 1840 production with Charles Kemble—the younger brother of John Philip Kemble and Sarah Siddons—as Charles Surface. This seems to be the sixty-five year old Kemble's final stage performance. We can also point to an 1867 staging with the great Henry Irving (1838–1905) as Joseph Surface.

34. For example, Samuel Phelps, Eaton O'Donnell, and Henry Compton as Sir Peter and Mary Warner and Charlotte Cushman as Lady Teazle. Lady Sneerwells of the period included the likes of Helen Matthews, Eleanor Bufton, and Harriet Coveney.

35. During this period, the likes of Virginia Bateman, Ada Cavendish, Adelaide Neilson, and Teresa Furtado acted Lady Teazle; Mrs. Bernard Beere and Cicely Nott depicted Lady Sneerwell; and W. H. Stephens, Benjamin Webster, James Fernandez, and William Chippendale took on the role of Sir Peter. A December 1880 production at Sadler's Wells featured Farren, Jr. as Crabtree, Hermann Vezin as Sir Peter, and Virginia Bateman as Lady Teazle—the latter two American-born. Clearly the most interesting of these performances was the one at the Prince's Theatre in February 1885, which included Farren, Jr., Herbert Beerbohm Tree as Sir Peter, and Lillie Langtry as Lady Teazle.

36. *The Athenaeum,* January 18, 1890, 94. Other than being the husband of Winifred Emery, Cyril Maude (1852–1951) was an exceptionally fine comic actor. Serving a turn with Frederick Harrison as manager of Theatre Royal, Haymarket from 1896 to 1905, Maude would later twice tour the United States and appear in several films (the last in 1947). In April of 1942, the Haymarket mounted a special performance of scenes from *The School for Scandal*, with Vivien Leigh playing Lady Teazle, to honor Maude on his 80th birthday. Four photographs of the two of them depicting Sir Peter and Lady Teazle are in the National Portrait Gallery.

37. Her notoriety stemmed, of course, from her affair with the prince of Wales between 1877 and 1880 and with the Earl of Shrewsbury, Prince Louis of Battenberg, and Arthur Clarence Jones

immediately afterward. Oscar Wilde suggested that she turn to acting, and in December 1881 she débuted in *She Stoops* at the Haymarket. See her autobiography *The Days I Knew* (New York: George H. Doran, 1925), and Laura Beatty, *Lillie Langtry: Manners Masks and Morals* (London: Chatto & Windus, 1999).

38. Her reputation would be secured in 1893, when she starred in Arthur Wing Pinero's *The Second Mrs. Tanqueray*. Campbell would go on to memorable Shakespearean productions at the Lyceum with Johnston Forbes-Robertson as well as a notable turns as Ibsen's Hedda Gabler. Although too old for the character when she appeared as Shaw's original Eliza Doolittle, there was little doubt she was the choice, since few actresses could rival her popularity with London audiences—and especially since Shaw wrote the part for her. See Margot Peter, *Mrs. Pat: The Life of Mrs. Patrick Campbell* (New York: Alfred A. Knopf, 1984).

39. *Saturday Review,* April 11, 1891, 442.

40. All three of these actors were closely associated with Daly, the American theatre manager and playwright whose artistic vision often offended audience members and critics alike, especially when his company toured England. Shaw, for one, objected to Daly's cuts in and controversial stagings of the American's Shakespeare productions. During his long career as an actor (1889–1924), Bourchier appeared in a good many Shakespearean parts. His wife Violet Vanbrugh (1867–1942), who performed for over fifty years, also distinguished herself in Shakespeare, particularly in such roles as Ophelia, Rosalind, and Portia in *The Merchant of Venice.* The same may be said of their theatrical colleague Ada Rehan (1860–1916), who began acting at fourteen and would spend over twenty years with Daly's company. Rehan was acclaimed for her Rosalind, but even more adored for her Viola and Kate in *The Taming of the Shrew.*

41. *The Athenaeum*, November 18, 1893, 705.

42. Forbes-Robertson (1853–1937) would become the long-sought heir to Irving in many important roles, most notably Hamlet (which he did not begin playing until he was in his mid-forties, although he continued in the part until he was 63, even starring in a silent film version three years earlier). Forbes Robertson was also an acclaimed Romeo and Othello, often in the 1890s appearing with Stella Campbell, with whom he had a brief love affair. Shaw had utter praise for Forbes-Robertson's talents and wrote the role of Julius Caesar for him in *Caesar and Cleopatra* (written in 1898). See Ralph Berry's entry on Forbes-Robertson in the *Oxford Dictionary of National Biography.*

43. *The Athenaeum,* June 27, 1896, 852.

44. Born in St. Petersburg in 1835 while his family was working for the English Ambassador to Russia, Fernandez appeared with the likes of Henry Irving, Ellen Terry, Charles Mathews, Lillie Langtry, Charles Wyndham, and the American Edwin Booth. Tilbury (1863–1950) went on to appear in many films, including an "Our Gang" (or "The Little Rascals") comedy in 1936.

45. Matthison (1875–1955) became a member of Greet's company and played Rosalind to his Touchstone in the same year they did *Scandal.* Two years later she would travel with Greet's company to New York, where she garnered considerable attention and praise as Rosalind and as the character Everyman in Greet's production of the fifteenth century morality play. When she returned to England, Irving invited her to play Portia to his Shylock on his farewell tour. See the Sydney Higgins's website "The Golden Age of British Theatre (1880–1920)," last modified June 13, 2009, http://www.the-camerino-players.com/britishtheatre/index.html.

46. *The Athenaeum*, June 23, 1900, 796.

47. Lewis (1855–1935) joined the D'Oyly Carte Opera Company in 1882, although almost exclusively as an understudy. (His leaving allowed Henry Lytton a place in Gilbert and Sullivan history when the role of Robin Oakapple in *Ruddigore* fell open very shortly after Lewis left the company.) Lewis continued performing in musical comedy but added straight comic roles to his *repertoire*. Later made a Dame of the British Empire, Lilian Braithwaite (1873–1948), had her London debut in *As You Like It* in 1900. She appeared in Hitchcock's 1927 film *Downhill* and in Noel Coward's influential drama *The Vortex*. She would also earn acclaim in the early 1940s for her role in the long-running *Arsenic and Old Lace*. As an actress, Viola Compton was largely overshadowed by her sister Fay Compton. Viola's grandfather was the significant theatre personage Henry Compton and her father the actor/manager Edward Compton. Rounding out the theatrical accomplishments of the Compton's, Viola's mother, the actress Virginia Bateman, played Lady Teazle opposite Hermann Vezin in 1880.

48. *The Athenaeum,* September 21, 1907, 344.

49. Tree began acting professionally in 1878. In 1886 he played both Iago and Sir Peter Teazle for F. R. Benson's company at Bournemouth, one hundred miles southwest of London. He began his coordinated career as actor/manager in 1887 at the Comedy Theatre in London's West End—and soon after took the reins of the then flagging Haymarket Theatre, which he restored to preeminence. In the later 90s, he managed Her [later His] Majesty's Theatre and helped finance its rebuilding. His dedication to Shakespearean productions rivaled and then surpassed that of Irving and the Lyceum. Tree was also a pioneer in the depiction of Shakespeare on film, beginning in 1899 with three brief moments from *King John*—in which he appeared and which he directed—the first filmed record of a Shakespeare play. In 1911 Tree portrayed Cardinal Wolsey in a five-scene film treatment of *Henry VIII*. Finally, in 1916 he played Macbeth in D. W. Griffith's film (now lost). See Madeleine Bingham, *The Great Lover: The Life and Art of Herbert Beerbohm Tree* (New York: Atheneum, 1979); and Hesketh Pearson, *Beerbohm Tree: His Life and Laughter* (London: Methuen, 1956).

50. *The Athenaeum*, April 17, 1909, 474–75. Of further interest is the fact that a former Sir Peter, Hermann Vezin, took on the role of Rowley in a number of the performances of this run.

51. Even though some felt Tree's acting style was by now reflective of another era and others noted his excessive use of theatrical make-up, a reviewer of his 1913 performance noted that Tree played Sir Peter differently, as man of fifty, not as an older and more addled character as others had traditionally performed him (*The Athenaeum,* April 19, 1913, 444).

52. Sir Peter's ward Maria was performed by Marie Hemingway, who was very briefly married to Claude Rains of *Casablanca* and *Invisible Man* fame. Coincidentally, Rains made his stage debut as a boy singer in a 1900 production of *Sweet Nell of Old Drury Lane.*

53. He, and not Lon Chaney, was the first actor to play the character Mr. Wu on both stage and film.

54. Terry's most significant period parts were Charles II in *Sweet Nell of Old Drury Lane,* Benedict in *Much Ado*, and Charles Surface in *Scandal.*

55. Ainley later played the exiled Duke Senior in the 1936 film of *As You Like It,* which starred Laurence Olivier as Orlando.

56. Collier (1878–1955) began acting at age three, playing Peaseblossom in *A Midsummer Night's Dream*. Tree would later cast her as Cleopatra to his Antony in Shakespeare's play (1908). In 1916 she would make her second tour of the United States with Tree, and while there appeared in four films, doing Lady Macbeth to Tree's Macbeth in one of them. Collier would later have roles in talking films, coaching and becoming fast friends with the likes of Katherine Hepburn and Marilyn Monroe. For Collier's biography see Higgins, "The Golden Age of British Theatre (1880–1920)."

57. Vanbrugh (1872–1949) commenced her career in 1888 with Phebe in *As You Like It,* followed by Titania in *A Midsummer Night's Dream*. In 1891 Vanbrugh moved to the London stage, appearing in J. M. Barrie's *Ibsen's Ghost* and joining Beerbohm Tree's company two years later. (She continued to appear in Barrie's plays over the next two decades.) In the 1930s she was featured in ten films, sharing the screen with Douglas Fairbanks Jr., Marlene Dietrich, and Henry Fonda, most notably. She received her DBE in 1941. See Sydney Higgins, "The Golden Age of British Theatre (1880–1920)."

58. Holmes-Gore would die five months later, at the age of 44, killed at the Battle of Gallipoli. He also appeared in the 1915 film adaptation of Anthony Hope's *The Prisoner of Zenda*, which also featured Henry Ainley.

59. The Old Vic began as the Royal Coburg Theatre in 1818. In 1880 it was formally dubbed The Royal Victoria Hall. At the time of this production The Old Vic was under the management of the redoubtable Lilian Baylis (1874–1937).

60. Shepherd (1882–1958) was not quite thirty-three when he played Sir Peter in this production. He would later appear as Clemenceau in the 1931 film *The Dreyfus Case,* which starred Cedric Hardwicke in the title role.

61. Thorndike (1882–1976) acted on stage (and in film) throughout the next four decades—including the movie version of Shaw's *Major Barbara* (1941), bowing out in a TV drama with Anthony Hopkins in 1970. (She made her Broadway debut in 1910.) During the First World War, when a number of male actors were in service, Thorndike added to her *repertoire* such parts as Lear's Fool, Prince Hal, and Puck. She was made a DBE in 1931. See Jonathan Croall, *Sybil Thorndike: A Star of Life* (London: Haus Publishing, 2008).

62. As an impresario, Greet (1857–1936) sought a simpler Shakespeare production (including the warmly received "scene-less" *Twelfth Night* while touring America in 1904) as a reaction to the more elaborate and occasionally garish offerings of the day. See Winifred Isaac, *Ben Greet and the Old Vic: A Biography of Philip Ben Greet* (London: Greenback Press, 1964).

7

NAUMACHIA AND THE STRUCTURE OF *THE CRITIC*

Daniel J. Ennis

DESPITE *THE CRITIC'S* THREE-ACT structure, most discussions of the afterpiece divide it into two halves, just as the full title of the play suggests that it has two parts: *The Critic, or a Tragedy Rehearsed* (1779). The first half consists of Act I and most of Act II, the Dangle-Sneer-Plagiary-Puff commentary on the contemporary stage, not strictly parody, but satire broadly conceived: Horatian, topical, and character-driven. The second half is made up of Act II, scene ii and most of Act III, and consists of the rehearsal of the parodic heroic tragedy *The Spanish Armada*. Reviews of *The Critic* in the wake of its November 1779 debut establish this bifurcation: *The Morning Post* provides an account of the Dangle portion of the play, and then offers extended commentary on "the rehearsal of [Puff's] tragedy," which occupies "the remainder of the piece."[1] *The Public Advertiser* calls the second half of *The Critic* "The Rehearsal of the Tragedy."[2] *The Morning Chronicle*, echoing the afterpiece's full title if not its capitalization, dubs this portion of *The Critic* "The *Tragedy rehearsed*."[3] This treatment of the latter half of the play as a distinct dramatic unit is a common and enduring feature in the body of criticism surrounding *The Critic*. It is true that *The Critic* falls conveniently into two halves, but another way to look at the play is to see it in three parts—the two recognized sections and a framing device, which might be called, to use Dangle's line, "the fleet and the nation." *The Critic* begins and ends with questions of naval conflict and national destiny.

The Critic's frame consists of the first moments of the play's very first scene, Mr. and Mrs. Dangle's conversation about national and theatrical politics, and the very last moments of the play, a *naumachia* consisting of the dialogue-free spectacle of the English fleet defeating the Spanish Armada.[4] In effect, Sheridan brackets the satire of the Dangle-Sneer-Plagiary-Puff interaction and the burlesque of heroic tragedy as embodied in "The Tragedy Rehearsed" with the serious matter of Britain's contested maritime supremacy and, by extension, her continued existence as a nation. Sheridan's responses to the military crisis that attended the war with France that grew out of the American Revolution have been discussed in detail by other scholars, most recently and incisively by Robert W. Jones,[5] but there is more to be gleaned from the fact that *The Critic* opens with hints of news about the fleet and closes with an idealization of the Royal Navy, invoking and thwarting invasion(s) that were a frighteningly real possibility for the Britons of 1778–1780. Paula R. Backscheider, in *Spectacular Politics: Power and Mass Culture in Early Modern England*, demonstrates the special agency of texts composed in the midst of social crises, and establishes how such texts participate "in the negotiations that would assimilate change and reestablish ideological, and therefore social, stability." Often such texts employ an "idealized English self-image" and thus allow "the entire culture to agree on what its people were like" and, among other things, "what 'community' would mean."[6] Backscheider draws upon a wide variety of texts that constitute "mass culture" in the eighteenth century, but her formulation, when applied to *The Critic*, reveals how Sheridan's framing device foregrounds the nation's security concerns and raises questions about the community's duty in such a crisis. By invoking the Royal Navy at the very beginning of *The Critic*, and then closing the frame with the *naumachia* at the very end of the play, Sheridan consociates his satire of "theatrical politics" and his parody of heroic tragedy with the power of spectacular patriotism.

The opening of *The Critic* finds Mr. and Mrs. Dangle at home: he reading the newspapers, she carping on her husband's pretensions as a theatre impresario and bewailing his lack of patriotic vigor. Mr. Dangle complains that the newspapers devote too much space to the news of the war with the French and Americans:

> DANGLE. [*reading*] 'BRUTUS to LORD NORTH.'—'Letter the second on the STATE OF THE ARMY'—Pshaw! 'To the first L—dash D of the A—dash Y.'—Genuine extract of a Letter from ST. KITT'S.'— 'COXHEATH INTELLIGENCE.'—'It is now confidently asserted that Sir Charles Hardy.'—Pshaw!—Nothing but about the fleet, and the nation!7

In order to lay bare *The Critic's* frame, the references to the Royal Navy oblige a closer reading, even at the risk of treading some familiar ground. David Crane, in an otherwise penetrating analysis of this scene, neglects to mention the references

to the Royal Navy, summarizing these lines as "on the subject of the state of preparedness of the army to meet the immediate threat from France in the autumn
of 1779."[8] But it is the naval allusions in this speech that connect this opening
scene with the final moments of *The Critic*. Two particular items on Mr. Dangle's
list emphasize the importance of the fleet during the invasion scare. "To the first
L—dash D of the A—dash Y" refers to John Montagu, Fourth Earl of Sandwich,
who as First Lord of the Admiralty had been subject to a cannonade of unsolicited
advice and abuse regarding his management of the war at sea. The script indicates
that Mr. Dangle reads the editorial elisions literally, each dash enunciated. Mr.
Dangle's mannered pronunciation of the typography of the newspaper suggests he
is either so uninformed a citizen that he is unable to identify the First Lord of the
Admiralty, or so disinterested in the subject that he cannot be bothered to replace
the dashes and utter the syllables. "The First Lord of the Admiralty" becomes the
gaps and-silences-strewn "first L—dash D of the A—dash Y."

Mr. Dangle's pattern of mentioning the war only to dismiss it continues in
his abortive reading of an item related to the security of the English Channel: "It
is now confidently asserted that Sir Charles Hardy." Mr. Dangle starts to recite the
lede of the newspaper item, but breaks off with his percussive "Pshaw," unwilling
to devote any more time to the non-theatrical Sir Charles Hardy. Hardy, as the
commander of the Channel Fleet, would have been best placed to shield Britain
from the threat of French invasion, and the item, "confidently asserted," teases the
audience with its incompleteness: who is doing the asserting? And what was being asserted? That the French fleet, long rumored to be crammed with troops and
lurking in the English Channel, has returned to port? That Hardy has finally met
them in battle? That Hardy has failed to intercept? On September 5, 1779, Horace
Walpole wrote to Horace Mann, "We heard of Sir Charles Hardy off Plymouth
and yesterday off Portsmouth," but that there was no news of the location of the
combined Franco-Spanish fleet. Walpole expresses frustration with the lack of information on the positions of the respective fleets, complaining that "I have told
you all the little I know, disrobed of the reports and lies of each new day....I write
rather to abstract the small truth there is in newspapers."[9] Mr. Dangle—like Walpole, dependent on the newspapers—reads just enough of the report to establish
its import, but the item is left, well, to "dangle." Unable to provide satisfaction in
this matter, the audience is shown Mr. Dangle's fundamental—and unmanly—
flaw: he hates "all politics but theatrical politics."[10] Mrs. Dangle implies that her
husband's interest in the theatre is both enervating and disloyal. Mr. Dangle, she
declares, lacks "spirit."[11]

Mrs. Dangle's dissatisfaction with her husband is presented as a function of his lack of patriotism, but continuing the subtextual assertions of Mr. Dangle's impotence, she covers him with abuse, declaring he is a gossip whose house has been transformed into "the motley rendezvous of all the lackeys of literature." The Dangle home, then, *viz* the eighteenth century's fantasy of Roman values, is not the hearth and sanctuary, but a disorderly meeting-place for "candidate actors, and poets without character." Mrs. Dangle's drawing room is filled not just "with misses and ma'ams piping hysteric changes on Juliets and Dorindas, Pollys and Ophelias," but also with "the probationary starts and unprovoked rants of would-be Richards and Hamlets!" Thanks to the opera, the Dangle home has been beset by "signors and signoras" whose un-English warbling suggests the sound of a foreign invasion. Mrs. Dangle complains of the opera singers "sliding their smooth semibreves, and gargling glib divisions in their outlandish throats," and declares that such a chaotic scene would be a likely hiding place for "foreign emissaries and French spies" who, "disguised like fiddlers and figure dancers," would be well-placed to undermine the security of Great Britain.[12] Mr. Dangle, by dangling about the stage and allowing danglers in his home, and by hoping, as Mrs. Dangle says, that the invading French will bring a theatrical troop with them, falls far short of what Backscheider would call "the idealized English self-image." Mr. Dangle's world is already a multi-ethnic motley of quivering men and hysterical women, a preview of post-invasion England, should Sir Charles Hardy fail in his duty. Hardy was a septuagenarian veteran of the Seven Years' War who had come out of retirement to command the channel fleet and face the French threat. Whatever the criticisms of Hardy as a tactician (and there were many), he was at sea doing his duty, and his absent presence in the opening of *The Critic* stands in contrast to the fey, flaccid inaction of Mr. Dangle.[13]

The frame thus established, *The Critic* shifts to other terrain, and it is only at the end of the play that the fleet—idealized—is reintroduced as patriotic spectacle. In most readings of *The Critic*, the sea-battle, since it exists only in stage directions, is taken as the conclusion of the "Tragedy Rehearsed." The dialogue of *The Critic*, however, is warrant enough to consider Puff's battle as separate from his tragedy. Tilburnia has delivered her "mad speech" and has left the stage:

Sneer: And pray what becomes of her?

Puff: She is gone to throw herself into the sea, to be sure—and that brings us at once to the scene of action, and so to my catastrophe—my sea-fight, I mean.

Sneer: What, you bring that in at last?

Puff: Yes—yes—you know my play is *called* the *Spanish Armada*; otherwise, egad, I have no occasion for the battle at all.[14]

Sneer, a veteran theatre-goer, expresses surprise that there is to be a sea-battle. For him, the generic conventions of the tragedy have already been fulfilled, with Tilburnia's death the logical end-point of the genre, exeunt omnes bearing bodies. Puff, however, has put the spectacular cart before the generic horse: calling his play *The Spanish Armada* allows him to attach a patriotic demonstration to a play that is already complete (although wretched) without such a final scene. *The Critic*'s parody of heroic tragedy ends with Tilburnia's suicide; onstage there is one more bit of foolery when the actor playing the Thames bungles the procession of rivers, but with the *naumachia*, Sheridan returns to the frame of "the fleet and the nation" and signals a change in mood: The tragedy is over, let the spectacle begin.

Scholars have been successful in tracing characters, speeches, and even particular phrases from *The Critic* back to their dramatic origins: The recognition scene of Tom Jenkins in *The Spanish Armada* parodies a similar incident in Richard Cumberland's *The West Indian*. Puff's Beefeater steals a line from *Othello*. Tilburnia's character is drawn not just from *Hamlet* but also from Thomas Otway's *Venice Preserved*.[15] But sifting through Nathaniel Lee and Nicholas Rowe, Elkanah Settle and even John Dryden himself, one cannot find an eighteenth century reparatory tragedy that incorporates a *naumachia* and thus provides a model for the spectacle that concludes *The Spanish Armada*. Restoration stagecraft could not support such displays, the memorable-but-static scene-paintings for William Davenant's *Siege of Rhodes* notwithstanding. The same holds true for Sheridan's fresher targets, the tragedies of his own era such as Henry Jones's *The Earl of Essex* (1753), John Home's *Douglas* (1756), and Cumberland's *The Battle of Hastings* (1778). Sheridan as manager had produced some of these plays; for example, *The Battle of Hastings* was staged at Drury Lane just a year before *The Critic* was composed. However, just as was the case with Restoration heroic drama, none of the tragedies written by Sheridan's contemporaries incorporate a *naumachia*; the ravings of Orestes (*The Distrest Mother*) and Old Norval (*Douglas*) gave no opening for an appearance by the fleet. Heroic tragedies produced in the 1770s featured plenty of opportunities for soldiers on the march (e.g. Edwin's "If you are with me, warriors, strike your shields" speech in *The Battle of Hastings*), but nary a Jack Tar nor a canvas ocean. When Dangle asks if there is to be a battle, Puff responds, "Yes, yes, you will have a battle at last: but, egad, it's not to be by land, but by sea—and that is the only quite new thing in the piece."[16] In Sheridan's theatre, sea-battles on stage were not new. Attaching a *naumachia* to a *tragedy* was Puff's innovation.

To find the model for Puff's sea-fight, then, we must look not to the high form of tragedy, with its Aristotelian endorsement and surfeit of cultural capital, but to the lowers steps of the eighteenth-century dramatic ziggurat: masques, pantomimes, and afterpieces. These short pieces were the vehicles through which naval spectacles were introduced to the stage; tragedies filled a different role.[17] In the 1770s, the estimable combination of David Garrick (as what we might call producer-director) and Philippe Jacques De Loutherbourgh (in his capacity of designer-technical director) discovered and exploited an audience demand for ships on the stage. Garrick's October 1773 revival of *Alfred*, a masque that had not been performed in twenty-two years, was made an unexpected hit at Drury Lane by the inclusion of a naval spectacle of unprecedented detail and effect.[18] Ralph G. Allen documents how such displays, inspired by the King's review of the fleet at Spithead in July 1773, became a staple of the London stage; within weeks of the fleet review, the Haymarket offered up "an admirable transparent representation of the fleet"[19] and Covent Garden countered with a new pantomime that included "a fleet of ships, with every sail crowded and full."[20] Drury Lane could not be left out, so Garrick took *Alfred* in hand and added touches that connected the great ninth-century king to Britain's latter-day naval supremacy. Garrick amplified the role of the hermit-seer character, having him conjure up for the titular King a vision of the future glory of the eighteenth-century Royal Navy. The most famous of *Alfred*'s songs, Thomas Arne's "Rule Britannia," was restored to its original length, reversing a trend evident in previous *Alfred* revivals wherein the song had been truncated.[21]

Such revisions launched a thousand scaled-down ships. The next season Garrick, eager to further amortize the expense of De Loutherbourgh's technical achievement, added a naval review to an old Shadwell play, thus transforming *The Fair Quaker of Deal* into *The Fair Quaker*; the play's setting was moved from Deal to the naval town of Portsmouth so as to give plausible excuse for the appearance of the fleet.[22] Garrick and De Loutherbourgh also inserted a regatta scene (almost surely drawing on the properties of the *Alfred* naval review) into the venerable pantomime *Queen Mab* in 1775. That regatta turned up in two other productions during the 1775–1776 season, each time giving new life to a stale repertory piece.[23] The ships and ocean backdrops were added to Drury Lane's stock of scenery, props, and effects, and with a bit of preparation a fleet could be brought to the stage in short order. Very early in its generic development, then, the Georgian *naumachia* was employed as an autonomous theatrical element, a crowd-pleaser that did not demand much in the way of plot support or motivation and could be attached to a ready script on the flimsiest of pretences.

By the time he composed *The Critic*, Sheridan was well aware that naval spectacle had become an increasingly prominent and financially successful element of his theatre. When he took over the management of Drury Lane from Garrick in 1776, Sheridan leaned on De Loutherbourgh heavily, emphasizing spectacles in the repertory in order to compensate for the loss of the services of England's most popular actor.[24] *The Fair Quaker* was revived, fleet and all, and Sheridan ensured that the scenes and properties necessary for a *naumachia* did not lay unused for long. *Queen Mab* was staged on October 8, 1778, and October 5, 1779, and other afterpieces that used the stock ships, ocean-scenes, and fleet transparencies, such as Garrick's *Harlequin's Invasion* and Edward Phillips's *Britons, Strike Home, or, The Sailor's Rehearsal*, saw revivals in the months immediately preceding the debut of *The Critic*.

There is no reason to believe that Sheridan welded a sea-fight to the end of *The Critic* because it would contribute to his elaborate takedown of heroic tragedy. In autumn 1779, Sheridan had little to gain by mocking *naumachia* as theatrical decadence, especially when such mockery might be misread as an attack on the Royal Navy as an institution. Between the disconcerting reports about the Admiralty's ineffective response to the French entry into the Channel that summer and the sudden fame of the American Privateer John Paul Jones, who on September 23, 1779 had humiliated the Royal Navy in a spectacular battle off Flamborough Head, Sheridan had material ready and sufficient to satirize the Royal Navy. Had he done so, he would have risked a severe reaction from patriotic theatre-goers, and perhaps, given the Licensing Act, some unwanted attention from the Lord Chamberlain's office.

These factors have not prevented critics from asserting that the battle at the end of *The Critic* was presented with a satiric edge. V.C. Clinton-Baddeley proposes an ingenious—but ultimately unconvincing—reading:

> Battles had often been burlesqued before—but usually by making them fatuous. Sheridan made the joke the other way round, burlesquing not with a minimum but with an excess of patriotic splendor.[25]

In the same vein, Allen calls the *naumachia* in *The Critic* "a witty satirical battle scene," but his comment is in passing, and he offers no evidence of the battle itself being presented in a way that audiences might perceive as ironic, much less subversive.[26] Mark Auburn also believes there is satire to be had in the *naumachia*, proposing that with Puff's sea-fight, "the audience, with its appetite for spectacle, becomes the unspoken subject of satire, satisfied with noise, battle, and claptrap."[27] Yet there is nothing to suggest that the spectacle was *received* as "claptrap" and no reason to believe that Sheridan was limning the battle with subtext—and on a mundane level, it is difficult to figure how such subtext might be injected into the scene. These readings tend to project Sheridan's assault on heroic tragedy onto the *naumachia*, but if indeed the "satire" of Puff's sea-fight was somehow tied up in its excess (Clinton-Baddeley's argument) or slyly directed at the spectators (Auburn's position), there is still the problem of motivation. For Sheridan to countenance a farcical naval battle at Drury Lane after a summer of invasion fears would have been to invite the hissing of the pit and the quick damning of *The Critic*.

If the *naumachia* were to be treated as a continuation of *The Critic's* parodic mode, then we ought to find evidence of Puff's sea-fight being held up to ridicule, just as the rhetorical flights of fancy in the speeches of Don Ferolo Whiskerandos and the "profound" silence of Lord Burleigh demolish the pretensions of the heroic mode. But eighteenth-century reviewers of *The Critic* did not sense that the naval battle was anything more than a straightforward demonstration of an effective Drury Lane set-piece. As Auburn himself points out, "early critics lavishly praised De Loutherbourgh's scene and effects for their realism, not their mockery of theatrical effect."[28] As an emerging genre, the rules of the Georgian *naumachia* were still inchoate in the late 1770s, but one audience expectation was clear: naval spectacles were serious business. Despite the fact that they were often attached to pantomimes and afterpieces (and in the case of *The Critic*, the sea-fight is attached not to a tragedy, but to an afterpiece, a sort of double in-joke), they were not played for laughs, and there was a high bar for realism and detail.[29] Allen points out that the theatre reviews of the day treated the sea-fight seriously, and it certainly is the case that the production values of the spectacle were consistent with other, similar displays.[30] Since the sea-fight would have taken place not on the forestage—that liminal space where winks and asides could drive a metatheatrical satire home—but behind the proscenium line, where the grooves in the stage floor could be used to guide the ships, it is hard to see what would have been overtly parodic in the *naumachia*.

One of the reasons otherwise penetrating scholars have been led to assert that Puff's "magnificence" was an elaborate send-up of naval spectacles is the frustrating lack of detailed accounts of the *naumachia* in question. From *The Critic* itself, we have a mere stage direction:

> *Flourish of drums—trumpets—cannon, &c., &c. Scene changes to the sea—the fleets engage—the musick plays—'Britons strike home.'—Spanish fleet destroyed by fire-ships, &c.—English fleet advances—musick plays 'Rule Britannia.'—The procession of all the English rivers, and their tributaries, with their emblems, &c., begins with Handels water musick—ends with a chorus, to the march in Judas' Maccabaeus.—During this scene, Puff directs and applauds every thing[.]*[31]

That there are satirical elements in this description cannot be denied: the procession of the rivers had already been marked for ridicule, and it is easy to imagine Thomas King's Puff capering about the stage, milking his "direction" for laughs. But the "*fleets engage*" stage direction would have triggered a series of stage effects, and those effects would have had a particular resonance to an audience conditioned to seeing the Royal Navy *always* triumph on the London Stage. A Drury Lane promptbook from 1782, first brought to light by F. W. Bateson, contains further information on the battle-scene, and again suggests that in the matter of the sea-fight nothing unpatriotic was allowed, and no British sailors were ridiculed, much less harmed:

> Whistle & Ring above & below.—A Few Bars of "To Arms"—to shew Scene, then "Britons strike home"—during which the Fleet Fire—1st. Fire Ship P.S. Sails to 1st Spanish Ship O.P. and sinks her. 2nd. Fire Ship Sails to Mid : Spanish Ship She Blows up, after which Spanish Fleet Retreat, and British Fleet advance.[32]

The "flourish of drums" of 1779 either was or very quickly became a very specific metrical pattern: the drum tattoo of "To Arms," a musical signal imported from the Royal Navy and used to indicate impending action. Such martial staccato would have contrasted favorably with the operatic "sliding" of "smooth semibreves, and gargling glib divisions" about which Mrs. Dangle complains in the opening scene of *The Critic*. The drumming gives way to Henry Purcell's "Britons Strike Home," a patriotic song that had drawn waves of nationalistic applause in 1778 and 1779 revivals of *Bonduca*. "Britons Strike Home" serves as the soundtrack for the motion of the ships; it is not implausible that the listening audiences would have silently supplied the familiar verse:

> To arms, to arms! Your ensigns strait display:
> Now, now, now, set the battle in array.
> The oracle for war declares;
> Success depends upon our hearts and spears.[33]

The choreographed victory makes a gesture at realism (the Royal Navy did indeed best the Spanish Armada by means of fire ships), but also provides an abstract of naval conflict; one Spanish ship sinks, another blows up (one presumes by means of De Loutherbourgh's ingenious pyrotechnics), and the British vessels chase the Spaniards from the scene. The effect created here parodies nothing, and is reminiscent of Roland Barthes' classic meditation on professional wrestling:

> The public is completely uninterested in knowing whether the contest is rigged or not, and rightly so; it abandons itself to the primary virtue of the spectacle, which is to abolish all motives and all consequences: what matters is not what it thinks but what it sees.[34]

What viewers of *The Critic* saw, night after night, was Britannia *always* triumphant.

The history of the composition of the play also suggests Sheridan, by necessity, contemplated a shift out of the parodic mode when he scribbled the words "She is gone to throw herself into the sea, to be sure—," thus sending Tilburnia to her clichéd, watery doom. Puff admits that he's shifting genres at the close, noting that he is "blending a little of the masque" with his tragedy.[35] The eighteenth-century actor-singer Michael Kelly's widely repeated account of the writing of the conclusion of *The Critic* provides interpretive signposts:

> Two days previous to the performance of *The Critic*, the last scene was not written; Dr. Ford and Mr. Linley, the joint proprietors, began to get nervous and fidgety, and the actors were absolutely *au désespoir*, especially King, who was not only stage-manager, but had to play Puff.[36]

These circumstances help account for the shift in tone that occurs when the death of Tilburnia is juxtaposed with the signal for patriotic display. Having written himself into a dramaturgical cul-de-sac—his heroine dead, heroic tragedy well and truly mocked—Sheridan faced the challenge of every satirist, from Aristophanes to Tina Fey: how to end the joke? Since one of the running gags in *The Critic* is the actors' destructive revisions of Puff's original script, the tragic material presented onstage in *The Critic* has no arc, no coherence, and thus points to no satisfying ending, even taking into account the low bar of satisfaction associated with burlesque conclusions.[37] Sheridan stalled. Kelly reports that King and Linley locked Sheridan in the green room with "a table, with pens, ink, and paper, a good fire, an armed chair at the table, and two bottles of claret, with a dish of anchovy sandwiches" and refused to release him until he provided *The Critic* with a final scene.[38] Kelly tells this story with relish, and it shows us an attractive Sheridan—disorganized and indolent, perhaps, but also good natured and talented. We are told that "Sheridan took this decided measure in good part; he ate the anchovies, finished the claret, wrote the scene, and laughed heartily at the ingenuity of the contrivance."[39]

"Wrote the scene" suggests that Sheridan crafted something scene-like—situation, dialogue, plot, dénouement. But if we take Kelly's account at face value and it was indeed the final pages of *The Critic* that were lacking, and thus Sheridan was locked into the green room with the script completed only up to Tilburnia's suicide, it is likely that Sheridan ate the anchovies, finished the claret, and wrote *"Flourish of drums,"* knowing that a *naumachia* was an easy way out. He had, in a store-room somewhere in the depths of Drury Lane, an impressive collection of miniature ships outfitted with full white sails and functional cannons. In the scene-shop, there were expansive and expensive canvases, his gifted scene-painter's tempests and grey rolling breakers. Visuals covered, the aural solution was within reach as well. Thumping anthems could be drawn from the Drury Lane repertory, and, as Eric Rump points out, *Judas Maccabeus* had already been performed three times in the spring of 1779, meaning that Drury Lane's musicians could work up their patriotic medley with a minimum of fuss.[40] Given what we know of Sheridan, his work habits, and his patriotism, it is difficult to see how and why this ending is "burlesque" (Clinton-Baddeley),[41] "satirical" (Allen),[42] or "claptrap" (Auburn).[43] It was an ending, hit upon under comfortable duress, formed from visual and aural bits of the Drury Lane repertory, and suitable for a play composed in a time of war. The *naumachia* provided a dramaturgical "reset" that allowed the audience to accommodate an England that produced both Dangles and Drakes, Puffs and Raleighs.

At the opening of *The Critic* the fleet is invoked but absent, just as it was for Britons in the summer of 1779. With accounts of the naval war sporadic and often contradictory, delivered by dispatch boat from Hardy's storm-beaten flagship or rumored through London thanks to the merchant ships that plied the English Channel and counted the French sails on the horizon, Dangle's newspaper reading reenacts a familiar scene for a certain class of Georgian Londoner. By bringing a material fleet onstage in the last scene of *The Critic*, Sheridan answers with wordless action the wordiness of the static opening scene in which a character, seated, repeats fragments of accounts of a war. De Loutherbourgh's *naumachia*, the descendent of the *Alfred* naval review first put on stage by Garrick in 1773, was the harbinger of a new type of theatre, one where smoke and color and noise would eventually supersede poetry and declamation. As Backs-cheider points out:

> Pyrotechnics give an intense and immediate kind of stimulation and gratification that delivers excitement and relieves boredom. Such effects often "carry" a large part of the fantasy and bear great responsibility for absorbing the spectators' experiencing the imaginary world without continually comparing it to their own lived experience or "reality." At a deeper level they are evidence to the spectators of the author's skill and control, signs that they can "trust" and put themselves in the creator's hands.[44]

At some point, Sheridan had to close the gap between theatre-goers (his paying audience) and patriots. Having set up Dangle as an effete bystander with deca-dent values and poor taste, Sheridan silences him at the end of the play. Dangle has no more lines after the Thames enters, but no stage direction sends him off-stage; he must watch, mute, as the action in the English Channel unfolds. Puff himself, the author who loses control over that which he created, can dance on the margins of the *naumachia*, but he "applauds every thing"—the naval victory being the one thing in *The Spanish Armada* with which he is satisfied. Having shaken the public's trust in the stage throughout *The Critic*, Sheridan' decision to bring out the fleet and strike up the band was the most reassuring gesture he had available, a way to reestablish the bond between theatre and citizenry. As Crane points out, the audience of *The Critic* was "already disposed for patriotism."[45] By bypassing language and emphasizing spectacle, Sheridan is able to side-step the question of how going to the theatre contributes to the war effort. It does not, but nautical spectacles—flags flying, cannons banging, trumpets blaring—sug-gest otherwise.

After Sheridan's death, the accounts of *The Critic's* relationship to Sheridan's theatrical practice take on an historical cast, with *The Critic* acting as the teleo-logical anchor of the Sheridan canon—a play by a playwright looking backward at his completed "Major Works." In his 1825 biography of Sheridan, Thomas Moore draws a bright line between 1779, the year *The Critic* made its debut, and 1780, the year Sheridan was elected to Parliament, and thus demarcates the end of Sheridan's career as a playwright and the beginning of his career as a politician. Moore declares that it was a good thing that after *The Critic*, Sheridan shifted his emphasis in from writing for Drury Lane to stumping for Westminster. After all, as a dramatic writer, "Mr. Sheridan would possibly never had exceeded what he had already done" by 1779. Moore claims that had Sheridan continued to write for the stage, he might have ended up "being left, like Alexander, to sigh for new worlds to vanquish."[46] This stance had been a model for almost two centuries of commentary on Sheridan's career. *The Critic* stands as Sheridan's great statement on dramaturgy and his last legitimate performance as a playwright. John Loftis labels it "Sheridan's final important play."[47] V. C. Clinton Baddeley notes that the play appeared "like a summary, at the end of an era."[48] In the words of Christine S. Wiesenthal, the play is a "final, ringing affirmation" of Sheridan's view of comedy, and thus Sheridan's career as a writer of comedies "ends with a happy blare and a bang."[49] But *The Critic* can be understood not only as the culmination of Sheridan's most productive period as a playwright, but as a pivot point, a moment when Sheridan's artistry captured his complicated and contradictory position as both playwright and manager. *The Critic*'s frame—naval anxiety answered by naval victory—provides a structure of feeling through which we can better understand how, in Georgian London, spectacle and war and patriotism and opposition were always already dancing a high-stakes quadrille.

Notes

1. *The Morning Post*, November 1, 1779, review reprinted in Sheridan, *The Dramatic Works of Richard Brinsley Sheridan*, ed. Cecil Price, 2 vols. (Oxford: Clarendon Press, 1973), 2:476.

2. *The Public Advertiser*, November 1, 1779, quoted in Sheridan, *Dramatic Works*, 478.

3. *The Morning Chronicle*, November 2, 1779, quoted in Sheridan, *Dramatic Works*, 480.

4. *Naumachia*, a Latin term for the massive recreations of naval battles popular in first-century Rome, was usefully redeployed to help delineate Georgian nautical set-pieces by Gillian Russell in her *The Theatres of War: Performance, Politics and Society, 1793–1815* (Oxford: Clarendon Press, 1995). I adopt her sense of term here, applying it to "naval spectacles" such as the one that concludes *The Critic*. In the 1770s, a *naumachia* generally featured model ships, pyrotechnics, and musical accompaniment. At Drury Lane, these effects were supplemented by painted backdrops, canvas "seas," and the occasional transparency. Other theatres pushed the technology further later in the century; Sadler's Wells featured a water tank. Sheridan's engagement with the form did not end with *The Critic*. His 1794 production *The Glorious First of June* was the apotheosis of the Georgian Drury Lane *naumachia*.

5. See Robert W. Jones, "Sheridan and the Theatre of Patriotism: Staging Dissent during the War for America," *Eighteenth-Century Life* 26, no. 1 (2002): 24–45.

6. Paula R. Backscheider, *Spectacular Politics: Theatrical Power and Mass Culture in Early Modern England* (Baltimore: Johns Hopkins University Press, 1993), 237–38.

7. Sheridan, *The Critic*, in *Dramatic Works*, 2:497.

8. David Crane, "Satire and Celebration in *The Critic*," in *Sheridan Studies*, eds. James Morwood and David Crane (Cambridge: Cambridge University Press, 1995), 87.

9. Horace Walpole to Horace Mann (September 5, 1779), in Horace Walpole, *The Yale Edition of Horace Walpole's Correspondence*, ed. W. S. Lewis, 48 vols., New Haven, CT: Yale University Press, 1937–1983, 24:512. Walpole's distrust of the reliability of the newspapers was probably shared by Sheridan, whose Puff fancies himself a naval strategist. When he is not puffing the plays of his friends or writing his own, Puff composes uninformed nautical commentaries: "I have some little matters here to send to the papers, and a few paragraphs to scribble before I go.—Here too are some political memorandums—I see; ay—To take PAUL JONES, and get the INDIAMEN out of the SHANNON—reinforce BYRON—compel the DUTCH to—so!—I must do that in the evening papers, or reserve it for the Morning Herald...." (*The Critic*, in *Dramatic Works*, 2:518). "Byron" is Admiral John "Foul-Weather Jack" Byron, the poet's grandfather.

10. Dangle thus turns to the newspaper with the most extensive theatrical coverage, *The Morning Chronicle*. Mrs. Dangle's response is telling: "Yes, that's your gazette." Price, in his edition of *The Critic*, leaves the word "gazette" un-capitalized and un-italicized, following the typography of the 1781 edition of *The Critic*, but in so doing, he suggests that Mrs. Dangle is speaking generically, with "gazette" as a generic name for a newspaper (cf Samuel Johnson's definition: "a paper of news"). But other editions of *The Critic* (Knight in 1924, Kronenberger in 1957) capitalize the word.

"Yes, that's your *Gazette*" is a plausible reading, as it is likely that some audience members in 1779 heard "gazette" and supplied the capital "G" themselves, thus taking Mrs. Dangle's comment to be particularly cutting; for her husband, *The Morning Chronicle* is his *London Gazette*, the paper of record where one might find official (if not definitive) accounts of the state of the nation.

11. Robert W. Jones points out that Mrs. Dangle's enthusiasm for the war effort, like her husband's obsession with the theatre, is informed by a desire to be fashionable (26).

12. Sheridan, *The Critic*, in *Dramatic Works*, 2:499.

13. "The criticisms have often shaped the perception of Hardy as an over-cautious, incompetent commander, but many such remarks were motivated by blatant factionalism—notably those of his captain of the fleet, Richard Kempenfelt, who sought to advance himself, and of the likes of Thompson and Captain Walsingham of the *Thunderer*, who were trying to ingratiate themselves with Sandwich's rival, Lord George Germain." See *Oxford Dictionary of National Biography*, s.v. "Hardy, Sir Charles, the younger (*bap.* 1717, *d.* 1780," by J. D. Davies, http://oxforddnb.com [accessed September 30, 2011]).

14. Sheridan, *The Critic*, in *Dramatic Works*, 2:549.

15. Peter Knox-Shaw makes the Tiburnia connection to *Venice Preserved* in *Jane Austen and the Enlightenment* (Cambridge: Cambridge University Press, 2004), 56 n201.

16. Sheridan, *The Critic*, in *Dramatic Works*, 2:536.

17. The one exception may be *Eliza*, a Richard Rolt/Thomas Arne opera from 1754 that featured a recreation of the defeat of the Spanish Armada.

18. The ship models were made by the renowned marine artist Dominique Serres and were "complete with all their rigging, masts, and nautical detail." Christopher Baugh, "Philippe de Loutherbourg:

Technology-Driven Entertainment and Spectacle in the Late Eighteenth Century," *Huntington Library Quarterly* 70, no. 2 (June 2007): 251–68.

19. *The London Chronicle*, August 10–12, 1773. Quoted in Ralph G. Allen's "Topical Scenes for Pantomime," *Educational Theatre Journal* 17, no. 4 (December 1965): 290.

20. *Whitehall Evening Post*, October 30, 1779. Quoted in Allen, "Topical Scenes," 292.

21. Eric S. Rump, "Sheridan, Politics, The Navy and the Musical Allusions in the Final Scene of *The Critic*," *Restoration and 18th-Century Theatre Research* 6, no. 2 (Winter 1991): 33.

22. Allen, "Topical Scenes," 292. Both versions were often subtitled *The Humours of the Navy.*

23. Allen, "Topical Scenes," 296.

24. Ralph G. Allen, "Irrational Entertainment in the Age of Reason" in *The Stage and the Page: London's "Whole Show" in the Eighteenth-Century Theatre*, ed. George Winchester Stone, Jr. (Berkeley: University of California Press, 1981), 97–98.

25. V. C. Clinton-Baddeley. *The Burlesque Tradition in the English Theatre after 1660* (London: Methuen & Company LTD, 1952), 77.

26. Ralph G. Allen, "Topical Scenes," 297.

27. Ralph G. Allen, "Topical Scenes," 316–17.

28. Ralph G. Allen, "Topical Scenes," 317.

29. Crane points out that the sea-battle is both the conclusion of *The Spanish Armada* and the conclusion of *The Critic*; thus both plays "become in the end the same play" ("Satire and Celebration," 94).

30. Ralph G. Allen, *The Stage Spectacles of Philip James De Loutherbourg*, PhD diss. (Yale University, 1960), 213. Allen is referring to reviews in *The London Packet*, November 1, 1779; *General Advertiser*, November 1, 1779; *The Lady's Magazine*, November 1779; and *Westminster Magazine*, November 1779. Allen himself is convinced that the sea-fight is intended to be ironic, and seems surprised that contemporary reviewers didn't "get" the joke (210–14).

31. Sheridan, *The Critic*, in *Dramatic Works*, 2:550.

32. F. W. Bateson, "Notes on the Text of Two Sheridan Plays," *The Review of English Studies* 16, no. 63 (July 1940): 316. "O.P." is "opposite prompter" and "P.S." is "prompter side."

33. Francis Beaumont and John Fletcher, *Bonduca: A Tragedy*, adapted by George Colman (London: George Cawthorn, 1796), cf n9, 40, http://books.google.com (accessed March 1, 2011).

34. Roland Barthes, *Mythologies*, trans. Jonathan Cape (New York: Farrar, Strauss, and Giroux, 1972), 15.

35. Sheridan, *The Critic*, in *Dramatic Works*, 2:549.

36. Michael Kelly, *Reminiscences of Michael Kelly of the King's Theatre and Theatre Royal Drury Lane*, ed. T. E. Hook, 2 vols. (London: Henry Colburn, 1826), 2:308.

37. The default ending of such productions was a dance (Buckingham's *Rehearsal*, John Gay's *What D'Ye Call It*), but Henry Fielding's *Tom Thumb* contained seven murders and a suicide in its final moments.

38. Kelly, *Reminiscences*, 2:309. One presumes there was a chamber-pot as well.

39. Ibid, 2:308–9.

40. Rump, "Sheridan, Politics," 33.

41. Clinton-Baddeley, *The Burlesque Tradition* 77.

42. Allen, 297.

43. Mark S. Auburn, "Richard Brinsley Sheridan." In *Restoration and Eighteenth Century Dramatists: Third Series*, edited by Paula R. Backscheider. *Dictionary of Literary Biography*. Vol. 89. Detroit: Gale Research, 1989, 316–17.

44. Backscheider, *Spectacular Politics*, 237–38. Backscheider is actually using "pyrotechnics" here as an analogy for feats of authorly technique. But, in Sheridan's case, it is literal pyrotechnics: the cannons on the ship models did indeed fire.

45. Crane, "Satire and Celebration," 95.

46. Thomas Moore, *Memoirs of the Life of the Right Honourable Richard Brinsley Sheridan*, 5th ed., 2 vols. (London: Longman, Rees, Orme, Brown, and Green, 1826. Reprint, New York: Greenwood Press, 1968), 1:280.

47. John Loftis, *Sheridan and the Drama of Georgian England* (Cambridge, MA: Harvard University Press, 1977), 103.

48. Clinton-Baddeley, *Burlesque Tradition*, 79.

49. Christine S. Wiesenthal, "Representation and Experimentation in the Major Comedies of Richard Brinsley Sheridan," *Eighteenth-Century Studies* 25, no. 3 (Spring, 1992): 328–29.

8

THE LEES AND THE SHERIDANS

An Unexamined Connection

Steven Gores

THE CAREERS OF Thomas and Richard Brinsley Sheridan are
well known, as are the Sheridan family's ties to the Linley family, to David Garrick,
and to the Kembles and the Siddonses. One relation that has gone unnoticed is the
link between the Sheridans and the Lees. In fact, both Thomas and Richard—as
well as various other Sheridans—interacted with members of the Lee family on an
increasingly familiar level. The Lee-Sheridan connection was multigenerational,
and spanned over fifty years, from 1751 to 1807. This connection proved ben-
eficial to both families on personal and professional levels. Establishing Richard's
continuing involvement in this family connection should prove a corrective to
commonplace depictions of him as having left Bath and family concerns behind
as he increasingly became absorbed in politics and Parliamentary power struggles.
In fact, his continuing acknowledgment of the Lees demonstrates that he was very
much embedded in what might be called the Lee-Sheridan-Linley family alliance.

There is an obvious disparity in the degrees to which the Lees and the Sheridans are remembered in literary and theatrical history. The story of Richard Brinsley Sheridan's success as a playwright and theatre manager-owner has been told
by scholars and writers as diverse as Thomas Moore, Margaret Oliphant, Oscar
Sherwin, Madeleine Bingham, and Fintan O'Toole. Richard's father, Thomas, has
also been featured in accounts of his son's life, of course, but he has also been the
subject of some scholarly attention in his own right, most notably in Esther Sheldon's *Thomas Sheridan of Smock-Alley*.[1] In contrast, though the Lees also played a
significant role in theatrical and literary developments of the late eighteenth and
early nineteenth centuries, they have received scant attention. John Lee remains
nearly unrecognized for his accomplishments as an actor, author, and provincial

stage manager. His daughters Sophia and Harriet are better remembered by literary historians, but they, too, have been largely left out of the canon of eighteenth-century and Romantic-era literature.

John Lee and his wife Anna were the first Lees to establish a connection with the Sheridan family. Both were actors who broke in at the Richmond theatre in the 1740s, then moved on to Drury Lane and Covent Garden, with stints at Smock Alley; John was also, from 1752 to 1756, the pioneering theatre manager at Edinburgh's Canongate theatre, and he later managed twice at Bath. He was a good friend of Charles Macklin, and an inveterate rival of David Garrick.[2] Of John and Anna's five children, Sophia (1750–1824) and Harriet (1757–1851) are by far the most well known: the two of them wrote popular novels, plays, and an influential short story collection. Among their friends they counted Hester Lynch Thrale Piozzi, Sarah Siddons, the Linleys, and the painter Sir Thomas Lawrence. Unfortunately, Harriet is perhaps best known by scholars of Romanticism for the offer of marriage she received from William Godwin.

The history of the Lee-Sheridan family alliance begins in 1751, when Thomas Sheridan hired Anna Lee to act at his Smock Alley theatre in Dublin. Promised lead roles, she was relegated to the shadows by the surprise success of Peg Woffington.[3] Meanwhile, constrained by contract to Garrick, John Lee was forced to stay for the season at Drury Lane. It must have been difficult for Anna to be in Dublin alone—she had a one-year-old in tow, and she was most likely in Ireland for the first time. On Anna's benefit night in May, John travelled to Dublin to act Romeo to Anna's Juliet, but their first appearance together at Smock Alley went virtually unnoticed. John Lee surely resented the way Thomas Sheridan had treated his wife, but he was eager to move on to Edinburgh, where he had agreed to take over management of the Canongate theatre.

Despite any lingering resentments, the Lees were back at Smock Alley four years later: John had negotiated a complicated contract with Thomas Sheridan that guaranteed him and Anna a sum of £400, plus more if they appeared in certain roles during the season. Sheridan's letters to John Lee also offer the possibility of John replacing Sheridan as Smock Alley manager so that the latter could retire.[4] Unfortunately for the Lees, Thomas Sheridan acted in his own best interest—he did not schedule the plays that would have benefitted the Lees, and he retreated from giving up Smock Alley to John. Near the end of the season, a pamphlet war broke out, with Lee publishing *Letters from Mr. Lee to Mr. Sheridan* in an attempt to expose Sheridan's double-dealing. John and Anna left for Covent Garden in the fall of 1757, with no further satisfaction from Thomas Sheridan.[5]

Safe to say, it was not an amicable parting between the two families, but, based on later events, there must still have been some basis for friendship that persisted in spite of the men's public quarrel. It is tempting to speculate that Anna Lee and Frances Sheridan had bonded—if not over the theatre, over their children. By the time of their second engagement in Dublin, the Lees had four children, three of whom are known—Sophia, Charlotte, and John Alexander; the Sheridans had three children—Charles, Richard, and Alicia, or "Lissy," as she was called. The eldest two—Sophia and Charles—were the same age, and Richard was just a year behind them. It is tempting—if anachronistic—to imagine little toddler Sophia Lee having a playdate with Charles and Richard Sheridan, while their doting but exhausted mothers look on and perhaps have time to laugh at the excesses of their husbands. While this imaginary scene is undoubtedly too contemporary to hold true, it remains possible that the similarity of their situations drew Anna Lee and Frances Sheridan together.

However, if the ladies were friends, they were not destined to meet again. When the Lees and the Sheridans next crossed paths, thirteen years later (1770), Thomas's wife Frances had already been dead for four years.[6] And when, in September of 1770, Thomas Sheridan travelled to the Lees's home base of Bath, his arrival there coincided with the Anna's death.[7] Thomas' arrival on the scene spotlighted a reversal in the families fortunes: whereas he had lost his theatre and his wife, and had been forced to flee to France to escape prosecution for debt, John Lee had finally achieved some financial and family stability since accepting the managership of Bath's Theatre Royal in 1768.[8] Anna's death surely offered an opportunity for Thomas Sheridan to condole with John and renew their acquaintance on a different footing.

It is probable that the path to reconciliation between the two men was also paved by Richard Brinsley Sheridan's courtship of the singer Elizabeth Linley, a Bath native. The Sheridan-Linley courtship is one of the most fascinating parts of Richard Brinsley Sheridan's life, and it has been described, discussed, and analyzed intensively by all of his biographers.[9] Nonetheless, all accounts leave out a peripheral, yet important detail: this love affair very likely brought Richard Sheridan not only closer to the Linleys, but also to the Lees. Sophia Lee was a favorite of Elizabeth Linley's mother, Mary (1729–1820), and Sophia was a frequent presence in the Linley household.[10] It is probable that Sophia and Richard met there for the first time as teenagers, if not at Bath's Theatre Royal, where John Lee was manager. A further connection between the Lees and Sheridans was likely founded through John Palmer, the owner of the Theatre Royal. Years later, Palmer became an intermediary between Sophia and Richard when the latter became manager-owner at Drury Lane, so it also seems likely that at this time both generations of Lees and Sheridans socialized at the Palmer household, which was known as a meeting place for theatrical and literary visitors to Bath.[11]

In any case, after the Sheridan-Linley courtship, evidence of a growing connection between the Lees and the Sheridans is easy to find. In April of 1773, Sophia wrote an "Epithalalium" to celebrate the marriage of Richard Sheridan and Elizabeth Linley.[12] In it, she praises Richard's sacrifices for Elizabeth:

> Long, Oh, long, may he receive,
> All the transports love can give;
> While conscious worth, which soothed his care,
> And shed a ray of peace,
> O'er the wan visage of Despair,
> Will give the bliss increase.
> And those, sweet Maid, to whom great Heav'n,
> The crown of virtue thus has giv'n,
> In its full light the wondrous blessing see,
> "And live for him alone who more than died for thee."

It would be pretty to imagine the Lees, Linleys and Sheridans celebrating this marriage together, but the reality was far different. Some time after Anna's death in 1770, John Lee abandoned his position as manager of the Bath Theatre Royal and left for London, where he fell into debt.[13] From July 1772 to July 1774, he and his children lived in prison; in March of 1774 his only son, John Alexander, died. John Lee was finally freed from King's Bench prison only through the Insolvency Act passed by Parliament. He and his daughters had fallen out of the circle of theatrical and artistic friends they had become accustomed to in Bath.[14]

Though others may have attempted to help the Lees as well, Richard Sheridan's effort—whether on his own impetus or his wife's—is well documented. In 1775, Richard tapped John Lee to play the comic Irish character Sir Lucius O'Trigger in his new play, *The Rivals*. This choice seems inexplicable if viewed only through the theatrical lens: Sheridan, a theatre aficionado, certainly knew that John Lee specialized in tragic roles, and that Lee had never tried to portray a stage Irishman. Furthermore, the Irish-born Richard Sheridan also knew several actors who had made their careers portraying stage Irish. The only way to rationalize his choice is by invoking the Lee-Sheridan family alliance. Sheridan wrote this play with specific actors in mind, so why did he cast Lee as a comic Irishman? He knew that Lee needed help to get back on his feet, no matter how unsuitable the role. Unfortunately, Sir Lucius O'Trigger was beyond John Lee's abilities, and his poor performance is one reason why *The Rivals* initially failed to please audiences.[15]

The Lee-Sheridan connection was next developed through a third party— the actress Sarah Siddons. When John Lee and his daughters returned to Bath in the aftermath of his O'Trigger debacle, he found work at the Theatre Royal. There he was united in starring roles with Siddons, who had, like Lee, come to the provinces to redeem her reputation after an inauspicious start in London. In 1779 they played Beatrice and Benedick in *Much Ado about Nothing*, Macbeth and Lady Macbeth, Pierre and Isabella in *Venice Preserved*, and Shylock and Portia in *The Merchant of Venice*, among other paired roles.[16] Meanwhile, in London, Richard Sheridan had already used his success as a playwright to leverage himself into the position of part-owner and stage manager of Drury Lane theatre.[17] Thomas Sheridan saw Siddons performing in Bath and wrote very positively about her to his son Richard, who soon recruited her to return to the London stage. In her second attempt at the London market, she was a complete success and was arguably the greatest star of the late eighteenth-century stage. While she was in Bath, she numbered the Lee sisters among her friends, and she was always grateful for the support she received from the community at large there. As far as the Sheridans are concerned, it is likely that they might have been glad—at some points—to distance themselves from the Lees, but professional ties and personal connections with the Lees through Siddons and others continued to multiply for them, especially in Bath.

Just as the Sheridan family seemed poised to leave the Lees behind in fame and success, the Lee family's theatrical reputation was redeemed, not by John, but by his daughter Sophia. While in prison with her father, she wrote a play manuscript that became the greatest comic hit of 1780. For many years afterwards, Sophia Lee was known as the celebrated author of *The Chapter of Accidents*.[18] The success of this play allowed her to truly re-establish the Lee family in Bath, where in January of 1781 she and her sisters Charlotte, Harriet, and Anne opened a school for girls called Belvedere School.[19] Sophia's success permitted the Lees to return to equal status in Bath with the Linleys and the Palmers. Sophia "was Mrs. Palmer's most intimate friend," so it is likely that she was often at the Palmer household, where frequent visitors included actors such as Dimond, Siddons, Blisset, and Murray, and writers and managers such as Richard Sheridan, George Colman, Richard Cumberland, and Thomas Holcroft.[20] During the early 1780s, even the adolescent Robert Southey visited the Palmers in the company of his aunt.[21]

Unfortunately, John Lee did not have long to enjoy his daughter's success or the family security that she had made possible. He became ill in late 1780, and in 1781 died, according to the *Bath Chronicle*, of a "mortification of the bowels." He left behind him not only Sophia, age thirty-one, and Harriet, age twenty-four, but also their siblings Charlotte (age unknown), Anne, probably age twenty-two, and George, age twenty.[22] Like his fellow patriarch Thomas Sheridan, he had a reputation for being cantankerous and arrogant on occasion, but he was well known in Bath, and his children were liked—it is easy to imagine that his death acted as a catalyst to assure the Lee siblings of a place in the Palmer-Linley-Sheridan network of friends and associates.

Perhaps spurred by her first theatrical success with *The Chapter of Accidents*, Sophia Lee began to market a new work in 1781 that would bring her into close contact with the Sheridans and the Linleys. Thomas Sheridan's deceased wife, Frances, had been an author in her own right—one of her best-known efforts was the oriental tale *Nourjahad*, originally published posthumously in 1767. Sophia, aiming to create a musical adaptation of *Nourjahad* for the stage, wrote to Thomas to approve her project. In her letter, she announces that she is depending upon Mr. Linley for the music accompanying her libretto, and—for undisclosed reasons—she asks that her authorship remain anonymous.[23] She also explains that she had actually started work on adapting *Nourjahad* before *Chapter of Accidents* was accepted for the stage, and that she had been forced to put it aside to focus on finishing *Chapter*. In choosing *Nourjahad* as her first literary effort, Sophia Lee may simply have taken a liking to the Oriental material, or she may have chosen it deliberately as an homage to a woman whom she admired.

For unknown reasons, Sophia's adaptation of Frances Sheridan's story, titled *The Illusion, or the Trance of Nourjahad*, was put aside again. It did not appear on the London stage until 1813, and even then it was not credited to Sophia Lee.[24] The reasons for this lengthy delay and the continued withholding of Sophia Lee's authorship—well after Thomas Sheridan was dead and Richard had for years been absent from the theatre world—remain mysterious. What stands out clearly is Sophia's desire to honor Frances Sheridan by bringing *Nourjahad* to the stage, a gesture that surely reinforced her connection to the Sheridan family.

As Sophia's literary star continued to rise, she used her fame to honor family friends, including Richard Sheridan. *The Recess*, a historical novel published in three volumes over the period 1783–1785, was Lee's second critical and popular success. She dedicated the book to Sir John Elliott, the physician who attended her mother, brother, and father in their final illnesses. As a follow-up to *The Recess*,

Sophia published in 1787 a long poem entitled *A Hermit's Tale*, which seems to have had at least a touch of Sheridan's hand: in a letter to her publishers, Cadell and Davies, she says that she is coming to London to "obtain from Mr. Sheridan a copy the margin of which (he told me) he had noted."[25] Lee dedicated the poem to him, acknowledging her "grateful sense of the distinction your praise has given to those [talents] you were pleased to find in me."[26] *A Hermit's Tale* was popular enough to go to a second edition in 1787, and it was immediately pirated in Dublin for the Irish audience. While there are no other records of Richard Sheridan and Sophia Lee working together in this way, this example shows how close the families had become, both personally and professionally.

When the Lee sisters returned to writing for the stage, they naturally chose to patronize Sheridan's Drury Lane Theatre. In November of 1787, Harriet's first comedy, *The New Peerage*, appeared at Drury Lane. It featured audience favorites Tom King and Elizabeth Farren, and Mr. Linley provided the music. When it was printed, Harriet dedicated it to King, and the prologue was contributed by Richard Cumberland, a frequent visitor to the Palmer's house in Bath. While not a great hit like *The Chapter of Accidents*, *The New Peerage* had a respectable run of nine performances and was also performed at the Lees' home theatre in Bath, John Palmer's Theatre Royal.[27] Harriet's first dramatic effort was clearly "taken care of" by a network of family friends—especially John Palmer, Thomas Linley, and Richard Sheridan.

The Lee sisters did not successfully use their theatrical connections again for nearly a decade, but when they did, they again sought the aid of Richard Sheridan.[28] In 1795, Richard accepted Sophia's tragedy *Almeyda; Queen of Granada* for production at Drury Lane, surely because of their personal connection but also because Sophia wrote it specifically as a vehicle for Drury Lane's resident female star, Sarah Siddons. Since Sarah Siddons' two-year residence at the Bath Theatre Royal, she and the Lee sisters had become good friends. Despite all her personal connections at Drury Lane, Sophia was unable to get *Almeyda* staged until late in the season, in April of 1796: Sheridan had a large backlog of playwrights to whom he had made promises, and he was certainly too busy with his parliamentary career to pay much attention to the theatre.[29] Unfortunately, *Almeyda* ran for only five nights and was never seen again on the stage, though both eighteenth-century and modern critics have praised it.[30] Neither Harriet nor Sophia had another play staged until 1807, when Sophia saw her comedy *The Assignation* once again play at Drury Lane.

Offstage, personal connections between the Lees and the Sheridans deepened during the late 1780s, as the Lees were introduced to Richard's youngest sister, Betsy. Though she was nearly Harriet's age, she had apparently little memory of or contact with the Lee sisters until she came to live in Bath during the mid-1780s. By May of 1789, while staying in Richard's London home, she writes casually to her sister Alicia that they had Miss Lee (Sophia), Mr. and Mrs. Linley, and John Philip Kemble to dinner. Newly married to Henry LeFanu, Betsy reports that her husband is "deeply engaged reading [Sophia's novel] *The Recess*."[31] Once again in Bath for Christmas 1789, Betsy invites Mr. Linley and both Sophia and Harriet to dinner; in January, she tells Alicia that she will pass her compliments on to Sophia.

The Lee-Sheridan family alliance was reinforced in 1793, when Richard Sheridan's close friend and brother-in-law Richard Tickell died suddenly, leaving three orphaned children in Sheridan's care. In fact, Tickell's only daughter, Elisabeth or "Betty," had been living in the Sheridan household ever since Mary (Linley) Tickell's death in 1787. Then Elizabeth Sheridan—who had been devoted to her young nephews and niece—died in 1792, and different plans had to be made for their care and future.[32] Tickell's daughter, Betty, was placed at Belvedere, the Lee sisters' school for girls in Bath. This was perhaps an obvious choice, given not only the friendship—dating back to childhood—between Richard and the Lee sisters, but also given Sophia's close friendship with Mary Linley, the girl's grandmother.[33] Elizabeth Linley Sheridan treasured Betty as a reminder of her beloved sister; when Elizabeth was on her death bed at Bristol Hot Wells, she called on her family in Bath to bring not only her son Tom to her, but also Betty. Though Betty was only a niece through marriage to Richard Brinsley Sheridan, she was treated as a daughter by his dead wife, and she was the daughter of his great friend Richard Tickell—surely Sheridan was called upon, at least, to endorse the Lee sisters as her educators and caregivers. Installing Betty Tickell at Belvedere School was probably viewed by the Sheridans and Linleys as keeping her inside the family circle.[34]

Also, if family ties weren't enough to dictate Betty's residence at Belvedere, the school itself had become the pre-eminent girls' school in Bath. It was a place where girls were sent to prepare themselves to enter the marriage market, a school whose theatrical and dance performances were attended by elite audiences. This was due in part, at least, to the fame and literary reputation of Sophia and Harriet Lee. Belvedere's enrollment was always completely full: "application had to be made some time before for the admission of pupils; . . . they might double the number [of girls], if they had accommodation."[35] It is no surprise that six years later, in 1799, the Drury Lane star Siddons also placed her daughter, Cecilia, at Belvedere.

During her stay at Belvedere, Betty Tickell became Sophia's special charge, and their friendship lasted well beyond her years at Belvedere School. In September of 1798, Betty Tickell was still in Sophia's care—the poet Anna Seward met the two of them taking the waters at Matlock Baths in Derbyshire.[36] In May of 1799, Mrs. Piozzi reports that Sophia Lee is in London escorting "a lovely little Girl of her own bringing up: an Orphan Daughter of Tickell the Wit."[37] As Mrs. Piozzi makes clear a few lines later, Sophia was in charge not only of "bringing up" Sheridan's niece, but of bringing her out on the marriage market. Sophia Lee was, in fact, acting as surrogate mother for Betty, showing how integrated the Sheridan, Lee, and Linley families had become.

In 1800, Sophia also was drawn into the business of Jane Linley's courtship by her friend, the matriarch Mary Linley. Jane was Richard Sheridan's sister-in-law and the youngest of the Linley siblings. After all her experience with the older daughters, Mary Linley was still—as much as possible—attempting to control Jane's choice of suitor and the terms of their marriage. In a letter to Jane, she claims to have "consulted my friend Miss Lee" and to have come up with a plan regarding a financial settlement. Both Jane and her suitor, Charles Ward, doubted that Mary's plan had been shared with anyone, so they wrote to Sophia, who confirmed their doubt, writing in return that "Mr. Ward . . . was in the right to be incredulous."[38] Sophia's position in this matter shows her importance to the Linley family: by both generations, she is called upon as a reliable advisor in the most intimate family negotiations. Perhaps in part thanks to Sophia Lee's honesty, Jane Linley and Charles Ward were married in spite of Mary Linley's interference. Still, Jane and her new husband were frustrated in one regard: they had wished for her niece, Betty Tickell, to come and live with them as they set up their new household. At that, Mary Linley put down her foot—Betty was to stay at Belvedere School, which was only a short walk from her own Bath residence. Sophia and Mary Linley's friendship persisted, probably because of Sophia's long-term intimacy with Mary, and her acceptance of her friend's faults.[39]

Despite the familial ties that brought Richard Sheridan and the Lee sisters together, there can be no denying that his parliamentary career and increasingly dissolute behavior distanced him from his old friends and even closer relations. Even the Linleys were distressed by his alienation and ill-treatment of them, as reflected in a series of letters held in the British Library. In one dated April 1793, William Linley complains about the family members being unpaid for their work at Drury Lane: "My sister is almost left destitute, both in respect to money and the necessaries of life. How should it be otherwise when the last five months we have scarcely received a shilling from the theatre? My mother [Mary, Sophia's friend] has good spirits, else, I believe, she would not be alive."[40] Under these circumstances, it is easy to credit Clementina Black's suggestion that the Lees received Betty Tickell as a non-paying boarder at Belvedere: even if they expected payment for taking on Betty, it is highly unlikely that the Linleys would have been able to pay or that Richard Brinsley Sheridan would have paid attention to their request.

Sheridan's financial delinquency ultimately resulted in a huge change at Drury Lane, which undoubtedly affected the Lees, as well. In 1802, after years of being unpaid for months on end and constantly threatening to quit, the two greatest tragedians of the eighteenth-century English stage—John Philip Kemble and his sister Sarah Siddons—left Drury Lane for Covent Garden, where Kemble assumed duties as manager. The long-term presence of the Linleys at Drury Lane had ended earlier: Mr. Linley—the former music director at Drury Lane—had died in 1795, while his wife, Mary, had retired as Drury Lane's wardrobe mistress. This was the effective end of the working relationship that Sheridan had continued not only with his two stars, but also with the Linley clan, the Lees, and most of his Bath connections.

However, despite Richard Sheridan's inattention to literary, theatrical, and family business, the Lees tried to maintain their old connections to Drury Lane. In a letter dated Christmas 1806, Sophia informs Betty—now known as "Eliza" Tickell—of her business in the city connected to the staging of her new play, *The Assignation*, at Drury Lane.[41] Amid the excitement of viewing preliminary readings of the play, Sophia reports that Eliza's grandmother, Mary Linley, often accompanies her, and that they have visited with Mr. Kemble and the painter, Thomas Lawrence. Unfortunately for Sophia Lee, the excitement of having a new play on the stage lasted less than one performance: due to what the audience perceived to be a satiric attack on Lord Admiral Nelson—who had become an icon since his death at Trafalgar in 1805—*The Assignation* was cried down and was never performed again.[42] This marks the end of the Lees' professional connection to Drury Lane.

There is no record of Sheridan's reaction to the disastrous production of *The Assignation*, most likely because his own personal and political affairs were in such disorder. There is, however, a connection of sorts: both disasters were the result of politics. Sophia Lee had, perhaps inadvertently, hit a nerve with her portrayal of the naval hero "Admiral Baltick," understood by audiences as Lord Nelson; Sheridan had reached the limits of public tolerance for his dissolute behavior and his association with increasingly unpopular Whig party policies, in spite of his attempts to distance himself from them. Ironically for Sheridan, Sophia's comic naval character gave offense on the Drury Lane stage during the year in which Sheridan was serving as Secretary of the Navy. While Sophia Lee could simply bow out of the theatrical business and, at age of 57, could retreat to a private life of lady-like gentility, for Sheridan everything depended on keeping his position as a Member of Parliament. He was heavily in debt, and could only remain safe from his creditors through the exercise of parliamentary privilege. He was locked into the political life—there was no retreating from it.[43]

The story of Sheridan's final seven years has been recited endlessly as a lesson in total collapse. Briefly, in 1809 Drury Lane burned down and Sheridan lost control of the theatre's management. In 1812 he was voted out of Parliament, and lived out the rest of his life in abject poverty, constantly threatened by imprisonment for debt. In fact, in 1813 he was briefly imprisoned for debt, like Sophia's father had been years ago—it was a humiliation that his own father, Thomas Sheridan, though similarly plagued with debts, had managed to avoid in his time. There is no record of contact between Richard Sheridan and the Lees until his death in 1816. Narratives of his final years focus almost myopically on his status as a living lesson in how the mighty can fall and how it is unwise to depend upon the gratitude and friendship of courtiers and princes.[44]

Sophia and Harriet Lee, who never mixed with courtiers and princes, succeeded in living quietly and with dignity into old age. They sold Belvedere School to a friend, the Rev. Dr. Thomas Broadhurst and his wife; they moved to Clifton, a fashionable suburb of Bath's big-city neighbor, Bristol; they kept busy with their wide circle of friends and with the burgeoning family of their brother, George Augustus Lee. They were wealthy, thanks not only to their literary endeavors and their girls' school, but also due to investments they had made. Whereas Sophia retreated from the literary world, Harriet continued to essay the theatre as late as 1825, when her play *The Mysterious Stranger* was produced at Covent Garden, to positive reviews but an indifferent audience.[45] Sophia passed away in 1824, having outlived her near-contemporary Richard Sheridan by eight years, and Harriet lived to see her ninety-third year, 1850.

In contrast to Thomas and Richard Sheridan, or even John Lee, the Lee sisters' personalities have not been well recorded or discussed. While all three of the aforementioned "patriarchs" have been dissected psychologically, the Lee sisters remain mysterious—yet, they were consistently included in a variety of social circles, and they remained "in the mix" with younger generations. The early cataloguer of the Gothic, Montague Summers, reports that many of his contacts have fond memories of Harriet: "I have known more than one person who was acquainted with and had very distinct memories of the old lady, a brilliant conversationalist to the last, with a fund of interesting anecdotes."[46] Similarly, friends of the artist Sir Thomas Lawrence could not understand his devotion to the much older Lee sisters, especially Sophia. The Lee sisters' plays, novels, and their story collection called *The Canterbury Tales* had a long life in the nineteenth century, and earned them readers of the Romantic generation, including Lord Byron and Mary Shelley. Reclaiming the Lees as part of a Bath-based nexus of theatrical and literary connections makes it clear why—even in old age—they appealed to a broad range of people who were often much younger than themselves.

The Lees were an important part of the Bath milieu out of which the Sheridans and the Linleys emerged. It is also clear that, as much as they benefitted professionally from their connections to both families, the Lees also served as stalwart family friends over five decades. Restoring them to their place in the lives of the Sheridans, Linleys, and Siddonses broadens and enriches existing accounts of the Sheridan era at Drury Lane, and, in general, of literary culture in the second half of the eighteenth century.

For Richard Brinsley Sheridan, the Lee sisters might be seen—retrospectively, of course—as a bellwether in his life and career. They represent the kind of personal-professional collaborative network that marked his earlier life as poet, playwright, and theatre impresario. The literary fruits of that Bath-based network include, on his side, *The Rivals*, *The Duenna*, and *School for Scandal*; on the Lee side, *The Chapter of Accidents*, *A Hermit's Tale*, *The Trances of Nourjahad*, *The New Peerage*, *Almeyda*, and *The Assignation*. Of these, the Lees and the Sheridans were actively involved together in producing *The Rivals*, *A Hermit's Tale*, *The Trances of Nourjahad*, and *The New Peerage*. As the Lees and the Linleys slowly faded from Richard Sheridan's life, he traded the Bath network for one based on Parliament and the Royal Court, but he long retained an allegiance to his Bath-based friends and family. The Linleys have always been recognized as a part of his early success; now the Lees may be added to that picture.

Notes

1. Esther K. Sheldon, *Thomas Sheridan of Smock-Alley, recording his life as actor and theater manager in both Dublin and London, and including a Smock-Alley calendar for the years of his management* (Princeton, NJ: Princeton University Press, 1967).

2. A letter from Lee to Macklin testifies to the closeness of their connection, as Lee apologizes most profoundly for not yet having the money to pay a debt he owes to Macklin. John Lee, Letter to Charles Macklin, June 15, 1752. MS. Harvard Theatre Collection, Cambridge, MA.

3. Woffington was, of course, a very experienced and successful actress on the London stage, but she was not part of Thomas Sheridan's plans for the Smock Alley season: it was a surprise when she suddenly appeared in Dublin and made herself available. See Sheldon, *Thomas Sheridan*, 172–73.

4. While this is not the place to argue John Lee's case as an eminent but forgotten actor, it is interesting that Madeleine Bingham notes how "Under Garrick's management [at Drury Lane] actors like Spranger Barry, Charles Macklin and John Lee could demand up to one-third of the night's receipts above £80" (Madeline Bingham, *Sheridan: The Track of a Comet* [New York: St. Martin's, 1972], 137).

5. For more on Thomas Sheridan's ambitions, difficulties, and machinations as Smock Alley manager, see Sheldon's *Thomas Sheridan*, and for his treatment of the Lees, see Bingham, *Sheridan*, especially 224–27.

6. It is possible that the Lees and Sheridans met again sometime during the period 1757–1759, when both John Lee and Thomas Sheridan acted sporadically in Jonathan Rich's Covent Garden company. It was at this time—in 1758—that Frances Sheridan gave birth in London to her fourth child, Elizabeth (Betsy), while in 1757 Anna Sophia Lee gave birth to Harriet, possibly in London.

7. Anna Lee died on Sept. 3, 1770, in London. In the introduction to her edition of Sophia Lee's *The Recess or, A Tale of Other Times* (Lexington: University of Kentucky Press, 2000), ed. April Alliston asserts that Anna Lee lived for six more years (xxvi), but I have been unable to confirm that claim.

8. For more on the Bath theatre, see Arnold Hare and Kathleen Barker, *Theatre Royal Bath: A Calendar of Performances at the Orchard Street Theatre, 1750–1805* (Bath: Kingsmead, 1977). Strangely, this account almost entirely erases John Lee's role in the Bath theatre management.

9. In this work, see Jack E. DeRochi, "The Many Lives of Richard Brinsley Sheridan," chap. 1, which examines at length four distinctive biographical treatments of Richard's elopement with Elizabeth (Eliza) Linley.

10. See Clementina Black, *The Linleys of Bath* (London: Martin Secker, 1926). Many Sheridan biographers treat Mary Johnson Linley as a vulgar and money-grubbing matriarch, effectively embracing Samuel Foote's satiric send-up of her as a bawd named "Mrs. Linnet" in his 1771 play *The Maid of Bath*. This portrayal cleanses Elizabeth and Thomas Linley of any taint from Elizabeth's early engagement to the wealthy but elderly Walter Long, but it seems simplistic. A more balanced portrayal of Mary Johnson Linley is offered by Margot Bor and Lamond Clelland, *Still the Lark: A Biography of Elizabeth Linley*, (London: Merlin, 1962).

11. For more on John Palmer, who later became influential in developing the postal service, see Charles R. Clear, *John Palmer of Bath, Mail Coach Pioneer* (Poole: Blandford Press, 1955).

12. This unpublished manuscript poem is held by descendants of the Lees. The names of the newly married couple have been left blank, so it is impossible to be definitive, but the date of the poem and the family background makes the context clear.

13. Charles R. Clear asserts that Lee was removed from management by John Palmer because Lee's excessive strictness with his actors resulted in a strike. This is possible, of course, but it seems unlikely, given the intimacy between the Palmers and Lees. Lee's last documented performance at the Bath Theatre Royal was on January 28, 1771, when he played King Lear for his benefit night. Alliston claims that Lee left the Bath theatre management under a cloud because he had schemed to buy land in Bath and build his own theatre (Lee, *The Recess*, xxvi).

14. It is still technically possible that the Lee siblings may have attended the wedding festivities, since they were not bound to stay in the prison with their father—they could come and go freely, within

certain schedule restrictions. Richard Sheridan and Elizabeth Linley were married in London, where she had come to perform in the Lenten Oratorios.

15. In fact, John Lee's failure as O'Trigger is the only way in which the Lees have figured in the biographical treatment of Sheridan. Scapegoating John Lee has been the generally accepted practice in Sheridan biographies, as exhibited by Kenelm Foss, who describes Lee being hit by a rotten apple hurled by "disgruntled Hibernians" and claims that Lee then responded by addressing the audience personally in an Irish brogue, asking "'Is it me or the matter?'" (Kenelm Foss, *Here Lies Richard Brinsley Sheridan* [New York: E. P. Dutton, 1940], 112). Even James Lynch cites John Lee's "poor acting" as a general example of how faulty performance can damn an excellent play (James J. Lynch, *Box, Pit, and Gallery: Stage and Society in Johnson's London* [New York: Russell & Russell, 1953], 156). More equitably, Joseph Cove gives four reasons for the audience's negative reaction to *The Rivals*: "the play was far too long; . . . Lee failed hopelessly as Sir Lucius; . . . Shuter, who played Sir Anthony Absolute, knew hardly a line of his part; and . . . the character of Sir Lucius was objectionable" (Joseph W. Cove, *Sheridan, His Life and His Theatre* [New York: Morrow, 1948], 46). On the other hand, in his *Retrospections of the Stage* (London: Colburn & Bentley, 1830), John Bernard goes so far as to accuse Sheridan of falsely blaming Lee for the play's initial poor reception. To be fair to Lee, some audiences truly appreciated his acting; writing in 1780, after having seen John Lee and Sarah Siddons in *Venice Preserved*, Frances Burney declared herself enchanted by Lee's performance of Pierre.

16. It is certain that Siddons owed her later London success to her experience at Bath; how much she owed specifically to John Lee is impossible to gauge.

17. In 1776, Richard Sheridan, his father-in-law Thomas Linley, and another partner bought David Garrick's half share in Drury Lane; in 1778, Sheridan bought the remaining half share.

18. Performed first in August 1780 at the Haymarket, the play was published the same year and was in its fourth edition by 1782. It was also translated into French and German editions. In 1796 *The Chapter of Accidents* was included in *Bell's British Theatre*; in 1823 it was part of William Oxberry's New English Drama series (London: W. Simpkin and R. Marshall).

19. It appears that the Lees moved back to Bath from London in 1778, with John patching together an income from directing girls' school theatrical productions, offering private elocution lessons, and acting occasionally in the Bath and Bristol theatres.

20. John Francis Meehan, *More Famous Houses of Bath and District* (Bath: B. & J. F. Meehan, 1906), 73.

21. Ibid., 64.

22. George Augustus Lee is the only member of the Lee family to have no known connection to the Linleys and Sheridans, and to not have attempted any literary or theatrical productions. It is possible that he spent a good deal of time away at school. In his maturity he was an innovator in the milling industry, and he became a very wealthy industrialist.

23. From a letter dated August 25, 1781, held in the Berg Collection, New York Public Library.

24. Nicoll lists *Illusion*'s author as unknown in his "Handlist of Plays, 1800–1850" (Allardyce Nicoll, *Early Nineteenth-Century Drama, A History of English Drama: 1660–1900*, 7 vols. [Cambridge University Press, 1952–1959]). When it first appeared at The Lyceum, it was rumored to have been penned by Lord Byron; over time it has come to be ascribed to Samuel Arnold, manager of

The Lyceum, with music by Michael Kelly. Arnold apparently had some connection to the Lees, for he based his musical drama *Foul Deeds Will Rise* on Harriet's "The Traveller's Tale: Montford" a work derived from *The Canterbury Tales*.

25. Letter dated December 3, 1786, presently held in the Osborn Collection, Yale University Library. Lee asserts that she is coming in person to meet with Sheridan because he is such a poor correspondent.

26. From a copy held by the Newberry Library, Chicago. Sophia Lee, *A Hermit's Tale* (London: T. Cadell, 1787).

27. The published version also went through two 1787 editions. Harriet Lee, *The New Peerage: Or, Our Eyes May Deceive Us* (London: G. G. J. and J. Robinson, 1787).

28. Harriet Lee chose to submit her 1795 gothic drama, *The Mysterious Marriage*, to George Colman's Haymarket theatre instead of Drury Lane, perhaps because her sister's *Almeyda* had already been accepted at the latter. She was unsuccessful in getting the play staged until 1821, but it was published in 1798 to critical approval, with a preface blaming Colman for refusing to produce it.

29. The tale of Sheridan's neglect of theatre-related work has been told many times. He often did not open his mail for weeks, he ignored both bills and bank-notes, and "as for the heap of play manuscripts, John Philip Kemble, one of his managers at Drury Lane, referred to it as a 'funeral pile'" (Fintan O'Toole, *A Traitor's Kiss: The Life of Richard Brinsley Sheridan, 1751–1816*, [New York: Farrar, Straus and Giroux, 1998], 198). It is also worthy of note that, in the 1795–1796 season, Sheridan invested a good deal of money in bringing the Shakespearean forgery *Vortigern* to Drury Lane, which distracted from other new productions and caused a very skeptical attitude in audiences.

30. Thomas Campbell remarks that *Almeyda* "was respectfully received, and even applauded. Nor can I perceive why it should not be more popular than many tragedies that keep possession of the stage" (Thomas Campbell, *The Life of Mrs. Siddons*, 2 vols. [New York: Benjamin Blom, 1972], 269). More recently, Paula Backscheider has called *Almeyda* "a marvelous vehicle for a great actress" (Paula R. Backscheider, *Spectacular Politics: Theatrical Power and Mass Culture in Early Modern England* [Baltimore: Johns Hopkins University Press, 1993], 203).

31. William LeFanu, ed., *Betsy Sheridan's Journal* (New York: Oxford University Press, 1960), 180.

32. Richard Sheridan was further stricken by the death of his wife's infant daughter in 1793. He had taken a house in the village where his departed wife's nursemaid lived, so the baby could have the same care that Elizabeth had as a child. Margaret Oliphant claims that Sheridan had "made a little goddess of [the baby], worshipping her with every baby rite that could be thought of" (in Margaret Oliphant, *Sheridan, English Men of Letters*. ed. John Morley. [New York: Harper and Brothers, 1887], 155). Recent scholarship has made it clear that the baby was not his, but rather the product of Elizabeth's affair with Lord Edward Fitzgerald.

33. Some of Sheridan's early biographers, including John Watkins, assert that Tickell was opposed to his daughter attending Belvedere School; they also claim that Tickell married Sophia Lee after the death of his first wife, Mary (Linley), which is completely wrong. Sheridan's niece, Alicia Lefanu, took pains to show that they had conflated Sophia Lee with a Miss Leigh who became Tickell's second wife. See Alicia LeFanu's *Memoirs of the Life and Writings of Mrs. Frances Sheridan* (London: G. and W. B. Whittaker, 1824).

34. Alliston claims that Sophia Lee literally "adopted" Betty Tickell (Lee, *The Recess*, xxxiii), but I have found no evidence to support that claim.

35. Susan Mein Sibbald, *The Memoirs of Susan Sibbald (1783–1812)*, ed. Francis Paget Hett (London: John Lane, 1926), 34.

36. Seward is disappointed that Betsy has not inherited the Linley voice, but she enjoys her time with Sophia: "Miss Lee and I loitered an whole hour, one amber morning . . . . We were in interesting conversation, which she is eminently capable of supporting" From Anna Seward, *The Letters of Anna Seward*, ed. Archibald Constable, 6 vols. (New York: AMS Press, 1975), 5:150.

37. See vol. 3 (1993) of Edward Bloom and Lillian Bloom, eds., *Correspondence of Hester Lynch Piozzi, 1784–1821 (formerly Mrs. Thrale)*, 6 vols. (Newark, NJ: University of Delaware Press, 1989–2004).

38. Clementina Black's *The Linleys of Bath* (London: Martin Secker, 1926), 260.

39. In evaluating Mary Linley's character, it is difficult not to be influenced by the almost universally negative opinions of Linley and Sheridan biographers. They have variously called her "domineering" and "shifty and provoking" (Black); "miserly" (Fitzgerald); "a trial" (Sherwin), "coarse," "vulgar," "lowly-born," and "a bustling termagent" (Foss); and "vulgar and parsimonious" (Bingham); etc. The only dissenters are Bor and Clelland, who, in *Still the Lark*, admit that Mary's thrift "border[ed] on meanness,' yet claim that she was "comely" and "had a sweet singing voice" (18–19). In defense of her aggressive posture regarding Jane's courtship, it must be noted that she was without her husband's advice for perhaps the first time. Thomas Linley had died in 1795, leaving her alone to care for her younger children—no doubt she missed his presence in approving of and negotiating with suitors.

40. Quoted in Percy Hetherington Fitzgerald's *The Lives of the Sheridans*, 2 vols. (London: R. Bentley and Son, 1886), 2:30.

41. This letter is in private collection by descendents of the Lee sisters.

42. *The Assignation* is also supposed to contain a satire on Nelson's lover, Emma Lyon, Lady Hamilton. Whether Sophia Lee intended this satire is unknown, but it is possible that she met Emma Lyon in London in 1778, when Emma was a servant in the Linley household. See Bingham's *Sheridan: The Track of a Comet*, 269.

43. Sheridan's Parliamentary status was continually in jeopardy during this period: in 1806 he gave up his long-held Stafford seat to take the spot of his deceased Whig colleague Fox, representing Westminster; in 1807 he was defeated in Westminster but was lucky to receive a seat representing Ilchester.

44. Perhaps the exception to this pattern is O'Toole's *A Traitor's Kiss*, which depicts Richard Sheridan as a heroic victim of his patriotic embrace of Irish nationalism.

45. *The Mysterious Stranger* is Harriet Lee's adaptation of her own novella entitled "The German's Tale: Kruitzner." Byron, who greatly admired this tale, had pre-empted her in 1822 by writing his own theatrical adaptation, which he called *Werner*.

46. Montague Summers, *The Gothic Quest: A History of the Gothic Novel* (New York: Russell and Russell, 1964), 167.

9

SHERIDAN'S COURTROOM DRAMAS

The Impeachment of Warren Hastings and the
Trial of the *Bounty* Mutineers

Glynis Ridley

F ROM 1788-1795 THE IMPEACHMENT TRIAL of
Warren Hastings, former British Governor General of India, was a fixture of the
London political scene, its longevity exhausting audiences, journalists, legal teams
and, finally, its House of Lords jury, one quarter of whom died in the course of the
proceedings. One of the very few constants during this time was the prosecuting
figure of Richard Brinsley Sheridan, whose literary celebrity had gained his election to the House of Commons in 1780. And though easily capable of giving a
virtuoso performance, Sheridan was to share the limelight on this particular stage
with Edmund Burke, at times forming a double act intended to grind Hastings
the more completely into the ground. Yet while the opening of the trial on 13
February 1788 was *the* social event of the season, and admission to the public
seating harder to obtain than any ticket for a West End play, London audiences
grew increasingly weary of the Hastings Impeachment as it dragged on, with no
prospect of resolution in sight. In all that has been written on the subject of the
Impeachment and Sheridan's theatrical antics in the courtroom of Westminster
Hall, it has been assumed that the Impeachment proceedings ultimately failed
because the trial became a self-sustaining world, seen as increasingly marginal as
the years went by. This chapter will suggest that, rather than considering the Impeachment as a self-contained drama, Sheridan's most celebrated speeches during
the trial represent his constantly evolving sense of the Hastings trial in relation to
other entertainments—specifically other criminal cases—engaging the attention
of London society. In particular, this paper will focus on Sheridan's rhetoric as it
may be seen in dialogue with the trial of the *Bounty* Mutineers.

The impeachment proceedings opened on 13 Februrary 1788, in an atmosphere of expectation and publicity that would stand comparison with any
televised celebrity trial today. Westminster Hall, now part of the Commons—and
scene of famous trials including that of Charles I—was made to resemble an
eighteenth-century stage: indeed, a watercolor of the impeachment opening shows
two floor-level boxes for royal spectators, screening them from the eyes of those at
ground level, and protecting crowned heads from the packed galleries above.[1] A
full complement of royal princesses was, after all, present—all wearing diamond
tiaras. Members of the House of Lords sat in the full regalia of their offices, flank-
ing the royal boxes and separated from lesser mortals crowding the rails behind
them. To use a modern phrase, Sheridan and Burke needed to "open big" and they
did so with some of the greatest lines of Sheridan's career. To appreciate the great
difference between Sheridan's rhetoric and that of Burke, it will be helpful to quote
both men in the order in which they spoke. Here is Burke:

> I impeach him in the name of the English nation, whose ancient honour
> he has sullied. I impeach him in the name of the people of India, whose
> rights he has trodden under foot, and whose country he has turned into
> a desert. Lastly, in the name of human nature itself, in the name of both
> sexes, in the name of every age, in the name of every rank, I impeach the
> common enemy and oppressor of all.[2]

Leaving aside the irony of Burke's concern for the "rights" of the "people of India"
(when he would famously deny that the "swinish multitude" of Britain could lay
any claim to any "rights"), it is clear that Burke's syntax privileges a vaguely defined
affront to England's honor over anything specific suffered by her Indian subjects.[3]
Burke's opening salvo is comprised entirely of emotive abstractions. As Paine
would observe of Burke's rhetoric, "he pities the plumage but forgets the dying
bird"—Burke's descriptors float free of any obvious reference point.[4]

Sheridan's opening statement is a complete contrast to Burke's. Where
Burke talks in terms of generalities, Sheridan makes a series of specific assaults on
Hastings' character:

> In his mind all is shuffling, ambiguous, dark insidious, and little; all
> affected plainness, and actual dissimulation;—a heterogeneous mass of
> contradictory qualities; with nothing great but his crimes, and even those
> contrasted by the littleness of his motives, which at once denote both his
> baseness and his meanness, and mark him for a traitor and a trickster.[5]

Sheridan's opening charge consists of a single sentence in which a series of semi-colons give him the opportunity to pause and catch his breath, as he lays a potentially lethal rhetorical trap. For Sheridan constructs Hastings as fundamentally untrustworthy: his "plainness" is not to be taken as straightforward honesty, but as an "affectation"; the manipulative calculation of a "trickster" who will con his audience if only they will let him. Having constructed Hastings' outward demeanor as a contrivance, Sheridan makes it impossible for Hastings to protest his innocence, the assembly having been assured that Hastings is all plausibility. Beneath his apparently respectable and innocuous exterior, Hastings is supposed to hide his "little" personal ambition: the word "little" is chosen and repeated to good effect since, tragically for Hastings' victims, it can be contrasted with the "great" consequences of his base actions. It is noticeable, however, that Hastings' victims—both the starved and starving masses of India and the East India Company stockholders—are not mentioned at all. Sheridan's opening statement is an *ad hominem* attack, framing anything that Hastings or his counsel might subsequently do or say as inherently untrustworthy. The power of Sheridan's first sentence surely owes much to his experience of writing for the stage. Read aloud, the lines' careful construction for the ear is obvious in the sibilance of "insidious," "plainness," "heterogeneous," "littleness," "baseness," "meanness." This similarity of the endings of adjacent or parallel words is a textbook illustration of the rhetorical figure *homoioteleuton* and, as with the use of all such figures, it is instructive to examine the end to which it is used. Given that Sheridan would repeatedly characterize Hastings as an arch-deceiver, leading to his apotheosis as the serpent in the Garden of British India, the repeated sibilance of words chosen to describe Hastings reduces him to a hissing snake well in advance of the connection being made explicit. Exploring the aural qualities of Sheridan's opening speech, one could also note how the words "ambiguous" and "dark insidious" generate a half-rhyme, as though we are listening to lines of verse rather than carefully crafted prose. Burke and Sheridan both "opened big," but Sheridan was the oratorical star.

Whether the audience in Westminster Hall perceived any disconnect between the Mephistophelean character conjured up by this rhetoric and the unremarkable figure of Hastings sitting before them was surely, to a large degree, dependent upon whether any observer understood the complexities of the case well enough to be able to formulate a view on the legitimacy of the prosecution's case. Impeachments are a hot ticket when expectations run high that there will be some extraordinary piece of evidence offered by a highly placed official, or a confession from the accused, breaking down under duress. The reality is rather more mundane: a mountain of evidence, claim and counter-claim, much of which must be contextualized in local, national, and perhaps even international terms. Though the rhetoric of the prosecution's opening salvos was one of emotive generalizations followed by an artfully constructed character assassination, the specifics of the prosecution's case were of course complex. Two years into the trial, Burke would take four days to explain Indian history, culture and geo-politics to a bemused and increasingly bored audience, in order that they might better understand one of the charges against Hastings. While Hastings has been the subject of dedicated volumes and articles examining his time in India, and any summation of Burke's four-day marathon of the charges laid against him necessarily risks over-simplification, Sheridan's rhetorical set-pieces are best understood when contextualized in light of key elements of the prosecution's case. So was Hastings charged with sins of commission or omission? The charge was "high crimes and misdemeanors." Broken down into separate areas, the substance was that during Hastings' time in office (from 1772–1785), a ratcheting up of taxes in Bengal had criminally coincided with a famine (1773–1774) that left one-third of the population of Bengal—some five million people—dead from starvation. Another famine in 1783–1784 killed more than a fifth of the population of the Indian plains. Bookending Hastings' rule, the famines and the weight of human misery they produced were of less interest to a certain sort of East India Company shareholder than the complete collapse of Company stock during this time. And to all intents and purposes, the East India Company was British rule in India.

Compounding the sense that Hastings was out of his depth, in 1773 he had accepted an offer of 40 million rupees from the Nawab of Oudh for British forces to fight the Rohillas: a migratory Afghan people settled in the Nawab's lands. The mercenary expedition cost nearly as much as the promised sum, which was never paid by the Nawab. When the East India Company was forced to turn to the government for financial assistance, and was unable to pay its annual dividend, Hastings became the proverbial lightning rod for all criticism of the British in India. As Niall Ferguson says of the impeachment, it "was more than the public humiliation of a chief executive before a meeting of disgruntled shareholders. In truth, it was the whole basis of the company's rule in India that was on trial."[6] All this said, however, we should beware facile judgments of Hastings' character and actions, for he resists easy assumptions about the colonizer's view of the colonized. An accomplished scholar of Persian before his arrival in India, Hastings learned four separate Indian languages during his time there. He was not someone who, in E. M. Forster's memorable formulation, "had learnt the lingo, but only to speak to the servants, so . . . knew none of the politer forms and of the verbs only the imperative mood."[7] Intelligent, articulate and infinitely curious about the world, this was the man Sheridan's prosecuting theatrics had to prove guilty.

To Sheridan's contemporaries keeping up with the trial, there was no doubt as to which of his speeches repaid further study. In 1790, following Burke's disastrous, near week-long account of Hastings' ill-conceived dealings with the Nawab of Oudh, on whose behalf Hastings had engaged British military forces in an internecine war for no discernible gain, the prosecution badly needed to regain its momentum. It fell to Sheridan to salvage the sinking ship and his resulting speech—known as the Speech on the Begums (that is, princesses) of Oudh—is widely cited by his contemporaries as one of the greatest oratorical performances of the eighteenth century. And "performance" is an apposite word for a speech that had already enjoyed a partial "dress rehearsal" three years previously. For what is rarely discussed in relation to Sheridan's Impeachment tour-de-force is that he had first tried out the emotional impact of what would become his most celebrated speech on 7 February, 1787, when trying to persuade the House of Commons that impeachment was an appropriate vehicle for the prosecution of Hastings's perceived crimes. No complete transcript of Sheridan's speech to the Commons is known—in contrast to his later speech on the Begums of Oudh made at the impeachment trial—and Sheridan's biographers have therefore typically reconstructed his rhetorical tour-de-force before the Commons from his own extensive notes and various memoranda made by his contemporaries. His speech on the same subject made at the impeachment in 1790 is far better attested from the trial records. Accepting the record as not necessarily complete then, it is evident that Sheridan was able to make two wholly distinct—though equally effective—indictments of Hastings, calculating the content of each according to the audience, and choosing as the defining framework for each speech a field of imagery that resonated with the concerns of the moment. In February 1787 before the Commons, Sheridan's rhetoric appears to have returned time and again to the (inter)national ramifications of financial impropriety on the part of governments, institutions, and individuals:

> nations have been extirpated for a sum of money, whole tracts of country laid waste by fire and sword, to furnish investments; revolutions occasioned by an affidavit, an army employed in executing an arrest; towns besieged on a note of hand, a prince expelled for the balance of an account, statesmen occupied in doing the business of a tipstaff, generals made auctioneers, a truncheon contrasted with the implements of a

counting house; and the British Government exhibited in every part of Hindostan holding a bloody scepter in one hand and picking pockets with the other.[8]

Though the last clause of this sentence is explicit in making British policy in India its ostensible subject, Sheridan's word choice can be shown to have evoked other national contexts for his hearers. Implied criticism of the notorious profligacy of the Price Regent (the future George IV) might be inferred from the reference to "a prince expelled for the balance of an account"—but such an inference could only be made in ignorance of the friendship existing between Sheridan and the Prince Regent at this time. Rather, a letter written by Horace Walpole to the Countess of Ossory makes it clear that Sheridan's contemporaries saw the power of his speech to lie in its evocation of a range of financial woes plaguing Britain's arch-imperial rival, France. Walpole writes of Sheridan's speech:

> one heard everybody in the streets raving on the Wonders of that speech; for my part I cannot believe it was so supernatural as they say—do you believe it was, Madam? How should such a fellow as Sheridan who has no diamonds to bestow, fascinate all the world?[9]

Walpole's reference to Sheridan as a would-be giver of "diamonds" is puzzling when the letter—and the speech to which the letter refers—is considered apart from its surrounding socio-political context, but the currency of Walpole's image and the power of Sheridan's rhetoric to which it pays homage makes perfect sense against the backdrop of the mismanagement of French royal financial affairs in the first half of the 1780s. For when Walpole cast Sheridan as a persuasive speaker despite having no diamonds to offer his hearer, he clearly expected the Countess to understand an allusion to the infamous "Diamond Necklace Affair" which was known across European court circles.[10] On 11 August 1784, the cardinal bishop of Strasbourg, Louis, Prince de Rohan, became the unwitting lead actor in a drama at the French court, when he played out the final scene he had been duped into performing. Always disliked by Marie Antoinette, Rohan had been persuaded that he could finally curry favor with his queen if he would be willing to act as go-between in her secret purchase of a fabulous necklace of over 500 diamonds. But the veiled woman Rohan met in the Versailles palace grounds who "authorized" him to make the 1.6 million livres purchase on her behalf was a prostitute playing a queen. When the royal jewelers finally sought out their promised payment, the sting unraveled. Imprisoned on the direct order of Louis XVI, Rohan had to be released after the Paris *Parlement* debated his case on 31 May 1786 and found him not guilty by a majority of 26 to 23. The ten thousand-strong crowd that made its way to the Bastille to demand Rohan's release seemed emblematic of a wider unease in the country. The monarchy was perceived to be morally if not physically bankrupt and, to the alarm of the international currency markets, French Controller-General Calonne thought his country's finances in such a serious state that he proposed Louis XVI seek the endorsement of a financial reform package from his Assembly of Notables: a body that had last met in 1626. When Sheridan's 1787 speech on the Begums of Oudh asked its hearers to contemplate Britannia as a morally and financially impoverished ruler of India, it simultaneously allowed them the luxury of feeling morally superior to an even more unstable France.

The speech on the Begums of Oudh that Sheridan delivered at the impeachment trial in June 1790 was equally celebrated but obviously different to its precursor. The reasons for that difference can readily be gauged. In 1790, Sheridan had both to prosecute the legal case against Hastings, but also to distinguish his own part in the prosecution from that of Burke. On one level, this was relatively straightforward. Burke took four days to explain the complexities of Indian regional and dynastic politics to a bemused audience at Westminster Hall, making no concessions to his hearers' limited ability to empathize with what they heard. Sheridan therefore attempted to refocus attention away from the abstractions of Burke to something more concrete. One of the points of Burke's exhaustive explanation of Indian politics and culture had been to convince the House that, when Hastings agreed to send British soldiers to fight a migratory Afghan people on behalf of the Nawab of Oudh, Hastings knew that the Nawab was engaged in a regional power play that was also a dynastic battle, and that would rob the Nawab's surviving female relatives of the power they enjoyed. Rather than asking Hastings' judges to dwell upon the suffering of millions of Indian peasants on the plains, Sheridan attempted to engage the sympathy and harness the outrage of his audience by collapsing the cultural distance between England and India in a sentimental tableau. Here is Sheridan in full flow:

> the design of obliging the Nabob [of Oude] to plunder those unfortunate Princesses (his mother and grandmother) of their treasures . . . and seize upon their ministers, throw them into a dungeon, there load them with chains, and keep them for many months close prisoners, suffering incredible hardships, was first entertained by the Governor General.[11]

That the "Nawab" has here become the "Nabob" is surely no accident—a regional ruler (mis)identified by a term commonly used disparagingly in relation to eighteenth-century Britain's nouveaux riche who had gained their money in the furthest outposts of empire.[12] In the mouth of the creator of Mrs. Malaprop, however, the substitution of "Nabob" for "Nawab" looks like deliberate policy. And the Nabob Sheridan paints for his listeners is the worst villain imaginable from the contemporary literature of sentimentality, a brute who will not only "plunder" his own mother and grandmother, but who will imprison them and "*load* them with *chains* . . . for many *months*." To compound his villainy, the innocent women for whom this base treatment was designed are "princesses"—one imagines Sheridan holding the viewer's line of sight in the direction of the royal boxes where, according to Macaulay, the "fair-haired young daughters of the house of Brunswick" were sitting.[13] The Nawab of Sheridan's creation is not only the unnatural child and grandchild of helpless female relatives but—worse still following the events of 1789—he is a regicide, and very much the creature of Hastings, who is credited with first entertaining this senseless chain of events.

For the spectator astute enough to realize that it would make no sense for Hastings to plot to imprison the Nawab's female relatives, the dawning realization that this is probably Sheridan's affecting hyperbole is surely less important than the image Sheridan has conjured—a very human reference point at the centre of a prosecution case sadly unable to paint the starving fate of millions in similarly resonant terms. Having suggested Hastings as the architect of the Nawab's regional land grab, Sheridan builds on this foundation to raise Hastings up as a Governor-General turned power broker. A contemporary pamphlet account of Sheridan's speech comments on the way in which "[Mr Sheridan] burst out into a tone of eloquent and empassioned expressions on the character of Mr Hastings and worked . . . to a climactic crescendo" as he " . . . called upon gentlemen to say, if there was any thing in Machiavel, any treachery upon record, if they had ever heard of any cold Italian fraud, that could in any degree be put in comparison with the disgusting hypocrisy and unequalled baseness that Mr Hastings had shewn . . . he appeared to be a mixture of the trickster and the tyrant . . . [and] he could no more go straight forward to his object, than a snake could be made to proceed without writhing in curves."[14] In this comparison, the apotheosis of Hastings is complete: worse than anything dreamt of by Machiavelli, he is a "base" "trickster"—not the first time Sheridan has used either word of Hastings, a man for whom the most fitting comparison is a snake. In short, Sheridan creates—or, rather, recreates—Hastings as the Satanic tempter in the garden of British India. And why, Sheridan asked his audience, should they care:

Was Parliament misspending its time, by enquiring into the oppressions practiced on millions of unfortunate persons in India . . . ? Was it a misuse of their functions to be diligent in attempting, by the most effectual means, to wipe off the disgrace that stood affixed to the British name in India, and to rescue the national character from lasting infamy?[15]

This is surely one of the most effective rhetorical questions ever posed, for dozing parliamentarians and spectators in the public gallery could sit a little taller and believe that their goal was the salvaging of "the national character" itself. As Sheridan assured the House, they "proved to all the world, that, however degenerate an example of the conduct of Englishmen some of the British subjects had exhibited in India, that the people of England . . . were anxious to do justice, by redressing injuries, and punishing offenders, however high their rank, however elevated their station."[16] Sheridan's speech creates and then rides a wave a popular indignation. His hearers may have cared little about the lives—and deaths—of ordinary Indians under Hastings' rule, but Sheridan makes Hastings' crime nothing less than the single-handed destruction of Britannia's reputation.

If Sheridan's rhetoric was calculated to flatter his parliamentary peers who moved the impeachment, and their hereditary opposite numbers, members of the Lords, who sat in judgment on Hastings, Sheridan also appears to have been acutely conscious of its effect on the public gallery. The general public's reaction to the performance was summed up in an anonymous snatch of verse, remarkable for its consistent use of an eleven-syllable line:

> The gallery folk, who, misled by the sport
> Conceived 'twas a playhouse, instead of a court,
> And thinking the actor uncommonly good,
> They clapp'd and cry'd 'Bravo' as loud as they could,
> Then Edmund gave Sherry a hearty embrace
> And cry'd, as he spluttered all over his face,
> "At supper this night thou shalt have the First Place."[17]

Even if the reader is being invited to laugh at "the gallery folk" who have no understanding of the difference between a theatre and a courtroom, the doggerel insists upon the power of Sheridan's rhetoric to generate an affective response in his fellow prosecutor: by definition, a more sophisticated and dispassionate auditor. Given that Burke's *Reflections on the Revolution in France* was composed in the first half of 1790, and published in November of that year, and given that one of the most affecting images Burke aims for is that of Marie Antoinette, who bears "her own captivity, and the exile of her friends, and the insulting adulation of addresses, and the whole weight of her accumulated wrongs, with a serene patience, in a manner suited to her rank and race," it is tempting to speculate that Burke learned much from his experience of watching Sheridan paint the wrongs done to the princesses of Oudh.[18]

If the rapidly evolving situation in France provided one source of imagery and a contextual framework for Sheridan's speeches, then another context was surely provided by a drama that unfolded across late spring and early summer 1790 much nearer to home. In March 1790, Lieutenant William Bligh, late of His Majesty's ship, *The Bounty*, presented himself to the Lords of the Admiralty and reported his ship lost to mutiny after its visit to Tahiti. Bligh's meticulously maintained log confirmed the incredible story he told: of mutiny among his forty-five man crew, and of being cast adrift in the Bounty's largest cutter with seventeen men who remained loyal to him. With rations enough for only five days, Bligh successfully navigated the cutter across 3,618 miles of ocean to the port of Coupang in the Dutch East Indies, taking forty-eight days on starvation rations and losing only one man. As His Majesty's ship *Pandora* was readied to go in pursuit of the mutineers, London could not get enough of the sensational aspects of The Bounty story. The Royalty Theatre quickly premiered *The Pirates; Or, The Calamities of Captain Bligh*, promising audiences Tahitian dances and "the attachment of Tahitian women to . . . British sailors," the "whole to conclude with a correct view of that superb monument of British benevolence Greenwich Hospital"—the royal naval hospital.[19] Patriotic celebrations of the imperial venture were very much the order of the day. Before mutineer Fletcher Christian's relatives spun Bligh as a sadistic tyrant, he was a national hero. For the prosecution at Hastings' impeachment, it was clear that their trial was losing ground to the *de facto* trial of the absent Bounty mutineers already begun in the press.

Fanny Burney's diary for May 1790 tells us that she attended Hastings' impeachment, but, while on her way to Westminster Hall with her brother, James Burney, a well-connected ship's captain who had sailed with both Cook and Bligh, the Burneys' were hailed by William Windham, a member of Parliament active in Hastings' impeachment. Burney's recollection is as follows:

> "But what officers you are!" Windham cried to Captain Burney. "You men of Captain Cook; you rise upon us in every trial! This Captain Bligh—what feats, what wonders he has performed! What difficulties got through! What dangers defied! And with such cool, manly skill"![20]

It is hard not to catch a note of jealousy in Windham's greeting. For the drama of the mutiny on the Bounty—and its dramatic afterlife—combined a heady mix of English men and Tahitian women, caught between the claims of duty and the urges of rebellion. Whatever the injustices they had suffered, and no matter how much pathos Sheridan tried to derive from their situation, the princesses of Oudh were as nothing in the popular imagination compared to seductive Tahitian women and a wronged captain of His Majesty's Navy. Bligh was, temporarily, the hero of the hour, but the villains of his particular drama were present in London only as recreated by actors. (When ten of *The Bounty* mutineers were recaptured and brought to London as prisoners in the summer of 1792, the nation had to wait until 12 September for all the admirals due to preside at the court martial to be back from active duty. In the absence of actual testimony, the prisoners' motives and actions were the predictable subject of romantic speculation and fevered rumor.) Yet if *The Bounty* mutineers were temporarily unavailable for public scrutiny, Hastings was all too present. Admiralty House and The House of Commons would receive a hero and a villain respectively. Together they constituted a complete drama. Responding to the dynamics of a shifting public interest—away from the Hastings impeachment, now already a year old—and towards *The Bounty* story, Sheridan's hyperbolic rhetoric in the speech on the Begums of Oudh cleverly constructed Hastings as an embodiment of the three greatest moral failings ascribed to *The Bounty* mutineers.

Leaving aside the capital charge of mutiny (the proof of which depended upon showing a man's active involvement in seizing control of *The Bounty*), the court of public opinion held the mutineers to be guilty of three more intangible charges, which Sheridan astutely laid at Hastings' door. The speech on the Begums of Oudh did, after all, require those sitting in judgment on Hastings to recognize that only a guilty verdict could "rescue the national character from lasting infamy": like the mutineers, Hastings presented some hazily formulated affront to the very notion of empire. Perhaps this was because Hastings was, like the mutineers, a subordinate assuming power he had not the right to assume. And from this construction of Hastings's character, it was but a short step to link him to the most infamous subordinate ever to protest his status—Hastings being repeatedly likened by Sheridan to the fallen angel turned tempter of mankind, that "trickster," "tyrant," and serpentine "tempter," Satan himself. But try as Sheridan might to paint an affecting royal family drama at the center of the Nawab's power-play against his female relatives, Hastings' role as arch deceiver was eclipsed by the characterization Bligh offered of his first lieutenant, Fletcher Christian.

In his popular *Narrative* account of the mutiny, Bligh reported that "when they were forcing me out of the ship, I asked him [i.e. Christian], if this treatment was a proper return for the many instances he had received of my friendship."[21] Motioned at gunpoint to the ship's launch, Bligh pleadingly cried out, "Consider Mr Christian, I have a wife and four children in England, and you have danced my children upon your knee." Christian's response at this point, as reported by Bligh, has caused endless speculation as to its meaning: "[H]e appeared disturbed at my question, and answered with much emotion. 'That!—captain Bligh,—that is the thing—I am in hell—I am in hell.'" Sheridan's contemporaries found his speech on the Begums of Oudh delivered in June 1790 the most affecting oration they had heard—until the villainy of Hastings was almost immediately eclipsed in the popular consciousness by speculation on the machinations of Fletcher Christian. It would therefore be wrong to see a declining public interest in the impeachment of Warren Hastings as simply a verdict on the length and nature of the proceedings. The impeachment trial was undeniably long and certainly longer than it need have been. But it should never be considered in isolation from contemporary current affairs, especially other trials that captured the public imagination.

Indeed, the trial of the Bounty Mutineers began a decade of notorious court proceedings that made legal dramas of central importance to a wider audience than ever before. In 1792 and 1793, a series of Sedition Trials were staged against a range of Britons charged with promoting radical political propaganda. The accused included a number of booksellers and, most conspicuously, Thomas Paine, tried *in absentia* on account of his authorship of the *Rights of Man* (1791). The British government's determination to quash the burgeoning radical movement culminated in the 1794 Treason Trials, in which Thomas Hardy, John Horne Tooke and John Thelwall faced capital charges for their writings. During all this time, Sheridan and Burke were at the center, not only of the impeachment of Hastings, but of the written and verbal battles waged around the cause of political reform. This paper has focused on Sheridan's widely acclaimed speech on the Begums of Oudh, but a more complete examination of Sheridan's oratory in the impeachment trial would necessitate an examination of its interplay with the full range of Sedition and Treason Trials of 1792–1794, with whose workings Sheridan was demonstrably familiar.[22]

David Womersley has characterized the audience for Restoration drama as one so used to seeing "a rapid sequence of plays" that spectators "must have thereby been encouraged to contrast and compare what was placed before them, to have developed habits of mental juxtaposition."[23] To be sure, Sheridan's comedies of manners are separated from their Restoration antecedents by at least a century, yet audience habits of identifying allusions and references cannot have been very different. And while the audiences Sheridan played to in Westminster Hall included those in the gallery, mocked by the satirists, Sheridan's rhetoric also fell on the ears of those for whom the impeachment was another entertainment, playing alongside court gossip, the unfolding story of the mutiny on The Bounty and, ultimately, the Treason Trials. This audience undoubtedly compared and contrasted turns of phrase, and understood allusions made to the range of spectacles entertaining London society at the time. Womersley concludes that the pursuit of anything that might be defined as success with such an audience results in a drama that "can without gross distortion be conceived as Darwinian . . . a ceaseless mutation of dramatic species." During the impeachment's seven-year long run, Sheridan's rhetoric demonstrates the acute awareness of a playwright schooled in this competitive dramatic atmosphere. To continue to engage its audience, including those sitting in judgment on Hastings, the impeachment had to compete successfully against a range of compelling human dramas. In the case of the trial of the Bounty mutineers and the Treason Trials, the defendants—unlike Hastings—battled for their lives. Sheridan could write his own script, but not the scripts of those public spectacles unfolding around him, against which the impeachment proceedings were implicitly weighed and ultimately found wanting.

Notes

1. The watercolor is "A View of the Tryal of Warren Hastings," by Edward Dayes, 1789. It is held in the British Library [Shelfmark: P376].

2. Quoted in Niall Ferguson, *Empire: How Britain Made the Modern World* (London: Allen Lane/ Penguin Press, 2003), 55.

3. Edmund Burke, *Reflections on the Revolution in France*, ed. J. C. D. Clark (Stanford: Stanford University Press, 2001), 242.

4. Thomas Paine, *Rights of Man* (London: J. S. Jordan, 1791), 51.

5. Ferguson, *Empire*, 55.

6. Ibid., 53. A very different view of the relationship between the impeachment and British colonial ambitions in India can be found in Nicholas B. Dirks, *The Scandal of Empire: India and the Creation of Imperial Britain* (Cambridge, MA: Harvard University Press, 2006). For Dirks, the "moral spectacle" of the impeachment helped to legitimize the notion of British sovereignty over India (125), and the legal proceedings were therefore a cause of the success of British imperial ambitions, rather than a consequence of them.

7. E. M. Forster, *A Passage to India* (Orlando: Harcourt, 1924), 42.

8. Quoted in Alice Glasgow, *Sheridan of Drury Lane* (New York: Frederick A. Stokes Co., 1940), 171.

9. Quoted in Madeleine Bingham, *Sheridan: The Track of a Comet* (New York: St Martin's Press, 1972), 236.

10. The following account of the Diamond Necklace Affair summarizes the version of events given in Colin Jones, *The Great Nation: France from Louis XV to Napoleon* (New York: Columbia University Press, 2002), 336–42.

11. Richard Brinsley Sheridan, *The Speech of R. B. Sheridan, Esq. On Wednesday, the 7th of February, 1787, In bringing forward the Fourth Charge against Warren Hastings, Esq. Relative to the Begums of Oude.* 2nd ed. (London, 1787), 12.

12. For a history of the term "nabob" see Jill H. Casid, *Sowing Empire. Landscape and Colonization* (Minneapolis: University of Minnesota Press, 2005), 49.

13. Thomas Babington Macaulay, *Essay on Warren Hastings*, ed. Alexander Mackie (London: Longmans, Green & Co., 1892), 169.

14. *The Speech of R. B. Sheridan, Esq. On Wednesday, the 7th of February, 1787, In bringing forward the Fourth Charge against Warren Hastings, Esq. Relative to the Begums of Oude.* 2nd ed. (London, 1787), 42–45.

15. Ibid., 5.

16. Ibid., 6.

17. Quoted in Nicholas K. Robinson, *Edmund Burke: A Life in Caricature* (New Haven: Yale University Press, 1996), 101.

18. Burke, *Reflections*, 237–38.

19. Caroline Alexander, *The Bounty: The True Story of the Mutiny on the Bounty* (New York: Penguin, 2004), 164–65.

20. Fanny Burney, *Diary and Letters of Madame d'Arblay*, ed. by her niece [Charlotte Barrett], 7 vols. (London: H. Colborn, 1842–46), 3:101.

21. Bligh's account of events was published in the instant bestseller: William Bligh, *A Narrative of the Mutiny, on Board His Majesty's Ship Bounty; and the Subsequent Voyage of Part of the Crew, in the Ship's Boat, From Tofoa, one of the Friendly Islands, to Timor, a Dutch Settlement in the East Indies* (London, 1790). The last conversation between Bligh and Fletcher Christian—including Christian's enigmatic last words—is discussed in Alexander's *The Bounty: The True Story of the Mutiny on the Bounty* (cf. n19), 140–1r.

22. For Sheridan's knowledge of the trials and the specifics of their language, see John Barrell, *Imagining the King's Death: Figurative Treason, Fantasies of Regicide 1793–1796* (Oxford: Oxford University Press, 2000), 224–25; 325; 426.

23. David Womersley, ed., *Restoration Drama: An Anthology* (Oxford: Blackwell, 2000), viii.

10

PIZARRO'S SPECTACULAR DIALECTICS

Sheridan's Bridge to the Cosmopolitical Future

Daniel O'Quinn

L ET'S GO OUT ON A LIMB and say that eighteenth-century theatre ended on the evening of 24 May 1799, when the curtain at Drury Lane rose on Richard Brinsley Sheridan's *Pizarro*. As the culmination of a century of dramaturgical and scenographic innovation, the play points towards developments that would define nineteenth-century theatrical practice. But rather than describing the play as a watershed, I'm inclined to see it as a cataract separating two aesthetic and political regimes. Although it is set in the past and allegorizes the present, *Pizarro* demands that its audience leap into the future. This precarious declaration is part of an overall rhetoric of precarious leaps that takes its inspiration from the play's most famous and ambitious scene. I am referring to the extraordinary mountain torrent and collapsing bridge that not only stunned audiences during its initial presentation—and almost killed Kemble and its operators on opening night—but also lived on in subsequent set designs.[1] Unfortunately for theatre history, the visual record of De Loutherbourg's scene has been lost, and the print descriptions of it that remain are hopelessly vague. I am going to make a virtue of that loss by arguing that its disappearance is curiously apt, for it is a crucial mechanism in a utopian dialectic whose effectiveness relies on getting beyond the bridge. Explaining that sentence is going to take some time and effort. This essay attempts to think about the utopian possibilities set into motion by Sheridan's play by taking up the admittedly utopian gesture of theatre history which attempts to reconstitute, from incomplete evidence, past performance.

To bridge the gap in our knowledge we can turn to the remarkably thick record of response to the play. *Pizarro* was both the most popular and most critiqued play of the age. No play in the late eighteenth century generated as many lengthy reviews, as much criticism and as much visual satire as *Pizarro*.[2] Much of this printed material focuses on the play's sensational success as a loyal play in a time of political crisis, on its complex adaptation of the politically and morally suspect Kotzebue for the British stage, and on the rather surprising fact that it should come from the pen of Sheridan. Politically, Sheridan was both hailed as a patriot and ridiculed as an apostate—or worse, as a cynic. Aesthetically, the critics on opening night praised the play's innovative integration of tragedy, spectacle and music. For others, the play's generic hybridity signalled a profound threat to theatrical legitimacy, and hence to conventional definitions of the British theatrical heritage. Sheridan was seen by many as a traitor to the very theatrical and political traditions that his earlier plays and speeches had exemplified.

This paradoxical response to Sheridan's play had its counterpart in the response to his oratory on the Great Mutiny of 1797. The mutiny of sailors at Spithead and the Nore was arguably the moment of gravest crisis for the nation during the Revolutionary War, and Sheridan's response to it foreshadows much of his rhetorical strategy in *Pizarro*. From the outset, Sheridan and Fox were deeply and loudly critical of the Admiralty and of the ministry's response to the demands of the sailors. It is not surprising therefore that they and other members of the opposition were satirized by the government's propagandists as behind the entire affair.[3] When Sheridan made his famous speech of 2 June 1797 in which he supported the government against the sailors, pro-government satirists and commentators were either stupefied or simply continued to impugn the opposition.[4] What they couldn't countenance was a nationalist response to the crisis that was nevertheless critical of the state. In Sheridan's speech he calls for all members to join together against the mutiny, but in the same breath states—as he did on numerous occasions before—that the entire affair was of the government's making.[5] If the ministry and admiralty had dealt with the sailors in a reasonable and conciliatory way, then the mutiny would not have escalated. Thus he paradoxically calls for a unified House to take action against the sailors in order to rectify a situation pushed to the level of crisis by the ministry. In short, he is asking all members to join the government to correct the government's mistake. And this position, although internally contradictory, is completely in keeping with Sheridan's critique of Pitt's management of the war.[6] In his speeches, Sheridan—and Fox, for that matter—repeatedly asserts that the lack of provisions, the escalation of hostilities, the financial encumbrances and the intractability of the conflict were the result of bad policy.[7] From this point onward, Sheridan remained rigorously critical of both the threat posed by the Directory (and eventually by Bonaparte) *and* the threat posed to the nation by the ministry's incompetence abroad and its incursions on liberty at home. The mutiny thus was read as a symptom of a larger problem that could only be solved through an inconsistent response: in this time of crisis, Whig would have to support Tory and yet maintain an ongoing critique of government policy. This is why Sheridan could both support the ministry on the mutiny and join Fox in secession shortly afterwards. Two years later, *Pizarro* was staged at Drury Lane to great acclaim and it is, I believe, the next logical but nevertheless counterintuitive step in this complex counterpolitics.

Of the Political Possibilities of Tonight's Performance

After taking the town by storm, *Pizarro* was the occasion of one of the most auspicious Royal Command performances in the history of British theatre. With the closing of Sheridan and Kemble's production of *Venice Preserv'd* in 1795, the King refused to attend a play at Drury Lane for four years. Short of revoking the theatre's license, the King's boycott was an extreme statement of the state's disapprobation not only of the theatrical institution, but also of Sheridan's politics. With widespread reports that *Pizarro* was generating enthusiastic expressions of loyalty from its audiences, the King arranged to return to Drury Lane on 5 June 1799. The following report from *The Star* gives a detailed account of the King's performance and what I would argue is a complex form of counter-performance managed by Sheridan himself:

> This elegant house never possessed a more splendid and numerous audience than last night, drawn together by the double attraction of the presence of the ROYAL FAMILY, and the popular play of *Pizarro*. The whole of the boxes were taken before the doors opened, and it was by accident only a single seat could be procured. Some of the first fashion were seated up one pair of stairs. . . . The lower boxes were crowded with Nobility.
>
> The difficulties of entering the galleries and pit were of course excessive; the crowd was dreadful; several Ladies fainted, and one falling down near the door, was much bruised. On opening the box doors, the crowd was as great as on the first night of *Pizarro*; the railing was burst off; and the windows, which had been repaired, were again broken to give air. Ladies in full dress were struggling to enter, and hundreds less courageous were standing in the lobbies and round the doors; and Ladies and Gentlemen after paying to go to the boxes, clambered over to the Pit. Notwithstanding the confusion was so great, and that the avenues are

none of the best, we don't find that any accident happened, or that any person was injured. The Royal Box, with the stair case and room adjacent, were fitted up in a most sumptuous stile, with richest shrubs and flowers.—The first of the Royal Party that entered were the Duke and Duchess of YORK, who seated themselves in one of the private boxes on the KING's side, amidst the universal greetings of the numerous and splendid auditory. Mr. SHERIDAN immediately followed their Highnesses to pay his respects to them, which being observed by the audience, his conduct was warmly applauded by every part of the House. Their MAJESTIES and PRINCESSES appeared soon after in the State Boxes. On their entrance the roar of acclamation from all parts of the Theatre was prolonged for nearly ten minutes. All the principal singers belonging to the Theatre then came forward, and the Duke of YORK's band being ranged on the stage, sang *GOD save the King*, which was promptly encored. The loyal and affectionate manifestations having subsided, the Play commenced, the Sentiments of which, appropriate to the times, seemed to make a very deep impression upon the exalted visitors, while they electrified the audience. The patriotic speech of *Rolla* to his countrymen, in the Temple of the Sun, was interrupted by a thunder of applause, which suspended the performance nearly five minutes. Several other passages had a similar effect. Where the Peruvian's attachment to his Sovereign, and that Sovereign's love for his people were so glowingly described, the Royal Pair were affected even to tears.

Between the Tragedy and the Farce, *Rule Britannia* was sung with great effect; and at the conclusion of the Entertainment, *God Save the King*, was played, while their MAJESTIES were departing. . . . Mr. SHERIDAN, Mr. RICHARDSON, and Mr. GRUBB, the Proprietors, walked before their MAJESTIES to their box, with each two candles, and conducted them in the same way to their carriages. . . . No performance in any Theatre, ever went off with great *éclat* than that of last night.[8]

I have recorded this review at length in order to draw attention to the carefully managed and rehearsed political performance of the Royal party. The presence of the Duke of York's band on stage indicates that much of this was got up in advance by the Royal household. In light of the controversy sparked by the last time George III attended a play by Sheridan—this was the performance of *The Rivals* at Covent Garden in 1795—it is not surprising that the Royal household attempted to control the performance of these songs. And from all reports the Duke of York's band did its job remarkably well. But it may well be that this was precisely what Sheridan was counting on.

When the Crown's representatives are on stage, the commercial theatre's relation to the state is made manifest and a certain anachronism kicks in. *The Star's* account of the performance indicates that the audience that evening was composed almost exclusively of the nobility. The theatrical space of Drury Lane has been transformed into a near simulacrum of court. I have added the qualification here because the review is fascinated by the degree to which the foremost figures in the nation behave in a manner more suited to the mob: "Ladies and Gentlemen" are pressing on the stairs and even clambering over the boxes into the pit. After all this confusion, Sheridan, Grubb and Richardson, carrying tapers, lead the King and Queen from their sumptuous seats which were themselves fitted up from the properties of the theatre. The entire gathering, entrance and departure is highly reminiscent of a court masque, of a kind of theatrical performance which hypostatized sovereign power not only by allegorizing the benevolence and power of the King, but also by transforming the social space of performance to enact sovereignty. Is there a more accurate characterization not only of this scene of performance, but of *Pizarro* itself? The music, the highly intricate allegories, the complex and elaborate sets, properties and visual effects were widely recognized as the epitome of a new form of theatrical spectacle, but that same spectacle has its origins in the court masque. Aesthetically, De Loutherbourg's most prominent forebear was Inigo Jones. One glance at a contemporary rendering of the play's most magnificent set should clinch the filiation. (See fig. 10.1) The procession and the very scenography of The Temple of the Sun from act two, scene two brings the allegorical types of the King and the ministry into a space of unparalleled grandeur.

But if De Loutherbourg was one of Sheridan's primary artistic collaborators on this show, then it is important to remember that his primary political collaborator, Charles James Fox, regularly referred to the ministry as "The Court" during this period.[9] Much of the criticism of *Pizarro* has focussed on its generic instability and has argued for generic innovation. What happens if we take our cues from Sheridan's actions in Drury Lane on this evening, and think of the play as an anachronism, as a belated masque? Or more precisely, could Sheridan be staging—if only on this night—a parody of a masque that aims to demonstrate the distance between the historical actors and their allegorical counterparts? This would imply that George III is less a constitutional monarch than an absolutist king who is most entertained when he is the focus of all

Figure 10.1.   *The Temple of the Sun*, by Edward Orme, 1800. Courtesy of the Trustees of the British Museum.

representation both political and theatrical. If so, then the politics of allegory itself, which have been so crucial in a time of intense state censorship, are being mobilized in a new—yet curiously old—way by Sheridan.

The primary effect of such an intervention would be to highlight not only how George III and Pitt do not live up to the standards of Atiliba and Rolla, but also the degree to which they and the audience are caught in the thrall of a particularly dangerous delusion. This is precisely what is at stake in some of the most biting visual satires of the command performance. *Pizzaro a New Play or the Drury-Lane Masquerade* shows Sheridan dressed as Pizarro with candles leading the King, Queen and the Princesses to their boxes. (See fig. 10.2) Along with requests to play "God Save the King" more and more loudly, Sheridan asks that a rather conspicuous stone marked "Maidstone Loyalty" be moved out of the way "to make room for the best and wisest of sovereigns."[10] The King, for his part, declares "No no no Jacobins here all Loyal all Loyal. Charming man the Author eh charming man, never saw him in such a good light before" and the Princesses state they "never saw that General at Court." In the background we see the band and audience members (including Fox) hailing the King. This satire aligns Sheridan with the character allegorically tied to Napoleon in order to undercut his supposed loyalty. Clear signals are given to the viewer that Sheridan's loyalty is an act either staged for cynical ends (a note in the foreground suggests that he has his eyes on a peerage) or something more sinister. The more sinister possibility is coded into the response of the Royal family. They don't seem to see that Sheridan is merely acting. The masquerade is the truth in the King's eyes, and the Princesses misrecognize Sheridan's costume as a British military uniform—in spite of the fact that, according to the play's allegorization of the war with France, Sheridan's Spanish dress aligns him with Bonaparte. If Sheridan is attacked for pandering, then the King, Princesses and audience are ridiculed for their gullibility—or worse, for their stupidity. This separates the viewer from the represented audience and asks that they consider both the judgement of the King, and the expressions of loyalty to such a monarch. Sheridan emerges as the only character in the satire that needs a costume, because George III and the audience either are already masquerading as sovereigns and patriots, or perhaps worse, unable to discern masquerade from reality.

A similar thread of critique runs through prints representing the Royal family's departure from the theatre.[11] In *Returning from Pizarro!!* the King rattles on about the playwright's loyalty, but a particularly dangerous looking Sheridan leads the royal party into a dark passageway full of a "pack of Jacobin Rascals." (See fig. 10.3) Again, the satirist's attempt to capture the danger posed by Sheridan's implied

Figure 10.2.   *Pizzaro a New Play or the Drury-Lane Masquerade*, by S. W. Fores, 1799. Courtesy of the Trustees of the British Museum.

Figure 10.3.   *Returning from Pizarro!!* by William Holland, 1799. Courtesy of the Trustees of the British Museum.

duplicity and sedition requires not only a diminution of the King's judgement, but also a startling re-characterization of the audience on that evening. Perhaps picking up on multiple reports of the general confusion on the stairs and the unseemly actions of the nobility, the audience members in the passageway are designated Jacobins. Is this because they are behaving like the mob which assaulted the King's carriage four years earlier—note the breaking of windows which appears in almost all the reviews of the command performance—or because at this moment in time, when one of the most vehement critics of the Crown dons the cloak of loyalty, the distinction between loyal and seditious, noble and base is radically destabilized? [12]

In all of these images, the King emerges as a particularly easy mark whose stupidity or narcissism impair his aesthetic and political judgement. The implications of the satire are no doubt disturbing, but they seem gentle when compared to the treatment of Pitt in a remarkable print entitled *Rolla's Address to the Peruvian Army*. (See fig. 10.4) The print presents verbatim Rolla's famous speech from the second act of the play—which is itself a rehearsal of Sheridan's famous speech on the Begums charge—that was so important to the early phases of the impeachment of Warren Hastings ten years earlier. The choice of speech is important because, as Andrew McCann has persuasively argued and I have also suggested elsewhere, it is rhetorically indebted to Burke's dramatic analysis of politics that was so crucial to the rhetorical excess of *Reflections on the Revolution in France*.[13] But the speech is now visually attributed to a highly effeminate Pitt dressed as Rolla before an equally effeminate army of Peruvian/British soldiers. As we will see, Sheridan's play scrutinizes Burke's deployment of effeminacy in no uncertain terms, and I would argue that this satire is responding to Sheridan's critique of Burke's rhetoric in quite specific ways. All of the figures in the foreground that comprise Pitt's war cabinet wear rouge, feathers and earrings.[14] On the right of the image, we are presented with Fox and others under the flag of Libertas on the not too distant shore of France. The print rather bluntly declares that Pitt is an especially unlikely candidate for the mantle of heroic martial masculinity characterized by Rolla, and—by extension—Sheridan himself in an earlier oratorical guise.

Like the image of the King's arrival and departure from the command performance, this satire suggests either that Pitt is, at best, an actor pretending to be Rolla, or that the audience, in their approbation for Rolla's speech, misrecognizes Rolla's true patriotic sentiment for the persona of the Minister. Pitt's reluctance to attend the play may indicate that he recognized the danger of the former representational trap, but what are we to make of the latter aspect of the play's reception? For it suggests that the audience's expressions of loyalty are not to Pitt, but to

Figure 10.4. *Rolla's address to the Peruvian army*, by William Holland (pub), 1799. Courtesy of the Trustees of the British Museum.

Sheridan's earlier critique: not only of Hastings governance in India, but also of Tory foreign policy. This implies that the audience is demonstrating loyalty not to the ministry, but to a type of Whig politics that explicitly projected a form of patriotic commitment to the constitution that was at variance not only with the Pitt government's incursions on political and civil liberties during the mid-1790s, but also with George III's perceived flirtations with absolutism from as early as 1783.

This is actually thematized in the speech itself, in a passage that caught the eye of more than one pro-government critic. After the famous vultures and lambs trope that was lifted wholesale from the Begums speech, Rolla declares,

> Be our plain answer this: The throne WE honour is the PEOPLE'S CHOICE—the laws we reverence are our brave Fathers' legacy—the faith we follow teaches us to live in bonds of charity with all mankind, and die in hope of bliss beyond the grave. Tell your invaders this, and tell them too, we seek no change; and least of all, such change as they would bring us.[15]

As Loftis argues, "the speech is unambiguous in its simple allegorical equation of the Spanish and Pizarro with the French and Bonaparte," but this lack of ambiguity is partially cancelled by the proliferation of allegorical relations.[16] As Julie Carlson notes

> At a minimum, Rolla's speech answers to five alarms of invasion. Besides those sounding between Peru and Spain, India and England, and England and France, Rolla's speech also raises alarms over the literary invasion of England by Germany in the 1790s and the perpetually immanent invasion of Ireland by England in the same years.[17]

As Carlson goes on to argue, this rallies the audience to two contradictory judgements regarding England, because England goes from victimizer to victim as the speech passes from the Hastings trial to the boards of Drury Lane. But this contradictory deployment of an us/them rhetoric is even more troubled than either critic suggests. When Rolla talks of serving a monarch who is the people's choice, we are in remarkably anti-Pittite territory. At the 1798 meeting of the Whig Club, the Duke of Norfolk and Fox himself got themselves in trouble making toasts to "Our Sovereign the People," for which Pitt petitioned the King to sanction Fox.[18] Within short-term memory, there is little to prevent this utterance from becoming a radical declaration of the people's right to check the actions of their king. Cobbett in fact wrote vociferously against the speech for precisely this reason.[19]

In a slightly more long-term view, this sounds remarkably like the characterization of Fox as "the man of the people" in the early 1780s that caused so much consternation during the debate over the India Bill in 1783 and the subsequent election of 1784.

Rolla's speech, like its oratorical forebear, is loyal less to George III and Pitt than it is to Foxite notions of the ideal constitutional monarch and to Fox himself in the early years of opposition to Pitt. In other words, Rolla's speech belatedly pledges allegiance to Whig principles that are here misrecognized by large portions of the audience as somehow manifest in those very figures who most oppose them. The radicalism of Sheridan's play lies in the fact that an increasingly obsolete form of British political identity, whose pastness is figured by the primitivism of the Peruvians, is called upon to do battle with George III and Pitt's corrupt incursions on the constitution. To add to Carlson's list of invasions, Sheridan posits the present ministry invading the constitutional past of Britain and figures forth a self-styled army of Whigs to defend British liberty. In this reading, there is little separating Pitt and Bonaparte; the former is an internal threat to the political legacy that constitutes the present state and the latter is an external threat who has emerged from a revolution itself indebted to British notions of constitutionalism.

What is remarkable is that the audience's allegiance to the content of Rolla's speech ratifies a type of political identity that the Tories had been highly effective in discrediting throughout this period. At the time of *Pizarro*'s first performances, the Allies were doing well on the Continent and the opposition's fortunes were arguably at their lowest point during the war of 1793–1801.[20] Unable to govern in the House, Sheridan achieved something quite startling. Through the power of allegory and a certain belatedness in the audience's ideas of political liberty, he was not only able to reinvigorate a type of Whig patriotism that had been effectively dead for some time, but also marked the failure of Tory rule to live up to this constitutional standard. But more importantly, Rolla's speech and its reception suggest that the audience's patriotic identifications were not tied to Pitt's ministry, but rather to a mythic constitutional past which Fox, Sheridan and—in an earlier guise, Burke—argued was the essence of Whig opposition to Tory governance. For Sheridan, this may be all for the good, but it also suggests that the audience was just as much to blame as the ministry itself for the perilous state of the nation. From Sheridan's position in opposition, the people seem unable to discern the true constitution from Tory incursions on it, or the real sovereign ideal from the current monarch. Thus, patriotic approbation supersedes political judgement, and that in itself was a dangerous development which I believe Sheridan was attempting to counter or at least reveal in *Pizarro*. If the people and the government are unable to discern the history of the English constitution from Burke's bizarre interpretation of it in the *Reflections*, then all that is left is the brute force of the State in a time of war. And, in such a hegemonic climate, even critique is transformed into consent.

Such a reading fits the trajectory of Sheridan's theatrical and political career more persuasively than the general charges of apostasy, aesthetic failure or inconsistency.[21] Throughout his career, Sheridan never wavered from showing the distinction between social and political ideals and their corrupt manifestation. *The School for Scandal* is a complex demonstration of how one must read the distance between public representation and historical action. Similarly, if there is one thing which unites Sheridan's political actions and his parliamentary speeches, it is a rigorous Whig belief that the gulf between the incumbent leaders of the nation and the idea of sovereignty and governance they are supposed to embody threatens not only the constitution, but also the polity at large. By 1799 this carries with it an important corollary: that the people are losing their ability to discern patriotic fantasy and national reality, true Whig patriotism from the charade of Tory pragmatism. *Pizarro* needs to be understood not only in the context of Sheridan's Whig oratory, as John Loftis and Julie Carlson have conclusively demonstrated, but also in the context of a new political order in which Whig principles—especially in their Foxite manifestations—no longer have political purchase, but linger on in vestigial cultural forms. Sheridan's complex dramaturgical strategies, which occasioned much commentary at the time, are intimately tied to these spectres of Fox.

Miscasting, or The Utopian Politics of Citation

The only hesitations regarding the first performances of *Pizarro* among reviewers, aside from its ponderous length, were a number of rather strange dramaturgical decisions on Sheridan's part. Foremost among these was the apparent miscasting of the chief female roles:

> Mrs. SIDDONS and Mrs. JORDAN are evidently out of their places. The latter has, in *Cora*, stepped beyond the natural limits of her powers and genius. The glowing warmth of parental affection, the transitions from tenderness to madness, despair, disappointed love, and the most violent agonies, do not fall within her province . . .—*Cora* would have been a *chef d'oeuvre* in the possession of Mrs. Siddons, and *Elvira* would have found an adequate representative in Mrs. Powell.[22]

Dora Jordan was the foremost comic actress during this period, but the role of the much-suffering Peruvian mother Cora is anything but comic, so Sheridan chose to cast her against type. This was highlighted by the fact that the role of Cora was almost a compendium of the maternal qualities most frequently associated with Sarah Siddons's acting style. With Siddons on stage in the role of Pizarro's mistress Elvira, the audience would have been constantly reminded of the tendentiousness of Sheridan's choice, especially since Jordan was arguably the most famous mistress of her generation. As Laura Rosenthal has argued, the vast number of satires on her affair with the Duke of Clarence and the very publicity of their liaison meant that "audiences loved to watch Jordan, but they also loved to watch William watching Jordan; their relationship became incorporated into the evening's entertainment."[23] Casting Siddons as the ambitious mistress and Jordan as the tragic mother is thus almost chiastic in its effect: the very reversal reminds the audience of its artifice.

One explanation for this decision is that casting Jordan as Elvira would suggest that Pizarro is the type of the Duke of Clarence. Such an insinuation would not only trouble the allegorical linkage between Pizarro and Bonaparte, but also open Sheridan to charges that he was indecorously ridiculing a reasonably popular, if somewhat ridiculous, Prince.[24] But perhaps Sheridan's decision to have her play Cora—with the implication that the Duke can be aligned with Alonzo—is less defensive and more strategic. Jordan famously had ten children by the Duke, so it is hardly a stretch to see her as the mother. But it is extremely difficult to see her as the wife. There is an irreducible disjunction between Jordan's social and theatrical identity and the character she is asked to portray. It is basically the same type of miscasting employed by the satirical prints discussed above. Pitt makes a poor Rolla, George III is neither as wise nor as beloved by his subjects as Ataliba, and likewise the Duke of Clarence falls short of Alonzo's dedication to his country and his wife. Each of the historical figures shares enough positional similarities with their respective characters for a comparison to be made, but these similarities are mobilized to signal the palpable difference between figure and referent. This allows Sheridan to be resolutely patriotic, but unbeholden to the present regime.

With some sense of the strategic possibilities in the chiastic casting of Jordan and Siddons, we can turn to the more complex issues raised by the character of Elvira. After the first wave of reviews, critics opposed to Sheridan's play—and they were legion—were particularly displeased with the character of Elvira. Samuel Argent Bardsley records his objections as follows:

> That a cloistered recluse should, on the first mention of Pizarro's exploits, conceive a violent attachment for his Person and Character, is an extravagant

supposition; but that she should afterward by seduced by this illiterate, fero-
cious, and every way unpolished Adventurer—(the *murderer* of her *Brother*
by his sword, and of her *Mother* through Grief) . . .—is an outrage against
probability, and in contradiction to the best feelings of the human mind.
None but an abandoned character could have acted like Elvira. Yet she is
depicted as possessing sensibility, moral feeling, a high tone of sentiment,
and great powers of Mind![25]

Bardsley's objection turns on what he refers to as the "inconsistency of this heteroclite character."[26] In his estimation, it is not possible that the Amazonian qualities
attributed to her in the first act could be reconciled with the lofty sentiments of
her remorse in acts three and five. It is difficult to say how much of this objection
is simply a matter of his discomfort with Elvira's palpable threat to normative
femininity—she is heteroclite by any late eighteenth-century standards—but there
is something conspicuous about Elvira's changing relation to the men and the situations in the play that merits further consideration.

Act one of *Pizarro* establishes the play's political allegory: the first thing we
find out about Elvira is that she is attached to Pizarro not out of desire for material gain, but out of "passion, infatuation" (I.i.657). Elvira loves Pizarro because
his martial masculinity accords with her own preexisting fantasy of male heroism.
As she states,

> *Elv.*: When first my virgin fancy waked to love, Pizarro was my country's
> idol. Self-taught, self-raised, and self-supported, he became a hero; and
> I was formed to be won by glory and renown. 'Tis known that when he
> left Panama in a slight vessel, his force was not an hundred men. Arrived
> in the island of Gallo, with his sword he drew a line upon the sands, and
> said, "Pass those who fear to die or conquer with their leader." Thirteen
> alone remained, and at the head of these the warrior stood his ground.
> Even at the moment when my ears first caught this tale, my heart ex-
> claimed, "Pizarro is its lord!" (I.i.658)

Elvira's passion for Pizarro arises from the narration of past actions and thus is
mediated by representation. Significantly, in a speech that follows closely upon this
one, Pizarro describes the precipitous attachment between Alonzo and himself in
almost identical terms:

> *Piz.*: Often I had talked to him of our first adventures—what storms
> we struggled with—what perils we surmounted.—When, I say, of these

things I spoke, the youth, Alonzo, with tears of wonder and delight, would throw him on my neck, and swear, his soul's ambition owned no other leader. (I.i.659)

Both Elvira and Alonzo are drawn to Pizarro by the power of heroic narrative, and thus their primary attachment is to a preexisting fantasy of character whose rough contours correspond to models of masculinity endemic to early eighteenth-century heroic narrative. This means that there is an irreducible gap between the phantasmatic object of desire and the historical or "real" figure to which it is attached. That gap constitutes a point of vulnerability in these relationships, and the play's multiple narrative strands arise out of two successive ruptures in that attachment.[27]

Alonzo is the first to break with the seductive power of narrative. Under the influence of Las Casas, Alonzo is persuaded "to forego his country's claims for those of human nature" (I.i.659), and attempts to convince Pizarro, through an argument based on "justice and humanity" that "the Peruvians [are] our innocent and unoffending brethren" (I.i.659). Pizarro's analysis of the rupture and his subsequent account of Alonzo's behaviour is revealing:

> *Piz.*: But when he found that the soft folly of the pleading tears he dropt upon my bosom fell on marble, he flew and joined the foe: then, profiting by the lessons he had gain'd in wrong'd Pizarro's school, the youth so disciplined and led his new allies, that soon he forc'd me. . . . in base retreat and foul discomfiture to quit the shore. (I.i.659–60)

Pizarro's tale extracts "tears of wonder and delight" from Alonzo, but Alonzo's pleading tears have no effect on Pizarro. Is this because the former are elicited by narrative and the latter are the product of moral reflection? The rupture between Alonzo and Pizarro is based on competing and irreconcilable definitions of community. For Pizarro, and even the potentially traitorous Valverde, the nation constitutes the primary locus of identification and loyalty. For Las Casas and Alonzo, the category of human nature trumps all other forms of allegiance and constitutes the ground on which a certain Christian cosmopolitical identity is forged. And this cosmopolitanism is secured not only by the moral and military affiliation between Alonzo and the Peruvians, but also by the bonds of blood. The intermarriage between Alonzo and Cora and their child turns a certain idea of the human into flesh and blood. This is why the endangerment of the baby is so crucial to the play's spectacular dynamics.

However, in order to secure this nascent cosmopolitanism, the Peruvians need to be re-figured not as obdurate heathens but as Christians *avant la lettre*. In a speech singled out by *The Oracle* as "one of finest and most impressive in the whole Piece," Las Casas berates Pizarro and his generals for avariciously planning to attack

> a King, in whose mild bosom your atrocious injuries even yet have not excited hate! but who, insulted or victorious, still sues for peace. Against a People who never wronged the living Being their Creator formed: a People, who, children of innocence received you as cherish'd guests with eager hospitality and confiding kindness. Generously and freely did they share with you their comforts, their treasures, and their homes: you re-paid them by fraud, oppression and dishonour. (I.i.661)

In its indictment of European relations with the colonized, the speech is remarkably similar to passages in Sheridan's "Speech on the Begums Charge" and Burke's "Speech Opening the Impeachment of Warren Hastings." Like his oratorical forebears, Las Casas attempts to render non-European peoples present by equating otherwise incommensurable social, familial and cultural structures.[28] Peru, here and elsewhere in the play, is the epitome of natural Christian religion in spite of the repeated but almost vestigial presence of the Sun God.[29] And yet, it is precisely the "naturalness" of this Christianity that prevents Las Casas's account from becoming anything but an ideal portrait of Britain. It is difficult for even the most fervent patriot to equate Britain with "a People who never wronged the living Being their Creator formed" (I.i.661). Thus the overarching political allegory is here qualified in important ways. Alonzo, Las Casas and eventually Elvira first cry for and then act on behalf of an ideal "People"—the same "people" who, in Rolla's speech, choose their King. Just as Rolla is not Pitt, the Peruvians are not Britons—or at least not yet.[30] The shift in affective investment from the narrative of Pizarro's heroism to the ideal "People" figured forth in Las Casas' speech—and subsequently embodied in Rolla and then the endangered child—constitutes a shift from one heroic ideal to another. But the shift in attachment or cathexis from Pizarro to Rolla to child requires an intermediary process that Las Casas and Elvira call "reflection."

When Elvira refuses to leave the Spanish warriors' colloquy, Pizarro allows her to stay on the condition that she remains silent.[31] Her response is I believe crucial to both the dramaturgical motive and political import of the remainder of the scene: "[t]hey only babble who practise not reflection. I shall think—and thought is silence" (I.i.660). Elvira is silent until Las Casas' portrait of Spanish rapacity and Peruvian innocence finally elicits the tears for which Siddons was so famous (I.i.661). Like Alonzo before him, Las Casas cries in his attempt to persuade Pizarro of the humanity of the Peruvians, and his tears elicit sympathetic tears from Elvira that resonate, not only throughout the play, but also with Burke's famous account of Siddons's tears in *Reflections on the Revolution in France.*

Reflections on the Revolution in France frequently mobilizes the power of emotion by conforming historical events to the form of sentimental tragedy.[32] Burke's success in this regard had tangible political effects, for the palpable weaknesses in his constitutional arguments were drowned out by the rhetorical effects of sentiment. What interests me is that the repeated scenes of crying in the first act of *Pizarro* mimic Burke's argument so carefully. Like Las Casas' teachings, the narration of the narrow escape of Marie Antoinette from her boudoir elicits contradictory responses. It supposedly provokes exultation among Dr. Price and his associates, and it provokes tears from both the narrator and from those readers of the tale with whom the narrator affiliates himself. Defending his own tears, Burke argues that he feels for the Queen

> because it is *natural* I should; because we are so made as to be affected at such spectacles with melancholy sentiments upon the unstable condition of mortal prosperity, and the tremendous uncertainty of human greatness; . . . . We are alarmed into reflexion; our minds . . . are purified by terror and pity; our weak unthinking pride is humbled, under the dispensations of a mysterious wisdom. (175)

This double naturalization insists that "in events like these our passions instruct our reason," but from here he declares the normativity of specific passionate responses in order to pathologize those who do not share his feelings of sympathy. It is with such a pathology in mind that Burke admits, first hypothetically and then directly, that he has cried:

> Some tears might be drawn from me, if such a spectacle were exhibited on the stage. I should be truly ashamed of finding in myself that superficial, theatric sense of painted distress, whilst I could exult over it in real life. With such a perverted mind, I could never venture to show my face at a tragedy. People would think the tears that Garrick formerly, or that Siddons not long since, have extorted from me, were the tears of hypocrisy; I should know them to be the tears of folly. (175–76)

The attribution of perversion to those who exult in a scene that should extort tears needs to be read against the curiously conditional nature of his argument. The opening sentence offers a hypothetical Burke, one who *might* cry, if he saw such a spectacle on the stage. Placing himself in the place of Price *et al.*, this same Burke would be ashamed if similar events in real life called forth feelings of exultation. For Burke, contradictory response is perverse. The shame lies in the inconstancy of the affect, for the tears shed in the theatre must not have been the result of natural feelings of sympathy—since the real events occasion no such affect—but rather of effeminacy. These tears are now a sign of "painted distress" that attests to the effeminate artifice of not only those enthusiastic for the French Revolution, but also those who question the moral significance of sympathy.

Throughout act one Sheridan stages scenes of judgement similar to those employed by Burke to naturalize his political reflections on the French Revolution. And he does so with the very actress whom Burke deployed to make his case. What happens, then, if we read the entire act as a rehearsal of Burke's political logic? As Burke suggests, Alonzo and Elvira cry when presented with Las Casas' representation because it is natural that they should—the Peruvians are innocent, the Spaniards are cruel and rapacious. But both Alonzo and Elvira demonstrate prior allegiance to the phantasmatic heroism of Pizarro that is itself derived from a passionate response to narrative. And that prior aesthetic response is figured in the play as non-normative: Pizarro frequently refers to Elvira as more masculine than many of his soldiers—"In love thou art thy sex's miracle—in war the soldier's pattern" (III.ii.684). Sheridan is using the sentimental logic of Burke's argument to discredit sentimentality as a tool for political or social ends. This, I believe, fits with Sheridan's long-standing critique of sentimental drama and helps to explain why Siddons in particular is cast in this role. Her deployment by Burke is here invoked to haunt his political legacy. When Almagro declares that Las Casas and Elvira cry because they are both women and thus incapable of constancy of affect, he, like Burke, uses the charge of effeminacy to argue that emotional inconstancy is an explicit symptom of treason. Only this time the audience is witness to "good" treason. This carries with it the implicit charge that Alonzo, whose emotions and actions foreshadow the emotional development and future actions of Elvira, is no less heteroclite. It is Pizarro and his minions whose political and aesthetic response remains rigorously consistent. What Sheridan is demonstrating here is that Burke's political analysis, or to use the word used by everyone involved, reflection, can be used to justify "unnatural" ends. By separating nature from moral good Sheridan effectively destroys Burke's attribution of normative response.[33]

For many critics, and not only conservative ones, there was something deeply unsettling about the disjunction between Elvira's political and sexual inconsistency and the nobility of her speeches and actions.[34] The critic at *Anti-Jacobin Review* is predictably the most extreme in its censure, for not only is he aghast that "one of the most reprehensible characters that was ever suffered to disgrace the stage . . . goes off unpunished," but also maintains that "Elvira is nothing less than a complete Godwinian heroine, stark staring *Mary* all over!"[35] As Donahue states, "This condemnation—a case of guilt-by-association with Mary Wollstonecraft— illustrates the perennial connection in the popular mind between unorthodox political belief and immoral conduct, in this instance between British radicalism and German "immorality."[36] But there is more at stake here when one takes Sheridan's casting into account. Siddons was rarely, if ever, associated with sexual impropriety off the stage, but some of her most famous roles subsumed past vice into present enactments of virtuous suffering. Like many of the tragic heroines in Siddons's repertoire, Elvira combines vice and virtue into a complexly flawed character. It is the progression from one to the other that draws the audience to her and makes her a compelling dramatic figure. By casting Siddons as Elvira, the implication is that the normative response figured forth by Burke is itself based on political inconsistency because only inconsistency can give rise to the tragic affect necessary for the passions to instruct the reason.[37] In this light, consistency, whether political or theatrical, is the province not only of absolutism and cruelty, but also of ineffective theatre. And *Pizarro* is an object lesson in how inconsistency, whether at the level of character, plot, or genre, can generate affect.

Alonzo and Elvira both turn on Pizarro and Spain, but their treason is justified by an investment in precisely the kind of cosmopolitical formation based on "right, justice and humanity" that Burke and other conservatives resist so vociferously. In the overall trajectory of the play, unwavering allegiance to the nation of the kind advocated by Pizarro and Burke is shown to be literally a dead end. Suddenly Elvira's statement that her reflection will be based on "thought" gains political purchase, because it implies that her "inconsistency" is a result not of passionate identification with Las Casas' representation of the Peruvians, but with a reasoned analysis of the morality of the Spanish cause. Passion does not instruct her reason, but rather constitutes the corruption from which her judgement must be salvaged. An important distinction emerges here: Alonzo and Elvira are seduced by a passionate and precipitous identification with narratives of Pizarro's heroism, whereas their defection from his influence is the result of a process of moral education, one of whose key features is the instigation of measures to reform moral evil.

This allows Sheridan to elicit patriotic feeling against Pizarro/Bonaparte—thereby implicitly prophesying the French leader's demise—*and* argue against the forms of nationalist identification called for by conservative propagandists. This double argument recognizes how crucial it is that in overcoming France Britain not become France, that Pitt or the King not become Bonaparte in order to resolve the war, for such a development would result in a victory for absolutism at home that may not be all that different from servitude to an absolute foreign ruler. As we will see, the alternative future lies in the hands of Rolla.

If this seems too subtle for a play whose modus operandi is often all too blunt, consider Elvira's speech in act three wherein she explicitly broaches the question of sympathetic response. With Alonzo captured, Elvira attempts to convince Pizarro to either release him out of mercy or to "let him arm, and bid him to the field on equal terms" (III.ii.682). However, she does not argue, as Alonzo does, that acting otherwise is "inhuman", rather she asks only that he be true to the heroic narrative that sparked her infatuation:

> *Elv.*: Pizarro, I demand not of thee virtue—I ask not from thee nobleness of mind—I require only just dealing to the fame thou hast acquired; be not the assassin of thine own renown. . . . Do not an act which, howe'er thy present power may gloss it to the world, will make thee hateful to all future ages—accursed and scorned by posterity. (III.ii.683)

Pizarro's personal hatred for Alonzo threatens to undermine the heroic tale that constitutes the basis of Elvira's passion for him, and is thus doubly damaging. It destroys his story for posterity and reveals that Elvira is committed not to the man but the heroic representation of him. When that is revealed, the scene of moral judgement is presented in terms that specifically mimic Burke's scene of conditional sympathetic judgement:

> *Elv.*: Pizarro, scorn not my words—beware you slight them not!—I feel how noble are the motives which now animate my thoughts—who *could* not feel as I do, I condemn—who, feeling so, yet *would* not act as I SHALL, I despise! (III.ii.685)

Is this not precisely how Burke stages his critique of Dr. Price and the Revolution Society presented above? Secure in the nobility of his thoughts, Burke condemns those who do not feel like he does and despises those who do but act otherwise. The only problem is that this speech is a prelude, not to an act of loyalty or love, but to Elvira's explicit declaration of vengeance.

Like those critics of Burke who perceived an erotic attachment to Marie Antoinette at the heart of his historical analysis, Pizarro ridicules Elvira's commitment to virtue as displaced love for Alonzo. Her response is chilling:

> *Elv.*: 'Tis well! 'tis just I should be humbled—I had forgot myself, and in the cause of innocence assumed the tone of virtue. 'Twas fit I should be rebuked—and by Pizarro. Fall, fall, ye few reluctant drops of weakness—the last these eyes shall ever shed. How a woman can love Pizarro, thou hast known too well—how she can hate, thou hast yet to learn . . .—Come, fearless man—now meet the last and fellest peril of thy life—meet! and survive—an injured woman's fury, if thou canst. (III.ii.685)

Elvira's transformation from lover to vengeful assassin at the end of the third act marks the turning point in the play, for the heroic narrative which instantiated her love has been subsumed into a larger narrative of her hatred. But this shift does not entail a rupture with the fantasy of heroic masculinity; rather, her hatred is fueled by Pizarro's infidelity to that obsolete narrative. As she retells the story of Pizarro's heroic deeds once again, they are suddenly deployed as evidence of her own potential greatness in overcoming him (III.ii.685).

Sheridan demonstrates that the conviction with which Burke judges Price *et al.*, and with which Elvira judges Pizarro, is not based on moral principles but rather on narratives whose erotic and political investments are not incidental but foundational. Passion for an idealized sovereign such as Marie Antoinette is no less phantasmatic than Elvira's infatuation with Pizarro, and thus we are forced to ask what prevents some reflecting subject from turning on his idealized leader when history—or in Sheridan's words "posterity"—ruptures the affective economy. The idealization of George III as Ataliba within this very play stages the political problem quite eloquently, for the audience is forced to distinguish the real threat to Britain's political stability from conservative fantasies of sedition. If the King or his ministry start (or continue) behaving in a way that "assassinates" the very renown generated by their propagandists—and by this play—then the polity or the audience will turn on these characters with hatred and vengeance. Revolution in these terms is a response to the Crown's failure to live up to the ideal of sovereignty. This is what I believe is at stake in the deployment of femininity in the print *Rolla's address to the Peruvian army*. (See fig. 10.4)

In this context, *Pizarro's* patriotism becomes subversive. It occasions loyalty, but it establishes political ideals—in this case, Whig ideals—that will become the benchmark against which future political action on behalf of the Crown will be measured. The more effectively the play can draw its audience to the ideal figures, then the more forceful will be its reaction if the Crown disappoints their patriotic fantasy. Sheridan may be promulgating a form of utopian identification aimed at destroying the present State when it fails to live up to the standard of heroic fantasy. This leaves us with two revolutionary paths, now allegorically affiliated with a form Britishness distinct from Tory nationalism: that followed by Elvira, and that followed by Alonzo. They are both occasioned by sympathy with innocence, but the former devolves into vengeance, while the latter develops into cosmopolitical interracial love. Significantly, both paths need to come together to kill Pizarro and then the former needs to be superseded by a tableau of domestic sentiment.

Spectacular Dialectics, or Bridging the Tragic Whig Past to the Cosmopolitical Future

The miscasting of Dora Jordan and Sarah Siddons opens up a situational reading of *Pizarro* that can account for the play's aesthetic, historical and political inconsistency. But that reading relies on a recognition of the dialectical potential not only of utopian narrative, but also of generic hybridity. Frederic Jameson has written extensively about the former in *Archeologies of the Future*, and his suggestion that it is not the particular vision of alternate political and social arrangements that constitutes the power of utopian thinking, but rather the formal disruption of actuality that generates a countermomentum of ongoing critique is germane to my analysis of *Pizarro*. In historical moments when economic and political formations seem to negate the possibility of oppositional positions—and this may well describe the situation of England in 1799—utopian projections force the audience to "concentrate on the break itself: a meditation on the impossible, on the unrealizable in its own right."[38] Sheridan does not stage his utopian vision of Britain in the future, but rather adapts it from the work of a foreigner and locates it in a conspicuously non-European past. And he is not the first political writer to envisage America as a locus of an alternate political and social order to that of a corrupt European state. What interests me is that this utopian gesture is connected to the past, but the significance of that connection will not be apparent until later in my argument.

Without discounting the financial motives behind adapting Kotzebue, the fact that Sheridan goes to precisely the kind of theatre most associated by conservatives with social levelling and moral vice should give us pause. Not only does Sheridan re-form this material into what one critic referred to as a "performance . . . in every respect conducive to virtue in its principles, feelings, and actions," he also explicitly adopted dramaturgical techniques that he himself did so much to discredit in *The Critic*.[39] It as though Sheridan specifically takes up the prevailing opinions about both Kotzebue's and his own work and turns them inside out. In my opinion, this same structure of reversal—already identified in the casting of the principal female characters—applies to Sheridan's casting of himself. The satires on Sheridan's supposed defection from the opposition take up precisely this issue, but what one discovers when one looks closely at the attacks on Sheridan is that they are far more equivocal than one might suspect. For example, in *Trying on a Turn'd Coat!!* Pitt fits Sheridan in court dress, but the lining retains the blue and buff of Whiggery so that Sheridan can turn back when it is to his advantage. (See fig. 10.5) But the etching also suggests that it is Pitt the tailor who makes it possible for Sheridan to turn his coat back and forth. The satire is primarily on Sheridan for ostensibly changing his political views, but it also attacks the ministry and supposed loyalists for being willing to recognize such an inconsistent client.[40]

What all this suggests is that political and aesthetic inconsistency are the point of Sheridan's complex intervention. As we have seen, the play thematizes political inconsistency, but its very enactment in the field of culture engages with this issue. *Pizarro* is a play seemingly inconsistent with Sheridan's past theatrical practice. Its political allegories are internally incoherent, so any attempt to simplify the play's political message requires a negation of a series of political counternarratives (some of which are associated with Sheridan's critique of the state and some of which are not). As Julie Carlson has indicated, the Britain allegorized in the play is simultaneously victim and victimizer, and disentangling these figural implications does serious violence to the play's relation to history. This is most evident in the way that Sheridan's own political oratory is deployed in the play. It is my contention that all of these inconsistencies—whether they be internal to the play, or part of the para-theatrical world in which it is performed—are activated to force the audience to focus on the break with the present that is most forcefully felt in the gap between the patriotism elicited by *Pizarro* and that which is supposed to inhere in the state form. That gap is crucial to understanding the importance of generic, familial, national and political hybridity at the heart of this play, and the way that these hybrid elements elicit patriotic identification with a national fantasy that has the potential to hollow out the claims of the Tory state and replace it with something politically unrealizable in 1799.

It should come as no surprise that contemporary criticism focussed on various forms of inconsistency and hybridity. After Elvira's moral judgement is staged

Figure 10.5. *Trying on a Turn'd Coat!!* etching by William Holland (pub), 1799. Courtesy of the Trustees of the British Museum.

for the audience and *Pizarro* enters its final two acts, grandiloquent speeches are subsumed into increasingly spectacular and improbable scenes. One could even argue for an accelerating departure from drama based on dialogue towards a theatre of visual effects, processions, battles and tableaus.[41] For many critics this shift seriously challenged the play's claim to be a tragedy and this generic question animated much of the immediate criticism of *Pizarro*. For example, Bisset's overwhelming endorsement of the play's aesthetic and moral value stages its entire argument in terms of naturalness and probability, but the famous bridge scene forces him into an "as if" construction. If we behave "as if" the bridge scene were credible, then we could maintain the play's status as a tragedy, which is to concede that the play exceeds the narrative limitations of tragic action.[42] Dutton's conservative lampoon of the play's myriad narrative improbabilities is more direct in its critique. He underscores the improbability of the battle scene where the Peruvians defeat the heavily armed Spanish with sticks, of Elvira's sudden appearance with just the sword needed for Alonzo to slay Pizarro, and finally of the "*tragico-comico-fancico* representation of the funeral obsequies of Rolla": "It was, it seems originally intended to close this solemnity with a dance, or Peruvian *hop*, round the bier; but this part of the ceremony, as being *too atrocious a murder* of the dignity of the tragic muse to be publicly exhibited, was reserved for private rehearsal behind the scenes."[43] By styling the funeral that ends the play as a "tragico-comico-fancico representation," Dutton is merely repeating one of Burke's most memorable critiques of the French Revolution. For Burke, the Revolution's historical innovation corresponded to an infraction in the laws of tragedy. By cutting itself off from the traditional laws of the Ancien Régime, France has devolved into the "unnatural" genre of tragi-comedy: "Everything seems out of nature in this strange chaos of levity and ferocity. . . . In viewing this monstrous tragi-comic scene, the most opposite passions necessarily succeed, and sometimes mix with each other in the mind; alternate contempt and indignation; alternate laughter and tears; alternate scorn and horror" (92–3). For Burke, such conflicts in sympathy weaken the ideological links that secure "the great chain of society" and portend social disintegration. For Dutton, the popularity of *Pizarro*'s generic innovation is a symptom of social illness.

Both Bissett and Dutton's arguments indicate, from opposite critical positions, that the spectacles of the bridge scene, the battle, the death of Pizarro and the funeral tableau (act five, scenes two, three and four respectively) have a supplemental relation to the tragic narrative. Spectacle in *Pizarro* often clinches the elicitation of tragic emotion and yet, like all supplemental relationships, it also undoes the play's cathartic claims. This paradox is perfectly captured in Dutton's faux-legislation "that, to render a tragedy truly tragic, it is indispensably necessary to murder, not only the principal dramatis personae, but the tragedy itself."[44] What interests me here is that the critics are drawn directly to the paradoxical gap between the play's ideal objectives as tragedy and the pragmatic necessity of spectacle to suture audience response. Bissett is forced to imagine a more perfect narrative, where Rolla's rescue of the child could be possible, let alone probable, and Dutton falls back into a rehearsal of a past argument regarding revolution that can only pathologize the patriotic response to the play. Both critics find themselves either enacting or recognizing the possibility of a critique of the present actuality.

Much about this critical situation is resonant, but nothing more so than the auspicious placement of the bridge scene in this supplemental relation. It is, quite literally, the bridge between the tragic fable and the scenes that call the play's generic claims into question. Act five opens in the midst of a dreadful storm with Cora, "wild and distracted," first bewailing the loss of Alonzo and subsequently of her nameless child. Through Rolla's actions both her husband and her child are returned to her, but the scene is crucial for establishing the depth of sentiment that unites this interracial family. Cora's anguish is intended to generate sympathy for her plight, and nothing could be more anxiety-provoking than the abduction of her child. With the bonds of the family suitably threatened by the Spanish soldiers, it falls to Rolla to snatch up and save the child of his friend and beloved.

If we look at the play's structure, act five, scene one is the negative repetition of the first scene of act two. Also set in a "wild wood," act two, scene one establishes the sentimental bonds of the family:

Cora: Now confess, does he resemble thee, or not?

Al.: Indeed he is liker thee—thy rosy softness, thy smiling gentleness.

Cora: But his auburn hair, the colour of his eyes, Alonzo—O! my lord's image, and my heart's adored! [*Pressing the Child to her bosom*]

Al.: The little daring urchin robs me, I doubt, of some portion of thy love Cora. At least he shares caresses, which till his birth were only mine.

Cora: Oh no, Alonzo! A mother's love for her dear babe is not a stealth, or taken from the father's store; it is a new delight that turns with quicken'd gratitude to HIM, the author of her augmented bliss. (II.i.666)

This sentimental dialogue goes on considerably longer and it subtly prepares the ground for Rolla's citation of the Begums speech in the next scene, for Sheridan's oration famously turned on precisely this kind of idealization of maternal love and filial piety. But it is striking that the introduction of the exemplary Peruvian family focuses so intently on the corporeal manifestation of the child's mixed parentage. To each parent, the child exhibits traits of their beloved, and this strengthens not only the love for their son but also the erotic ties between the parents. This both underscores the hybridity of the child and suggests that it is almost a dialectical resolution of the social, cultural and racial differences which otherwise constitute the grounds for violent conflict in the play. Pizarro's violent attempt to extirpate or enslave the Peruvians contrasts with Alonzo's amatory conquest of Cora: the former is characterized as destructive and avaricious, whereas the latter is idealized and, from this point onward, constantly under threat. In this context, the inter-racial union of Alonzo and Cora figures forth a political child who is nurtured in a household of natural religion and natural rights, but who owes its life to Sheridan's Whig principles. The child inherits a kind of politics that is impossible in the present, but which can nevertheless operate as a stance from which to critique the current actuality where more direct dissent has been discredited or criminalized.

Clearly, the Alonzo/Cora union troubles any straightforward allegorical equation of Spain with France and Peru with England. In terms of the play's alle-gorical equation of Pizarro and Bonaparte—and, because we can't simply insert Pitt here—Rolla and some undisclosed British leader, the fruit of the Alonzo/Cora union constitutes an amatory resolution to national conflict that lies beyond anything put forward by the ministry. Alonzo and Cora's child is an icon not only of a utopian form of cosmopolitanism that has not yet achieved maturity, but also of present vulnerability. In other words, the child, in its very potential, projects a cosmopolitan reconciliation of the present conflict into the future. And yet the preservation of the possibility for this future state relies on the intervention of a figure who, in his very words and deeds, embodies past Whig sentiment.[45] It is Rolla who saves the future, and in so doing, memorializes not only his but Sheridan's political past.

Rolla's citation of Sheridan's oratory links him to a particularly "hot" moment in Whig resistance to George III's flirtations with absolutism, because much of Sheridan, Burke and Fox's attack on Hastings was aimed at demonstrating the threat of "arbitrary power" to the English constitution. Because Sheridan's cited speech has a two-fold target—it takes aim at both Hastings's imperial rapacity and the Ministry's tacit acceptance of this kind rule—it reads doubly in the play. It is an apt call-to-arms against conquest that has the capacity to figure forth the French threat to British liberty. And yet it also has the potential to suggest, like Fox and Sheridan did so often in Parliament, that British liberty has long been under attack at home. As John Loftis points out, these kind of sentiments are not confined to Rolla: Alonzo justifies his treason by stating that "I have not warred against my native land, but against those who have usurped its power. The banners of my country, when first I followed arms beneath them, were Justice, Faith, and Mercy" (III.iii.681).

This political opposition to Pizarro, borne out of an adherence to principles of justice, faith and mercy, are the grounds of the highly eroticized and sentimental friendship between Alonzo, Rolla and Cora. When Rolla is first introduced in act two, scene one, he is hailed by Cora as "my friend, my brother!"; likewise Alonzo greets him with "my friend, my benefactor! how can our lives repay the obligation which we owe to you" (II.i.667). Alonzo and Rolla share not only a belief in principles of justice and humanity, but in a fashion completely in keeping with Burke's notion of "connexion" in *Thoughts on the Present Discontents*—which Fox so powerfully mobilized against Burke during debate on the Quebec Bill—they also cultivate their friendship so as to achieve active political ends.[46] The play repeatedly emphasizes that the strength of the Peruvian resistance to the technologically superior Spaniards rests on the combined efforts of Alonzo and Rolla. In this regard, they conform, almost to the letter, to notions of friendship advocated by Fox and which Burke left behind in early 1791.

But Sheridan elaborates on the friendship further. Alonzo and Rolla share a homosocial bond based on their shared desire for Cora. It is important to remember that Rolla risks his life to save first Alonzo and then Alonzo's child. The obligation referred to by Alonzo above is Rolla's decision to sublimate his desire for Cora and bless their marriage, but Sheridan leaves the erotic attachment intact throughout the play. Within this friendship, Rolla's barely suppressed desire for Cora is repeatedly legitimized by allusions to Rolla's relation to the child. Early on, Cora herself suggests that the child should look on Rolla as his father (II.i.667), but later in the play, when acting on Alonzo's request that he marry Cora should she become a widow, Rolla finds himself repudiated:

> *Cora*: For that love thou seekst; whose blossoms are to shoot from the bleeding grave of thy betray'd and slaughter'd friend!—But thou hast borne to me the *last words* of my *Alonzo*! Now hear *mine*—Sooner shall this boy draw poison from this tortured breast—sooner would I link me to the pallid corse of the meanest wretch that perish'd with Alonzo, than he call Rolla father—than I call Rolla husband! (III.ii.11–17)

Cora's repudiation of Rolla—however unmerited—is significant because it empha-sizes that Rolla is only ever and only will be the friend. And it is as a friend and not a husband or a father that he will die. As a friend, he can figuratively take the place of the father—he can even offer care that the father is incapable of providing—but ultimately Cora declares an irreducible distinction between Rolla and the child that is ultimately biological. This biological distinction is, I believe, meant to fig-ure a political distinction between the nationalist implications of Sheridan's Whig oratory and the utopian intercultural possibilities deposited in the child. This firmly separates Rolla's Whig qualities from the child's cosmopolitical potential, and yet it also suggests that of all the characters in the play he is the one needed to the guarantee the survival of the baby. In other words, a Whig representative will save the future, but the future is constitutionally distinct from the Whig past and the Tory present. In fact the emergence of this new political ideal will kill not only Rolla, but also Pizarro. And with their demise, the play predicts the neces-sary death and supersession of both national combatants—Britain and France in their current absolutist forms—and both political combatants—Whig and Tory constituencies as they were defined in the late eighteenth century.

This is why Rolla dies, not at Pizarro's hands, but incidentally during an attempt to save the future, here embodied by Cora and Alonzo's baby. What is so resonant is that this interracial and cross-cultural child figures forth a cosmopoliti-cal reconciliation that is paradoxically a return to Fox's fantasy of a post-revolu-tionary Europe based on Whig principles. Sheridan's key recognition is that such an anticipatory return necessarily involves the loss of the friend and, with him, the demise of the notion of party on which Whig action is based. Thus the audience is affectively bound to the loss of Foxite politics. Paradoxically, this becomes the core of patriotic identification in Tory times and may well constitute an extraordinary political and cultural victory for what is quickly becoming an obsolete form of politics. Patriotic response and by extension consent for Tory rule are negotiated through a kind of spectral Whiggery in which the current government is dead except as it is animated by Rolla's (Whiggery's) ghost. This effectively usurps Tory governance and makes it reliant on Whig principles.

But the loss of the friend has a further, more radical, connotation. The friendship between Alonzo and Rolla, like the love between Alonzo and Cora, crosses racial and cultural boundaries. Male friendship in the play can produce effective opposition to tyranny, but it cannot produce a child. In the figural economy of the play, this suggests that the political affiliation of Alonzo and Rolla cannot produce a way out of the present crisis because it cannot reproduce. In this context, race and sex become crucial political signifiers in the play, because they are precisely what prevent Rolla from ever being the father to Cora's child and what ultimately define his political fate. In the utopian rhetoric of the play, interracial friendship is sacrificed to guarantee the survival of a corporeally defined hybridity. This is resonant in light of Kathleen Wilson's argument regarding the emergent gap between the once-synonymous words "race" and "nation" at this historical juncture.[47] It is as though Sheridan is suggesting that the only way out of the current political conflict is to hybridize all social difference so that violence cannot be perpetrated on other peoples because alterity—or to use the word set into circulation by Las Casas, but never fully defined, "humanity"—has become the basis of identity. This implies something beyond a nationalist resistance to the State typical of Fox and Sheridan's oratory in the 1790s. Opposition here is taking on the extra-national quality of cosmopolitanism and in the process redefining the humanitarian principles of Whig politics.

At this point in an admittedly acrobatic argument, I want to turn our attention to the materiality of the bridge scene itself and turn it into an emblem for the entire discussion. What sense we have of the scene relies on three images, none of which can be conclusively connected to the first performances of the play. They all pertain to the moment when Rolla seizes the child from the Spanish soldiers. The first is Sir Thomas Lawrence's famous portrait of Kemble as Rolla holding the baby aloft in his left hand. (See fig. 10.6)

Everything about the strong diagonal composition of the image focuses attention on the baby. The halo of light in which the child is framed is symptomatic of his utopian function in the play: he exists separate from and above the dark action in which he is engulfed. And the composition contrasts him to the sword in Kemble's hand. The visualization of Rolla's heroism is complex because there are distinct visual echoes of Roman costume in this Peruvian warrior. This is true of other images of Kemble in the role circulating at the time (See fig. 10.7) and is a visual sign of the characters' proximity to any number of tragic heroes in the host of Roman plots which dominated eighteenth-century tragedy. The history of tragic Roman heroes on the eighteenth-century stage is not a happy one: the aesthetic failure of this legion of Roman plays and heroes is a commonplace of theatre history. And it is, I believe, significant that Rolla's Peruvian dress is little more than a modified Roman costume, for he is like his tragic forebears not only in his nobility, but also in his cultural obsolescence. As I have argued, the model of tragedy, largely enacted in Roman plots in this period, is rendered obsolete in this very scene.

This helps to explain the undecidability of Kemble's gesture as rendered by Lawrence. The sword is curiously poised. Is he about to slash his assailants? Or is

Figure 10.6.   *Rolla*, Henry Dawe, after Sir Thomas Lawrence, mezzotint, 1805. Courtesy of the Trustees of the British Museum.

Figure 10.7.   *We serve a Kind whom we love—a God whom we adore. Pizarro*, etching by
Robert Dighton, 1799. Courtesy of the Trustees of the British Museum.

the sword pointed at his own breast? The position of the hand, and the dramatic moment, indicate that it is the former. But the composition and overall flow of the scene point to the latter. He will die a sacrifice to the child in his other hand, and thus the sword pointed towards himself captures the overall import of this moment. Lawrence has rendered the very undecidability of Rolla's character: his gesture figures forth a threat to those who threaten the child *and* prefigures the sacrifice of himself that he is about to make on the bridge. The doubleness is apt, for it captures the paradox I have been outlining above. Rolla's heroism will both bring the tragic fable to its end and instantiate a new generic economy that undoes tragedy's civic claims. And out of the undecidable moment emerges the utopian sign around which this play's aesthetic and political challenges to present practice revolve.

The doubleness of Kemble's gesture and the triangular composition are crucial for understanding the iconicity of the child, and they inform the larger design of the scene. In an engraving of the command performance at Covent Garden in 1804 (See fig. 10.8) the bridge and the cataract are in an elevated central position in the background with Pizarro and the Spanish soldiers downstage right and Kemble and baby downstage left.

Since Rolla already has the child in his hand, the image illustrates the moment when he threatens to kill anyone who follows him (V.ii.22–3, 699). Presumably he would have been much closer to Pizarro and the soldiers downstage right for the early speeches of the scene when he is in chains. When Rolla seizes the child he exits stage left, re-enters upstage left on the rocks and is pursued by the soldiers who are under strict orders not to harm him. After struggling with some of the soldiers among the rocks, Rolla crosses the wooden bridge over the cataract, pursued by the soldiers, who shoot him. Even though he is injured, Rolla "tears from the rock the tree which supports the bridge, and retreats by the back ground, bearing off the child" (V.ii.699). He re-enters in the next scene to quickly return the child to Cora and die before the ensuing battle in scene iv.

Some sense of the blocking and the extraordinary effect of the collapsing bridge is captured in an engraving based on a performance of the play at the Theatre Royal Edinburgh in 1813. [48] (See fig. 10.9) Here we see Kemble escaping with the child and one of the soldiers falling with the bridge into the torrent. By placing Pizarro and Rolla opposite one another downstage at the crucial moment when Rolla seizes the child, the scene spatializes the fundamental political opposition in the play. But when Rolla exits and then ascends the rocks to the bridge, the audi-

Figure 10.8. *Covent Garden 1804*, engraving by J. Fitler, after Pugh. By permission of the Mander and Mitchenson Collection, University

Figure 10.9. *Scene from "Pizarro,"* from James R. Anderson, *An Actor's Life* (London, 1902).

ence is left with an absent spot downstage left. All of the remaining action occurs at a point above the stage, and the triangular effect perfectly captures the dialectical resolution of the opposition between Pizarro and Rolla. At the apex of the triangle we have Rolla, the child and soldiers. The soldier's bullet mortally wounds Rolla as he crosses the bridge. Likewise the soldiers are mortally wounded by the collapse of the bridge. The only survivors will be the child, who exits with Kemble upstage right and Pizarro downstage right. The audience is left contemplating an overall movement in which the child is borne aloft and everyone else either dies on the spot or dies in the ensuing two scenes. Rolla dies immediately in the next scene and Pizarro is killed in the following scene by the combined efforts of

Elvira and Alonzo. The spatial dynamics of the scene, wherein a direct opposition downstage leads to the sublimation of the child at the apex of the compositional triangle that is the bridge, materializes the utopian dialectic sketched out in the previous paragraph. The timbers that arch over the cataract metaphorically take us from the past to the future, and the collapse of the bridge figures forth the break with present actuality which lies at the heart of a string of utopian gestures in the play. The collapse of the bridge seals the fate of not only of those who threaten the child, but also the one figure who rescues him.

Significantly, this bridge from one political realm to another also marks a bridge from one aesthetic regime to another, because De Loutherbourg's remarkable painting and his ingenious mechanism inaugurate increasingly spectacular stage effects not only in the ensuing scenes, but also in subsequent melodramatic productions. The spectacular supplementation of the tragic fable becomes the most memorable aspect of the play and arguably what saves *Pizarro* from itself. With this leap over the perilous chasm into aesthetic domains more at home in the illegitimate theatre, *Pizarro* effected an audience response which was, at this moment of extreme state hegemony, beyond the scope of legitimate tragedy. Could we not argue that since tragedy's capacity to negotiate with social and political crisis was severely hampered by State intervention in both the theatre and everyday life, Sheridan adopted a hybrid form of theatre—like Rolla carrying Alonzo and Cora's hybrid child—in order to make him something other than himself? Just as Rolla sacrifices himself on the bridge to save the potential nascent in the interracial child, so too does Sheridan sacrifice his past theatrical and political personae in order to generate a countermomentum of ongoing critique of the political present. *Pizarro*, like Alonzo and Cora's child, is the child of an intercultural union that many observers thought would be treasonous, but which turned out to be more patriotic than conventional patriotism because it refuses to sacrifice humanity to the demands of the state. The strange amalgam of Sheridan and Kotzebue, which has so seriously damaged Sheridan's literary and political reputation, is just one in a string of sacrificial hybridizations thrown up by the play. In this light, the derogation of Sheridan's last play, like the dismissal of much of the melodrama that followed in its wake, has more to do with models of politics and aesthetics averse to inconsistency and hybridity. In other words, these dismissals, whether they come from the likes of Cobbett or from recent critics of Sheridan's oeuvre whose investments remain with a nationally defined literature, are equally indebted to the very social, cultural and political identities Sheridan may have been trying to get beyond.

The Remainder, or The Tears of the Crown

In this context, it is worth considering what gets left behind—the remainder left in the wake of the dialectical moment on the bridge above the perilous chasm. The play gives us two exemplary bodies, both of which die in equally improbable fashion. The much-criticized slaying of Pizarro, in which Elvira not only provides Alonzo with a much-needed sword, but also with the opportunity to prevail by interrupting Pizarro's concentration, elicits two key speeches. Elvira concludes her role in the play with a stirring evocation of Pizarro's counterexemplarity:

> *Elv.*: Cherish humanity—avoid the foul examples thou hast view'd—Spaniards returning to your native home, assure your rulers, they mistake the road to glory, or to power.—Tell them, that the pursuits of avarice, conquest, and ambition, never yet made a people happy, or a nation great.— [*Casts a look of agony on the dead body of* PIZARRO *as she passes, and exit.*]

She might be speaking directly to the Directory and, in that sense, she speaks as Sheridan believed the state should at this historical moment. Her utterance is markedly different than that of the monarch Ataliba: with the words "My brave Alonzo!" he doesn't even offer a full sentence and basically fades from the scene. In terms of the play's allegory, the current monarch fades away and is replaced by Alonzo, to whom the remaining Spaniards look for mercy. Ataliba is dramatically displaced until Rolla's body is brought on stage. This is interesting in light of Pizarro's expressed plans to keep a puppet leader on the throne after conquering the Peruvians. With Pizarro's military conquest over, Alonzo's amatory conquest appears to have the same result. The play's speeches end with Alonzo first speaking for Ataliba and then telling him what to do. In political terms, this points toward a post-Napoleonic world when a largely Whig-identified character takes charge of the state and the crown in a fashion that only Fox and Sheridan could dream of.

After Pizarro is killed by the combined efforts of Elvira's glance and Alonzo's hand, and Alonzo comes into power, tears are extracted from the King when an elaborate procession brings Rolla's lifeless body on stage (V.iv.702). The entire patriotic spectacle focuses on the loss of the benevolent Whig hero. It is an act of memorialization thoroughly traversed by Whig fantasies of the future because the king, in crying over Rolla's body, both figuratively and literally cries for Sheridan. By binding Ataliba to Alonzo, Cora and the child in a scene of sentimental mourning, Sheridan not only has the king weep for one who speaks words from Sheridan's political past throughout the play, but also subsumes the king into a cosmopolitical future in which his presence is vestigial at best. It is a future in which he will not speak, but will merely cry. And the ironic implication of course is that George III cries, as the reviews of the command performance indicate he did, for a fallen Whig hero who has just memorialized himself. George III's tears on the night of 5 June 1799 thus become a remarkably paradoxical sign. They may simply be the tears of narcissism. But, in the most radical interpretation, they suggest that he cries because—in going with Pitt and his bellicose ministry—he chose the wrong Rolla, and in so doing failed to live up to the ideal sovereignty envisaged not only the opposition, but also by the audience who shed tears for the fallen hero. They are tears which, like his seeming lack of concern over the ravages of war both at home and abroad, belatedly mark his distance from the polity and which open a gap in the present moment over which it is possible to imagine a genuinely new understanding of community. After too many years of war, the King's tears are shed for a future no longer possible, that nevertheless attests to the possibility of something yet to come.

Notes

1. The attribution of this design to De Loutherbourg now seems reasonably secure. For a discussion of its genesis and its afterlife in other plays, see Allan Jackson, "*Pizarro*, Bridges and the Gothic Scene," *Theatre Notebook* 51, no. 2 (1997): 81–91. Julie Carlson has recently suggested that the scene lives on as a form of anti-colonial visual countermemory in later plays concerned with slavery ("Race and Profit in English Theatre," in *The Cambridge Companion to British Theatre, 1730–1830*, eds. Jane Moody and Daniel O'Quinn [Cambridge: Cambridge University Press, 2007], 175–88).

2. For an extensive account of the visual satires associated with the play, see Heather McPherson, "Caricature, Cultural Politics, and the Stage: The Case of *Pizarro*," *Huntingdon Library Quarterly* 70, no. 4 (2007): 607–31.

3. For example Isaac Cruikshank's *The Delegates in Counsel, or Beggars on Horseback* depicts Sheridan, Fox and others inciting the sailors to Jacobinism. The print is predictably scurrilous and fails to adequately account for the complexity of the Whig position.

4. See Richard Brinsley Sheridan, *Speeches of the Late Right Honourable Richard Brinsley Sheridan*, ed. "A Constitutional Friend," 5 vols. (London: Patrick Martin, 1816), 4:424–28.

5. See Ibid., 4:397–410. Sheridan spoke on the matter four times prior to the speech of 2 June on May 8, 9, 23 and 26.

6. This position was shared by Fox throughout the 1790s. See Leslie G. Mitchell, *Charles James Fox* (London: Oxford University Press, 1992), 161–3.

7. See Conrad Gill's analysis of the Whig position (*The Naval Mutinies of 1797* [Manchester: Manchester University Press, 1913], 348–54) and especially his long citation from the *Morning Chronicle* June, 12 1797.

8. *The Star*, June 6, 1799. The opening and closing sections of this review are almost identical to the review in *The Morning Post and Gazetteer*, June 6, 1799.

9. See Stanley Ayling, *Fox: The Life of Charles James Fox* (London: John Murray, 1991), 196.

10. The phrase "Maidstone Liberty" refers to the political debacle following the trial of O'Connor when prominent Whigs including Fox and Sheridan acted as character witnesses for the defendent. This detail reminds us the play's complex relationship to Irish politics, but I will not be pursuing this issue in this essay.

11. Isaac Cruikshank's *The Return from Pizarro* (1799) renders the Royal Party's departure from the theatre in order to show Fox weeping over Sheridan's ostensible loyalty to the Crown.

12. See John Barrell, *Imagining the King's Death: Figurative Treason, Fantasies of Regicide, 1793–1796* (New York: Oxford University Press, 2000), 554–73.

13. Andrew McCann, *Cultural Politics in the 1790s: Literature, Radicalism and the Public Sphere* (Houndmills: Macmillan, 1999), 33–58.

14. Mary Dorothy George identifies Dundas, Grenville, Portland, and Windham in the foreground (*Catalogue of Political and Personal Satires Volume 7, 1793–1800. Preserved in the Department of Prints and Drawings in the British Museum*, 7 vols. [London: British Museum, 1942], 7:564).

15. Richard Brinsley Sheridan, *Pizarro*, in *The Dramatic Works of Richard Brinsley Sheridan*, ed. Cecil Price, 2 vols. (Oxford: Clarendon Press, 1973), 2:II.ii.669. All subsequent references to the play will be presented parenthetically by act, scene and page number.

16. John Loftis, *Sheridan and the Drama of Georgian England* (Cambridge, MA: Harvard University Press, 1977), 462.

17. Carlson, "Race and Profit," 362.

18. See Ayling, *Fox,* 199–200.

19. See Loftis, *Sheridan and Drama,* 466.

20. George makes this observation (*Catalogue of Political and Personal Satires,* 7:566).

21. Both Loftis' *Sheridan and Drama* (Cambridge: Harvard University Press, 1976) and William Cobbett's *The Political Proteus: A View of the Public Character and Conduct of R. B. Sheridan, Esq* (London: Cox, Son, and Baylis, 1804),76–94, indict Sheridan on these grounds. I have attempted to build a genealogy of Sheridan's theatrical practice that would lead to the complexity of this essay's reading of *Pizarro* in *Entertaining Crisis in the Atlantic Imperium, 1770–1790* (Baltimore: Johns Hopkins University Press, 2011).

22. *Evening Mail*, May 24–27, 1799. This passage appears verbatim in *The Star*, May 25, 1799 and a similar critique appears in the *The London Packet*, May 24–27, 1799.

23. Laura Rosenthal, "Entertaining Women: The Actress in Eighteenth-Century Theatre and Culture," in *The Cambridge Companion to British Theatre, 1730–1830*, eds. Jane Moody and Daniel O'Quinn, chap. 11, 159–74 (Cambridge: Cambridge University Press, 2007), 164.

24. In 1799 the Duke of Clarence was no longer in active service and despite attempts to connect him not only with a successful naval career, but also with Nelson's victory at Abu Qir, his public persona at this time was far from martial and anything but virtuous.

25. Samuel Argent Bardsley, *Critical Remarks on Pizarro* (London: T. Cadell and W. Davies, 1800), 28–9.

26. Ibid., 30.

27. This vulnerability is important because if we are to understand Pizarro as the type of Bonaparte, then it constitutes the all important point of resistance to his romantic claims on the imagination of his admirers (both sexual and political).

28. See Sara Suleri, *The Rhetoric of English India* (Chicago: University of Chicago Press, 1992), 49–74; and Daniel O'Quinn, *Staging Governance: Theatrical Imperialism in London, 1770–1800* (Baltimore: Johns Hopkins University Press, 2005), 165–221 for discussions of the deployment of sexuality in the Hastings oratory. See P. J. Marshall, *The Impeachment of Warren Hastings* (London: Oxford University Press, 1965) for the most cogent account of the proceedings.

29. Joseph Donahue, *Dramatic Character in the English Romantic Age* (Princeton, NJ: Princeton University Press, 1970), 142–4.

30. This was actually an issue of great concern to the conservative reception of the play. The Anti-Jacobin and others were quick to point out the religious distinction that prevents the Peru/Britain allegory from fully cohering. See Donahue, *Dramatic Character*, 149.

31. In the Harvard manuscript version of *Pizarro*, Las Casas' speech is introduced as a reflection: "What a dreadful reflexion! a Battle—against whom? against a King, that a few days ago offered peace—against a nation, that in innocence, and with purity worship their Creator in their accustomed way and manner." This precursor text is intriguing not only because it makes less of a connection between Peruvian worship and Christian deism, but also because it describes a future event as susceptible to "reflexion." The temporal disjunction makes the use of the word almost catachretic, but it is important to recognize that this same construction is used with less linguistic violence by Elvira shortly before Las Casas' speech.

32. Paul Hindson and Tim Gray, *Burke's Dramatic Theory of Politics* (Aldershot: Avebury, 1988), 13–27.

33. That this is demonstrated in a scene where the representatives of inconsistency are actually on the side of good—and on the British side of the allegory—turns the satirical knife even further, for the audience is asked to identify with that which is understood to be treasonous in any conventional understanding of the term.

34. Donahue, *Dramatic Character*, 147–48.

35. *Anti-Jacobin Review*, III (1799), 210. Quoted in Donahue, *Dramatic Character*, 147.

36. Donahue, *Dramatic Character*, 147.

37. This takes on further significance when we recognize that Sheridan was widely satirized for Elvira's supposed flaw. All of the graphic satires on the play, and much of the contemporary criticism, charge Sheridan with political inconsistency. He is mocked as an apostate, as one who is willing to surrender his political opinions for ready cash, as someone who has finally seen the error of his ways and as someone whose politics swing with the wind.

38. Frederic Jameson, *Archaeologies of the Future: The Desire Called Utopia and Other Science Fictions* (New York: Verso, 2005) 232.

39. Dr. Bisset in the *Historical Magazine*, June 1799, quoted in John Britten, *Sheridan and Kotzebue: The Enterprising Adventures of Pizarro . . .* (London: J. Fairburn, 1799),133.

40. Interestingly, this was what Pitt categorically refused to do during the mutiny crisis. Apparently Sheridan offered his services to Pitt at roughly the same time as his famous address to the House on June 2, 1799. Pitt refused the offer.

41. Gillian Russell, *The Theatres of War: Performance, Politics, and Society, 1793–1815* (Oxford: Clarendon Press, 1995), 54–9.

42. "Mr. Sheridan's *Pizarro*, as a fable, has unity of action; though, in the language of rhetoricians, an implex, instead of a simple story. The action is not only entire, but important and interesting; it tends to *improve our virtuous sensibility*. . . . Mr. Sheridan's Rolla we think a most masterly delineation of the best and highest moral qualities, tried in circumstances that required their *full* exertion; a combination of greatness and goodness of heroism, the kindest of affections, and the most exquisite sensibility, ministering to happiness. Excellent as the character of Rolla is, it does not transcend credibility. Feeling as he did, his attempt to snatch the child was perfectly natural; but, we must say, we think the escape through all the Spanish guards rather beyond the bounds of probability; although, if admitted to be credible, one of the most interesting scenes in the piece" (Britten, *Sheridan and Kotzebue*, 131–32).

43. Britten, *Sheridan and Kotzebue*, 136.

44. Ibid., 134–35.

45. See Loftis, *Sheridan and the Drama*, for a thorough discussion of Rolla's connection to Whig critiques of the government.

46. See my "Fox's Tears: The Staging of Liquid Politics," in *Spheres of Action: Speech and Performance in Romantic Culture*, eds. Alexander Dick and Angela Esterhammer (Toronto: University of Toronto Press, 2009), 194–221.

47. See Kathleen Wilson, *The Island Race: Englishness, Empire and Gender in the Eighteenth Century* (New York: Routledge, 2002), 1–28.

48. From James R. Anderson, *An Actor's Life* (London: Walter Scott Publising, 1902).

11

SHERIDAN AND WOMEN

Marianna D'Ezio

BORN INTO A FAMILY whose reputation and income were anchored in literature and the theatre, Richard Brinsley Sheridan's predisposition to theatrical activity was not unexpected. His father Thomas Sheridan was an actor and a manager, and Sheridan himself had always been surrounded by talented women writers, from his mother Frances Chamberlaine—a gifted authoress and playwright, albeit her work and biography still lack a comprehensive critical study—to his first wife Elizabeth Linley, a singer who managed to make a living from her public performances and contribute to realizing her family's financial independence. Furthermore, there was another society of women around Sheridan besides his family connections, comprising professional and amateurish playwrights who were pursuing their own way into the highly male-dominated arena of commercial theatres. Of the plays that premiered at Drury Lane during Sheridan's part-ownership of the theatre and his father's management in 1778–1781, twenty-six were written by women, including a whole generation of distinguished female playwrights like Hannah Cowley, Elizabeth Inchbald, and Elizabeth Griffith, as well as authoresses like Frances Burney who wanted to try their hand at writing for the stage.[1]

Official biographies of Sheridan have generally suggested that his role with regard to female theatrical productions was that of mentor.[2] At the time of Frances Burney's early attempts at writing for the stage, for example, when Sheridan had become the manager of Drury Lane, he nurtured her hopes by offering his assistance in producing her first play—the unstaged comedy *The Witlings* (1779)—and in trying to persuade her father, Charles Burney, to withdraw his ban concerning his daughter's passion for dramatic writing.[3] Burney writes an enthusiastic account of Sheridan's insistent request that she write a comedy, a naively flattering description of the great man who had "meditated to [propose this] to you the first Time I should have the pleasure of seeing you":

> As a manager who must, of course, be loaded with Pieces & recommendations, to urge me to write, & to promise to thank me for my Writing, instead of making a favour & a difficulty of even looking at it,—is it not truly good-natured & liberal minded?
>
> And now, my dear Susy,—if I should attempt the stage,—I think I may be fairly acquitted of presumption, & however I may fail,—that I was strongly pressed to try by Mrs. Thrale,—& by Mr. Sheridan,—the most successful & powerful of all Dramatic living Authors,—will abundantly excuse my temerity.[4]

In a similar tone, Elizabeth Griffith's "Advertisement" to her comedy *The Times*, first performed at Drury Lane on 2 December 1779, addressed Sheridan's father and "return[ed] thanks to my much-esteemed friend, Mr. SHERIDAN, senior, for his kind attention to the getting-up my Play, my ill health not permitting me to attend one Rehearsal."[5] For his part, Sheridan also wrote a conspicuous number of prologues and epilogues—to Elizabeth Craven's *The Miniature Picture*, for instance, acted at Drury Lane on 24 May 1780,[6] and to Hannah More's *The Fatal Falsehood*, first performed at Covent Garden on 6 May 1779[7]—ostensibly, as he wrote to Garrick, because he meant to be "vastly civil to female talent of all sorts."[8]

Taking the above into account, it would seem pertinent to disagree with Ellen Donkin, who argues that Sheridan maliciously sabotaged women dramatists' productions with the intention of undermining the idea of the woman playwright as professional.[9] Sheridan *was* critical of women's involvement in writing for the stage as well as in performing; however, evidence of and, more importantly, the reasons for Sheridan's attitude towards women's professionalism have yet to be fully demonstrated. One of the aims of this essay is precisely to shed light on Sheridan's often-misinterpreted connections with the professional women of his time, in order to assess his own personal and professional stance towards the female sex and to measure the impact of his ideas regarding women on the course of his own career as a dramatist.

Sheridan's relationships with the women in his life—whether aristocratic female representatives, professional women writers, or his two wives—mirrored the contradictions and eccentric aspects of his own character. From his clandestine, romantic marriage with Elizabeth Linley as a young and penniless son of an Irish actor to his entry into the fashionable world of the Whig patroness Georgiana, Duchess of Devonshire, his notorious "womanizing" has been frequently distorted.[10] Sheridan's notions of love and his idealistic self-representation as passionate hero are indeed much more complex and kaleidoscopic than they may seem. He possessed a strong yearning to be accepted into the high spheres of eighteenth-century society—one still reluctant to admit members of an intellectual middle class that was busy affirming its professional presence. And yet Sheridan was never a flatterer: he acquired his position amidst members of the upper classes with by his genius alone. From time to time, Sheridan took on the roles of public man, politician, gentleman, devoted husband, and affectionate lover, although his social and political ascent demanded in return the sacrifice of both Elizabeth Linley's and his second wife Hecca's sentiments. He could be relentless, impetuous, seductive, and even vengeful with the women he was determined to pursue, yet he was never vicious, and his female partners were always strong women with vivacious intellects and original minds. On the other hand, Sheridan consciously recognized the ambiguous character of his relationships with the female sex, and alternatively pictured himself as a candid lover consumed with "tormenting sensations," and as the "Serpent [that] found [its] way to the ear of slumbering innocence," learning with time to bargain his feelings for a much coveted place among the wits:[11]

> I have fixed to myself a walk in Life, for my entrance into which I shall work 'Oar and Sail' as the Devil did in Milton, and when I am in, if I can't make my way on, I shall deserve to be trod on.[12]

Both his wives would soon learn to "taste the forbidden fruit" in order to reconcile with his eccentric character and continue to live with him.[13]

Drawing liberally from his personal and professional relationships with women, Sheridan depicted and polished his ideal of the woman throughout his works: there is an interesting evolution of the female characters, especially in his comedies, that follows Sheridan's own involvement with Elizabeth Linley and the coterie of fashionable women of Devonshire House, coming full circle in the uncommon "new woman" of *The Camp* (1799). The character of Nell, notably underestimated among the female characters in Sheridan's theatrical production, is at the other extreme of Lydia Languish in *The Rivals* (1775). And yet these characters complement each other, thus offering a complete (and complex) notion of a Sheridanian female *alter ego* that, never finding full expression in a single character in Sheridan's works, was instead fragmented into a series of fictional women that combine together his own multi-faceted personality.

Writing to Mrs. Angelo from Bath in October 1770, Sheridan was probably already infatuated with the woman who would inspire so many characters in his comedies as well as some of the most adventurous episodes of his life, including duels, an elopement to France, and a secret marriage. He recounted that Bath was "no place for news," except for the fact that "there is a Mr. Linley here, a music master, who has a daughter that sings like an angel; perhaps you may have heard of her."[14] At that time, he wrote that most of the women he associated with at Bath were, to use a theatrical expression, "as ugly as Lions," and Elizabeth Linley was already a celebrity. The story of Sheridan's romantic elopement with "Eliza" to escape the persecutions of Captain Mathews, and of their consequent clandestine marriage in France, is well-known to Sheridan scholars and readers. As a matter of fact, more than witnessing the passion that Sheridan bore for Eliza—"my love is almost the only Feeling I have alive"—the fashionable milieu of Sheridan's love affair with her, made up of duels, gossip, speculations and newspaper paragraphs, turned into his first public performance and the ideal setting for his official entrance into the world *à la mode*.[15]

Before moving to Bath with his father in 1770, Sheridan was a solitary young boy, with some vague prospects of becoming a lawyer and a deep sense of revenge already rooted in his soul. His mother's death in 1766, the rivalry he had always felt with his brother Charles, and the ambiguous relationship with his father exacerbated his anxieties about finding himself strangled by an ordinary life that could domesticate that "brilliancy of genius" his sisters always ascribed to him.[16] The occasion of endorsing his concept of himself as the romantic hero offered by Eliza's situation and prompted by Sheridan's sisters could provide more excitement and popularity than simply laboring over the translation of some erotic fables from the Greek, or in writing a burlesque narrative of the amours of deities and mortals.[17] To Alicia and Betsy Sheridan, it would be obvious that "one so handsome, clever and bold had been designed by Nature to act the part of a knight of olden time," and Sheridan was captivated by this unexpected, romantic role he was called upon to play.[18] He and Eliza spent the following years in reciprocal adoration, opposed by their fathers, with secret encounters and exchanges of verse from both sides, and with Sheridan "doom'd to hope in vain / The joys that love requite,"[19] but at the same time involved in a whirlwind of "sordid encounters."[20] Thanks to Eliza, the boundaries between his private and public persona had blurred: he was ready to make the scene on the London stage.

Being in the spotlight, however, required some kind of social distinction: years later Sheridan would recognize that the society he wanted to join and from whom he craved acceptance was one "in which *Propriety* of *conduct*, and Purity and decorum of sentiments are only taunted at and reviled!"[21] But at the time of Sheridan's entrance into the world, representatives of the upper classes would still shun the multitude of playwrights, actresses, writers and performers from outside his circle of influential friends.[22] Associating actresses and literary women professionals in general with "Creature[s] of a mercenary Manager, The Servant[s] of the Town, and a licens'd mark for Libertinism" was in fact a prevailing opinion among aristocrats that labeled them as prostitutes, notwithstanding Sarah Siddons' successful efforts to rehabilitate the respectability of the profession.[23] Sheridan seemed to have established his own scale of respectability for women, ranging from the lowest station—actresses, with whom his theatrical activity at Drury Lane (1776–1809) occasioned him to meet and rehearse with on an almost daily basis—to numerous women playwrights, and to the highest rank of aristocratic women, including the Duchess of Devonshire, Lady Duncannon, and Maria Fitzherbert, royal mistress to George III. Chameleon-like, Sheridan cheekily learnt to rise from the ranks at all levels of London society, and the women who crossed his path became instrumental in the construction of his public character.

Sheridan had no birthright to be admitted to the society of Devonshire House, but his friendship with the Duchess became his passport to high society. "[D]espite the difference in their upbringing there was a similarity in their temperament," as they were both romantic dreamers and passionate lovers, and shared an instinctive aversion for compromise.[24] Their connection was intense: Sheridan could rely upon the Duchess in his gloomy days, and when reflecting on his life on the eve of Eliza's death he would intimately confide to the Duchess his deepest concerns on "the irregularities of all my Life and pursuits, the restless contriving Temper with which I have persevered in wrong Pursuits and Passions [. . .]."[25] The "reflexion worse to me than ever to those who have acted worse" did not prevent, however, his serious love affairs, notably with Frances Crewe and Harriet Duncannon (sister of the Duchess of Devonshire), both known to his wives.[26] On the verge of his death, his second wife, Hecca, would ask Lady Duncannon, then Lady Bessborough, to assist him at his deathbed: Sheridan had loved her passionately for almost twenty years, in spite of both his marriages and the fact that Lord Duncannon had threatened to divorce her and prosecute him. Like Georgiana, Harriet was the repository of the melancholy of his darkest moments. When "reflecting on many past scenes," he admitted, "there has been length of Life enough to bring regret."[27] The relationship between Sheridan and Lady Duncannon, however, was neither a romantic friendship nor a platonic infatuation: Sarah Ponsonby, one of the Ladies of Llangollen, reported that Sheridan and Harriet had been caught *in flagrante*.[28] Even after the scandal, and despite Lord Duncannon's sudden decision to leave England for Brussels with his wife, Sheridan would allusively write to her about ten years later to inform her that "Hecca has a cold, and I am staying with her this evening or I would come . . . "[29] His sexual relationship with Frances Crewe was instead publicly alleged by the verse dedication that Sheridan wrote for her and circulated among his friends, which has since been printed as the dedicatory poem to his *School for Scandal* (1777). Eliza also "participated" in the affair, since the name of "Amoret" that Sheridan used to refer to Mrs. Crewe was the sobriquet that Eliza herself had coined some years before in her poem "Laura to Silvio" to describe Crewe (as Amoret) courting the young poet Silvio (Sheridan):

> With gentle step and hesitating grace,
> Unconscious of her power, the fair one came;
> If while he view'd the glories of her face
> Poor Silvio doubted—who shall dare to blame?
> A rosy blush his ardent gaze reprov'd,
> The offer'd wreath she modestly declin'd
> [. . .] At last, unable to decide, he divides his garland among
> them—to Myra, the rosebuds; to Stella, the glowing carnations; to Flavia,
> the daffodils; to Jessie, the flower called Love-in-Idleness; to gentle Amoret,
> Violets and Eglantine. To Laura he gives a never-fading wreath of Myrtle.[30]

At the time of their first meeting, around 1775, Frances Crewe was one of the most beautiful and brilliant hostesses of London society, and Eliza indignantly tolerated her husband's intimate connection with her.[31] Sheridan's "Portrait," where he designated "the gentle Amoret" as the model for the "Daughters of Calumny," the "prim adepts in Scandal's School"[32] was not only, in O'Toole's words, "a peculiarly public form of love letters."[33] Rather, it was a public declaration of reverence and admiration in keeping with the moral conventions of the world of which he had then officially become a member: to be associated with the high spheres of fashionable society meant accepting and sharing its values, however immoral and dissolute they might appear. As Lady Teazle and Surface put it in *The School for Scandal*, since most aristocratic women did admit "a Lover" but "no farther than Fashion require[d]"—"a mere Platonic Cicisbeo, what every London wife is entitled to" (II.ii.384)—fashionable ladies would also, and often, transgress the boundaries of prudence and morality prescribed by gender conventions, as well as their male counterparts customarily did.

Sheridan was indeed performing the role of melodramatic Byronic hero in order to secure his position among the wits in the Devonshire House circle. On the one side, such connections contributed to his public success as a playwright. Patronizing his *premières* of *The School for Scandal* on 8 May 1777, and *The Critic* on 30 October 1779 at Drury Lane, and praising the latter as "vastly good" since "it occasioned peals of laughter ev'ry minute," not only did the Duchess of Devonshire *de facto* advertise Sheridan's plays but her presence was itself a remarkable sign of prestige and distinction.[34] She also supported Sheridan's early attempts to launch himself in a much-desired political career, helping him to stand as a Whig representative for Stafford in the summer of 1780, an office he maintained for more than thirty years. "It is no Flattery to say that the Duchess of Devonshire's name commands an implicit admiration whenever it is mentioned," he wrote in his thank-you note, acknowledging that Georgiana's assistance in his political ascent was crucial.[35] As for Sheridan, when the fashion for romantic sensibility reached the stage with John Philip Kemble and Sarah Siddons' acclaimed performances in Kotzebue's English version of *The Stranger* (1798), he wrote a song for the play, and Georgiana set it to music, more than twenty years after the commencement of their friendship.[36] It is easy to read Sheridan's lines in the light of the exclusive attachment he professed for Georgiana, whom he would depict as his sole, trustful confidante:

> I have a Silent Sorrow here,
> A Grief I'll ne'er impart;
> It breathes no Sigh, it sheds no Tear,
>   But it consumes my Heart!
> This cherish'd Woe, this loved Despair,
>   My lot for ever be;
> So, my Soul's Lord, the pangs I bear
>   Be never known by thee![37]

Parallel to the public, sophisticated role of romantic hero and *protégé* he interpreted for his aristocratic patronesses runs the story of Sheridan's relationship with women writers, and his supposedly unscrupulous conduct towards female playwrights. As early as 1779, in the first edition of her *Albina* "Mrs. Cowley charges the Managers of Drury-lane and Covent-garden theatres with unfair practices while [the tragedy] was in their hands."[38] The anonymous editor of a later edition of the play cautiously suggested that "similar charges have often been made by other authors: but, probably, they originated more in their own fancies than in the conduct of the Managers." The charge that Cowley put forward in the 1779 Preface to the tragedy of *Albina* was technically one of plagiarism. Besides her disappointment at Sheridan's personality and behavior—"I wrote to Mr. *Sheridan* [. . .] but of my letter not the least notice was taken," "I waited three hours, (which was rather longer than he had ever made me wait before)," "in apologies for negligence Mr. *Sheridan* is remarkably easy and successful"—she was now experiencing what she had "frequently heard, before I had any experience in this anxious warfare, [. . .] the danger when once an idea is afloat in the Theatrical Hemisphere, of its getting into other plays. Amidst the croud [*sic*] of Plots, and Stage Contrivances, in which a Manager is involv'd, *recollection* is too frequently mistaken for the suggestions of *imagination*."[39] Hannah More's *Percy* (1777) and *The Fatal Falsehood* (1779) were both staged while Cowley was still waiting to see *Albina* performed at either Drury Lane or Covent Garden: *The Fatal Falsehood* in particular, for which Sheridan wrote the epilogue, bore an astonishing resemblance to Cowley's play in "every essential circumstance in the Plot, and Character [. . .] [and] it was changed principally in those places which had been objected to in mine" by Sheridan himself.[40] Sheridan's "most injurious and unaccountable manner" could reflect a characteristic practice of theatre managers, as well as of playwrights.[41] As Hester Lynch Thrale asserted, however, "borrowing" from female playwrights seemed to be rather more blatant:

> I believe there are really very infamous Things done by the Managers with regard to the female Wits: the poor Girls are so easily brow beaten, & dare not tell how M[r] Such a one treated their Piece with Contempt for fear of incurring more Contempt; so then M[r] Such a one lays it by as worthless, & in a Year or two, (especially if the Wench dies,) brings out a Play of his own upon her Plot, or with a Character from her performance as suits him best. Sheridan certainly serv'd poor Miss Richardson so: She was a sick Milliners' prentice on Tower Hill, & very unlikely to battle with Managers, but the Fellow that does such dirty Tricks & then writes an Epilogue to ridicule Female Wits, and fright the Women from writing—*should hear* of it, & so he shall.—as for deserts, he *deserves* to be sent to the Justitia, as well as many a less elegant Thief.[42]

Mrs. Thrale openly accused Sheridan of having plagiarized Elizabeth Richardson's *The Double Deception* (1779) in the last lines of a poem she sent to the *Public Advertiser*:

> Did Sheridan receive no Billet
> Was the Duenna all his own?
> Or did he like a Scoundrel steal it,
> And palm his Theft upon the Town.[43]

Richardson's play ran for four nights at Drury Lane, was then withdrawn and never published, and therefore it is difficult to ascertain Sheridan's appropriations. The habit of borrowing was not, however, merely a matter of counterfeit. In the same way that Sheridan would send love letters to Hecca by copying them from letters he had written to Eliza, he would also rewrite, rephrase, adapt, and reuse his own writings. The first part of his prologue to Lady Elizabeth Craven's *Miniature Picture* reappeared in the prologue to *Pizarro* (1799), and a preliminary version of his epilogue to Hannah More's *Fatal Falsehood* had earlier occurred in *The Camp*.[44]

Of all the women writers with whom he had collaborated in his lifetime, however, Sheridan was mostly indebted to his mother. As O'Toole also suggests, his "appropriations" were a celebration of her work, an affectionate tribute to a mother with whom he had scarcely lived, and who died when he was only fifteen. "Filial piety! [. . .] the primal bond of society," he would declare in 1788 in his notorious speech during the trial of Warren Hastings; although he could not fulfill "that instinctive principle which [. . .] soothes, unbidden, each sense and sensibility of man," he wanted to show his mother "that gratitude which, softening under the sense of recollected good, is eager to own the vast, countless debt it never alas! can pay [. . .]."[45]

As a matter of fact, however, notwithstanding Sheridan's sympathetic consideration of his mother's career as a playwright, his "first wish in attempting a play [i.e. *The Rivals*] [. . .] to avoid every appearance of plagiary" did not seem to apply to Frances Chamberlaine's writings. And *The Rivals* was not the only one of Sheridan's comedies to draw situations and characters from Chamberlaine's works. Although I disagree with Elizabeth Kuti's attempt to deconstruct Sheridan's innovations and comic strategies so that Chamberlaine can fully emerge "as the acknowledged inspiration behind her son's plays," Sheridan's debt towards his mother's plays is undeniable.[46] From the character of Faulkland, directly borrowed from Chamberlaine's *Memoirs of Miss Sidney Bidulph* (1761) and the title of his *Trip to Scarborough* (1777), reminiscent of her *Trip to Bath* (unfinished; although this play has always been published as *A Journey to Bath*),[47] to the characters of Sir Oliver Surface in *The School for Scandal*, styled after Ned Warned in Chamberlaine's *Sidney Bidulph*, and particularly Mrs. Malaprop, based on Mrs. Tryfort in *A Trip to Bath*, one might attest that Chamberlaine provided more than naive inspiration to her son's own plays.[48] While Mrs. Malaprop, for example, was unwittingly shaping neologisms and using expressions like "progeny of learning" and "contagious countries," Mrs. Tryfort had already employed the exact same phrases. Rather than looking at Sheridan's borrowings of Chamberlaine's writings as mere "plagiarism" as Kuti puts it, however, I believe that Sheridan consciously wanted instead to provide his mother's work with the recognition she deserved, and to which she had aspired throughout her lifetime. Since plagiarism implies rewriting, Kuti acknowledges, Sheridan's "appropriations" indeed fostered the re-writing of his mother's plays with the precise purpose of establishing and even perpetuating her success. Such was Thomas Sheridan's tacit intention when he consigned the manuscript of his wife's *Trip to Bath* into Richard's hands in order to revise it, and thus the rewriting process might have become reciprocal, with Sheridan eventually rewriting passages of his mother's play rather than merely appropriating them. In fact, "to make Mrs. Malaprop, Sheridan added a vicious twist to his mother's gentle satire," and therefore a character that Chamberlaine had only—though admirably—outlined in her play eventually came to be perfected in Sheridan's own comedy.[49] Unsurprisingly, Richard was not alone in promoting and "rewriting" his mother's works. On 25 November 1813, an anonymous melodrama version of Chamberlaine's novel *The History of Nourjahad* opened at Drury Lane,[50] and most importantly, Alicia Sheridan Le Fanu adapted her mother's unpublished novel *Eugenia and Adelaide* (1739) for the stage.[51]

To her son Richard, Chamberlaine was a professional writer who struggled against contemporary social expectations to accomplish her writerly ambition, defying the gendered conventions of her time. The character of Sir Anthony Absolute in *The Rivals* and his coarse aversion to women's literacy remarkably hints at her father's prohibition of learning to read and write: "Had I a thousand daughters, by Heaven! I'd as soon have them taught the black art as their alphabet!" (I.ii.85). Sheridan's most vehement reply to Sir Anthony Absolute is to be found in his project of a "Royal Sanctuary," a sort of educational institute for unfortunate gentlewomen that he addressed to the Queen in a letter dated around 1772. Mrs. Malaprop's "instructions" concerning "what I would have a woman know" (I.ii.86) ironically put Sheridan's plan into practice:

> The Classes are to be distinguished only by age—none of Degree—for as their qualification should be Gentility, they are all on a Level. The instructors should be women, excepting for the Languages. Latin and Greek should not be learned. The frown of Pedantry destroys the blush of Humility! The Practical Part of Science, as of Astronomy, etc., should be [taught]. In History they would find, that there are other Passions in Man than Love. As for Novels there are some I would strongly recommend. But Romances infinitely more. The one is a representation of the Effects of the Passions as the[y] should be, tho extravagant. The other as

they are. The Latter is false[ly] called Nature, it is a figure of depraved and corrupted Society. The other is the glow of Nature. Therefore I would exclude all Novels that show Human Nature depraved. However well executed the Design will disgust. The Next Thing to be attended to is their accomplishments. They should be early be instru[ct]ed all in Dancing, and wools emboidery [*sic*] etc. Those whose Genius should lead to it in Musick and Poetry, and Drawing. Diversions. These are the happinesses. A well directed imagination, more than an improved Understanding, or honest disposition Promotes the welfare of individuals. They should ride and walk, the younger Part be invited to exercis[e] by the little Pastimes. Dancing and Concerts, always a Spirit of Emulation kept up by Prizes. In the Winter the French petit jeus at once entertain and quicken the genius. [. . .] Above all a Knowledge of Œconomy and the Management [of] a House should be inculcated.[52]

Sheridan's concerns about women's education were undoubtedly prompted by his mother's example and must be also considered in the light of the effect that female learning could have on men's conduct: "the influence that Women have over us," he admitted, "is as the Medium thro' [which] the finer arts act upon us, the incense of our Love and respect for them, creates the Atmosphere of our Souls, which corrects and melio[r]ates the beams of Knowledge, where it is not, the Night of Ignorance shall prevail."[53] His admiration for his talented mother and his choice to marry brilliant women—Eliza Linley, not only a celebrated singer and a beauty but also Sheridan's writing assistant,[54] and Hecca, an eccentric young woman who could not "help telling Sheridan everything that comes into my mind"[55]—and to always carefully select "bright" hostesses as his female companions was thus because "the Brighter they are the more shall we be illumined."[56] In other words, men would be safely considered irreproachable if they "fell," since "in Woman is the influencing power of Virtue [and] if Vice be Virtue misapplied, from her too comes the influence of Vice."[57] Therefore, virtuous women could, and ought to be, learned but only within the boundaries of the private space of their dressing rooms and their households, as, for example, Lydia Languish's readings, and Elizabeth Linley singing only for friends (and for free) after their marriage; in a public domain, their understanding and skills had to be negotiated with, and necessarily subdued to, men's achievements. Women's "private" accomplishments could thus easily turn into "public" vice, if they chose to become public performers, and "Like Wretches who work in unwhol[e]some Mines, their senses are corrupted in the operation of their Trade."[58] Accordingly, actresses were "vicious" women due to the very fact that they had *chosen* to move from the private to the public sphere, and had thus violated their own privacy to expose it to public appraisal and lure.

Actresses overturned the notion of patriarchal protection and challenged the ideal of man as a woman's gallant protector, guardian, and indeed possessor, and thus represented an overt transgression to established economic settlements for gentlewomen. An actress could make money out of her public display, as well as an authoress could make money out of publishing her own writings, and money matters were, as chance would have it, the most vulnerable side of their profession. Sheridan's biographers insistently emphasize that he never had any personal intercourse with actresses. The social respect he had acquired with his political career and his presence at Devonshire House and the fashionable London coteries had nurtured the illusion that he could also be regarded as a gentleman, and as such, liaisons behind the scenes would be compromising, although Samuel Rogers reported some rumors of the "indiscreet advances" that Sheridan made to Sarah Siddons.[59] Money was indeed a perfect means to "domesticate" the threat that actresses represented to female respectability, as Siddons learnt from Sheridan, who habitually did not pay her "either equitably or promptly."[60] She was, at last, driven to revolt:

> I have just received a letter, in the usual easy style, from Mr. Sheridan, who, I fancy, thinks he has only to issue his Sublime Commands, and that they will of course be obeyed. This time I believe, however, he will find himself mistaken, for Sid [her husband] does at last seem resolutely determined not to let me play till he has sufficient satisfaction, at least for the money which is my due [. . .].[61]

Again, in October 1796, Hester Lynch Thrale (then Mrs. Piozzi) tells of a "very good account of Sheridan's usage of Miss Lee,"[62] whom at first he refused to pay for her tragedy *Almeyda*, staged at Drury Lane on 20 April of the same year, with Sarah Siddons in the leading role of Almeyda.[63]

Such intriguing details from Sheridan's theatrical activity, together with his contradictory stance towards the women of his life would return to torment his mind, in later years, with "aching thoughts and bitter recollections all mix'd with much self reproach."[64] All of his writing career and his political performances had been influenced by his personal life and his ambiguous relationship with the female sex, and the female characters of his works inevitably reflect such ambiguities. Yet writing for the stage was also an occasion to fictionalize reality and observe it from a more critical viewpoint. Sheridan progressively transformed the conventional female image he had helped to shape—one typical of the comedy of manners and of the age of sensibility—into a more modern version of a woman who refused to be enslaved, either by passion or by the degenerate values in the same upper-class society he had adopted and that would eventually shun him. Between *The Rivals* and *The Camp*, between Lydia Languish and Nell, there are successive female characters that notably and sarcastically lampoon the upper class women of Sheridan's time.

The Rivals is at first sight the public homage he paid to his liaison with Eliza.[65] The premises of Sheridan and Elizabeth Linley's affair in Bath, the duels, the secret elopement, clandestine marriages, exchanges of letters, all served to acknowledge publicly what had only previously been rumored, and officially sanction Sheridan's own persona of gallant lover and romantic hero in spite of his social affiliation. Lydia and Absolute's "secret" affair is thus not so secret, since everything has already taken place in their relationship: their first meeting, the courtship, the exchange of vows and the promise of marriage. What matters here, what hampers and delays the actual consummation of their love and indeed offers a clear suggestion of Sheridan's very nature, is Lydia's romantic imagination. Lydia's readings, a careful selection of senti-mental novels and "romantic nonsense,"[66] her good breeding and her high-ranking social position ("She could pay the national debt as easily as I could my washer-woman! She has a lapdog that eats out of gold,—she feeds her parrot with small pearls,—and all her thread-papers are made of bank-notes!" [I.i.78]) have allowed her to carve out an idealized version of chivalrous love.[67] Mrs. Malaprop's obsessive use of the verb "to become" when referring to the "version" of Lydia that her contem-porary society, including Absolute, is expecting to see, clashes with Lydia's firm deter-mination that "Willingly, ma'am—I cannot change for the worse" (I.ii.85). Lydia's obstinacy unveils her reluctance at being treated "as an object," as Mrs. Malaprop is willing to do, and yet she will relentlessly have to yield to the "sad reverse" (V.i.135) of things, "to find myself made a mere Smithfield bargain of at last!" Love is reified and sacrificed to social status, and Lydia can only look back to the time of Absolute's courtship as "something like being in love." The conflicting dualism between ideal-ized love and the reality of compromise is clearly represented in the double nature of the character of Beverley/Absolute: Beverley's promises to Lydia lead to an excessively romantic and verbose declaration of love, but Beverley does not *exist*, and his words are but pure fabrication. Lydia's candor also features in "Lauretta's manner, so pure a bloom upon her charms,—something so interesting in her simplicity" (I.i.166) in Sheridan's two act farce *St. Patrick's Day*, first performed at Covent Garden on 2 May 1775.[68] O'Connor's description of Lauretta seems to contrast with that of the

London ladies, "so defended, such a circumvallation of hoop, with a breastwork of whale-bone that would turn a pistol-bullet, much less Cupid's arrows,—then turret on turret on top, with stores of concealed weapons, under pretence of black pins,— and above all, a standard of feathers that would do honour to a knight of the Bath." O'Connor compares her bloom with the "impudent," "everlasting blush" of "these quality Amazons," but at the same time he is also eager to admit his attraction "for the changeable rose," though, as he proudly—and also ironically—warns, "I admire modesty in women" (I.i.166–167). Modesty is indeed a quality that Sheridan's female characters soon learn to cast aside: the irresistible appeal of public high life—a charm that Sheridan himself had just tasted in London—renders Lauretta's segregation unbearable, and she begins to feel the constraints of being "shut up all day so like a nun" (II.ii.180).[69]

In Sheridan's first contribution to the Drury Lane repertoire, *A Trip to Scarborough*, Lydia Languish's dreaded "change" has finally come to its completion: women have now fallen to "an ebb taste" (I.ii.577) in terms of morality, fashion and luxury debauch them all, and husbands are "too fashionable [. . .] to pry into the secrets of [their] wives" (II.i.587).[70] The expectation that the comedy creates around the character of Miss Hoyden—the same expectation that was created around Lydia Languish before her appearance on stage—resolves in the *mise-en-scène* of a malicious, pragmatic woman who has learnt to consider love as a fashionable game and a means to do "what pleases me." Thus Berinthia, a young widow, is now able to instruct her friend Amanda on the reality that stands behind romantic dreams:

> *Berinthia*: Look you, Amanda, you may build castles in the air, and fume, and fret, and grow thin, and lean, and pale, and ugly, if you please; but I tell you, no man worth having is true to his wife, or ever was, or ever will be so. (III.ii.598)

Genuine dreams of love have been replaced by the pursuit of pleasure, and the object of contention between Tom Fashion and his brother Lord Foppington proves to be a mere coquette with only the ardent desire to get to London.

The character of Miss Hoyden evolves to become that of Lady Teazle in *The School for Scandal*, where the young "country wife," now in London, deceives herself into the illusions of being her own mistress:

> *Lady Teazle*: I ought to have my own way in everything, and what's more I will too—what! tho' I was educated in the country I know very well that women of Fashion in London are accountable to nobody after they are married.

Sir Peter: Very well! ma'am very well! so a husband is to have no influence, no authority?

Lady Teazle: Authority! no, to be sure—if you wanted authority over me, you should have adopted me and not married me [. . .]. (II.i.373)

While Maria's virtuous (though colorless) character remains in the background, Lady Teazle gradually exploits and then recognizes the limits of her supposed emancipation, explicitly suggesting men's responsibility for women's waywardness.[71] From Absolute's subscription to Lydia's romance, to Lauretta's father giving her "a runaway name," and to Sir Peter's mistrustful attitude, male characters shape women's reputation in society, and hence their conduct, as Lady Teazle put it: "I must sin in my own Defence—and part with my virtue to preserve my Reputation. [. . .] certainly this is the oddest Doctrine" (IV.iii.412).[72]

Sheridan's middle-class morality had thus been transported into aristocratic London settings, and then crumbles into a nonsensical "Doctrine" that corrodes femininity at all levels of society. In such context, "love has no share whatever" (I.i.361), says Lady Sneerwell: Sheridan's female characters, as well as himself, had to relinquish their original simplicity and their dreams to the negotiation of sentiments in their relationships with the other sex, following the logic of public display and commerce. In this subverted moral order, an outsider of high society like Sheridan could capitalize on and, indeed, manipulate its seductions and temptations in order to claim his niche; the characters of Lucy in *The Rivals*, Margaret (the Duenna), and Mrs. Coupler in *A Trip to Scarborough* exemplify that personal and social redemption for which Sheridan paid the price of his own morality.[73]

Between frivolous aristocratic women and shrewd social climbers stands Nell, the protagonist of *The Camp*, an afterpiece Sheridan wrote in October 1778, probably in conjunction with John Burgoyne and Richard Tickell.[74] Nell is not a gentlewoman, she has no title, and her way of dealing with the other characters is markedly harsh, rebellious, and most of all, unfeminine:

Nell: Tell Mr. Gage, will you, he's a pretty protector indeed; he's a disgrace to his Majesty's inkhorn—while he seizes with one hand, he smuggles with the other.—Why, no longer ago than last summer he was a broken attorney at Rochester, and came down here, and bought this place with his vote, and now he is both a smuggler and contractor. O my conscience, if I had the management of affairs, I would severely punish all such fellows who would be so base as to cheat a poor soldier.

> *2nd Woman*: If his worship was here, you dare not say so. Here he comes, here he comes. Now you'll change your note.
>
> *Nell*. Will I? you shall see if I do. No, no; I'll tell him my mind; that's always my way.[75]

Nell peremptorily asserts that she will not *change* her way, and vehemently criticizes the women around her, accusing them of "dress[ing] [their daughters] up thus only to make the better bargains" (I.i) when they go to the camp market to sell their goods. Mr. Gage, the owner of the property where the women work, insists on the importance of making good bargains, but Nell cannot be easily corrupted:

> *Gage*: Right—Soldiers are testy customers, and this is the market where the prettiest will always make the best bargains.
> All. Very true, very true.
>
> *Gage*: Te besure [*sic*]; I hate to see an awkward gawkey come sneaking into the market, with her damned half-price countenance, and is never able to get scarce double the value of her best goods.
>
> *Nell*: I can hold no longer: are you not ashamed you who are a contractor, and has the honour to carry his Majesty's inkhorn at your button-hole, to teach all these poor wretches all your court tricks.
> [. . .]
>
> *1st Man*: How durst you talk so saucily to his worship?
>
> *Nell*: Hold your tongue, or I'll throttle you, you sheep biter. (*collaring him*)
> [. . .]
>
> *Gage*: (*Aside*) Come, Nell, hold your tongue, and I'll give you a pound of smuggled hyson, and, throw you a silk handkerchief into the bargain.
>
> *Nell*: Here's a rogue! Bear witness neighbours he has offered me a bribe;—a pound of tea. No, Sir, take your pitiful present, and know that I am not to be bribed to screen your villainies by influence and corruption. (I.i)

Nell is a "foolish girl" because she refuses to accept a bribe and "follow the example of her betters," and therefore she is labeled as "mad."[76] Interestingly, Surface also accuses Lady Teazle of being "mad" when, from behind the curtains and off the (public) stage, she is free to reflect on her mistaken notions of "love."[77] Lydia Languish's betrayed expectations and dreams have finally been reassessed through Lady Teazle's experience, and uncompromisingly revenged in Nell's decisive denial of male authority.

Women's intellectual pursuits, as well as their ideal representations of love, were subdued to men's scrutiny, and their imagination limited within an already-debated concept of propriety. Sheridan may seem to have contributed to shape such "limits" in his managerial activity and with his attitude towards female playwrights and actresses; still, his was the attitude of the time, and also further proof of his own self-centered character. But in imagining the female characters of his comedies, he drew from his experience of social "outsider" to stage a powerful criticism of his contemporary aristocratic circles and, at the same time, endorse a defense of women's betrayed imagination in a society dominated by men and money. Indeed during all his life he tried to pursue both ideals—that of being a gentleman and of changing his social status through money. In neither of them was he successful. Through women's theatrical performance and representations of female personal experience he identified his own career and life—the life of a rebellious, romantic genius who struggled for public recognition and the fulfillment of his hopes and dreams in an era that was about to witness the revolutionary change which would transform its very foundations. And accordingly, the female characters of his plays reflect the social and personal expectations of women who eventually learn to domesticate their dreamy attitude into a more pragmatic approach to the reality of a deceitful and cruel society.

Unlike his female characters, however, Sheridan remained a dreamer, even in the years after he had ceased to write for the stage and had become obsessed with politics. Writing to his wife Hecca in 1796, in his visionary description of their idyllic, romantic life at Polesden Lacey, he finally realized that his greatest relief was not so much in enjoying the peace of his country estate with her, as rather in "the thought and Plan of this," in the construction of his own expectations, in the ever brilliant sparks of his genius and mind, in the "Hope and Happiness" of his own imagination:[78]

> So varying passions in my breast,
>   Its former calm destroy—
> By Hope and Fear at once oppress'd,
>   I tremble at my joy![79]

Notes

1. David D. Mann and Susan Garland Mann, eds., *Women Playwrights in England, Ireland, and Scotland, 1660–1823* (Bloomington: Indiana University Press, 1996), 403–17.

2. See, for example, Fintan O'Toole, *A Traitor's Kiss: The Life of Richard Brinsley Sheridan, 1751–1816* (London: Granta, 1997); and Linda Kelly, *Richard Brinsley Sheridan: A Life* (London: Pimlico, 1998).

3. A first extract of *The Witlings* appeared in Constance Hill, *The House in St. Martin's Street: Being Chronicles of the Burney family... With illustrations by Ellen G. Hill and reproductions of portraits, etc., etc.* (London: John Lane, 1907), but the entire comedy was edited for the first time in Clayton Delery's doctoral dissertation, (Fanny Burney, "*The Witlings*. A Comedy. By a Sister of the Order," ed. and sup. Clayton J. Delery [PhD diss., City University of New York, 1989]). The definitive edition is Peter Sabor's. See Fanny Burney, *The Witlings. A Comedy. By a Sister of the Order*, in *The Complete Plays of Frances Burney*, ed. Peter Sabor, 2 vols. (London: William Pickering, 1995), 1:1–101.

4. Frances Burney to Susannah Elizabeth Burney, January 11, [1779], in Fanny Burney, Lars E. Troide, and Stewart J. Cooke, eds., *The Early Journals and Letters of Fanny Burney*, 2 vols. (Oxford: Clarendon Press, 1988), 2:235–36. Sheridan was still at Drury Lane years later, when Burney had to withdraw her tragedy *Edwy and Elgiva* from the stage due to the failure of its first performance. *Edwy and Elgiva* was performed at Drury Lane on 21 March 1795, but "failed ignominiously" and was never re-acted nor published at that time. See Margaret Anne Doody, *Frances Burney: The Life in the Works* (New Brunswick, NJ: Rutgers University Press, 1988), 180.

5. Elizabeth Griffith writes, "But Mr. SHERIDAN's friendship, wherever professed, is not of modern growth." In "Advertisement," to *The Times: A Comedy. As it is performing at the Theatre Royal in Drury Lane* (Dublin: R. Marchband, 1779).

6. Elizabeth Craven, *The Miniature Picture; A Comedy in Three Acts: performed at the Theatre-Royal, Drury-Lane* (London: G. Riley, 1781), v–viii. Sheridan's prologue also appeared in the *Annual Register*, 1780.

7. Hannah More, *The Fatal Falsehood: A Tragedy. As it is acted at the Theatre-Royal, in Covent Garden. By the Author of Percy* (London: T. Cadell, 1779), vi–vii.

8. "And even to the affectation of it where the person is very handsome (for the grace of Venus which passes all understanding, atones for an abundance of frailty," R. B. Sheridan to David Garrick, January, 1779, quoted in Richard Brinsley Sheridan, *The Plays and Poems of Richard Brinsley Sheridan*, ed. R. Crompton Rhodes, 3 vols. (Oxford: Basil Blackwell, 1928), 2:277n2.

9. Ellen Donkin, *Getting into the Act: Women Playwrights in London 1776–1829* (New York: Routledge, 1995), 145.

10. Kelly, *Richard Brinsley Sheridan*, 165.

11. R. B. Sheridan to Thomas Granville, late September, 1772 and R B. Sheridan to Lady Duncannon, 1788–9, in Richard Brinsley Sheridan, *The Letters of Richard Brinsley Sheridan*, ed. Cecil Price, 3 vols (Oxford: Clarendon Press, 1966), 1:45; 1:208. Further references to Sheridan's correspondence will be from this edition unless differently stated.

12. R. B. Sheridan to Thomas Granville, November 38, 1772, in Sheridan, *Letters*, 1:66. Sheridan quotes from John Milton's *Paradise Lost*, bk. 2, l:942.

13. Elizabeth Linley to Mehitabel Canning, quoted in Clementina Black, *The Linleys of Bath* (London: Martin Secker, 1926), 155.

14. R.B. Sheridan to Mrs. Angelo, October 13, 1770, in Sheridan, *Letters*, 1:20.

15. R.B. Sheridan to Thomas Granville, late September 1772, in Sheridan, *Letters*, 1:45.

16. Alicia to Betsy Sheridan, November 9, 1818, quoted in W. Fraser Rae, *Sheridan: A Biography*, 2 vols. (London: Richard Bentley and Son, 1896), 1:75.

17. A selection of Sheridan's *Love Epistles of Aristaenetus* appears in Sheridan, *Plays and Poems*, vol. 3; and extracts from *Ixion* (1771) appear in Thomas Moore, *Memoirs of the Life of the Right Honourable Richard Brinsley Sheridan*, 5th ed., Vol 1. (New York: Redfield, c. 1858), 13–19.

18. Quoted in Rae, *Sheridan*, 1:169.

19. Quoted in Moore, *Memoirs*, 2:574.

20. Kelly, *Richard Brinsley Sheridan*, 51ff.

21. R. B. Sheridan to the Duchess of Devonshire, October, 1788?, in Sheridan, *Letters*, 1:184. In 1773 *that* society demanded some semblance of respectability, and a married woman singing for money was an ambiguous object of public display: according to O'Toole, "it was impossible to be a public man without being, in the first place, a gentleman. He could only move onto the public stage if Eliza moved off it" (O'Toole, *A Traitor's Kiss*, 82).

22. As far as Eliza was concerned, "No *Gentleman* of Character and Fortune ever yet took a Wife from behind the Scenes of a Theatre," he stated in a letter to his father-in-law, Thomas Linley, opposing his decision to allow Eliza's sister Mary to work for Garrick at Drury Lane, "to play the Coquet, the Wanton, to retail loose innuendos in Comedy, or glow with warm Descriptions in Tragedy; and in both to be haul'd about, squeez'd and kiss'd by beastly pimping Actors!" (R. B. Sheridan to Thomas Linley, 1775, in Sheridan, *Letters*, 3:293–94).

23. Ibid., 3:300.

24. Hugh Stokes, *The Devonshire House Circle* (London: Herbert Jenkins, 1917), 130.

25. R. B. Sheridan to the Duchess of Devonshire, 7 May 1792, in Sheridan, *Letters*, 1:245.

26. Ibid.

27. "What times and what changes have passed! You… what have been, what are your sufferings? what has the interval of my Life been, and what is left me—but misery from Memory and a horror of Reflexion? […] In the most melancholy hours I have ever known, for I never felt so without Hope on a point that interested us before, I find my mind turning towards you as the only creature whom I find it a relief to think of, or with whom it is an ease to me to communicate, or from whose words I can look for anything consoling or reconciling. O… however negligent, mysterious or unaccountable my conduct may have appeared to you let me now find that I am not deceived in the opinion I have of the unalterable kindness of your Heart and nature" (R. B. Sheridan to Lady Duncannon, March, 1792, in Sheridan, *Letters*, 1:239–40 and 242).

28. O'Toole, *A Traitor's Kiss*, 251.

29. R. B. Sheridan to Lady Bessborough, March, 1799, Sheridan, *Letters*, 2:106.

30. Elizabeth Linley Sheridan, "Laura to Silvio," in Sheridan, *Plays and Poems*, 3:200.

31. Thus Eliza wrote to Mehitabel Canning: "S. [i.e. Sheridan] is in Town—and so is Mrs Crewe—*I am in the country and so is Mr Crewe*—a very convenient arrangement is it not?" in T. H. Sallier, "Some Unpublished Letters of Mrs Sheridan to Mrs Canning," in *The Political Career of Richard Brinsley Sheridan*, eds. Michael Sadleir and Elizabeth Ann Sheridan (Oxford: Blackwell, 1912), 81–85.

32. R. B. Sheridan, "A Portrait: Addressed to Mrs. Crewe, with the Comedy of the School for Scandal." All quotations from Sheridan's plays, unless otherwise noted, are taken from Richard Brinsley Sheridan, *The Dramatic Works of Richard Brinsley Sheridan*, ed. Cecil Price, 2 vols. (Oxford: Oxford University Press, 1973).

33. O'Toole, *A Traitor's Kiss*, 138.

34. Earl of Bessborough (ed.), *Georgiana. Extracts from the Correspondence of Georgiana, Duchess of Devonshire* (London: John Murray, 1955), 44.

35. Quoted in Stokes, *The Devonshire House Circle*, 132.

36. August von Kotzebue, *Menschenhass und Reue* (1789), translated by Benjamin Thompson as *The Stranger* and first acted at Drury Lane on 15 September 1798. The music sheet entitled "the Favourite Song, sung by Mrs. Bland in *The Stranger*. The Words by R. B. Sheridan, Esqre., the Air by her Grace the Dutchess of Devonshire" was printed by Longman Clementi & Company in 1798, and only appeared in later editions of the play.

37. Sheridan, *Plays and Poems*, 3:255.

38. Anonymous, "The Life of Mrs. Cowley," in Hannah Cowley's *Albina, Countess Raimond. A Tragedy. By Mrs. Cowley. Adapted for Theatrical Representation, as performed at the Theatre-Royal, Hay-Market* (London: George Cawthorn, 1797).

39. Cowley, "Preface" to *Albina, Countess Raimond*, i-viii.

40. Ibid., vi. For further details, see also Donkin, *Getting into the Act*, 71–72.

41. Ibid., vii.

42. Katharine Balderston, ed., *Thraliana: The Diary of Mrs. Hester Lynch Thrale (Later Mrs. Piozzi) 1776–1809*, 2 vols. (Oxford: Clarendon Press, 1942), 1:421. Thrale's resentment probably originated in the fiasco of her own play *Two Fountains*, which Kemble "shelf'd" (*Thraliana*, 2:829).

43. Thrale, *Public Advertiser*, January 20, 1780, in Balderston, *Thraliana*, 1:420.

44. Sheridan, *Plays and Poems*, 3:277, n2.

45. Richard Brinsley Sheridan, *Speeches of the Late Right Honourable Richard Brinsley Sheridan. (Several corrected by himself.)*, ed. "A Constitutional Friend," 5 vols. (London: Patrick Martin, 1816), 2:117.

46. Maria Kurdi, "Interview with Elizabeth Kuti," *Irish Literary Supplement*, 23, no. 1 (Spring 2004): 11–12. See also Elizabeth Kuti, "Rewriting Frances Sheridan," *Eighteenth-Century Ireland* 11 (1996): 120–28.

47. Since the full text of Frances Chamberlaine's *Trip to Bath* is no longer extant, only three surviving acts of her play were first published in Richard Brinsley Sheridan and William Fraser Rae, *Sheridan's Plays Now Printed as He Wrote Them and His Mother's Unpublished Comedy 'A Journey to Bath,'* ed. W. Fraser Rae (London: D. Nutt, 1902). See the "Introduction," in Frances Chamberlaine Sheridan's *The Plays of Frances Sheridan*, eds. Robert Goode Hogan and Jerry C. Beasley (Newark, DE: University of Delaware Press, 198), 27.

48. For a full discussion of Sheridan's borrowings from his mother's plays *A Trip to Bath*, *The Discovery*, *The Dupe* and her novel *Memoirs of Miss Sidney Bidulph*, see Sheridan's *The Rivals, A Comedy. As it was first Acted at the Theatre-Royal in Covent-Garden*, ed. Richard Little Purdy (Oxford: Clarendon Press, 1935); and Jean Dulck, *Les Comédies de R. B. Sheridan* (Paris: Didier, 1962), esp.152–53.

49. O'Toole, *A Traitor's Kiss*, 87.

50. Anonymous, *Illusions; or, the Trances of Nourjahad; an Oriental romance, in three acts, founded on a Persian tale, written by Mrs. Sheridan, as now performed at the Theatre-Royal, Drury Lane* (London: J. Barker, 1813). The melodrama was firstly attributed to Byron, who indignantly denied any connection with it. In a letter to her sister Cassandra dated 5 March 1814, Jane Austen also recounted going to the play: "We were too much tired to stay for the whole of "Illusion" ("Nour-jahad"), which has three acts; there is a great deal of finery and dancing in it, but I think little merit," Jane Austen, *Jane Austen's Letters to her sister Cassandra and others*, ed. R. W. Chapman, 2nd ed. (London: Oxford University Press, 1952), 318.

51. "*Eugenia and Adelaide* [...] was published after [Frances Sheridan's] death, and adapted for the stage as a comic opera by Alicia, her elder daughter," H. Philip Bolton, *Women Writers Dramatized: A Calendar of Performances from Narrative Works Published in English to 1900* (London: Cassell, 2005), 307.

52. R. B. Sheridan to the Queen, 1772, in Sheridan, *Letters*, 1:55–6.

53. Ibid., 1:49.

54. "I know that you have been very busy writing for Sheridan—I don't mean *copying*, but *composing*:—it's true, indeed;—you must not contradict me when I say you wrote the much-admired epilogue to The Rivals [...]. What makes it certain is, that my *father* guessed it was *yours* the first time he saw it praised in the paper," Mary Linley to Elizabeth Linley Sheridan, 1774, quoted in Moore, *Memoirs*, 1:137–8.

55. "I thought women in general were shy of expressing their love to Men, if so I am peculiarly brazen and impudent, for I can't help telling Sheridan everything that comes into my mind, and certainly love comes a little into it," Esther Jane Ogle (Hecca) to R. B. Sheridan, 1794, quoted in F. O'Toole, *A Traitor's Kiss*, 310.

56. R. B. Sheridan to the Queen, 1772, in Sheridan, *Letters*, 1:51.

57. Ibid., 1:55.

58. R. B. Sheridan to Thomas Linley, 1775, in Sheridan, *Letters*, 3:295.

59. Roger Manvell, *Sarah Siddons: Portrait of an Actress* (London: Heinemann, 1970), 172–73.

60. Ibid., 172.

61. September 18, 1799?, quoted in Oswald G. Knapp, ed., *The Intimate Letters of Hester Piozzi and Penelope Pennington, 1788–1821* (London: John Lane, 1914), 184.

62. Hester Lynch Thrale Piozzi to the Reverend Daniel Lysons, in Edward Bloom and Lillian Bloom, eds., *The Piozzi Letters. Correspondence of Hester Lynch Piozzi, 1784–1821 (formerly Mrs. Thrale)* 6 vols. (Newark, NJ: University of Delaware Press, 1989–2004), 2:379. Sheridan eventually paid Sophia Lee the £450 she requested.

63. Sophia Lee, *Almeyda, Queen of Granada. A Tragedy, in Five Acts. As performed at the Theatre Royal, Drury-Lane* (Dublin: Brett Smith, 1796).

64. R. B. Sheridan to His Wife [Hecca], November, 1814, in Sheridan, *Letters*, 3:206.

65. First performed at Covent Garden on January 17, 1775.

66. Anonymous, Review of Mrs. Fogerty's *The Fatal Connexion* (1773), *London Magazine*, September, 1773. For a full description of the books that Lydia mentions in act two, scene two of *The Rivals*, see George Henry Nettleton, "The Books of Lydia Languish's Circulating Library," *Journal of English and German Philology* 5, no. 4 (1905): 492–500; E. E. Phare, "Lydia Languish, Lydia Bennet, and Dr. Fordyce's Sermons," *Notes and Queries* 11, no. 5 (1964): 182–83; and Frank W. Bradbrook, "Lydia Languish, Lydia Bennet, and Dr. Fordyce's Sermons," *Notes and Queries* 11, no. 11 (November 1964): 421–23.

67. On this point, the correspondence between Lydia Languish and Arabella in Charlotte Lennox's *The Female Quixote* (1752) is conspicuous.

68. "Ah! my soul, what a life will we then live! Love shall be our idol and support! we will worship him with a monastic strictness; abjuring all worldly toys, to centre every thought and action there. Proud of calamity, we will enjoy the wreck of wealth; while the surrounding gloom of adversity shall make the flame of our pure love show doubly bright. By Heavens! I would fling all goods of fortune from me with a prodigal hand, to enjoy the scene where I might clasp my Lydia to my bosom, and say, the world affords no smile to me but here—[*Embracing her*]" (III.iii.29–36).

69. In *The Duenna*, first performed at Covent Garden on November 21, 1775, Clara and Louisa discuss the same issue and reckon that "the character of a nun is a very becoming one at a masquerade: but no pretty woman, in her senses, ever thought of taking the veil for above a night" (III.iii).

70. An adaptation of John Vanbrugh's *The Relapse* (1697) and a tribute to Sheridan's mother, named after her *Trip to Bath* (1765), was first performed on February 14, 1777.

71. "Your own Arts have furnished [me] with the means" (IV.iii).

72. As Lauretta's mother, Mrs. Bridget Credulous, maintains: "Lauretta! ay, you would have called her so; but for my part I never knew any good come from of giving girls these heathen Christian names: if you had called her Deborrah [*sic*], or Tabitha, or Ruth, or Rebecca, or Joan, nothing of this had ever happened; but I always knew Lauretta was a runaway name" (II.iv).

73. "Now shall I try whether I can't play the fine lady as well as my mistress, and if I succeed, I may be a fine lady for the rest of my life," says the Duenna (I.iii).

74. For the story of the attribution of *The Camp* to Sheridan, see George W. Williams, "A New Source of Evidence for Sheridan's Authorship of 'The Camp' and 'The Wonders of Derbyshire,'" *Studies in Philology* 47, no. 4 (Oct. 1950): 619–28.

75. Richard Brinsley Sheridan, *The Works of the late right Honourable Richard Brinsley Sheridan*, collected by Thomas Moore (Leipsic: Ernest Fleischer, 1825), 223. Quotations from *The Camp* are taken from this edition, for reasons described in n76, below.

76. "Aye, aye, she's mad" (Sheridan, *The Works*, 224). The Moore edition has Gage accusing Nell of being mad, thus echoing Joseph Surface's accusation that Lady Teazle must be "mad" to refuse to compromise her marriage. Cecil Price, working from different sources than Moore, prints "Turned fool I think" (I.i.40).

77. Sheridan, *The Works*, (IV.iii).

78. R. B. Sheridan to Hecca, August, 1796, in Sheridan, *Letters*, 2:44.

79. Quoted in Richard Brinsley Sheridan and Alfred Howard, *The Beauties of Sheridan, consisting of Selections from his Poems, Dramas, and Speeches* (Boston: Printed by S.N. Dickinson, 1831), 53.

12

CARICATURING SHERIDAN

David Francis Taylor

G RAPHIC SATIRE PRESENTS US with an alternative perspective on Sheridan's complex, multifaceted and often paradoxical career as a playwright, theatre manager, and Whig politician. Few public figures received greater attention from caricaturists. He appeared in close to five hundred political prints between 1783, the year he entered government with the Fox-North Coalition, and his death in 1816, and perhaps only George III, William Pitt, and Charles James Fox—that is, the king, the prime minister, and the leader of the opposition—were subject to more insistent visual derision.[1] These satires provide an immense and detailed body of information about public perceptions of Sheridan across a thirty-year period; they embody a visual barometer of his shifting political fortunes, a counterbiography that writes his radical sympathies and theatrical endeavours as an iconography of power that was legible to a socially diverse metropolitan audience.[2]

In the early 1790s, for instance, following his endorsement of the French Revolution and vociferous campaign against the oppressive legislative programme of Pitt's administration, caricaturists habitually imaged Sheridan, along with the likes of Fox, as a sans-cultotte. Isaac Cruikshank's 1792 print, *Mad Tom's First Practical Essay on the Rights of Man* (See fig. 12.1) for example, depicts a hooded, conspiratorial Sheridan abetting Tom Paine's arson attack on the House of Commons, while James Gillray's *The Hopes of the Party* from 1791 (See fig. 12.2) imagines the execution of George III on a scaffold erected in the Strand, with Sheridan pinning the oblivious king's head in place and wishing he, rather than Fox, "had hold of the hatchet."[3] Such caricatures often proletarianize Sheridan; they refigure an advocate of reform as a Francophile, a Jacobin, a terrorist, a regicide, and deploy a discourse of xenophobic patriotism in order both to reflect and *inflect* the anxieties and ideological polarization of their public.[4] In this way, we must broach the art of graphic satire with a certain hermeuntic caution—as a self-consciously hyper-bolized and, on occasions, propagandic aesthetic. Yet it would be wrong to suggest that the grammar of caricature necessarily effaces political nuance. Caricatures, as I hope will become clear during the course of this essay, are complex visual records that combine an array of registers and allusive networks as a means of negotiating political moments and agents. Their iconography distils certain realities even as it wilfully distorts them. However exaggerated it might be, the picture of Citizen Sheridan that emerges from prints by the likes of Cruikshank and Gillray goes some way towards rehabilitating a figure whose committed reformism has too often been elided by critics and biographers.

Moreover, and more crucially in terms of my present discussion, graphic satires habitually theatricalize politics. Prints such as Gillray's 1791 *Weird Sisters; Minister's of Darkness; Minions of the Moon* (BM 7937)—which depicts Pitt, Henry Dundas, and Edward Thurlow as the witches of *Macbeth* (or rather, of Henry Fuseli's rendering of the tragedy)—illustrate the powerful nexus between graphic satire and drama in the period. "As the eighteenth century progressed," Jonathan Bates writes, "caricaturists more and more frequently viewed politics as theatre [. . .] the theatre itself was a constant point of reference in their work."[5] Unsurprisingly, then, Sheridan's almost unique professional bridging of playhouse and Parliament—"At once the *Atlas* of the stage and state," as a satirical poem of 1785 expressed it—made him a compelling and fertile subject for caricaturists.[6] As many as one in ten prints of Sheridan, as Marc Baer notes, made reference to the theatre in some manner.[7] In *Mad Tom's First Practical Essay*, for example, Sheridan exclaims: "Ca ira, Ca ira, Ca ira, thats your sort, now Master brown bread D—mn—n to scandal"—an utterance which interweaves French Revolutionary anthem, quotation from Thomas Holcroft's 1792 comedy *The Road to Ruin*, and, of course, reference to *The School for Scandal*.[8] As especially cogent contemporary portraits of neither a playwright nor a politician but of a playwright-politician, caricatures offer a direct and antidotal challenge to the bifurcated picture of Sheridan that continues to pervade much modern scholarship. Graphic satire, as we will see, understands and emphasizes the simultaneity and interconnectedness of Sheridan's theatrical and parliamentary activities.

Yet if Sheridan operates within the visual economy of caricature as a hiero-glyph of the theatricality of politics in Georgian London (an equation which is, of course, invertible), then his insistent and slippery presence in such prints also

Figure 12.1. Isaac Cruikshank, *Mad Tom's First Practical Essay on the Rights of Man*, 14 May 1792 (BM 8087). © Trustees of the British Museum.

Figure 12.2. James Gillray, *The Hopes of the Party, prior to July 14th*, 19 July 1791 (BM 7892). © Trustees of the British Museum.

serves to challenge such a prescription of eighteenth-century political culture. As I argue in my book *Theatres of Opposition*, caricatures of Sheridan coalesce and collide the registers of drama and politics in ways which problematize our understanding both of his public identity and, more broadly, of the dynamic relays between theatrical and parliamentary cultures that he can be seen to personify. In *Theatres of Opposition*, I look particularly at satires that depict Sheridan as either a Shakespearean character (parallels with the heavy-drinking, plebeian Bardolph of *Henry IV* were especially common) or as Harlequin.[9] In this present essay, I want to focus on a especially complex subset of caricatures of Sheridan to which I give less attention in the book: those prints which appropriate the vocabularies, personalities, and spectacles of Sheridan's own dramatic corpus. Graphic satires that not only engage in textual and iconographic invocations of Sheridan's plays but go as far as casting their author as his one of his own protagonists, offer a particularly complex mediation of Sheridan's presences within and across dramatic and parliamentary arenas. Here the playwright critiques the parliamentarian, the syntax of politics and the playhouse are at once intertwined and opposed, and the disjunctions and anxieties generated by a theatrical politics emerge with striking clarity.

Performative Politics and the Problem of Sincerity

From the first, graphic satirists sought, quite literally, to inscribe Sheridan's theatrical profession upon his political body. John Boyne's *Banditti* (See fig. 12.3), an attack on the Fox-North Coalition, deploys a simple visual pun by depicting Sheridan as a turbaned satyr. Contemporary lexicographers erroneously regarded the classical creature as the etymological origin of the word "satire," and Boyne's Sheridan thus comes to embody the very literature he writes. Such emblematism, moreover, also signifies difference that is both ethical and racial. Eighteenth-century reference guides to classical mythology commonly defined the satyr as a Dionysian apostle, a primitive creature of mischievousness, promiscuity, and, crucially, Indian origin.[10] In the symbolic form of satyr/satire, Sheridan not only becomes a reification of the suspect sensualism of the stage, but also a figure of oriental alterity. His turban, in this way, perhaps alludes as much to his suspect non-Englishness as to his support for Fox's India Bill—racial undertones that extend to Burke, the other Irishman in Boyne's print, who is portrayed as a Jesuit. Indeed, in a detail which superimposes the languages of theatre and race, the words "The School for Scandal" are written across Sheridan's turban. Boyne's caricature succinctly articulates the problematic identity of a Westminster politician who is also a dramatist and an Irishman. While subsequent prints negotiate and underscore Sheridan's connections with the play-house in more sophisticated ways, this design elicits the discursive paradox that, I want to suggest, underlies so many caricatural representations of Sheridan: Boyne's image of the satyr operates both to suture playwright and parliamentarian and, at the same time, to posit theatre as a semiotics of political otherness.

If *Banditti* reveals a graphic satirist grappling with an effective means of representing an agency that is at once political and theatrical, then *The Tombs of the Worthies* (See fig. 12.4), published just a few months later, establishes the pattern of appropriation and quotation that pervades caricatures of Sheridan thereafter. The print shows Sheridan and Burke, dressed in mourning clothes, weeping beside the tomb of Lord North and Charles James Fox, whose coalition had collapsed in late December 1783. The satire is rich in literary—and more particularly, theatrical—allusion. The epitaph on the tomb, "They were lovely in their lives and in their Death they were not divided," is taken from Addison's story of the lovers Theodosius and Constantia in *The Spectator* no. 164; an inscription below the Corinthian gallows at the head of the sepulchre, "Thus Gamesters united in Friendship are found," cites a song from *The Beggar's Opera* (Act III, scene ii); while both mourners are recognizable by the papers protruding from their jacket pockets—Burke carries a parchment labelled "Sublime & Beautiful," while Sheridan has with him a copy of *The Critic* and sheets headed "Theatrical Justice." It is within this allusive matrix that, for the first time in caricature, the figure of Sheridan quotes verbatim from one of his own plays: "Ah! Sure a Pair was never seen so justly form'd to meet by Nature" (from *The Duenna*).[11] The line is laced with irony, for the "Pair" on which it passes comment are in fact Isaac the Jew and Margaret, the eponymous Duenna of the play, who masquerades as her ward Louisa in order that she might escape the arranged marriage. Sheridan's lament thus inadvertently functions to elicit both the ill-matched nature of the Fox-North union—which, like that of Isaac and Margaret, is impelled by foolish ambition, blindness, and deceit—and also the duplicity and empty poeticism of Sheridan's own grief.[12] Like Carlos, who sings the line in the play fully aware that the Duenna is in fact "damn'd ugly," Sheridan is here offering sentiment "studied for the occasion" (Sheridan, *Dramatic Works*, 253); politics has become a mode of performance.

In *Tombs* Sheridan possesses no political language. In marked contrast to Burke, who is depicted in the act of declaiming a parodic version of an earlier Commons speech ("Alas, the best of K—gs"), Sheridan appropriates the vocabu-

Figure 12.3.   John Boyne, *Banditti*, 22 Dec. 1783 (BM 6281). © Trustees of the British Museum.

lary of his own dramatic writing as an ersatz grammar of politics. Yet this trafficking of the sentiments of stage farce into the sphere of (defunct) government is shown to evacuate political meaning rather than substitute for it. Judith Pascoe has written of the "charged double status of the theatrical gesture" in the Romantic period: "as an eye-catching public avowal of a particular political sentiment and as an incriminating indicator of falsity."[13] Graphic satirists, however, fundamentally elide the productive rhetorical and ideological tensions embodied in theatricality. In *Tombs*, theatre is no more and no less than a syntax of mimicry and dissimulation; Sheridan is here a "political proteus"—the appellation that William Cobbett would ascribe him in 1804. Indeed, Cobbett's sustained and unrivalled denunciation of Sheridan's parliamentary activities not only distils the prevailing criticisms levelled against him as a public figure by political opponents and satirists alike, but also reveals the potent antitheatrical prejudices which his career mobilized and aggravated—prejudices intricately woven into the satirical strategies of the

Figure 12.4. *The Tombs of the Worthies*, 27 Mar. 1784 (BM 6470). © Trustees of the British Museum.

caricatures I am discussing. That is, Cobbett's *Political Proteus* draws a correlation between two central allegations: first, that both Sheridan's rhetorical style and his dual role as MP and manager of Drury Lane operate to erode the boundaries between theatre and politic ("Your eulogists have [. . .] connected your playhouse performances with your parliamentary proceedings"); secondly, that Sheridan's political activity is ideologically confused and wilfully deceitful ("Misrepresentation I have long observed to be your *fort*").[14] Cobbett's polemic, like the satire of *The Tombs of the Worthies*, is thus firmly anchored in a conception of theatre as a powerful and insidious form of deception. The logic of critique is finally simple: if theatricality—both as a profession and as a mode of behavior and speech—is synonymous with dissimulation, then it follows that any kind of theatrical politics must therefore necessarily be a politics of hypocrisy.[15]

Recasting Sheridan's Comedies

Such antitheatrical anxieties take new and more complex shape in caricatures from the late 1780s onwards, as satirists begin not only to appropriate the words of Sheridan's dramas, but actively to cast the author as his own creations. During the Regency Crisis, in which his machinations on behalf of the Prince of Wales became a source of considerable public interest and consternation in equal measure, "Joseph Surface" gained currency as a popular epithet for Sheridan.[16] As a figure who employs sentimental platitudes as a masquerade for treachery and sexual seduction, *The School for Scandal*'s arch-hypocrite readily functioned as an free-standing trope of duplicity. When, in January 1789, an article in the Whig *Morning Post* implied that the Queen was altering bulletins of the King's health, William Dent responded with *Joseph Surface Posted* (See fig. 12.5).[17] In this print it is not Queen Charlotte but rather Sheridan, then press manager for the Foxites, who is shown to be disseminating "false reports"—as the paper he hands to one of his demon minions reads.[18] Grinning with a Machiavellian satisfaction and resting on the back of another demon, he pens an article accusing the Queen of "political interference." At the bottom of this work-in-progress is written, in larger script, "Scandal." Dent thus offers an ironic image of Sheridan as, simultaneously, the anti-hero and the author of [*The School for*] *Scandal*. As Foxite spin-doctor, he has collapsed distinctions not only between playwriting and politics but also between the satirizing and the purveying of newsprint fiction. This slippage is emblematized in both sexual terms—the postures Sheridan and the demon adopt in order for him to write the article homoeroticize the journalistic act—and in

Figure 12.5. William Dent, *Joseph Surface Posted*, 25 Feb. 1789 (BM 7510). © Trustees of the British Museum.

overtly ideological terms. In a detail in the right foreground of the caricature, and in what is surely a punning allusion to the character of Snake—the professional counterfeiter of Sheridan's comedy—two serpents, representing the *Morning Post* and *Morning Herald* (both Foxite publications), slither from a staff and cap of Liberty, respectively inscribed "Liberty of the Press" and "Licentiousness." It is a motif of infestation, in which the iconographies of Whiggism and the press/stage bleed into one another. Foxite Whiggism, Dent suggests, has been ideologically corrupted by its willing intercourse with the industries of journalism and theatre.

These complex satirical negotiations are given an ironic frame. In the border at the foot of the print, Dent announces that his portrait of Sheridan as the author of calumny is itself "Designed by Misrepresentation." Other deployments of "Joseph Surface" as a political soubriquet for Sheridan were, however, more sincere. William Combe's *Letters from a Country Gentleman*, published just a week before Dent's caricature in February 1789, attacked Sheridan for having "happily united in himself the avowed profligacy of Charles, with the sanctified hypocrisy of Joseph Surface [. . .] whose very appearance in Parliament is a libel upon the Constitution."[19] Indeed, for Combe, the flagrant theatricality of Sheridan's parliamentary speeches operated in precisely the same way as Joseph's discourse of sentimentalism to conceal a lack of substantive idealism: Sheridan, *Letters* asserts, "confined himself to sarcastic observations, railed at slanders! and attempted to ridicule what he did not think proper to refute." Satire and wit—the registers of the English stage comedy—once more serve as a language of the state. As Joseph Surface, Sheridan is the fraud, no more the man of political principle than his famous anti-hero is a man of sentiment.

The political duplicity embodied by the Sheridan/Surface caricature was to take on a more disturbing inflection the following year. In a debate in the Commons on 9 February 1790 which irrevocably irritated the ideological faultlines underlying parliamentary Whiggism, Sheridan and Burke clashed violently over the latter's diatribal image of the French Revolution. Sheridan contended that events in France in fact represented "as just a Revolution as ours [that of 1688], proceeding upon as sound a principle and a greater provocation" and accused Burke of valorizing "capricious despotism"—a charge which led Burke to proclaim that, "henceforth, his honorable friend and he were separated in politics."[20] In the wake of the debate, graphic satirists appropriated the Joseph Surface character as a means of depicting Sheridan as a dangerous radical posing as a genteel parliamentarian. In *Hopes of the Party*, for example, Sir Cecil Wray, standing on the far right of the scaffold, places his hand on Sheridan's shoulder, saying, "Here do give me a little room Joseph." Another Gillray print, *The Impeachment,—or—the Father of the Gang, Turnd Kings Evidence* (See fig. 12.6), depicts an imperious and paranoid Burke triumphantly exposing Sherida and Fox as as "abettors of revolution." A penitent Sheridan sobs: "Ha! what's that? miscreant Jacobites!—plots Conspiracies! Revolution! O! Damnation! we're all found out!—ah Joseph! Joseph! I fear you've brought up your Neck for a fine collar!" In John Nixon's *The Wrangling Friends or Opposition in Disorder* (BM 7855), published the same month, Sheridan stands on the sidelines of a Commons confrontation between Burke and Fox, shouting: "Oh Lord Oh Lord Order Order Order the man that betrays his friend &c &c.—School for Scandal"—a deliberate misquotation of Joseph's remark to Sir Peter Teazle, at the very moment Lady Teazle is famously concealed behind the screen, that "the man who can break through the laws of hospitality, and seduce the wife or daughter of his friend, deserves to be branded as a pest to society" (Sheridan, *Dramatic Works*, 415). The Jacobin-Joseph, the "man of character and

Figure 12.6 .   James Gillray, *The Impeachment,—or—the Father of the Gang, Turnd Kings Evidence*, May 1791 (BM 7861). © Trustees of the British Museum.

sentiment" exposed as covert revolutionary, offers a doubled trope of theatricality: as a *dramatis persona* it underscores Sheridan's profession as a playwright, while as a canonical archetype of hypocritical performance it further inscribes theatre as an economy of pretence and sensuality that is corrosive of political truth.

Perhaps the most complex caricature of Sheridan as one of his own characters, however, appropriates not *The School for Scandal* and its semiotics of socio-sexual subterfuge, but rather the self-consciously theatrical vocabulary and *personae* of *The Critic*. William Dent's *Election Compromise or a Cornish Hug in Westminster* (See fig. 12.7) depicts Sheridan as both Puff, the hack journalist-*cum*-playwright of his 1779 farce, and Bayes, the mock-Drydenian dramatist of Buckingham's *The Rehearsal* (1671)—Sheridan's source-text for *The Critic*. The print offers a commentary on the understanding reached between Pitt and the Lord Lauderdale in March 1790 that the Tories and Whigs would endorse only one candidate each in the upcoming Westminster election and thus avoid a repeat of the internecine contests of 1784 and 1788. Dent satirizes both the cosmetic nature and the constitutional ramifications of the political concord by showing the two candidates, Fox and Lord Hood, in the midst of an exaggerated homoerotic embrace ("My dear, dear Lord!!!," cries Fox; "Oh, my sweet Sir!!!" returns Hood) and trampling upon the "Freedom" and "Rights of the Electors." This contrived episode is presented to us as a theatrical snapshot—an image, as the print's subtitle indicates, of an "entire new Scene got up at a trifling expence, now in private Rehearsal and about to be produced on the Covent Garden Boards by the incomparable prime Manager of the Old House, in the Character of Bayes." Unlike those caricatural invocations of Joseph Surface, then, *Election Compromise* figures Sheridan as a playwright, dramatic character, *and* theatre manager—or rather, adding another layer of referentiality and harnessing the metatheatre of *The Critic*, as an actor performing all of these roles "in the Character of Bayes."

Sheridan here not only embodies but actively drills others in the practice of theatrical politics. Watching the embrace of the Fox and Hood, he exclaims:

> There's Situation—there's Characters—match them who can—there's stage effect—see how forcibly their Friendship appears after violent abuse—contrast has a happy Effect—egad, it will command notice on the day of public performance—as I am a Whig, and a Poet, and a long Speech maker and all that egad—

These lines establish the caricature as a specific parody of a scene in *The Critic* in which Puff, directing a rehearsal of his historical spectacular *The Spanish Armada*,

Figure 12.7. William Dent, *Election Compromise or a Cornish Hug in Westminster*, 30 Mar. 1790 (BM 7638). © Trustees of the British Museum.

has the hero Whiskerandos, his two competing lovers, and their uncles all draw swords upon one another—an absurd choreographic stalemate which nonetheless prompts the self-enraptured playwright to proclaim: "There's situation for you!—there's an heroic group!" (Sheridan, *Dramatic Works*, 544). Dent's caricatural travesty not only compares the Westminster agreement to this implausible dramaturgical "dead lock," but also posits Sheridan—who carries under his arm the script for "Election Coalition a Political Rehearsal by the Modern Bayes"—as the writer and orchestrator of the political sham enacted by Hood and Fox. Sheridan is "the prime Manager" of parliamentary role-play. Moreover, as "the Modern Bayes" (rather than the "modern Congreve," as he was more commonly known), Sheridan is cast as both Dryden, that "political proteus" of the Restoration world, and also Puff: the playwright and, crucially, party penman who in the first act of *The Critic* boasts of his propagandic commission "to establish the unanimity of the fleet in the Public Advertiser, and to shoot Charles Fox in the Morning Post" (Sheridan, *Dramatic Works*, 518). The print thus offers at once a forensic reading and a skillful inversion of the political satire at work in *The Critic*, depicting its author as the practitioner of the very party-puffing his play lampoons. In Dent's parody of a parody, Sheridan's own satirical strategy is reflected back at him.

Writing for Money: Pizarro

These images of Sheridan as the participant, the player, in texts from his own pen, foreground the rapidity with which his dramas were canonized, and the uses and abuses of this canonicity. Caricatures such as *Joseph Surface Posted* and *Election Compromise* deploy this cultural capital directly against Sheridan's career as a parliamentarian: that is, they harness the discourses and characters of Sheridan-the-dramatist as a means of deriding the agency and sincerity of Sheridan-the-politician. Such complex acts of literary hijacking function both to coalesce and bifurcate theatrical and parliamentary cultures. On the one hand, caricatures politicize Sheridan's comedies by reading their texts as allegories of political opportunism and hypocrisy. Equally, they offer a sequence of portraits that disclose the extent to which the contemporary public understood Sheridan's identity as the superimposition of "a Whig, and a Poet, and a long Speech maker." On the other hand, satirical prints elicit and augment the cultural disjunctions intrinsic to this theatrical politics—they polarize Sheridan's two professions by insistently pointing to playwriting and theatre management as activities which negate the authenticity of politics.

Moreover, if caricature's repeated inscription of dramatic politics as a politics of insincerity points to the powerful antitheatrical reflexes at work in Georgian society, then it also suggests the degree to which Sheridan's career in the Commons mobilized the entrenched social condescension of a political establishment which imaged itself as exclusively patrician. Theatre, in these prints, represents a form not only of mimicry but also of plebeian commerce. "In my opinion, it were sincerely to be wished," Cobbett wrote in *The Political Proteus*, "that members of Parliament followed no money-making profession whatever."[21] Nowhere is this antithesis of politics (as public interest) and theatre (as self-interest) more clearly expressed than in graphic satirists' collective response to Sheridan's late tragedy *Pizarro*.

In April 1798, alarmed by the increasing power and expansionist intent of republican France, Sheridan finally backed the war of which he had been so vociferously critical over the previous five years. First performed thirteen months later, *Pizarro*, a loose adaptation of Kotzebue's *Die Spanier in Peru*, appeared to offer a spectacular articulation of its author's new-found loyalism. Its dramatization of the Spanish conquest of Peru, of an aggressively imperialist (and Catholic) power's attempted invasion of an innocent and noble nation, was applauded by its contemporary public as a thinly veiled allegorization of the Anglo-French conflict— a cathartic exhibition of theatrical nationalism.[22] In particular, the speech of the Peruvian general, Rolla—"They follow an Adventurer whom they fear—and obey a power which they hate—we serve a Monarch whom we love—a God whom we adore" (Sheridan, *Dramatic Works*, 669)—became a set-piece of loyalist oration, and was even reprinted as a handbill entitled *Sheridan's Address to the People* in 1803. As I and others argue elsewhere—and as Daniel O'Quinn contends in this present collection—the tragedy's politics are in fact considerably more nuanced than they at first appear: just as the speech in which Sheridan first endorsed the war also reaffirmed his strident reformism, opposition to Pitt's ministry, and support of Irish independence, so *Pizarro* represents an intricate exercise in ideological negotiation.[23] In 1799, however, many statesmen were alarmed at the astonishing and suspect political volte-face that *Pizarro* seemed to embody. Fox declared the play to be "the worst thing possible," while a number of ministers regarded the drama as the shameless hijacking of a taxonomy of loyalism for commercial gain by a radical parliamentarian previously at the very forefront of the anti-war campaign.[24]

Political apostasy, then, was ostensibly embodied—even initiated—in a theatrical event: Sheridan appeared openly to be indulging in exactly the performative politics of which, as we have seen, satirists and opponents repeatedly accused him, and caricaturists were quick to depict Sheridan as his own despotic anti-hero.²⁵ *Doctor Pizarro Administering to His Patients!* (8 Jul. 1799, BM 9406), for instance, portrays Sheridan dressed as his conquistor-protagonist, prescribing a vial labelled "Essence of Loyalty" to Fox: "Don't be afraid, Sir, snuff it up freely," Sheridan tells his friend, "it will soon cure you."

Pizzaro A New Play or the Drury-Lane Masquerade (See fig. 10.2, page 198) responds to the command performance of the play on 5 June—the king's first appearance at Sheridan's theatre in five years. The print shows Sheridan, again costumed as Pizarro, proudly leading the royal party to their box. In an ostentatious and ceremonial display of patriotism he calls his orchestra to "play God Save the King d'ye hear" and announces that all must "make room for the best of Kings & wisest of Sovereigns!" Behind him, George III reassures Queen Charlotte: "No! no! no Jacobins here all Loyal all Loyal, Charming Man the Author eh! charming Man, never saw him in such a good light before." Yet the irony of this scene is that the light is manifestly *not* good, for Sheridan carries two candles to illuminate the way. Indeed, his pose here, as he holds a large candle before him, is a visual allusion to a different play: it precisely replicates the gestural conventions used by the period's actresses to perform Lady Macbeth in Act V scene i of Shakespeare's tragedy (See fig. 12.9), which documents Hannah Pritchard's iteration of this iconic scene. So

Figure 12.8.   *Pizzaro A New Play or the Drury-Lane Masquerade*, 11 Jun. 1799 (BM 9402). © Trustees of the British Museum.

Figure 12.9. *Macbeth*, Act V Scene I As Perform'd by Mrs Pritchard at Drury Lane Theatre, 1768. © Trustees of the British Museum.

immediately recognizable was this particular pose within eighteenth-century grammars of acting that it appears in caricature as late as 1821, in a print which casts Queen Caroline as Lady Macbeth.[26]

In *Pizzaro A New Play*, then, Sheridan's performance of multiple roles mobilizes a contradictory set of ideological signifiers. The loyalism of his words is undercut by a gestural vocabulary that denotes darkness, madness, regicidal guilt, and the stain of past sins that cannot be removed. If one of the bills strewn in the foreground announces that Sheridan is a "loyal author," then a second reminds us that this is "Maidstone Loyalty"—a reference to Sheridan's friendship with the Irish radical Arthur O'Connor, at whose trial for treason at Maidstone in May 1798 Sheridan had acted as a character witness. Patriotic politics is here at best costume-deep: as the print's title suggests, the loyalism of *Pizarro* is nothing more than a "Drury Lane Masquerade."

As Heather McPherson has shown, such images proliferated throughout the summer of 1799, but the first to caricature Sheridan as Pizarro, Gillray's *PIZARRO contemplating over the product of his new Peruvian Mine* (See fig. 12.10) is perhaps the most economic and acerbic in its satire.[27] Here Sheridan, corpulent and red-faced, stands on the Drury Lane stage and gloats over a helmet overflowing overflows with guineas. "Honor? Reputation?," Sheridan soliloquizes, "A mere Bubble!—will the praises of posterity charm my bones in the Grave?—'psha! my present purpose is all!—O, Gold! Gold! for thee I would sell my native Spain, as freely as I would plunder Peru." Sheridan, as is common

Figure 12.10.   James Gillray, *Pizarro Contemplating Over the Product of his New Peruvian Mine*, 4 Jun. 1799 (BM 9396).

in Gillray's prints of this period, is a grotesque personification of an avarice that negates political integrity.[28] Gillray transforms the opponent of Hastings into a colonial tyrant: the callous conquistador who plunders a nation for its gold becomes the mercenary writer who delightedly exploits national emergency for financial gain—an opportunist who would barter his allegiance to Britain as readily as he dramatizes it. Gillray mobilizes entrenched prejudices against the commercial stage and professional playwriting (here the cultural alter-ego of the art that would garner the "praises of posterity") as a vocabulary of political critique. In translating patriotism into spectacle, Gillray suggests, Sheridan has replaced a politics of honour with the slippery economics and cheap novelty of professional entertainment.

The second appearance of Gillray's Sheridan-Pizarro reappeared a few months later, in a print tellingly published in the *Anti-Jacobin Review*. *Pizzarro* (1 Oct. 1799, BM 9417) places even greater satirical emphasis on theatrical commercialism, with Sheridan shown awkwardly springing forward above the large disembodied head of the actor John Philip Kemble (who played Rolla). Under his left arm he carries two bags of money, while in his right hand he clutches a scroll inscribed:

> This season true my Principles I've sold,
> To fool the world & pocket George's gold,
> Prolific mine! anglo-peruvian food
> Provok'd my taste—and Candidate I stood,—
> While Kemble my support with LOYAL face
> Declares The PEOPLES CHOICE with stage-trick grace.

A caption at the foot of the print reaffirms, if further affirmation were needed, the satirical charge of this verse by reworking a line from the first act of the play: "In Pizarro's plans observe the Statesman's wisdom guides the *poormans Heart*" (my emphasis; the original line ends "the warrior's valour" [Sheridan, *Dramatic Works*, 662]). Such details specifically target the theatre as Sheridan's only source of income. According to the *Times* in 1787, Sheridan was "the poorest man in the House of Commons,"[29] while Nathaniel Wraxall acknowledged that Sheridan's "want of high birth and connexions" presented a constant "impediment" to his political ambitions.[30] Gillray mercilessly plays upon this socio-economic position: his image of Sheridan as Pizarro posits political apostasy, the elasticity and commodification of ideology, as the inevitable corollary of a parliamentarian whose class and well-known penury require him to fund his political activities through the industry of drama. Gillray received a government pension from 1797 and his debunking of Sheridan's new-found loyalty certainly represents an effective piece of propaganda on the part of an administration unsettled not only by the widespread praise of a radical politician's appropriation of a patriotic register over which they asserted exclusive ownership, but also by a figure who brought bourgeois professionalization into dangerously close contact with aristocratic hegemony.[31] Indeed, far more clearly than earlier caricatures of Sheridan as a political role-player, as a performer rather than a serious parliamentarian, Gillray's Sheridan-Pizarro distils systemic anxieties about the social and professional status of a figure who uncomfortably traverses—and transgresses—the boundaries of class and institution.[32]

Of course, a caricaturist's neglect was considerably worse than his attention, and the extent to which Sheridan's image, however distorted, proliferated across the metropolis over the course of three decades is an unequivocal index of his centrality to Georgian public life. Sheridan even purchased six impressions of Gillray's *Uncorking Old Sherry* (10 Mar. 1805, BM 10375), so delighted was he with the satire.[33] Equally, it is inherently difficult to locate stable meaning in caricatures: graphic satirists work in ways which necessarily blur distinctions between the strategies of deprecation and celebration. As I stated earlier, the frequency with which Sheridan's dramas feature as a caricatural language both testifies to and perpetuates his literary celebrity. Yet, in casting Sheridan as Joseph Surface, Puff, or Pizarro, political satires actively confer this cultural canonicity at the expense of parliamentary reputation. While neither the appropriation of dramatic texts and characters nor the representation of a politician as self-interested or duplicitous is in any way peculiar to graphic satires of Sheridan, the caricatures that have formed the basis of my present discussion are exceptional in the habitual manner in which theatre operates as a syntax of hypocrisy, avarice, and plebeian pretension. Prints of Sheridan *in* Sheridan do not simply theatricalize politics; rather they repeatedly marshal and reaffirm entrenched social and moral connotations of the theatre in ways that problematize and even seek to police political activity which emerges from—or is directly supported by—material theatrical enterprise. Politics, in these prints, is finally antitheatrical.

We might also consider how this graphically articulated antitheatricality challenges our understanding of the function of caricature within late eighteenth-century political culture. McPherson argues that prints served as a "counter-discourse," a vehicle, primarily oppositional in nature, through which "the political was conceived theatrically" in ways which destabilized aesthetic and institutional hierarchies alike.[34] Caricatures of Sheridan, however, suggest that such prints operated hegemonically: even while caricatures ridiculed politicians both in office and in opposition, they worked at a fundamental level to negate those elements that disquieted the aristocratic oligarchy with their social mobility, professional identity, and—as Boyne's *Banditti* illustrates—racial otherness. Certainly, as McPherson asserts, caricature visualizes politics theatrically, but, at least in Sheridan's case, this theatricality is traced in order to be exorcised from the polity in strident terms. Caricature's operation, here, is that of sanitization.

Indeed, the complex of discriminatory processes spinning around the eighteenth-century stage is visible in the very first print to caricature Sheridan in April 1783. *The Blessings of Peace* (16 April 1783, BM 6212), an anonymous satire on the negotiation of the peace treaty between Britain and newly independent America, shows statesmen in conference on both sides of the Atlantic. In the foreground, with the sun of the empire setting ominously behind them, British ministers surround the bewildered king. Near the center of the print, Sheridan turns towards Pitt the Younger saying, "The next Play I write [I] intend giving you a place in the Character of the Angry School Boy," to which the latter replies: "My Father's Spirit stirs within me and no Author or Manager shall Curb my will." This vignette is a visual paraphrase of the face-off that took place between Pitt and Sheridan during a Commons debate on the provisional treaty in February 1783. Answering Sheridan's call for the introduction of a number of amendments, Pitt asserted that

> no man admired more than he did the abilities of that right honour-
> able Gentleman, the elegant sallies of his thought, the gay effusions of
> his fancy, his dramatic turns and his epigrammatic point; and if they
> were reserved for the proper stage, they would, no doubt, receive what
> the honourable gentleman's abilities always did receive, the plaudits of
> the audience; and it would be his fortune 'sui plausu gaudere theatri'.
> But this was not the proper scene for the exhibition of those elegancies.
> (*Speeches*, 1: 47)

In his reply Sheridan inverted the terms of Pitt's charge, promising that should he return to playwriting he would "attempt an improvement on one of Ben Jonson's best characters, the character of the *Angry Boy* in the *Alchymist*." Sheridan's casting of Pitt as Kastrill, the adolescent who requires schooling in the art of quarreling, manifests an impressively urbane composure, but the institutional snobbery and social condescension resonant in Pitt's affirmation of parliamentary decorum nonetheless elicit the stigma of theatricality that impeded Sheridan throughout his career in the Commons. The son of a prime minister, soon-to-be prime minister, establishes himself as the defender of a gentrified politics of propriety, a "proper scene" which is threatened, in the incursive presence and "exhibitions" of a drama-tist, manager, and actor's son, by the contagion of the playhouse and its economies of irreverence, sensualism, disguise, and profit. It is at this precise political mo-ment that Sheridan enters the visual economy of caricature. Pitt's antitheatricalism and Sheridan's unapologetically dramatic response provide the originary motif of a suspect theatrical politics to which—as we have seen—satirical images of Sheridan repeatedly return over the following thirty years.

Notes

1. Sheridan ranks at number seven in the table detailing the number of caricatures of political personalities between 1778 and 1797 given in Nicholas K. Robinson, *Edmund Burke: A Life in Caricature* (New Haven, CT: Yale University Press, 1996), 194. However, Sheridan's ranking would certainly be much higher if we were to look at the years 1783 (when he first appeared in a political print) to about 1810.

2. There continues be a considerable debate among historians over the extent to which caricature may be defined as a truly 'public' form that reached a socially heterogeneous audience. See Todd B. Porterfield, ed., *The Efflorescence of Caricature, 1759–1838* (Farnham: Ashgate, 2011)—especially Portfield's introduction; Charles Press, "The Georgian Political Print and Democratic Institutions," *Comparative Studies in Society and History* 19, no. 2 (1977): 216–238; Roy Porter, "Seeing the Past," *Past and Present* 118, no. 1 (1988): 186–205; Eirwin E. C. Nicholson, "Consumers and Spectators: The Public of the Political Print in Eighteenth-Century England," *History* 81, no. 261 (1996): 5–21; Diana Donald, *The Age of Caricature: Satirical Prints in the Reign of George III* (New Haven, CT: Yale University Press, 1996), 1–21, 65; and Tamara L. Hunt, *Defining John Bull: Political Caricature and National Identity in late Georgian England* (Aldershot: Ashgate, 2003), 169, 293.

3. There are numerous caricatures of Sheridan as a sans-culotte, especially by James Gillray: see his *Guy Vaux Discovered in his Attempt to Destroy the King & the House of Lords—His Companions Attempting to Escape* (May 14, 1791, BM [British Museum] 7862), which shows Sheridan and Fox as the gunpowder plotters; *Sans-Cullottes Feeding Europe with the Bread of Liberty.* (January 12, 1793, BM 8290), in which Sheridan feeds John Bull with a loaf of liberty speared on a dagger's point; and also *Dumourier Dining in State at St. James's, on the 15th of May, 1793* (March 30, 1793, BM 8318), where Sheridan offers the French general, Dumourier, a deflated crown (metonymic of the king's head) on a platter.

4. For more on this caricatural strategy of proletarianizing reformists, see John Brewer, "'This monstrous tragic-comic scene': British Reactions to the French Revolution," in *The Shadow of the Guillotine: Britain and the French Revolution*, ed. David Bindman (London: British Museum, 1989), 19.

5. Jonathan Bate, *Shakespearean Constitutions: Politics, Theatre, Criticism, 1730–1830* (Oxford: Clarendon Press, 1989*)*, 28.

6. Anonymous, *The Beauties of the Brinsliead: or, a Sketch of the Opposition: a Poem* (London: John Stockdale, 1785), 9.

7. Marc Baer, "The Ruin of the Public Man: The Rise and Fall of Richard Brinsley Sheridan," in *Sheridan Studies*, ed. James Morwood and David Crane (Cambridge: Cambridge University Press, 1995), 157.

8. "That's your sort!" is the catchphrase of Goldfinch in Thomas Holcroft's 1792 play *The Road to Ruin*.

9. David Francis Taylor, *Theatres of Opposition: Empire, Revolution, and Richard Brinsley Sheridan* (Oxford: Oxford University Press, 2012).

10. See the entry for "Satyrs" in Anonymous, *The Gentleman and Lady's Key to Polite Literature; or a Compendious Dictionary of Fabulous History* (London: T. Carnan, 1783): "Pliny thinks these Satyrs were nothing else but a sort if apes, and that there were many of them in India which were very lascivious."

11. Richard Brinsley Sheridan, *The Dramatic Works of Richard Brinsley Sheridan*, ed. Cecil Price, Volume 1, (Oxford: Clarendon Press, 1973), 254. All references to Sheridan's play will be taken from this edition (henceforth Sheridan, *Dramatic Works*), the two volumes of which are paginated continuously.

12. This caricature is not the only example of a satirist politicizing the play's concern with masquerade and self-interest. Israel Pottinger's political parody of *The Duenna*, published in 1776, transformed Sheridan's comic opera into a critique of Britain's handling of the crisis unfolding in its thirteen American colonies. See my "'The Fate of Empires': The American War, Political Parody, and Sheridan's Comedies," *Eighteenth-Century Studies* 42, no. 3 (Spring 2009): 379–95.

13. Judith Pascoe, *Romantic Theatricality: Gender, Poetry and Spectatorship* (Ithaca, NY: Cornell University Press, 1997), 44.

14. William Cobbett, *The Political Proteus. A View of the Public Character and Conduct of R. B. Sheridan, Esq.* (London: Cox, Son, and Baylis, 1804), 16, 78.

15. A useful history of such negative conceptions is provided in Jonas Barish, *The Antitheatrical Prejudice* (Los Angeles: University of California Press, 1981).

16. See Charles Pigott, *The Whig Club: or, a Sketch of Modern Patriotism* (Londo: W. Priest, 1794), 36: "the public judged differently from the P[rince]; they applied to Mr. S–n a character from one of his own plays; and the name Joseph Surface has ever since been a substitute for his own."

17. *Morning Post*, January 18, 1789.

18. For more on Sheridan's role as press manager for the Foxite Whigs, see Lucyle Thomas Werkmeister, *The London Daily Press 1772–1792* (Lincoln: University of Nebraska Press, 1963), esp. 10–13, 98.

19. William Combe, *Letters from a Country Gentleman, to a Member of Parliament, on the Present State of the Nation*, 2nd ed. (London: John Stockdale, 1789), 59.

20. Richard Brinsley Sheridan, *Speeches of the Late Right Honourable Richard Brinsley Sheridan. (Several corrected by himself.)* ed. "A Constitutional Friend," 5 vols. (London: Patrick Martin, 1816), 2: 242, 245. Hereafter *Speeches*.

21. Cobbett, *Political Proteus*, 204.

22. Cobbett provides a notable exception to this body of public opinion. The play, in his view, represented an apologia for 'the creed of Price, Paine, O'Connor' (Cobbett, *Political Proteus*, 84).

23. See the fourth chapter of my *Theatres of Opposition*, 119–54, and also: John Loftis, *Sheridan and the Drama of Georgian England* (Oxford: Blackwell, 1976), 124–41; Sara Suleri, *The Rhetoric of English India* (Chicago: University of Chicago Press, 1992), 68–74; Christopher Reid, "Patriotism and Rhetorical Contest in the 1790s: The Context of Sheridan's *Pizarro*," in *Com-*

edy: Essay in Honour of Peter Dixon by friends and colleagues, ed. Elizabeth Maslen (London: Queen Mary College, 1993), 231–47; Gillian Russell, *Theatres of War: Performance, Politics and Society, 1793–1815* (Oxford: Clarendon Press, 1995), 56–58; Julie A. Carlson, "Trying Sheridan's *Pizarro*," *Texas Studies in Literature and Language* 38, nos. 3–4 (Fall-Winter 1996): 359–78; and Julie Stone Peters, "Theatricality, Legalism, and the Scenography of Suffering: The Trial of Warren Hastings and Richard Brinsley Sheridan's *Pizarro*," *Law and Literature* 18, no. 1 (2006): 15–45.

24. Quoted in Fintan O'Toole, *A Traitor's Kiss: The Life of Richard Brinsley Sheridan, 1751–1816* (London: Granta, 1997), 348.

25. The large number of caricatures generated by *Pizarro* have recently been discussed by Heather McPherson in "Caricature, Cultural Politics, and the Stage: The Case of *Pizarro*," *Huntington Library Quarterly* 70, no. 4 (2007): 607–31.

26. The print is Theodore Lane, *The whole truth, or John Bull with his eyes opened*, February 1, 1821 (BM undescribed).

27. Other prints of Sheridan as Pizarro include: Isaac Cruikshank's *The Return from Pizarro* (June 5, 1799, BM 9399); *Pizarro Returning from the Gold Mines of Peru!* (June, 1799, BM 9397); and *Returning from Pizarro!!* (June, 1799, BM 9398).

28. See, for instance, Gillray's *Doublures of Characters;—or Striking Resemblances in Phisiognomy* (November 1, 1798, BM 9261).

29. *Times*, February 7, 1787.

30. Nathaniel Wraxall, *Posthumous Memoirs of My Own Time* 3 vols. (London: R. Bentley, 1836), 3:314.

31. Lady Elizabeth Foster stated: 'The violent Ministerialists are angry at the loyalty of the Play' (quoted in Sheridan, *Dramatic Works*, 669).

32. See Christopher Clayton, "The Political Career of Richard Brinsley Sheridan," in *Sheridan Studies*, ed. James Morwood and David Crane, 131–50 (Cambridge: Cambridge University Press, 1995). Clayton judges Sheridan's parliamentary career to be an inevitable if honourable failure, given that he moved in a Whig party still controlled by aristocratic cliques to which he would always be an "outsider" (146).

33. See Richard T. Godfrey *English Caricature, 1620 to the Present: Caricaturists and Satirists, Their Art, Their Purpose and Influence: catalogue of an exhibition held at the Yale Center for British Art, The Library of Congress, Washington D.C., the National Gallery of Canada, Ottawa, the Victoria and Albert Museum, London.* (London: Victoria and Albert Museum, 1984), 88. It is worth noting here that during the 1770s Sheridan was likely himself an occasional caricaturist, working under the name Richard Sneer, who is credited with the socially satirical prints *Miss. Shuttlecock* (December 6, 1776, BM 5376), *The Back-Side of a Front Row* (June 1, 1777, BM 5430), and *Doleful Dicky Sneer in the Dumps* (April 1, 1777, BM 5435).

34. Heather McPherson, "Painting, Politics and the Stage in the Age of Caricature," in *Notorious Muse: The Actress in British Art and Culture 1776–1812*, ed. Robyn Asleson (New Haven, CT: Yale University Press, 2003), 187–89.

Alexander, Caroline. *The Bounty: The True Story of the Mutiny on the Bounty.* New York: Penguin, 2004.

Allen, Ralph G. "Irrational Entertainment in the Age of Reason." In *The Stage and the Page: London's "Whole Show" in the Eighteenth-Century Theatre,* edited by George Winchester Stone, Jr., 90–112. Berkeley: University of California Press, 1981.

———. *The Stage Spectacles of Philip James De Loutherbourg.* PhD diss., Yale University, 1960.

———. "Topical Scenes for Pantomine." *Educational Theatre Journal* 17, no. 4 (December 1965): 289–300.

Anderson, James R. *An Actor's Life.* London: Walter Scott Publishing, 1902.

Anonymous. *The Beauties of the Brinsleiad: or, a Sketch of the Opposition: a Poem.* London: John Stockdale, 1785.

———. *Female Innocence: or, a School for a Wife. As it is acted at Mrs. Lee's great booth, on the Bowling-Green, Southwark, by comedians from the theatres.* Southwark: G. Lee, 1732. http://galenet .galegroup.com/servlet/ ECCO (accessed February 13, 2012).

———. *The Gentleman and Lady's Key to Polite Literature; or a Compendious Dictionary of Fabulous History.* London: T. Carnan, 1783.

———. *Illusions; or, the Trances of Nourjahad; an Oriental romance, in three acts, founded on a Persian tale, written by Mrs. Sheridan, as now performed at the Theatre-Royal, Drury Lane.* London: J. Barker, 1813.

———. *The Imposter Unmasked; or the New Man of the People; with Anecdotes, never before published, Illustrative of the Character of the renowned and immaculate BARDOPHO. Inscribed without permission, to the superlatively honest and disinterested Man, R. B. S—R—D—N, Esq.* London: Tupper and Richards, 1806.

———. Review of *The School for Scandal. Saturday Review,* April 11, 1891, 442.

———. *The School for Daughters: or, The History of Miss Charlotte Sidney: In a series of original letters between persons in genteel life.* London:J. Bew, 1775.

———. *The School for Wives. In a Series of letters.* London, MDCCLXIII. [1763]. http://galenet.gale group.com/ECCO (accessed February 15, 2012).

Appleton, William W. *Madame Vestris and the London Stage.* New York: Columbia University Press, 1974.

Aristænetus. *Letters of Love and Gallantry.* London: Bernard Lintot, 1716.

Aristænetus, Nathaniel Brassey Halhed, and Richard Brinsley Sheridan. *The Love Epistles of Aristænetus: translated from the Greek into English Metre.* London: J. Wilkie, 1771.

The Athenaeum: A Journal of Literature, Science, the Fine Arts, Music, and the Drama, London: Athenaeum Press, 1828–1921.

Atkinson, J. Brooks. "Sheridan—Whom the Gods Loved." *The North American Review* 223, no. 883 (December 1926–Feburary 1927). 645–55.

Auburn, Mark S. "Richard Brinsley Sheridan." In *Restoration and Eighteenth-Century Dramatists: Third Series,* edited by Paula R. Backscheider. *Dictionary of Literary Biography.* Vol. 89. Detroit: Gale Research, 1989.

———. "Theatre in the Age of Garrick and Sheridan." In *Sheridan Studies,* edited by James Morwood and David Crane, 7–46. Cambridge: Cambridge University Press, 1995.

Austen, Jane. *Jane Austen's Letters to her sister Cassandra and others.* Collected and edited by R. W. Chapman. 2nd ed. London: Oxford University Press, 1952.

Avery, Emmet L., Charles Beecher Hogan, William Van Lennep, Arthur H. Scouten, and George Winchester Stone, eds. *The London Stage, 1660–1800.* 11 vols. Carbondale and Edwardsville: Southern Illinois University Press, 1960–1968.

Ayling, Stanley. *Fox: The Life of Charles James Fox.* London: John Murray, 1991.

Backscheider, Paula R. *Reflections on Biography.* New York: Oxford University Press, 1999.

———. *Spectacular Politics: Theatrical Power and Mass Culture in Early Modern England.* Baltimore: Johns Hopkins University Press, 1993.

Baer, Marc. "The Ruin of the Public Man: The Rise and Fall of Richard Brinsley Sheridan." In *Sheridan Studies,* edited by James Morwood and David Crane, 151–77. Cambridge: Cambridge University Press, 1995.

Balderston, Katharine, ed. *Thraliana. The Diary of Mrs. Hester Lynch Thrale (Later Mrs. Piozzi) 1776–1809.* 2 vols. Oxford: Clarendon Press, 1942.

Baldick, Chris. "Juvenilia." In *Oxford Concise Dictionary of Literary Terms.*132–33. Oxford: Oxford University Press, 2001.

Bardsley, Samuel Argent. *Critical Remarks on Pizarro.* London: T. Cadell and W. Davies, 1800.

Barish, Jonas. *The Antitheatrical Prejudice.* Los Angeles: University of California Press, 1981.

Barrell, John. "'The Dangerous Goddess': Masculinity, Prestige, and the Aesthetic in Early Eighteenth-Century England." *Cultural Critique* 12 (1989): 101–31.

———. *Imagining the King's Death: Figurative Treason, Fantasies of Regicide, 1793–1796.* New York and Oxford: Oxford University Press, 2000.

Barthes, Roland. *Mythologies.* Translated by Jonathan Cape. New York: Farrar, Strauss, and Giroux, 1972.

Bate, Jonathan. *Shakespearean Constitutions: Politics, Theatre, Criticism, 1730–1830.* Oxford: Clarendon Press, 1989.

Bateston. F. W. "Notes on the Text of Two Sheridan Plays." *The Review of English Studies* 16, no. 63 (July 1940): 312–17.

Baugh, Christopher. "Phillipe de Loutherbourg: Technology-Driven Entertainment and Spectacle in the Late Eighteenth Century." *Huntington Library Quarterly* 70, no. 2 (June 2007): 251–68.

Beatty, Laura. *Lillie Langtry: Manners Masks and Morals.* London: Chatto & Windus, 1999.

Beaumont, Francis, and John Fletcher. *Bonduca: A Tragedy.* Adapted by George Colman. London: George Cawthorn, 1796. http://books.google.com (accessed March 1, 2011).

Bessborough, Earl of, ed. *Georgiana. Extracts from the Correspondence of Georgiana, Duchess of Devonshire*. London: John Murray, 1955.

Bernard, John. *Retrospections of the Stage*. London: Colburn & Bentley, 1830.

Bickerstaff, Isaac. *The School for Fathers; or, Lionel & Clarissa. A Comic Opera. By Isaac Bickerstaff. Adapted for theatrical representation, as performed at the Theatres-Royal Drury-Lane and Covent-Garden. Regulated from the prompt-book, By Permission of the Managers*. London: J. Bell, 1791. http://galenet.galegroup.com/ECCO (accessed February 19, 2012).

———. *Songs Introduced in the New Dramatic Entertainment, called The Sultan; or a Peer into the Seraglio*. London, 1787.

———. *The Sultan, or Peep into the Seraglio. A Farce, in two acts*. London: C. Dilly, 1787.

Bingham, Madeleine. *The Great Lover: The Life and Art of Herbert Beerbohm Tree*. New York: Athenaeum, 1979.

———. *Sheridan: The Track of a Comet*. New York: St. Martin's, 1972; London: Allen and Unwin, 1972.

Black, Clementina. *The Linleys of Bath*. London: Frederick Muller, 1911. Reprint, London: Martin Secker, 1926, 1971.

Bligh, William. *A Narrative of the Mutiny, on Board His Majesty's Ship Bounty; and the Subsequent Voyage of Part of the Crew, in the Ship's Boat, From Tofoa, one of the Friendly Islands, to Timor, a Dutch Settlement in the East Indies*. London, 1790.

Bloom, Edward, and Lillian Bloom, eds. *The Piozzi Letters. Correspondence of Hester Lynch Piozzi, 1784–1821 (formerly Mrs. Thrale)*. 6 vols. Newark, NJ: University of Delaware Press, 1989–2004.

Boaden, James. *Memoirs of the life of John Philip Kemble, esq, including a history of the stage, from the time of Garrick to the present period*. Philadelphia: Robert H. Small, 1825.

Bolton, Philip H. *Women Writers Dramatized: A Calendar of Performances from Narrative Works Published in English to 1900*. London: Cassell, 2005.

Bor, Margot, and Lamond Clelland. *Still the Lark: A Biography of Elizabeth Linley*. London: Merlin, 1962.

Bradbrook, Frank W. "Lydia Languish, Lydia Bennet, and Dr. Fordyce's Sermons." *Notes and Queries* 11, no. 11 (November 1964): 421–23.

Brandon-Thomas, Javan. *Charley's Aunt's Father: A Life of Brandon Thomas*. London: Douglas Saunders, 1955.

Brewer, John. "'This monstrous tragic-comic scene': British Reactions to the French Revolution." In *The Shadow of the Guillotine: Britain and the French Revolution*, edited by David Bindman, 9–25. London: British Museum, 1989.

Britten, John. *Sheridan and Kotzebue: The Enterprising Adventures of Pizarro. . .* London: J. Fairburn, 1799.

Brown, Thomas. *The Works of Thomas Brown, in Prose and Verse; Serious, Moral, and Comical*, 2 vols. London: B. Bragg, 1707.

Brooke, Charlotte. *The school for Christians, in dialogues, for the use of children. By Miss Brooke*, Dublin, M.DCC.XCI. [1791]. http://galenet.galegroup.com/ECCO (accessed February 17, 2012).

Burke, Edmund. *Reflections on the Revolution in France (A Critical Edition)*. Edited by J. C. D. Clark. Stanford: Stanford University Press, 2001.

Burling, William J. *A Checklist of New Plays and Entertainments on the London Stage, 1700–1737.* Rutherford and Cranbury, NJ: Fairleigh Dickinson University Press; 1992.

Burney, Fanny. *Diary and Letters of Madame d'Arblay.* Edited by her niece [Charlotte Barrett]. 7 vols. London: H. Colborn, 1842–46.

———. "*The Witlings.* A Comedy. By a Sister of the Order." In *The Complete Plays of Frances Burney.* Edited by Peter Sabor. 2 vols. London: William Pickering, 1995.

———. "*The Witlings.* A Comedy. By a Sister of the Order." Edited and supplements by Clayton J. Delery. PhD diss., City University of New York, 1989.

Burney, Fanny, Lars E. Troide, and Stewart J. Cooke, eds. *The Early Journals and Letters of Fanny Burney.* 2 vols. Oxford: Clarendon Press, 1988.

Butler, Eliza Marian. *Sheridan: A Ghost Story,* New York: Richard Smith, 1931.

Byron, George. *Letters and Journals.* Edited by Rowland E. Prothero. 6 vols. London: J. Murray, 1922–24.

Campbell, Thomas. *Life of Mrs. Siddons.* 2 vols. London: Effingham Wilson, 1834. Reprint, London: E Moxon, 1839; New York: Benjamin Blom, 1972.

Carlson, Julie A. "Race and Profit in English Theatre." In *The Cambridge Companion to British Theatre, 1730–1830,* edited by Jane Moody and Daniel O'Quinn, chap. 12, 175–88. Cambridge: Cambridge University Press, 2007.

———. "Trying Sheridan's *Pizarro.*" *Texas Studies in Literature and Language* 38, nos.3–4 (Fall-Winter 1996): 359–78.

Casid, Jill H. *Sowing Empire: Landscape and Colonization.* Minneapolis: University of Minnesota Press, 2005.

Castle, Terry. *Masquerade and Civilisation: The Carnivalesque in Eighteenth-Century English Culture and Fiction.* London: Methuen, 1986.

Chatterton, Thomas. *The Complete Works of Thomas Chatterton: A Bicentenary Edition.* Edited by Donald S. Taylor in association with Benjamin B. Hoover, 2 vols. Oxford: Clarendon Press, 1971.

Chothia, Jean. *English Drama of the Early Modern Period, 1890–1940.* London and New York: Longman, 1996.

Choudhury, Mita. *Interculturalism and Resistance in the London Theater, 1660–1800: Identity, Performance, Empire,* Lewisburg, PA: Bucknell University Press, 2000.

Clayton, Christopher. "The Political Career of Richard Brinsley Sheridan," In *Sheridan Studies,* edited by James Morwood and David Crane, 131–50. Cambridge: Cambridge University Press, 1995.

Clinton-Baddeley, V. C. *The Burlesque Tradition in the English Theatre after 1660.* London: Methuen & Company LTD, 1952.

Clear, Charles R. *John Palmer (of Bath), Mail Coach Pioneer.* Poole: Blanford Press, 1955. Reprint, London: Blandford Press and Postal History Society, 1995.

Cobbett, William. *The Political Proteus: A View of the Public Character and Conduct of R. B. Sheridan, Esq.* London: Cox, Son, and Baylis, 1804.

Combe, William. *Letters from a Country Gentleman, to a Member of Parliament, on the Present State of the Nation.* 2nd ed. London: John Stockdale, 1789.

Cooper, Anthony Ashley Shaftesbury, Earl of. *Characteristics of Men, Manners, Opinions, Times.* Edited by Philip J. Ayres. 2 vols. Oxford: Clarendon Press, 1999.

Cove, Joseph W. [Lewis Gibbs, pseud.]. *Sheridan, His Life and His Theatre*. New York: W. Morrow, 1948.

Cowley, Hannah. *Albina, Countess Raimond; A Tragedy, By Mrs. Cowley. Adapted for Theatrical Representation, as performed at the Theatre-Royal, Hay-Market*. London: George Cawthorn, 1797.

Cox, Jeffrey N. *Poetry and Politics in the Cockney School: Keats, Shelley, Hunt And Their Circle*. Cambridge: Cambridge University Press, 1998.

Crane, David. "Satire and Celebration in *The Critic*." In *Sheridan Studies*, Edited by James Morwood and David Crane, 87–95. Cambridge: Cambridge University Press, 1995.

Craven, Elizabeth. *The Miniature Picture; A Comedy in Three Acts: performed at the Theatre-Royal, Drury-Lane*. London: G. Riley, 1781.

Critical Review. London: Archibald Hamilton, 1763, 1771, 1775.

Croall, Jonathan. *Sybil Thorndike: A Star of Life*. London: Haus Publishing, 2008.

Danziger, Marlies K. *Oliver Goldsmith and Richard Brinsley Sheridan*. New York: Frederick Ungar Publishing, 1978.

Darlington, William Aubrey Cecil. *Sheridan*. London: Duckworth, 1933.

D'Avenant, William. *The Works of Sir William D'Avenant*. 2 vols. London,1673. Reprint, reissued New York: Benjamin Blom, Inc., 1968.

Derrida, Jacques. *Spurs: Nietzsche's Styles*. Translated by Barbara Harlow. Chicago: University of Chicago Press, 1981.

Dibdin, Charles. *The Gipsies: A Comic opera, in two acts. As it is performed at the Theatre-Royal in the Haymarket*. London: T. Cadell and T. Sherlock, 1778.

———. *A Complete History of the English Stage*. 5 vols. London, 1800.

Dietrich, Richard F. *British Drama, 1890 to 1950: A Critical History*. Boston: Twayne Publishers, 1989.

Dirks, Nicholas B. *The Scandal of Empire: India and the Creation of Imperial Britain*. Cambridge, MA: Belknap Press of Harvard University Press, 2006.

Donald, Diana. *The Age of Caricature: Satirical Prints in the Reign of George III*. New Haven, CT: Published for the Paul Mellon Centre for Studies in British Art byYale University Press, 1996.

Donkin, Ellen. *Getting into the Act: Women Playwrights in London 1776–1829*. New York Routledge, 1995.

Donoghue, Frank. "Avoiding the 'Cooler Tribunal of the Study': Richard Brinsley Sheridan's Writer's Block and Late Eighteenth-Century Print Culture." *ELH* 68, no. 4 (Winter 2001): 831–56.

Donohue, Joseph W., ed. *The Cambridge History of British Theatre. Vol. 2, 1660–1865*. Cambridge: Cambridge University Press, 2004.

———. *Dramatic Character in the English Romantic Age*. Princeton, NJ: Princeton University Press, 1970.

Doody, Margaret Anne. *Frances Burney. The Life in the Works*. New Brunswick, NJ: Rutgers University Press, 1988.

Dowden, Wilfred S., ed. *The Journal of Thomas Moore*. 6 vols. Newark, NJ: University of Delaware Press, 1983–91.

Dulck, Jean. *Les Comédies de R. B. Sheridan*. Paris: Didier, 1962.

Durant, Jack Davis. *Richard Brinsley Sheridan*. Boston: Twayne Publishers, 1975.

———. *Richard Brinsley Sheridan: A Reference Guide.* Boston: G. K. Hall, 1981.

Dryden, John. *An Essay of Dramatic Poesy [Of Dramatick Poesie, an essay].* London, 1667.

Eyre, Edmund John. *Consequences; or, the school for prejudice. A comedy, of three acts. As performed at the theatres, Worcester, Wolverhampton, and Shrewsbury. By E. J. Eyre, Author of the Dreamer Awake; and the Maid of Normandy; or, the Death of the Queen of France, &c. Late of Pembroke College, Cambridge.* London, T. N. Longman, 1794. http://galenet.galegroup.com/ECCO (accessed February 13, 2012).

Fairer, David. *English Poetry of the Eighteenth Century, 1700–1789.* London: Longman, 2003.

Ferguson, Niall. *Empire: How Britain Made the Modern World.* London: Allen Lane/Penguin Press, 2003.

Fisher, Nancy. *"Thou Shalt not Steal." The School for Ingratitude: a comedy, in five acts.* London, 1798. http:/galenet.galegroup.com/ECCO (accessed January 18, 2012).

Fitzgerald, Percy Hetherington. *The Lives of the Sheridans.* 2 vols. London: R. Bentley and Son, 1886.

Forster, E. M. [Edward Morgan], *A Passage to India.* Orlando: Harcourt, Brace and Co., 1924.

Foss, Kenelm. *Here Lies Richard Brinsley Sheridan.* New York: E. P. Dutton & Co., 1940.

Garrick, David. "Epilogue" to The School for Wives. *Bell's British theatre. Consisting of the most esteemed English plays.* Vol. 7., London, 1797. http://galenet.galegroup.com/ECCO (accessed March 13, 2012).

Gatrell, Vic. *City of Laughter: Sex and Satire in Eighteenth-Century London.* London: Atlantic Books, 2006.

Gentleman, Francis. *The dramatic censor: or, Critical companion.* 2 vols. London: J. Bell, 1770.

George, Mary Dorothy. *Catalogue of Political and Personal Satires Volume 7, 1793–1800. Preserved in the Department of Prints and Drawings in the British Museum.* 7 vols. London: British Museum, 1942.

Gibbs, Lewis [Joseph W. Cove]. *Sheridan, His Life and His Theatre.* New York: W. Morrow, 1948.

Gill, Conrad. *The Naval Mutinies of 1797.* Manchester: Manchester University Press, 1913.

Glasgow, Alice. *Sheridan of Drury Lane: A Biography.* New York: Frederick A. Stokes, 1940.

Godfrey, Richard T. *English Caricature, 1620 to the Present: Caricaturists and Satirists, Their Art, Their Purpose and Influence: catalogue of an exhibition held at the Yale Center for British Art, The Library of Congress, Washington D.C., the National Gallery of Canada, Ottawa, the Victoria and Albert Museum, London.* London: Victoria and Albert Museum, 1984.

Green, Emanuel. *Richard Brinsley Sheridan and Thomas Linley: Their Residences at Bath, With a Notice of the Sheridan Grotto.* Bath: Herald Office, 1904.

Griffith, Elizabeth. *The Times: A Comedy. As it is performing at the Theatre Royal in Drury Lane.* Dublin: R. Marchband, 1779.

Groom, Nick, ed. *Thomas Chatterton and Romantic Culture*, with foreword by Peter Ackroyd. Basingstoke: Macmillan, 1999.

Haggerty, George E. "Keyhole Testimony: Witnessing Sodomy in the Eighteenth Century." *The Eighteenth Century: Theory and Interpretation* 44, nos. 2–3 (Summer–Fall 2003): 167–82.

Haley, David. *Dryden and the Problem of Freedom: The Republican Aftermath, 1649–1681.* New Haven, CT: Yale University Press, 1997.

Halhed, Nathaniel Brassey, and Richard Brinsley Sheridan. *Letters from Mr. H. B. Halhed to Mr. R. B. Sheridan.* Frampton: privately printed, 1872.

Hammond, Brean S. Review [untitled]. *The Review of English Studies, New Series* 38, no. 149 (February 1987): 83–84.

Hare, Arnold, and Kathleen Barker. *Theatre Royal, Bath: A Calendar of Performances at the Orchard Street Theatre, 1750–1805*. Bath: Kingsmead Press, 1977.

Harvey, Karen. *Reading Sex in the Eighteenth Century: Bodies and Gender in English Erotic Culture.* Cambridge: Cambridge University Press, 2004.

Hibernian Magazine or, compendium of entertaining knowledge. Dublin: T. Walker, 1771.

Higgins, Sydney. "The Golden Age of British Theatre (1880–1920)." http://www.the-camerino-players.com/britishtheatre/index.html (accessed May 20, 2012).

Highfill, Phillip, Kalman A. Burnim, and Edward. A. Langhans, eds. *The Biographical Dictionary of Actors, Actresses, Musicians, Dancers, Managers, and other Stage Personnel in London, 1660–1800.* 16 vols. Carbondale: Southern Illinois University Press. 1991.

Hill, Constance. *The House in St. Martin's Street: Being Chronicles of the Burney Family. . . With illustrations by Ellen G. Hill and reproductions of portraits, etc., etc.* London: John Lane, 1907.

Hindson, Paul, and Tim Gray. *Burke's Dramatic Theory of Politics.* Aldershot: Avebury, 1988.

Hogarth, William, John Reeves, and Evelyn J. Shirley. *The Analysis of Beauty: Written with a View of Fixing the Fluctuating Ideas of Taste.* London: J. Reeve, 1753.

Hume, Robert D., and Judith Milhous. "Isaac Bickerstaff's Copyrights—and a Biographical Discovery." *Philological Quarterly* 83, no. 3 (Summer 2004): 259–73.

———. "Playwright's Remuneration in Eighteenth-Century London." *Harvard Library Bulletin* 10, no. 2–3 (Summer–Fall 1999).

Hunt, Tamara L. *Defining John Bull: Political Caricature and National Identity in late Georgian England.* Aldershot: Ashgate, 2003.

Inchbald, Elizabeth. *Remarks for the British Theatre (1806–1809).* Delmar, NY: Scholars' Facsimiles and Reprints, 1990.

Isaac, Winifred. *Ben Greet and the Old Vic: A Biography of Sir Philip Ben Greet.* London: Greenback Press, 1964.

Jackson, Allan S. "*Pizarro*, Bridges and the Gothic Scene." *Theatre Notebook* 51, no. 2 (1997): 81–91.

Jameson, Fredric. *Archaeologies of the Future: The Desire Called Utopia and Other Science Fictions.* New York: Verso, 2005.

Johnson, Claudia D., and Vernon E. Johnson, eds. *Nineteenth-Century Theatrical Memoirs.* Westport, CT: Greenwood Press, 1982.

Jones, Colin. *The Great Nation. France from Louis XV to Napoleon.* New York: Columbia University Press, 2002.

Jones, Robert W. "A Matter of Honour: The Duel in Thomas Moore's *Life of Richard Brinsley Sheridan*," *Journal for Eighteenth-Century Studies* (forthcoming 2012).

———. "Sheridan and the Theatre of Patriotism: Staging Dissent during the War for America." *Eighteenth-Century Life* 26, no. 1 (2002): 24–45.

Kelly, Hugh. *The School for Wives: A comedy. As it is performed at the Theatre-Royal in Drury-Lane. Embellished with an etching, by Mr. Loutherbour.* 3rd ed. London, MDCCLXXIV [1774]. http://galenet.galegroup.com/ECCO (accessed February 19, 2012).

Kelly, Linda. *Richard Brinsley Sheridan: A Life*. London: Pimlico, 1998.

Kelly, Michael. *Reminiscences of Michael Kelly of the King's Theatre and Theatre Royal Drury Lane*. Edited by T. E. Hook. 2 vols. London: Henry Colburn, 1826.

Kershaw, Baz, ed. *The Cambridge History of British Theatre, Vol. 3., since 1895*. 3 vols. Cambridge: Cambridge University Press, 2004.COPYRIGHT 2008 Mid-America Theatre Association. This material is published under license from the publisher through the Gale Group, Farmington Hills, Michigan. All inquiries regarding rights should be directed to the Gale Group.

Knapp, Oswald G., ed. *The Intimate Letters of Hester Piozzi and Penelope Pennington, 1788–1821*. London: John Lane, 1914.

Knox-Shaw, Peter. *Jane Austen and the Enlightenment*. Cambridge: Cambridge University Press, 2004.

Kurdi, Maria. "Interview with Elizabeth Kuti." *Irish Literary Supplement* 23, no.1. (Spring 2004): 11–12.

Kuti, Elizabeth. "Rewriting Frances Sheridan." *Eighteenth-Century Ireland* 11 (1996): 120–28.

Langtry, Lillie. *The Days I Knew*. New York: George H. Doran, 1925.

Leacock, John. *The School forSscandal. A Comedy*. London, MDCCLXXIX [1779]. http://galenet.galegroup.com (accessed February 19, 2012).

Lee, Harriet. *The New Peerage: Or, Our Eyes May Deceive Us*. London: G. G. J. and J. Robinson, 1787.

Lee, Sophia. *Almeyda, Queen of Granada. A Tragedy, in Five Acts. As performed at the Theatre Royal, Drury-Lane*. Dublin: Brett Smith, 1796.

———. *The Chapter of Accidents*. Edited by William Oxberry. London: W. Simpkin and R. Marshall, 1823.

———. *A Hermit's Tale*. London: T. Cadell, 1787.

———. *The Recess, or, A Tale of Other Times*. Edited by April Alliston. Lexington: University of Kentucky Press, 2000.

Lefanu, Alicia. *Memoirs of the Life and Writings of Mrs. Frances Sheridan*. London: G. and W. B. Whittaker, 1824.

LeFanu, William, ed. *Betsy Sheridan's Journal*. New Brunswick, NJ: Rutgers University Press, 1960. Reprint, New York: Oxford University Press, 1960.

Loftis, John. *Sheridan and the Drama of Georgian England*. Oxford: Blackwell, 1976. Reprint, Cambridge, MA: Harvard University Press, 1977.

London Evening Post, London: John Miller, 1772.

Lynch, James J. *Box, Pit, and Gallery: Stage and Society in Johnson's London*. New York: Russell & Russell, 1953. Reprint, 1971.

M., T., "Memoirs of Richard Brinsley Sheridan, Esq." *The London Magazine, or, Gentleman's Monthly Intelligencer*. Vol. 47, November, 1778.

Macauley, Thomas Babington. *Essay on Warren Hastings*. Edited by Alexander Mackie. London: Longman, Green & Co., 1892.

Mangin, Edward. *The Imposter Unmasked: or the New Man of the People; with Anecdotes, never before published Illustrative of the Character of the renowned and immaculate BARDOPHO. Inscribed without permission, to the superlatively honest and disinterested Man, R. B. S—R—D—N, Esq.* London: Tupper and Richards, 1806.

———. *"A Letter to Thomas Moore, Esq." On the Subject of Sheridan's School for Scandal*. Bath: George Wood, 1826.

Mann, David D., and Susan Garland Mann, eds. *Women Playwrights in England, Ireland, and Scotland, 1660–1823*. Bloomington: Indiana University Press, 1996.

Manvell, Roger. *Sarah Siddons: Portrait of an Actress*. London: Heinemann, 1970.

Marshall, Gail, and Adrian Poole, eds. *Victorian Shakespeare: Theatre, Drama, Performance*. Basingstoke: Palgrave Macmillan, 2004.

Marshall, P. J. *The Impeachment of Warren Hastings*. London: Oxford University Press, 1965.

Matthews, Brander, ed. *Sheridan's Comedies: The Rivals and The School for Scandal*. New York: Thomas Y. Crowell, 1904.

McCann, Andrew. *Cultural Politics in the 1790s: Literature, Radicalism and the Public Sphere*. Houndmills: Macmillan, 1999.

McPherson, Heather. "Caricature, Cultural Politics, and the Stage: The Case of *Pizarro*." *Huntington Library Quarterly* 70, no. 4 (2007): 607–31.

———. "Painting, Politics and the Stage in the Age of Caricature." In *Notorious Muse: The Actress in British Art and Culture 1776–1812*, edited by Robyn Asleson, 171–94. New Haven, CT: Yale University Press, 2003.

Meehan, John Francis. *More Famous Houses of Bath and District*. Bath: B. & J. F. Meehan, 1906.

Mikhail, Edward Halim. *Sheridan: Interviews and Recollections*. New York: St. Martin's Press, 1989.

Mitchell, Leslie G. *Charles James Fox*. London: Oxford University Press, 1992.

The Monthly Review, or Literary Journal. London: R. Griffiths, 1771, 1775.

Moody, Jane, and Daniel O'Quinn, eds. *The Cambridge Companion to British Theatre, 1730–1830*. Cambridge: Cambridge University Press, 2007.

Moore, Thomas. *Memoirs of the Life of the Right Honourable Richard Brinsley Sheridan*, 5th ed., 2 vols. London: Longman, Rees, Orme, Brown, and Green, 1826. Reprint, New York: Redfield, c. 1858; New York: Greenwood Press, 1968.

More, Hannah. *The Fatal Falsehood: A Tragedy. As it is acted at the Theatre-Royal, in Covent Garden. By the Author of Percy*. London: T. Cadell, 1779.

Moretti, Franco. *Maps, Graphs, and Trees: Abstract Models For A Literary History*. New York: Verso, 2005.

Morning Chronicle, London: William Woodfall, 1772, 1775.

Morwood, James. *The Life and Works of Richard Brinsley Sheridan*. Edinburgh: Scottish Academic Press, 1985.

Morwood, James, and David Crane, eds. *Sheridan Studies*. Cambridge: Cambridge University Press, 1995.

Mullin, Donald, ed. *Victorian Plays: A Record of Significant Productions on the London Stage, 1837–1901*. New York and Westport, CT: Greenwood Press, 1987.

Mulrooney, Jonathan. "Reading Theatre, 1730–1830." In *The Cambridge Companion to British Theatre, 1730–1830*, edited by Jane Moody and Daniel O'Quinn. New York: Cambridge University Press, 2007.

Nead, Lynda. *The Female Nude: Art, Obscenity and Sexuality*. London: Routledge, 1992.

Neilson, Julia. *This for Remembrance*. London: Hurst & Blackett, 1940.

Nettleton, George Henry. "The Books of Lydia Languish's Circulating Library." *Journal of English and German Philology* 5, no. 4 (1905): 492–500.

Nicholson, Eirwin E. C. "Consumers and Spectators: The Public of the Political Print in Eighteenth-Century England." *History* 81, no. 261 (1996): 5–21.

Nicoll, Allardyce. *Early Nineteenth-Century Drama, A History of English Drama, 1660–1900*. 6 vols. Cambridge: Cambridge University Press, 1952–59.

———. Review [untitled]. *The Review of English Studies, New Series* 18, no. 71 (August 1967): 344–46.

Oliphant, Margaret. *Sheridan. English Men of Letters*. Edited by John Morley. New York: Harper and Brothers, 1887.

O'Quinn, Daniel. *Entertaining Crisis in the Atlantic Imperium, 1770–1790*. Baltimore: Johns Hopkins University Press, 2011.

———. "Fox's Tears: The Staging of Liquid Politics." In *Spheres of Action: Speech and Performance in Romantic Culture*, edited by Alexander Dick and Angela Esterhammer, 194–221. Toronto: University of Toronto Press, 2009.

———. *Staging Governance: Theatrical Imperialism in London, 1770–1800*. Baltimore: Johns Hopkins University Press, 2005.

O'Toole, Fintan. *A Traitor's Kiss: The Life of Richard Brinsley Sheridan, 1751–1816*. London: Granta, 1997, 1998. Reprint, New York: Farrar, Straus, and Giroux, 1998.

Oxford Concise Dictionary of Literary Terms. Oxford: Oxford University Press, 2001.

Oxford Dictionary of National Biography Online. Edited by H. C. G. Matthew and Brian Harrison. Oxford: Oxford University Press, 2004. http://www.oxforddnb.com/

Paine, Thomas. *Rights of Man*. London: J. S. Jordan, 1791.

Pascoe, Judith. *Romantic Theatricality: Gender, Poetry and Spectatorship*. Ithaca, NY: Cornell University Press, 1997.

Parker, John. *Who Was Who in the Theatre, 1912–1976: Biographical Dictionary of Actors, Actresses, Directors, Playwrights, and Producers of the English-Speaking Theatre*. Compiled from *Who's Who in the Theatre*, Vols. 1–15, 1912–1972. Detroit: Gale Research, 1978.

Peakman, Julie. *Mighty Lewd Books: The Development of Pornography in Eighteenth-Century England*. Basingstoke: Palgrave Macmillan, 2003.

Pearson, Hesketh. *Beerbohm Tree: His Life and Laughter*. London: Methuen, 1956.

Peter, Margot. *Mrs. Pat: The Life of Mrs. Patrick Campbell*. New York: Alfred A. Knopf, 1984.

Peters, Julie Stone. "Theatricality, Legalism, and the Scenography of Suffering: The Trial of Warren Hastings and Richard Brinsley Sheridan's *Pizarro*." *Law and Literature* 18, no. 1 (2006): 15–45.

Pigott, Charles. *The Whig Club: or, A Sketch of Modern Patriotism*. London: W. Priest, 1794.

Phare, E. E. "Lydia Languish, Lydia Bennet, and Dr. Fordyce's Sermons." *Notes and Queries* 11, no. 5 (May 1964): 182–83.

Porter, Roy. "Seeing the Past." *Past and Present* 118, no. 1. (1988): 186–205.

Porterfield, Todd B., ed. *The Efflorescence of Caricature, 1759–1838*. Farnham: Ashgate, 2011.

Press, Charles. "The Georgian Political Print and Democratic Institutions." *Comparative Studies in Society and History* 19, no. 2 (April 1977): 216–38.

Price, Cecil. "Hymen and Hirco: A Vision." *Times Literary Supplement*. July 11, 1958, 396.

Rae, W. Fraser. *Sheridan: A Biography*. 2 vols. London: Richard Bentley and Son, 1896.

———, ed. *Sheridan's Plays Now Printed as He Wrote Them and His Mother's Unpublished Comedy "A Journey to Bath"* London: D. Nutt, 1902.

Reid, Christopher. "Burke's Tragic Muse: Sarah Siddons and the 'Feminization' of the *Reflections*." In *Burke and the French Revolution: Bicentennial Essays*, edited by Steven Blakemore, 1–27. Athens.: University of Georgia Press, 1992.

———. "Patriotism and Rhetorical Contest in the 1790s: The Context of Sheridan's *Pizarro*." In *Comedy: Essay in Honour of Peter Dixon by friends and colleagues*, edited by Elizabeth Maslen, 231–47. London: Queen Mary College, 1993.

Reynolds, Frederick. *The Life and Times of Frederick Reynolds*. 2 vols. Philadelphia: H. C. Cary and I. Lea, 1826.

Rhodes, R. Crompton. *Harlequin Sheridan: The Man and the Legends*. Oxford: Blackwell, 1933.

Robinson, Nicholas K. *Edmund Burke: A Life in Caricature*. New Haven, CT: Yale University Press, 1996.

Rosenthal, Laura. "Entertaining Women: The Actress in Eighteenth-Century Theatre and Culture." In *The Cambridge Companion to British Theatre, 1730–1830*, edited by Jane Moody and Daniel O'Quinn, chap. 12, 159–74. Cambridge: Cambridge University Press, 2007.

Rump, Eric S. "Sheridan, Politics, The Navy and the Musical Allusions in the Final Scene of *The Critic*." *Restoration and Eighteenth-Century Theater Research* 6, no. 2 (Winter 1991): 30–35.

Russell, Gillian. *The Theatres of War: Performance, Politics, and Society, 1793–1815*. Oxford: Clarendon Press, 1995.

———. *Women, Sociability and Theatre in Georgian London*. Cambridge: Cambridge University Press, 2007.

Said, Edward W. *On Late Style: Music and Literature Against the Grain*. London: Bloomsbury, 2007.

Sallier, T. H. "Some Unpublished Letters of Mrs Sheridan to Mrs Canning." In *The Political Career of Richard Brinsley Sheridan*, edited by Michael Sadleir and Elizabeth Ann Sheridan, 74–85. Oxford: Blackwell, 1912.

Savin, Maynard. *Thomas William Robertson: His Plays and Stagecraft*. Providence, RI: Brown University Press, 1950.

Sedgwick, Eve Kosofsky. *Between Men: English Literature and Male Homosocial Desire*. New York: Colombia University Press, 1985.

Seward, Anna. *The Letters of Anna Seward: Written between the years 1784 and 1807*. Edited and published by Archibald Constable, 6 vols. Edinburgh, 1811. Reprint, New York: AMS Press, 1975.

Sheldon, Esther K. *Thomas Sheridan of Smock-Alley; recording his life as actor and theater manager in both Dublin and London, and including a Smock-Alley calendar for the years of his management*. Princeton, NJ: Princeton University Press, 1967.

Sheridan, Frances Chamberlaine. *The Plays of Frances Sheridan*. Edited by Robert Goode Hogan and Jerry C. Beasley. Newark, DE: University of Delaware Press, 1984.

Sheridan, Richard Brinsley. *The Dramatic Works of Richard Brinsley Sheridan*. Edited by Cecil Price. 2 vols. Oxford: Clarendon Press, 1966. Reprint, Oxford: Oxford University Press, 1973.

———. *The Duenna, An Opera. As it is performed in the Theatres Royal, by W. Oxberry*. London, 1820.

———. *The Letters of Richard Brinsley Sheridan*. Edited by Cecil Price. 3 vols. Oxford: Clarendon Press, 1966.

———. *The Plays and Poems of Richard Brinsley Sheridan*. Edited by R. Crompton Rhodes. 3 vols. Oxford: Basil Blackwell, 1928. Reprint, 1933.

———. *The Rivals*. Edited by Richard Little Purdy. PhD diss., Yale University, 1930. Reprint, Oxford: Clarendon Press, 1917.

———. *The Rivals, A Comedy. As it was first Acted at the Theatre-Royal in Covent-Garden*. Edited by Richard Little Purdy. Oxford: Clarendon Press, 1935.

———. *The Rival Beauties: A Poetical Contest*. London: W. Griffin, 1772.

———. *The School for Scandal*. Edited by Cecil Price. Oxford: Oxford University Press, 1971.

———. *The Speech of R. B. Sheridan, Esq. On Wednesday, the 7th of February, 1787 In bringing forward the Fourth Charge against Warren Hastings, Esq. Relative to the Begums of Oude*. 2nd ed. London, 1787.

———. *Speeches of the Late Right Honourable Richard Brinsley Sheridan. (Several corrected by himself.)* Edited by "A Constitutional Friend." 5 vols. London: Patrick Martin, 1816.

———. *The Works of the Late Right Honourable Richard Brinsley Sheridan*. Collected by Thomas Moore. Leipsic: Ernest Fleischer, 1825.

Sheridan, Richard Brinsley, and Alfred Howard. *The Beauties of Sheridan, Consisting of Selections from his Poems, Dramas, and Speeches*. Boston: S. N. Dickinson, 1831.

Sheridan, Richard Brinsley, and William Fraser Rae. *Sheridan's Plays Now Printed as He Wrote Them and His Mother's Unpublished Comedy 'A Journey to Bath.'* Edited by W. Fraser Rae. London: D. Nutt, 1902.

Sheridan, Thomas. *Captain O'Blunder: or, The Brave Irishman, A Farce*. London, 1771.

Sherwin, Oscar. *Uncorking Old Sherry: The Life and Times of Richard Brinsley Sheridan*. New York: Twayne, 1960.

Sibbald, Susan Mein. *The Memoirs of Susan Sibbald (1783–1812)*. Edited by Francis Paget Hett. London: John Lane, 1926.

Sichel, Walter. *Sheridan, From New and Original Material; Including a Manuscript Diary by Georgiana, Duchess of Devonshire*, 2 vols. London: Constable, 1909.

Smith, Dane Farnsworth, and M. L. Lawhon, *Plays about the theatre in England, 1737–1800: or, The self-conscious stage from Foote to Sheridan*. Lewisburg, PA: Bucknell University Press, 1979.

Snow, Edward. "Theorising the Male Gaze: Some Problems," *Representations* 25, no. 1 (1989): 30–41.

Stallybrass, Peter, and Allon White. *The Politics and Poetics of Transgression*. London: Methuen, 1986.

Stokes, Hugh. *The Devonshire House Circle*. London: Herbert Jenkins, 1917.

Suleri, Sara. *The Rhetoric of English India*. Chicago: University of Chicago Press, 1992.

Summers, Montague. *The Gothic Quest: A History of the Gothic Novel*. London: Fortune Press, 1938. Reprint, New York: Russell and Russell, 1964.

Taylor, David Francis. "'The Fate of Empires': The American War, Political Parody, and Sheridan's Comedies." *Eighteenth-Century Studies* 42, no. 3 (Spring 2009): 379–95.

———. *Theatres of Opposition: Empire, Revolution, and Richard Brinsley Sheridan*. Oxford: Oxford University Press, 2012.

Thicknesse, Ann. *The school for fashion, in two volumes. By Mrs. Thicknesse.* London, MDCCC [1800]. http://galenet.galegroup.com/ECCO (accessed February 17, 2012).

Thomson, James. *The Seasons.* Edited by James Sambrook. Oxford: Clarendon Press, 1981.

Thompson, James. "Sheridan, *School for Scandal,* and Aggression." *Comparative Drama* 42, no. 1 (2008): 89–98.

Timbs, John. *Lives of Wits and Humourists: R. Brinsley Sheridan, Richard Porson, Rev. Sydney Smith, Theodore Hook. James, and Horace Smith.* London: Richard Bentley, 1862.

Tomalin, Claire. *Mrs. Jordan's Profession: The Story of a Great Actress and a Future King.* London: Viking, 1994.

Treyssac de Vergy, Pierre Henri. *Nature: or, The school for demi-rapes. By Mr. Treyssac de Vergy.* London, 1771.

Troide, Lars E. "Trying Sheridan's *Pizarro*" *Texas Studies in Literature and Language* 38, no.3/4 (Fall/Winter 1996): 359–78.

Turley, Richard Marggraf. *Keats's Boyish Imagination.* London: Routledge, 2004.

Van Lennep, William, et al. *The London Stage: A Calendar of Plays, 1660–1800.* 11 vols. Carbondale: Southern Illinois University Press, 1960–1968.

Walpole, Horace. *Letters of Horace Walpole, Earl of Orford, to Sir Horace Mann: His Britannic Majesty's Resident at the Court of Florence, from 1760 to 1785.* 6 vols. Philadelphia: Lea and Blanchard, 1844.

———. *The Yale Edition of Horace Walpole's Correspondence.* ed. W. S. Lewis. 48 vols. New Haven, CT: Yale University Press, 1937–1983.

Watkins, John. *Memoirs of the Public and Private Life of the Right Honorable Richard Brinsley Sheridan, with a Particular Account of his Family and Connexions.* 2nd ed., 2 vols. London: Henry Colburn, 1817.

Weisenthal, Christine S. "Representation and Experimentation in the Major Comedies of Richard Brinsley Sheridan." *Eighteenth-Century Studies* 25, no. 3 (Spring 1992): 309–30.

Werkmeister, Lucyle Thomas. *The London Daily Press 1772–1792.* Lincoln: University of Nebraska Press, 1963.

Whitehead, William. *The School for Lovers. A Comedy, by William Whitehead, Esq. Adapted for theatrical representation, as performed at the Theatres-Royal, Drury-Lane and Covent-Garden. Regulated from the prompt-books, By Permission of the Managers.* London, MDCCXCIII [1793]. http://galenet.galegroup.com/ECCO (accessed February, 19, 2012).

Williams, Clifford J. *Madame Vestris: A Theatrical Biography.* London: Sidgwick and Jackson, 1973.

Williams, George W. "A New Source of Evidence for Sheridan's Authorship of 'The Camp' and 'The Wonders of Derbyshire.'" *Studies in Philology* 47, no. 4 (October 1950): 619–28.

Wilson, Kathleen. *The Island Race: Englishness, Empire and Gender in the Eighteenth Century.* New York: Routledge, 2002.

Wordsworth, William. *Early Poems and Fragments, 1785–1797.* Edited by Carol Landon and Jared Curtis. London: Cornell University Press, 1997.

Womersley, David, ed. *Restoration Drama. An Anthology.* Oxford: Blackwell, 2000.

Wraxall, Nathaniel William. *Posthumous Memoirs of My Own Time.* 3 vols. London: R. Bentley, 1836.

Mita Choudhury teaches eighteenth-century British literature and culture in the Department of English and Philosophy at Purdue University Calumet. She is author of *Interculturalism and Resistance in the London Theatre, 1660–1800: Identity, Performance, Empire* (Bucknell University Press, 2000) and coeditor, with Laura J. Rosenthal, of *Monstrous Dreams of Reason: Body, Self, and Other in the Enlightenment* (Bucknell University Press, 2002). Currently, she is working on a book entitled *Nation-space in Britain, 1660–1800.*

Marianna d'Ezio holds a PhD in English literature from the University of Rome, is the author of *Hester Lynch Thrale Piozzi: A Taste for Eccentricity* (Cambridge Scholars, 2010), and is the editor of the collection *Literary and Cultural Intersections during the Long Eighteenth Century* (Cambridge Scholars, 2008).

Jack E. DeRochi is associate professor of English at Winthrop University. He has published several articles on late-eighteenth-century drama and satire in publications including *Restoration and Eighteenth-Century Research* and *Studies in American Humor*. His essay on the emergence of the masculine gothic was included in *Prologues, Epilogues, Curtain-Raisers and Afterpieces: The Rest of the Eighteenth-Century London Stage* (University of Delaware Press, 2007).

Daniel J. Ennis is professor of English at Coastal Carolina University. He is the author of *Enter the Press-Gang: Representations of Naval Impressment in Eighteenth-Century British Literature* (University of Delaware Press, 2002) and edited, with Judith B. Slagle, a collection of essays entitled *Prologues, Epilogues, Curtain-Raisers and Afterpieces: The Rest of the Eighteenth-Century London Stage* (University of Delaware Press, 2007).

Emily C. Friedman is assistant professor of English at Auburn University, where she teaches and studies the history of the novel, theatre history, women writers, and the cultural history of the senses. Her work has appeared in *Eighteenth Century Fiction, The Burney Journal, Masters of the Marketplace: British Women Novelists of the 1750s,* and *Women's Writing,* among others. Her current book project examines olfactory data and the eighteenth-century novel.

Steven Gores is professor of English at Northern Kentucky University, where he teaches a wide variety of courses, including eighteenth-century theatre, the literature of Bath, and British narrative fantasy. His book, *Psychosocial Spaces: Verbal and Visual Readings of British Culture, 1750–1820* (Wayne State University Press, 2000), connects the novel to varied visual art forms including portrait miniatures and the crescent-style of row houses. He has also published on Austen, Fielding, and the *Harry Potter* series.

David Haley is professor at the University of Minnesota and writes about Early Modern politics and literature from Sidney to Sheridan. His books are on Shakespeare's courtly prudence in *All's Well That Ends Well* and on Dryden's fight against the rise of republican liberalism. A current project compares the several ways that Milton, Marvell, and Dryden used the book of Judges.

Robert W. Jones is senior lecturer in the School of English at the University of Leeds. He is the author of *Gender and the Formation of Taste in Eighteenth-Century Britain* (Cambridge University Press, 1998) and *Literature, Gender and Politics in Britain during the War for America, 1770–1785* (Cambridge University Press, 2011). He has also written essays on Thomas Chatterton, Anna Laetitia Barbauld, Sir Joshua Reynolds, Thomas Moore and the London Zoo. His current project is a book-length study of Sheridan and theatre provisionally titled *The Theatre of Richard Brinsley Sheridan: Drury Lane, Politics and Performance 1775–1787.*

Daniel O'Quinn is a professor in the School of English and Theatre Studies at the University of Guelph. He is the author of *Entertaining Crisis in the Atlantic Imperium, 1770–1790* (Johns Hopkins, 2011) and *Staging Governance: Theatrical Imperialism in London, 1770–1800* (Johns Hopkins, 2005). He also coedited the *Cambridge Companion to British Theatre, 1730–1830* (Cambridge University Press, 2007) with Jane Moody, and has edited the *Travels of Mirza Abu Taleb Khan*

(Broadview Press, 2008). His articles on the intersection of race, sexuality, and class in a range of cultural milieus have appeared in various journals.

Glynis Ridley is a graduate of the universities of Edinburgh and Oxford, at both of which she specialized in eighteenth-century studies. She is now professor of English at the University of Louisville, Kentucky. She is the author of *The Discovery of Jeanne Baret* (Crown, 2010), a biography of the first woman to circumnavigate the globe on Bougainville's expedition of 1766–1769, and she was guest editor of a special edition of the *Journal for Eighteenth-Century Studies* 33:4 (December 2010) on "Animals in the Eighteenth Century." She is just beginning work on a new book entitled *A Cultural History of the Dog*.

David Francis Taylor is assistant professor of English at the University of Toronto. He is author of *Theatres of Opposition: Empire, Revolution, and Richard Brinsley Sheridan* (Oxford University Press, 2012) and has published articles in *Eighteenth-Century Studies*, *European Romantic Review*, and *New Theatre Quarterly*. He is coeditor of the forthcoming *Oxford Handbook to the Georgian Playhouse*.

John A. Vance is emeritus professor of English at the University of Georgia. He has published articles on Milton, Swift, Pepys, Dryden, Cibber, Garrick, The Wartons, Johnson, and Boswell. His books include the monographs *Joseph and Thomas Warton* (Twayne, 1983), *Samuel Johnson and the Sense of History* (University of Georgia Press, 1984), and *William Wycherley and the Comedy of Fear* (University of Delaware Press, 2000); as well as *Joseph & Thomas Warton: An Annotated Bibliography* (Garland, 1983) and with Donald Greene *A Bibliography of Johnsonian Studies, 1970–1985* (University of Victoria, 1987). He has also edited *Boswell's "Life of Johnson": New Questions, New Answers* (University of Georgia Press, 1988). He remains an active playwright, actor, and director, having directed and appeared in Sheridan's *School for Scandal*.